SQL Server™
DTS

Contents At a Glance

SQL Server™ DTS

Steve Hughes, Steve Miller, Jim Samuelson,
Marcelino Santos, and Brian Sullivan

**New
Riders**

www.newriders.com

201 West 103rd Street, Indianapolis, Indiana 46290
An Imprint of Pearson Education
Boston • Indianapolis • London • Munich • New York • San Francisco

SQL Server™ DTS

Copyright © 2002 by New Riders Publishing

Trademarks

Warning and Disclaimer

Publisher
David Dwyer

Associate Publisher
Al Valvano

Executive Editor
Stephanie Wall

Managing Editor
Kristy Knoop

Acquisitions Editors
Ann Quinn
Karen Wachs

Development Editor
Laura Loveall

Product Marketing Manager
Stephanie Layton

Publicity Manager
Susan Nixon

Senior Editor
Lori A. Lyons

Copy Editor
Kathy Simpson

Indexer
Chris Morris

Manufacturing Coordinator
Jim Conway

Book Designer
Louisa Klucznik

Cover Designer
Brainstorm Design, Inc.

Cover Production
Aren Howell

Proofreader
Katherine Shull

Composition
Marcia Deboy

TABLE OF CONTENTS

About the Authors

How did we all get together to write this book? All of us came to Magenic for different reasons. Some of us came because Magenic was the top Microsoft Partner and we wanted to see whether we could be good enough to be among the best. Others came to Magenic for the opportunity to build a database consulting practice that helps businesses solve their toughest data problems. Others came to Magenic to be able to focus on one thing and become really good at it. Regardless of the reason, all of us wanted to be a part of the most dynamic and energetic company in the industry, to solve tough problems, and to help our peers in the field.

When SQL Server 7.0 first came out, Microsoft bundled a great tool called Data Transformation Services (DTS). At the time there was very little information about DTS. It seemed like nobody was writing about it. There were no books and few magazine articles. Marcelino and Jim had both been working on several projects where DTS was the perfect solution, and they decided to write a white paper. Its goal was to help other technologists learn DTS. This white paper ended up being presented at PASS99, and it was on the venue for TechEd2000 when New Riders approached us about expanding the white paper into a full book. That was when we sat down at Magenic and thought about what kind of book we would like to read and what kind of book would help us with our jobs. Our hope is that we accomplished that goal and that you find this book helpful.

Steve Hughes graduated from Bethany College of Missions in 1996 with a degree in Cross-Cultural Studies. He worked at Bethany House Publishers where he designed a warehouse management system using Microsoft tools. Steve has since become a Microsoft Certified Professional with MCSD, MCDBA, and MCSE certifications. He now works as a consultant in the Enterprise Data Services practice at Magenic Technologies, Inc.

Steve Miller is a Senior Business Intelligence Consultant with Magenic Technologies (www.magenic.com) in Minneapolis, MN. In addition to his development responsibilities, he has presented numerous seminars showcasing Microsoft Business Intelligence tools, on a regional basis through Microsoft's For Developers Only Series, and at the national level TechEd 2000. Steve also regularly presents to various database user groups, and he instructs at The University of Minnesota and Normandale Community College.

Steve has more than 15 years experience in the software and financial analysis industries. He holds a B.S. degree in Applied Economics from the University of Minnesota and is a Microsoft Certified Solution Developer (MCSD).

Jim Samuelson is the Enterprise Data Services Practice Manager for Magenic Technologies (www.magenic.com) and has been actively involved with Decision support and Business Intelligence Systems for more than 12 years. Jim speaks on a variety of database and software topics at local, regional, and national events. Jim holds a B.S. degree in Agricultural Business and an MBA in Finance & Management Information Systems. He currently serves on the Microsoft Business Intelligence Partner Advisory Council.

Marcelino Santos is an MCDBA, MCSD, and MCSE working as a Senior Consultant at Magenic Technologies (www.magenic.com). He is focused on data modeling and SQL Server technologies, including database design and implementation, performance tuning, DTS, and OLAP. He has an M.S. in Computer and Information Systems from Boston University in Brussels (Brussels, Belgium).

Brian Sullivan is a Senior Consultant in Magenic Technologies Enterprise Data Services group. He has more than 20 years experience as project lead, business analyst, and software developer. He has specialized in integration of new technologies, data migration, and productivity tool building. Prior to his exposure to DTS, he was involved in developing numerous systems required for the ETL of data between disparate systems. Brian has his Microsoft Certified Database Administration (MCDBA).

About the Technical Reviewers

These reviewers contributed their considerable hands-on expertise to the entire development process for *SQL Server DTS*. As the book was being written, these dedicated professionals reviewed all the material for technical content, organization, and flow. Their feedback was critical to ensuring that *SQL Server DTS* fits our reader's need for the highest-quality technical information.

Ted Daley, MCSE 2000, MCDBA 2000, MCT 2000, is a senior consultant, trainer, and member of the Data Warehousing Practice at CIBER, Inc., a company that specializes in data warehousing and business intelligence solutions. His consulting and training efforts are focused on Microsoft SQL Server 2000 and Analysis Services on the Windows 2000 Server platform. He can be reached at `tdaley@ciber.com`.

Mary Hooke is the president and founder of Distinctive Development, LTD (`www.distinctivedevelopment.com`). Located in New York City, Distinctive Development creates custom software applications for a variety of industries. Mary is also a contributing editor for *Visual Basic Programmer's Journal* and regularly writes articles on DTS and other SQL Server and programming related topics.

Acknowledgments

Steve Hughes—I would like to thank all those people who have helped me progress in my career, helping me to get to the point where I could write a book like this. Thanks to Terry Hughes, my dad, for the great advice. Thanks to Werner Godt, shipping manager at BHP, for his vision and confidence in me. Thanks to Ed Jankowski, my father-in-law, for an opportunity to learn from his experience. Thanks to Kari Koehler, Principle Consultant, Magenic Technologies, for showing me the ropes on SQL Server. Thanks to my wife, Sheila, and my kids, Kristyna, Alex, and Andrew, for putting up with the late hours and lost weekends to see the writing of this book through. Most importantly, thanks to God for giving me the ability to do any of this.

Steve Miller—I would like to thank Maryanne for her support on this project.

Jim Samuelson—My deepest thanks go to my wife, Jane. Your encouragement and faith in me has allowed me to pursue my dreams. Your unending patience, sacrifice, and constant belief in me, is an example of true love. I also must thank Terry Lindgren, who has been my mentor and friend for the last ten years. Terry, without your encouragement and guidance, I would not have the life I have today.

Marcelino Santos—Thanks, Grace!!! Thanks to Bob Owen at Peregrine Capital for giving me the opportunity to "blaze the trail" with DTS on my trusty server "Tarzan" for the better part of a year. Thanks to Jim Samuelson for asking me to help write the DTS white paper and inviting me to be part of this book.

Brian Sullivan—I would like to dedicate this book to my father, William Sullivan.

The Group—All of us would like to thank all the New Riders editorial staff, especially Laura Loveall, Ann Quinn, Karen Wachs, and Leah Williams for their help and expertise. You took a group of techies who knew nothing about writing a book and showed us how to turn our ideas and knowledge into something that can be helpful. We would also like to thank Ted Daley, Mary Hooke, and Euan Garden, who have made significant contributions to the technical quality and consistency of the book; your influence is in every page. Finally, we must thank Greg Frankenfield and Paul Fridman for creating a unique company called Magenic Technologies. We have never before seen a gathering of such great talent formed into one company focused on one thing—using Microsoft Technologies to build high-impact solutions. We have learned so much from everyone at Magenic.

Tell Us What You Think

As the reader of this book, you are the most important critic and commentator. We value your opinion and want to know what we're doing right, what we could do better, what areas you'd like to see us publish in, and any other words of wisdom you're willing to pass our way.

As an Executive Editor for the Web Development team at New Riders Publishing, I welcome your comments. You can fax, email, or write me directly to let me know what you did or didn't like about this book—as well as what we can do to make our books stronger.

Please note that I cannot help you with technical problems related to the topic of this book, and that due to the high volume of mail I receive, I might not be able to reply to every message.

When you write, please be sure to include this book's title and author as well as your name and phone or fax number. I will carefully review your comments and share them with the author and editors who worked on the book.

Fax: 317-581-4663
Email: stephanie.wall@newriders.com
Mail: Stephanie Wall
            Executive Editor
            New Riders Publishing
            201 West 103rd Street
            Indianapolis, IN 46290 USA

Preface

The first law of thermodynamics in essence states that energy cannot be created nor destroyed. It seems the same rule applies to data. In many of our systems, data is neither created nor destroyed—but it is pumped around an awful lot. We have data in legacy systems, we have data in our ERP systems, and we have data in our Web-based systems; and let's not forget we still have departmental and desktop systems data. In addition to numerous storage locations, it is typically stored across heterogeneous hardware platforms. With the advent of Internet business-to-business partnerships, no data can exist on the outside of our firewalls (and unfortunately, on the other side of someone else's firewall).

In an ideal world, all the data our applications need would exist in their database of choice. Rather than wait for that day, we will inevitably move data from one database to the next. To that end, Microsoft includes DTS with SQL Server. This would leave you to believe that data pumping from SQL server is all it's good for.

This book challenges you to think about solving broader application integration problems with this extremely useful product. With the experiences of Jim Samuelson, Steve Hughes, Steve Miller, Marcelino Santos, and Brian Sullivan, they give you not only new ways to use the product, they present real-world solutions you can use right out of the box. They give you ways to integrate with the emerging opportunities presented by XML tools embedded in Commerce Server 2000 and BizTalk, as well as concrete answers to everyday data warehousing tasks.

I know this book will give you a great foundation for levering the DTS technologies presented and a new way of thinking about your data movement and transformation problems.

Greg Frankenfield
CEO & MSDN Regional Director
Magenic Technologies, Inc.
April 23, 2001

Introduction

SQL Server Data Transformation Services (DTS) is a Microsoft product that is designed to move and manipulate data. It also has a nice graphical designer. So, you can create simple or complex workflows that pull data from any number of data sources; clean, manipulate, and integrate the data; and then push the data into any number of data destinations. These repositories of data can be large DBMSs like SQL Server, Oracle, or Sybase; small DBMSs like Access, Paradox, or dBase; or even applications like Excel or Exchange. DTS also has an open COM interface. So, you can write programs that build and control your DTS Applications (called packages). DTS is an independent application and does not need SQL Server to run.

I have found that DTS is a powerful and flexible tool that easily handles all kinds of data transformation problems.

Scope and Audience

The goal of this project is to create a book that can be used both as a reference book and an "idea" book on DTS. The scope of this book is to cover the breadth of DTS across all of its capabilities and show you how those capabilities can be used in combination with other technologies to solve a wide variety of system and application problems. We show how DTS interacts with other technologies, such as Message Queuing. We cover how to write programs using the DTS engine, and we will even show you how to customize DTS by building your own Tasks that you can reuse in many packages. We do cover some data warehousing, but to do only that would limit the discussion of the tools, capabilities, and the vast possibilities where DTS can be a vital and complementary component in a system or application design (see Figure I.1).

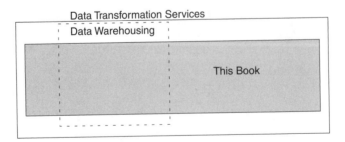

Figure I.1 DTS is more than just a data warehouse tool, and the scope of this book is to cover the world of DTS.

The primary audience for this book is anyone who has to move data. If you are a beginner with DTS, you will be challenged because we jump right into the product and building packages. If you have experience with DTS, our goal is to expand your knowledge both in breadth and in depth. As long as you have basic programming skills and basic database skills, you will be able to follow along with the book. We do use a lot of the Microsoft development technologies such as SQL Server tables and databases, SQL statements, stored procedures, VBScript, and Visual Basic programming. We will provide many examples and code snippets to help you on your way to learning and maximizing your knowledge of DTS.

All of our examples and code snippets have been packaged together and are at www.magenic.com/publications or www.newriders.com. We encourage you to use them while you are reading the book or whenever possible to aid in your work. Please refer to the inside back cover of the book for more information on the Web site and the files it contains.

Organization and Layout

The book is organized in four major sections: a reference section, a section on automation, a data warehousing and data mining section, and a case study section.

Part I, "Data Transformation Services—The Tool"

Part I covers all the components of DTS in both SQL Server 2000 and SQL Server 7.0 (connections, tasks, steps, and packages). This section is geared to providing you with a thorough understanding of all the DTS parts.

- Chapter 1, "DTS in the ETL World," talks about the world of data extraction, transformation, and loading. We compare DTS to other data movement technologies like BizTalk, Bulk Load, bcp, replication and Message Queue. We will also discuss DTS as a complement to major technologies such as Commerce Server 2000.

- Chapter 2, "DTS—An Overview," introduces you to DTS by building a simple, yet creative package that will use many features in DTS to publish data into a several Excel spreadsheets.

- Chapter 3, "Connections," covers all the connections that come with DTS.

- Chapter 4, "DTS Tasks." There are a lot of tasks available for use in DTS. This chapter covers the Data Movement Tasks: Transform Data Task, Data Driven Query Task, Bulk Insert Task, and the Multiphase Data pump.

- Chapter 5, "More DTS Tasks," covers all the other tasks that come standard with DTS, such as Execute SQL Task, ActiveX Script Task, Execute Process Task, Dynamic Properties Task, Message Queue Task, the Transfer Tasks, Analysis Services Task, and the Data Mining Task.

- Chapter 6, "DTS Workflows," covers all the features and capabilities of workflows, including where you can add custom scripting.
- Chapter 7, "Package," is about the Package and all of the properties, methods, and storage locations.
- Chapter 8, "Putting It All Together—An Extended DTS Example," builds and discusses a realistic production-ready DTS package that must do many things to support the business requirements.

Part II, "Automating Data Transformation Services"

Part II is all about creating, running, and responding to DTS packages using Visual Basic.

- Chapter 9, "Building a Package Using Visual Basic," is about using Visual Basic to create a fully operational DTS package that uses an ActiveX Script Task, the Data Transformation Task (with scripting), and workflow.
- Chapter 10, "Interacting with a Package Using Visual Basic," takes you through a variety of situations, such as processing all the files in a directory, processing email messages, loading XML data, and log processing, to show you best practices in working with a DTS package and how to handle DTS Events and Error Handling.

Part III, "DTS and the Business Intelligence Process"

Part III introduces you to data warehousing and Analysis Services. Then it discusses the DTS components and the data warehouse process, including issues and solutions.

- Chapter 11, "Introduction to Data Warehousing and Analysis Services," covers the Data Warehouse, the terminology, and the process. It also covers the components in SQL Server Analysis Services.
- Chapter 12, "Building a Data Warehouse with DTS and Analysis Services," walks you through the data warehouse process by highlighting the issues and showing you solutions to some common situations.
- Chapter 13, "DTS Data Mining," teaches you the basics of data mining and walks you through the new data mining features of Analysis Services and the DTS Prediction Task.

Part IV, "Using the Tool—Case Studies"

Part IV is composed of a series of chapters that will help you understand how to use DTS components in a variety of ways and with other technologies.

- Chapter 14, "Custom Error Logging with DTS," shows you an alternative to the DTS error logs to raise and store data problems.
- Chapter 15, "Managing Distributed Databases with DTS and Message Queues," walks you through the new Message Queue tasks by simulating a system that processes XML based purchase orders via a Message Queue.
- Chapter 16, "Creating Your Own Custom Task," shows you the Visual Basic code needed to create your own Custom Task complete with a property page. You will create a task that generates an HTML table from an SQL Statement and then stores the file to disk.
- Chapter 17, "Executing a DTS Package from a Stored Procedure." Sometimes you need a package on demand. This chapter walks you through a stored procedure that will execute a DTS Package.
- Chapter 18, "Data Lineage," shows you how to set up DTS to fully log your data so that you have a record of its history and transformation.

Conventions

This book follows a few typographical conventions:

- A new term is set in *italic* the first time it is introduced.
- Program text, functions, variables, and other "computer language" are set in a monospaced font—for example, `Main()` and `DTSTransformStat_Error`.

This book mainly covers information on SQL 2000, but it also provides some comparisons to SQL 7.0. All of the SQL 7.0 material appears in the following format:

> Information about SQL 7.0 appears in this format.

How to Use This Book

This book is designed to be both a guide and a reference manual. It can be read sequentially, and you can easily go to a particular topic to get the key information you need and move on.

For the beginner to DTS, I encourage you to read Part I of the book sequentially. Then you can read the chapters in Parts II through IV that spark your interest or address your current situation.

For the experienced DTS user, I encourage you to scan Part I, and concentrate on the portions that add value to your knowledge. Then you can read the chapters in Parts II through IV that spark your interest.

For all users, we hope this book will be useful to you as a quick reference to key components on DTS. We also hope that it gives you design ideas that can help you solve your data migration problems.

Good luck, and have fun with DTS. And don't forget, "Applications come and go, but your data lives forever!"

I

Data Transformation Services—
The Tool

1

DTS in the ETL World

WHEN WE FIRST HEARD OF SQL Server's Data Transformation Services (DTS), it was described as the perfect tool for loading data into a data warehouse, which is a task for which it seemed to be well suited. The first time we had an opportunity to use DTS, however, came from the need to translate data from an old application to a dramatically improved re-architecture. Our second experience involved processing Microsoft Exchange log files to perform analysis on email traffic across an entire multinational corporation. Although DTS was the best solution for that project, it still was not a data warehouse (but it would have been fun to do one). After doing a third nondata warehouse application for which DTS was the best solution, addressing the current technical problem, we started to see the world of possibilities for DTS. It became clear that DTS is much more than a data extraction, transformation, and load-ing (ETL) tool for building a data warehouse. DTS is a flexible data-movement engine that is completely open for customization and integration into a slew of products and systems.

You may have read about DTS, or you may have used DTS when it first came out with SQL Server 7.0. You might ask, "How can a mere feature inside SQL Server be so big?" In this book, you will see how and why DTS has grown both inside SQL Server and outside of it.

The goal of this book is to give you a solid foundation in DTS and to provide sample code showing the use and the various features of DTS. Many of these examples show techniques that are useful for moving and processing data. The book also covers how to use DTS to help you build and maintain data warehouses.

DTS and Traditional Technologies

Any discussion of DTS should include an overview of existing technologies, show what has been working to this day (albeit in a limited way), and what can now be done easily and efficiently with DTS. More important, the discussion should include which technologies DTS *cannot* replace.

BCP

Bulk Copy Program (BCP) is the original bulk insert utility for SQL Server. BCP is a powerful utility that allows you to import and export data to and from SQL Server tables. Although BCP does not require knowledge of SQL, users need to know the structure and data types of the source or target table.

In SQL 7.0, Microsoft added the `BULK INSERT` statement to Transact-SQL. This new statement allowed the DBA to use SQL to load data into SQL Server instead of having to use the command line and BCP. Although Bulk Insert provides many of the same features as BCP, it does not replace BCP; it only gives the DBA an alternative to loading data into SQL Server. Also, as the name suggests, BCP does not support exporting SQL Server tables into text files. The functionality of Bulk Insert has been encapsulated in a built-in DTS task called the *Bulk Insert Task*.

Although DTS can do almost everything BCP can, many people will continue to use it for its simplicity and speed.

Replication

Replication was an early advance in database technology that received significant attention from the database and business world. Being able to move and synchronize data between and among servers was suddenly a big deal. Unlike DTS, replication does more than just transport data. Depending on the replication model, data can be synchronized even with multiple updates coming from different locations.

You use replication when data needs to be "published" from one source to multiple locations. It may be appropriate when you need to distribute the data on a regular basis, or when you need replication to support some sort of offline distributed database capability. You especially need it when multiple locations each have a copy of the data and can update their copies. This is because replication can take care of synchronizing their updates.

Replication is not easy and should not be underestimated. Although you can use DTS as a replication tool across heterogeneous databases, carefully plan any proposed DTS solution. Using DTS for replication can easily take enormous resources to fully implement across several levels.

Transact-SQL (T-SQL)

A little overlap exists between what DTS can do and what T-SQL can do. Some T-SQL functionality, such as Bulk Insert, is implemented as DTS Tasks. On the other hand, a significant amount of T-SQL can be used within DTS tasks. By and large, however, DTS and T-SQL are two different sets of tools that accomplish a very basic common set of goals: access data, transform data, and store data. Following is a list of the main differences:

- DTS can be either graphical or scripting, whereas T-SQL is mostly scripting.
- DTS allows many kinds of scripting, whereas T-SQL is one type of script.
- DTS is designed to work primarily with any OLE DB or ODBC-compliant data source. T-SQL, which can be executed on almost any relational database, is predominately designed to work with SQL Server databases.

Could DTS replace T-SQL completely? The answer is no. Although you can use DTS to accomplish some database-creation and management functions with much less effort, many important core uses of T-SQL, and SQL in general, make it a vital portion of any major database.

DTS and Today's Technologies

Figuring out how DTS stands with respect to competitive ETL tools is equally important. DTS is already playing significant supporting roles in other Microsoft products including Commerce Server and BizTalk Server, to mention a few.

DTS and Commerce Server

Commerce Server 2000 (CS2000) is the latest version of Microsoft's solution for building and managing business-to-consumer and business-to-business Web sites. A major feature of this solution is the capability to mine data compiled by the transactional part of the system. This means extracting, transforming, and loading the data into a data warehouse. It also means being able to analyze the data to perceive trends, forecast customer behavior, identify critical situations, and provide management with information that it needs to manage the business.

CS2000 relies on SQL Server 2000 for both transactional and data-warehousing database support. The cornerstone of CS2000 is its capability to track customer profiles. It is capable of performing *explicit* profiling in which the customer is asked to provide consumer information. CS2000 also can track the activity of all Web site users. All of this information is stored in Profiles. CS2000 then relies on a special DTS task to import the profiles into the data warehouse.

Although this is one of the most important roles that a DTS task assumes in a CS2000 installation, it is not the only one. Several other custom DTS tasks are made available when you install CS2000. Each task performs a specific function to help you manage every aspect of data manipulation, analysis, and reporting in a dynamic commerce solution.

DTS and BizTalk Server

BizTalk is an enterprise application integration (EAI) and a business-to-business solution offered by Microsoft. It acts as a gateway that enables a business to send and receive electronic data and documents to and from its systems or trading partners. BizTalk can work with CS2000 to manage the data translation, encryption, digital signing, transport, and tracking of orders placed on a CS2000 Web site.

On the surface, BizTalk appears to be very similar to DTS, but it is not. The following list highlights the main differences:

- BizTalk is application and process integration, and DTS is data integration.
- BizTalk works best at the transaction level. Although DTS can operate at the transaction level, its sweet spot is high-volume bulk data loads.
- BizTalk responds to events or messages, whereas DTS usually runs on batch schedules.

Real-World Scenarios Used in This Book— About Sparks Electronics

Before you dive in to get the details on DTS, take a moment to learn about a scenario presented in this book. One of the goals of this book is to provide real-world scenarios where DTS can be used. Therefore, several of the examples were developed around a fictitious company called Sparks Electronics.

Sparks Electronics is a PC integrator and distributor. Incorporated in 1995, the company began assembling and reselling PCs for the lucrative military market. Company headquarters and the original plant are located in Minneapolis. In the past three years, Sparks Electronics has expanded sales to include the private-label market, which required opening two additional assembly plants in California. In 1998, when Sparks was having trouble getting printer cables of sufficient quality at a reasonable price, it entered into a partnership with a Mexican firm to produce these cables.

Bob Smith, a shipping manager at the Minneapolis plant, recently acquired a copy of SQL Server. For a manager, he has a great deal of technical knowledge. Bob knows that he can improve his data and reporting processes by using the DTS product in SQL Server.

Summary

This chapter discussed some areas in which DTS may be used, examined alternative and complementary technologies, and introduced the sample scenario.

Chapter 2, "DTS—An Overview," walks you through a more detailed example that uses DTS to solve problems for Sparks Electronics.

2

DTS—An Overview

THE DTS PACKAGE IS A DATA transformation application. A package can be as simple as running bulk copy to load a comma-delimited file into a SQL Server database or as complex as coordinating the combined work of many packages that extract, cleanse, and load data for a business intelligence system.

This chapter briefly introduces you to the power and flexibility of DTS by building a sample package. We do not expect you to understand everything you see and use here, but we hope you will be challenged and your interest sparked by the possibilities DTS offers.

This chapter discusses major DTS components and shows you how to build a package using many DTS features. The chapter does not discuss the DTS Import/ Export Wizard; it starts where the Wizard leaves off. Chapters 3 through 7 will cover the DTS tools in detail. Chapter 8, "Putting It All Together—An Extended DTS Example," will put all the pieces together and show you how to build a package that is production-ready.

DTS Import/Export Wizard

The Import and Export Data functionality in SQL Server is a wizard that automates the building and execution of a DTS package. The Wizard is useful and very flexible. You might use it on a regular basis to migrate data from one repository to another.

The wizard is useful for quickly loading one or many tables or views into a data repository. The source data can come from any OLE DB or ODBC-compliant data source. You can use SQL to join or filter the source data. If the source is a SQL Server database, you can bring in any SQL Server object from the source, such as stored procedures, user-defined data types, triggers, users and roles, and more.

The wizard is well laid out and very straightforward. Because it is well documented in other books and SQL Server Books on Line (BOL), this book does not cover it.

The DTS Package

The package specifies work to be performed by DTS. The package contains connections to data sources, tasks to work on the data or perform other functions, and workflow to manage the sequence of work. The connections can be established to any number of OLE DB, ODBC, or text-file formats. You can accomplish work through standard tasks or customize those tasks by using a Windows scripting language such as VBScript, JScript, or ActiveState PerlScript.

The workflow can execute the tasks in parallel or branch them conditionally based on the success, completion, or failure of a previous task. Packages can participate in transactions and sometimes can be rolled back entirely when errors arise. In essence, the DTS package has the interface and the plumbing to build complex data transformations and package workflow that can handle a variety of situations, which range from upgrading an application's data to performing the heavy cleansing and transforming requirements of data warehousing.

Connections

Connections create a tie to a data repository. DTS is a stand-alone application that comes with SQL Server but does not require SQL Server to be used as either the data source or the data destination. The standard data connections that come with DTS can be grouped into five major categories:

- Database management systems like SQL Server or Oracle

- File system databases like Microsoft Access, dBase, or Paradox

- Applications like Microsoft Excel

- Text files

- Other connections. You can incorporate any third-party OLE DB or ODBC connection, such as Sybase or IBM DB2, or even a custom-built OLE DB provider by using a language such as Visual C++ or Delphi. The coding for building your own provider is beyond the scope of this book, but you can find information at www.microsoft.com/data.

For more information on connections, refer to Chapter 3, "Connections."

Tasks

Tasks describe a unit of work that can be performed by the DTS package. DTS comes with a wide variety of standard tasks:

- Executing SQL statements

- Executing programming scripts

- Sending emails

- Handling high-speed data loads

- Executing other packages

- Interacting with Message Queue

- Interacting with Analysis Services

You can even create your own custom task by using a programming language such as Visual Basic or Visual C++. For more information on tasks, please see Chapter 4, "DTS Tasks," Chapter 5, "More DTS Tasks," and Chapter 16, "Creating Your Own Custom Tasks."

Workflow

Workflow specifies how each task in the package gets executed, including its sequence with respect to the other tasks. Workflow determines whether a task is executed simultaneously with other tasks or conditionally upon the completion, success, or failure of one or more previous tasks. Be careful—task concurrency is affected by the package property that sets the maximum number of tasks executed in parallel and determines whether the task is written free-threaded or not. For more information on package properties, please see Chapter 7. For more information on workflow, please see Chapter 6, "DTS Workflows."

Building a Package

In the next few pages, you will build a DTS package involving a real situation. The example has been used to show DTS flexibility rather than the DTS fast data load features. Because SQL Server 2000 included many enhancements to the DTS application, the DTS interface will vary in a few places, depending on which version of SQL Server you are using. This chapter highlights those places and shows you both versions of SQL Server (7.0 and 2000). Chapter 8 expands on this example, discussing additional DTS features and capabilities for making a package ready for production.

The Scenario

The package you will build here is based on the distributor that was introduced in Chapter 1, "DTS in the ETL World." The shipping manager, Bob, wants to know how he is doing compared with his budget. Unfortunately, his budget is in Excel, and it is at the product-group level, while his actual shipments are, of course, in a set of normalized tables recorded at the transaction level. Bob is pretty good with Excel and, therefore, wants his reports in Excel so that he can do some "what-if" analysis.

To demonstrate some of the flexibility inherent to DTS, the first report you will create for Bob will be Sparks Electronics: Shipping Actuals by Month in Units (see Figure 2.1). The second report will be a snapshot comparison of actual shipments for current month and year to date (YTD) against Bob's budget (see Figure 2.2). You will extract the month and year that Bob wants to do his analysis for from his Reports spreadsheet.[1]

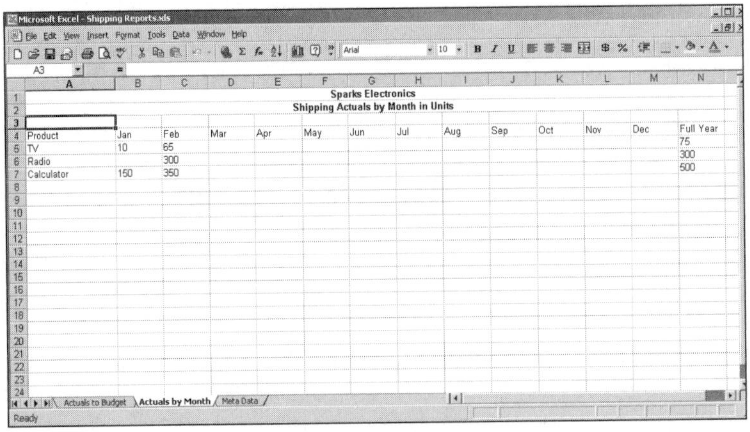

Figure 2.1   Actuals by Month Excel spreadsheet report created by DTS package.

Package Design

As in any development project, you need to lay out your application processes before you start coding. Your package for Bob will use the following steps:

1. Create the connections to your data sources and destinations.

   In this scenario, you will need three connections: one connection for inventory actuals, one for the shipping budget, and one for creating the shipping reports.

2. Create a task to prepare your destination to accept new data; then extract the month and year for which you need to create your reports.

---

1. All data files and scripts used in this book are available for download from http://www.magenic.com/publications or http://www.newriders.com. The self-extracting ZIP file will create a directory structure starting with DTS2000. You can extract the files to any drive or directory, but all file references in this book will be based on C:\DTS2000\.

3. Create some transformation tasks to integrate the budget information from the Excel spreadsheet and the actuals data in the Access database into the destination spreadsheet.

   You will need to convert the row-based transaction data in the normalized tables of the Access database to the column-based data that is common in spreadsheets.

4. Finally, you will need to put into place some conditional error handling to notify yourself when a problem with your package arises.

When complete, your package should look like Figure 2.3.

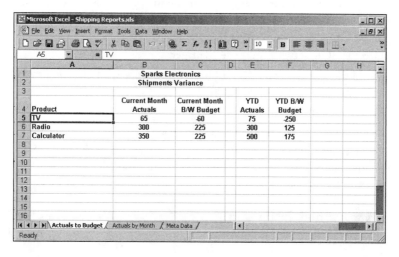

Figure 2.2   Shipments Variance Excel spreadsheet report created by DTS package.

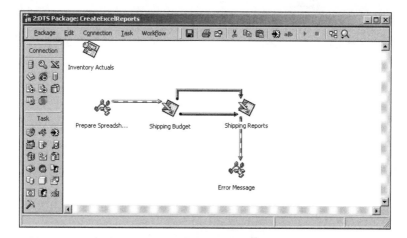

Figure 2.3   Complete DTS package for example.

> **Sample Package: Author's Note**
> The package you will be creating has been designed to help show available DTS features and is not the most efficient solution to the problem.

Step 1: Create the Basic Package

The first step is to determine where the package is to be stored. Packages can be stored locally (in SQL Server system tables); they can be stored in the Meta Data Services, as a structured storage file directly on disk, or even as a Visual Basic module. These storage options and their advantages/disadvantages are discussed further in Chapter 7.

For this example, you will create a new local package:

1. Open the SQL Server Enterprise Manager.

2. Expand the tree under the server you want to work with until you find Data Transformation Services (see Figure 2.4).

3. Select Data Transformation Services.

4. Click the Action menu and select New Package.

   This command brings up an empty DTS Designer window. The DTS Designer window allows you to create the data connections graphically, define the tasks you want the package to perform, and specify the task order of execution.

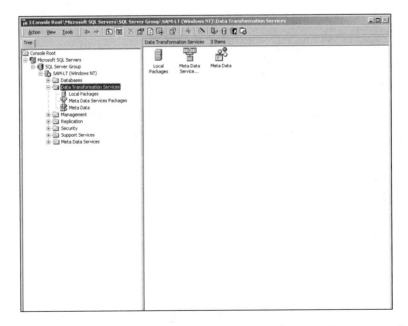

Figure 2.4   SQL Server Enterprise Manager with Data Transformation Services expanded.

DTS Designer Window

The Designer window is the workspace where you create or edit a DTS package. The DTS Designer allows you to create the data connections you need, define the tasks you want the package to perform, and specify the workflow or the sequencing of those tasks.

Using the Import/Export Data Wizard to Build a DTS Package

One way to see what a complete package looks like is to use the Import/Export wizard and save the package. After you save the package, you can view it in the Designer window to see what the wizard created.

5. Save the empty package by clicking the Package menu and selecting Save.

   You will be prompted to supply a name: `CreateExcelReports` (see Figure 2.5). You can specify storage type and location. The default is SQL Server, which stores all the information about the package in a SQL Server internal table called `sysdtspackages`. For more information on storage options, see Chapter 7.

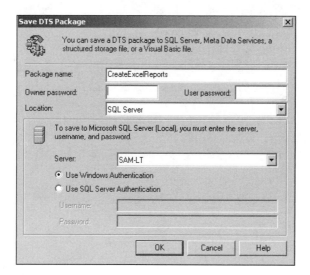

Figure 2.5   Save DTS Package dialog box.

Step 2: Create the Data Connections

Creating your connections first and setting them along the top of the package helps you easily see all the data repositories that you're interacting with and control the number of connections that you make. In this example, the first connection will be with the Actuals data stored in an Access database called Manufacturing.mdb.

You can create a data connection in one of four ways:

- Dragging the appropriate database connection from the Connection toolbar on the left side of the screen.
- Single-clicking the appropriate database connection in the Connection toolbar on the left.
- Using the Connection menu from the menu bar.
- Right-click on the workspace inside the DTS Designer main panel, and select Add Connection from the shortcut menu.

Using whichever method you desire, create a new Microsoft Access connection (see Figure 2.6).

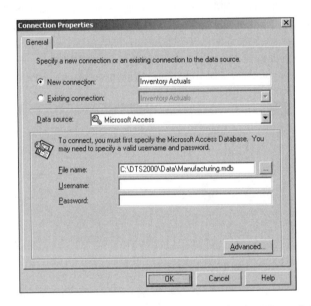

Figure 2.6   DTS Connection Properties dialog box for the Microsoft Access database called Manufacturing.mdb.

Because this connection is the first one in the package, the Existing Connection option is grayed out. For the Connection Name, type **Inventory Actuals**, and for File Name, locate the Manufacturing database file that you copied to your hard drive (Manufacturing.mdb). The data connection with Microsoft Access allows both read and write access to the database, depending on the permissions granted to you by the database administrator.

Now create a connection to both the Shipping Budget spreadsheet and the Shipping Reports spreadsheet (see Figure 2.7). Because both Microsoft Access and Excel are file-based applications, the Excel connection works just like the Access connection.

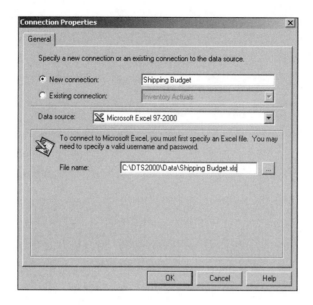

Figure 2.7   DTS Connection Properties dialog box for the Shipping Budget Excel spreadsheet.

After you create one connection, you can have the other connection objects reference the existing connection by choosing the Existing Connection option. This procedure will come in handy in large, complex packages, where you can have many tasks reuse existing connections to a particular data repository. This practice keeps the number of open connections to a minimum, and makes it easier to change the source data system. (When you update the original connection, all the connections that reference it are updated.) By reusing a connection, however, you are forcing serialization for the tasks that use that connection. For this example, this connection will be a new one. For more information on connections, please see Chapter 3.

Now create a second Excel connection, this one for Shipping Reports. Figure 2.8 shows the package with all three connections.

After you have set up the data connections, you can start creating the tasks to do the work.

Step 3: Create Global Variables

A *global variable* is a place to store information temporarily. All global variables are at the package level, which means they are available to all tasks in the package. You can create global variables ahead of time in the DTS Designer window or create them at run-time by using any of the tasks that use scripting. For a complete discussion of global variables, please see Chapter 7.

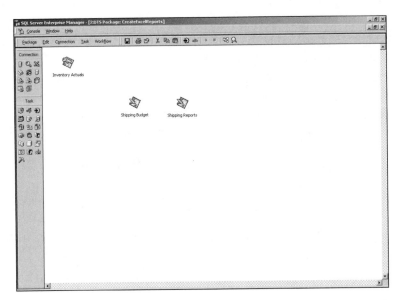

Figure 2.8 DTS package with all three connections.

For this project, you will create three global variables by using the DTS Designer window. Follow these steps:

1. Right-click an open space in the DTS Designer window, and select Package Properties.

2. Select the Global Variables tab inside the DTS Package Properties dialog box.

3. Click New.

4. Type **ActualsThroughMonth** in the Name field, set the Type to Int (Integer), and set Value equal to zero.

5. Repeat steps 3 and 4 for the remaining global variables:

   - Name = CurrentYear, Type = Int, Value = 0
   - Name = ErrorMessage, Type = String, Value (leave blank)

   The third global variable will be used to store any errors that occur in processing (see Figure 2.9).

6. Click OK to close the dialog box.

In reality, this method is not a good one for handling errors, because it is only a single string value, and some processes may raise multiple errors. For your purposes, however, this method will work. For more information on error handling, please see Chapter 7 and Chapter 14, "Custom Error Logging with DTS."

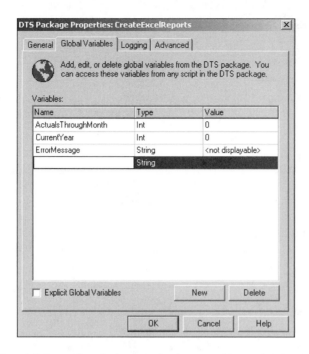

Figure 2.9   Global Variables tab, showing the three variables needed for the example.

Step 4: Prepare Spreadsheet and Extract Reporting Date

Before you load new information into the spreadsheet reports, you will need to purge the old data and then get the month and year for the reporting period. Excel has two major interfaces with which you can interact: the OLE DB interface and the Object Model interface. The Excel OLE DB connection allows SQL statements to read, insert, and update Excel spreadsheets just like a traditional database. The other major interface is the Excel object model. You can use the Script Task to interact with Excel either directly on a cell-by-cell basis or by executing an Excel VBA macro. Each option has its strengths and weaknesses.

For this exercise, you will use both options. You will prepare the spreadsheet by executing a macro and then, by interacting on a cell-by-cell basis, move through an Excel table, looking for the key names ActualsThroughMonth and CurrentYear. Table 2.1 shows what the spreadsheet table looks like.

Table 2.1 **Excel Spreadsheet Table with a List of Key Names and Associated Values**

Variable Name	Value
ActualsThroughMonth	3
CurrentYear	2000
Owner	Bob Smith

Tables like Table 2.1 are a nice way to store key data in Excel. Excel functions, Excel formulas, VBA, and even SQL Select statements can reference the values easily.

To get started, drag an ActiveX Script Task from the toolbar to the Designer work surface. Double-click the task to open it, and set its Description to Prepare Spreadsheet. The Script Task has a function called Main where you can write your script. The steps the script must take are:

1. Create an instance of the Excel application, as follows:

```
Dim xlApp
   Set xlApp = CreateObject("Excel.Application")
```

   By default, Excel will not be visible, and because you don't need the user to interact with it, you won't turn on visibility.

2. Open the workbook that contains the reports, as follows:

```
xlApp.Workbooks.Open "C:\DTS2000\Data\Shipping Reports.xls"
```

3. Execute the macro called "ResetReports", as follows

```
xlApp.Run ("ResetReports")
```

4. Cycle through each cell in the range named ActualsMetaData until a cell contains the string "ActualsThroughMonth" or "CurrentYear", using this code:

```
For each c in xlApp.Range("ActualsMetaData")
     If c.Value = "ActualsThroughMonth" or c.Value = "CurrentYear" Then
```

5. When either string is located, save the value of the cell to the right in the appropriate global variable, as follows:

```
DTSGlobalVariables(c.Value).Value = c.offset(0,1).Value
```

   Because the global variable has the same name as the Excel spreadsheet key name, you can use the cell value to specify which global variable to use.

6. Close the workbook, save the changes, and close Excel, as follows:

```
xlApp.ActiveWorkbook.Close True
xlApp.Quit
Set xlApp = Nothing
```

7. Tell DTS that the script ran successfully by setting the function Main equal to DTSTaskExecResult_Success, as follows:

```
Main = DTSTaskExecResult_Success
```

The only other option that you can use for a script-return value is DTSTaskExecResult_Failure, which tells DTS that the script failed. Chapter 4 will cover script tasks in more detail, and Chapter 7 will cover how DTS handles error-return codes.

Figure 2.10 shows the ActiveX Script Task with all the scripting necessary to open Excel, execute a macro, and then pull data from it.

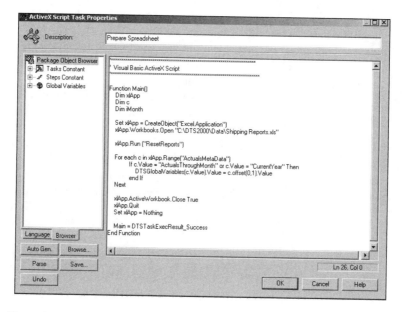

Figure 2.10   DTS VBScript task with script to interact with an Excel spreadsheet.

VBScript versus Visual Basic for Applications

When working with applications like Excel, you can use the script task to manipulate the file directly, or you can have a VBA macro embedded in the application and use the script task to execute the macro. Each method has strengths and weaknesses:

- **VBScript**—You might use this method when you're performing simple modifications, when the document that you're working with is being created from scratch, when you want the code to be in one central location, or when VBA macros are switched off to protect against malicious viruses.

- **Visual Basic for Applications**—You might use this method when you want a great deal of work to be done within the application, when performance is critical, or when you want the more robust development environment and easier debugging.

Step 5: Load Actuals Data

This step is where you map the Shipping Actuals data from the Access database to the Excel reports. The heart of the typical DTS package is the Transform Data Task. You can create any number of source-to-destination transformation mappings. You can do field-by-field copy, multiple source fields to a single destination field, single source to multiple destinations, and multiple source fields to multiple destination fields. You can do straight copy, or you can write scripts that test and manipulate the data before inserting it into the destination. You can have the Transform Data Task process the record, skip the record, or raise an error. For more information on this task, please see Chapter 4.

As in most technical situations, you can move data in several ways, and each method has advantages and disadvantages. For this example, you will read in a shipping category from the budget spreadsheet, look up the actuals from the Access database, and load the category name and actual amount into the Excel spreadsheet. This method is one way to supply only the categories that Bob wants and pivot the row-based transaction data into column-based summary data.

This method has two drawbacks: You must be careful that the spreadsheet has the exact product category references to match against the Access database, and this method is not the fastest way to load data. For each product category and for each month, the task will do a lookup against the Access database to get the actuals. This method may not be the fastest, but it does allow you to use the lookup feature. Because only a few product categories are involved, this method is acceptable. For a more thorough discussion of the lookup function, with some creative uses, please see Chapter 14.

Your package should look like Figure 2.11.

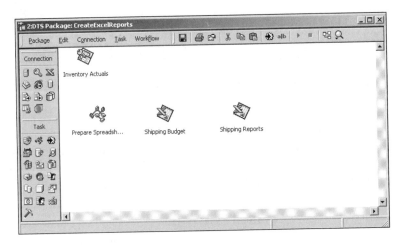

Figure 2.11   Partially completed DTS package.

Click the Transform Data Task button on the toolbar. You will be prompted to select a source connection. Click the Shipping Budget Excel connection. Next, you will be prompted to select the destination connection. Click the Shipping Reports icon. The Designer window will put in a gray workflow arrow, showing work going from Shipping Budget to Shipping Reports.

> SQL Server 7.0 users will need to preselect the source and destination connections. Hold down the Ctrl key, select the Shipping Budget as the source connection, and select Shipping Reports as the destination connection. Click on Workflow from the menu bar on top of the DTS Designer and click on Add Transform. The Designer window will put in a black workflow arrow, showing work going from Shipping Budget to Shipping Reports.

Double-click the arrow to view the properties of the Transform Data Task (see Figure 2.12). Make sure that the Source tab is selected. Type **Load Actuals** in the Description text box. Below the word Connection, select Table/View as the type. Clicking on the arrow to the right of the Table/View field produces a drop-down list showing Budget and 'Budget Sheet&'. Budget is a named range in Excel and 'Budget Sheet&' is the entire workbook.

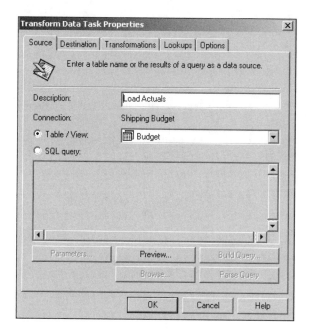

Figure 2.12   Source tab for the SQL Server 2000 Transform
Data Task using the Shipping Budget connection.

The Source tab is slightly different for SQL Server 7.0 (see Figure 2.13).

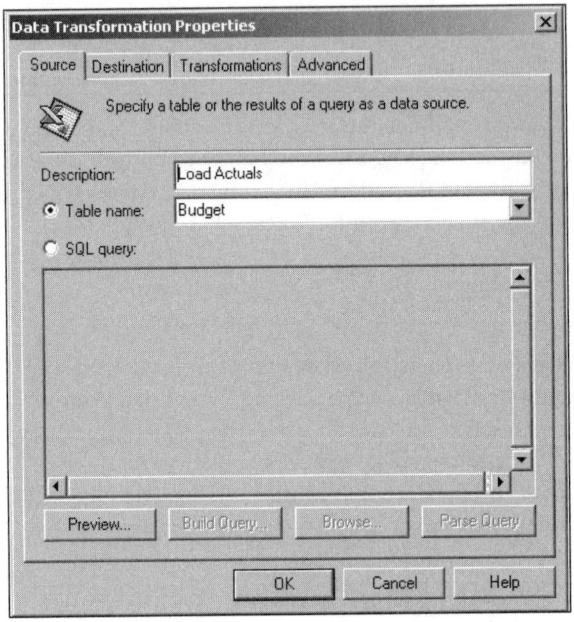

Figure 2.13 SQL Server 7.0 Source tab for the Transform Data Task using the Shipping Budget connection.

Select the Destination tab; then select the table name Actuals, which is also a named range in the Excel workbook. If necessary, the Transform Data Task can create a new sheet in the workbook that the connection is tied to, but because the sheet already exists, you will use it.

You will see Product, Jan, Feb, Mar, and so forth, in the Name column of the Table list. These names come from the first row of the named range. As you can see in Figure 2.14, you are making Excel act like a simple database.

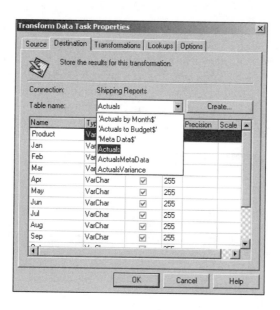

Figure 2.14   Destination tab for the SQL Server 2000 Transform Data Task using the Shipping Reports connection.

The Destination tab is slightly different for SQL Server 7.0 (see Figure 2.15).

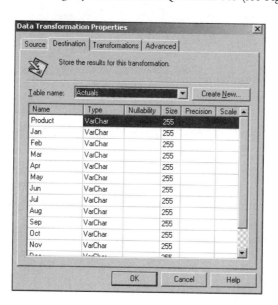

Figure 2.15   Destination tab for the SQL Server 7.0 Transform Data Task using the Shipping Reports connection.

Before you start mapping out the field-by-field transformations, you need to define two lookup queries. Lookup queries are a useful feature of DTS; they allow you to use a parameterized SQL statement to return zero to many values. You can use these queries to look up a value corresponding to a given ID, for example. Lookup queries can do more than just lookups, however; they also can execute any valid SQL statement, including inserts and stored procedures. You can specify lookups on the Lookups tab (see Figure 2.16).

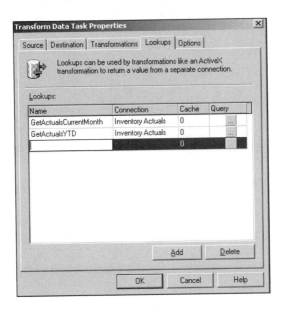

Figure 2.16   Lookups tab for the Transform Data Task in SQL Server 2000.

> SQL Server 7.0 users can find the lookup function in the Advanced tab by clicking the Lookups command button.

Click the Add button, type the name **GetActualCurrentMonth**, specify the connection Inventory Actuals, and then click the ellipsis button in the Query column to display the Query Builder. This screen is the same Query Builder available for the SQL Statement Task. Following is the query you need to run. This lookup will join the

Order, Order Details, and Product tables; constrain the rows selected by three parameters (Product Name, Actuals Month Number, and Current Year); and cumulate the quantity into a single total.

```
SELECT SUM([OrderDetails].[Quantity]) AS CumTotal
FROM ([Order] INNER JOIN OrderDetails ON [Order].[OrderID] =
[OrderDetails].[OrderID]) INNER JOIN Product ON [OrderDetails].[ProductID] =
[Product].[ProductID]
WHERE ([Product].[ProdName] = ?) AND (YEAR([Order].[ShippedDate]) = ?) AND
(MONTH([Order].[ShippedDate]) = ?);
```

The lookup query can accept any number of input parameters; in this case, you need three.

Now create the second lookup function, and name it `GetActualsYTD`. Specify the connection as Inventory, and click the ellipsis button to enter the Query Builder. This query will be almost exactly like the preceding one, but this time, instead of selecting only the transaction for the specified month, you will use all records up to the specified month for the current year, as follows:

```
SELECT SUM([OrderDetails].[Quantity]) AS CumTotal
FROM ([Order] INNER JOIN OrderDetails ON [Order].[OrderID] =
[OrderDetails].[OrderID]) INNER JOIN Product ON [OrderDetails].[ProductID] =
[Product].[ProductID]
WHERE ([Product].[ProdName] = ?) AND (YEAR([Order].[ShippedDate]) = ?) AND
(MONTH([Order].[ShippedDate]) <= ?);
```

The next step is to configure the column-level transformations. Click the Transformations tab and view the mappings between the source and destination columns in the two tables as follows:

1. Notice that DTS will try to match the columns of data in the source table to the destination columns, but because all you need from the source data at this time is the list of products in the budget, click the Delete All button to remove all the default mappings.

2. Click New to bring up the Create New Transformation dialog box.

3. Select ActiveX Script; then click OK.

4. Type **Copy Actuals** in the Name text box.

5. Select the Source Columns tab. You see a list of all the columns in the source database.

6. Double-click Products to make sure that it is selected.

7. Go to the Destination tab, and select all the destination columns by double-clicking the available column names.

   Be careful to select the columns from the bottom up. The data pump inside the Transform Data Task will reference columns in the opposite order from the order in which you select them (last in, first out). This system is important due to the way that you are going to reference the fields in your scripting. Figure 2.17 shows how the order should look.

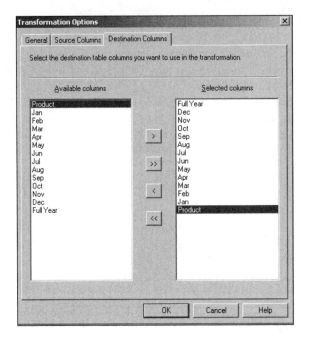

Figure 2.17   Selecting the destination columns for a particular transformation.

8. Go back to the General tab, and click Properties.

   You get a screen similar to the one for the ActiveX Script Task. You can write any script you want to aid in your manipulation of the data.

SQL Server 7.0 users can select the Transformations tab to map the source data to the destination data.

DTS will try to match the columns of data in the source table to the destination columns, but because all you need from the source data at this time is the list of products in the budget, remove all the default field mappings. To do so, hold down the Shift key, select the first field in the Destination Table fields list (Products), scroll down to the bottom of the list, select the last field (Full Year), and press the Delete key.

9. Click New to bring up the Create New Transformation dialog box and select ActiveX Script; then click OK.

10. Change the new transformation type from Copy Column to ActiveX Script, and click New.

Figure 2.18 shows how the tab should look just before you click the New button.

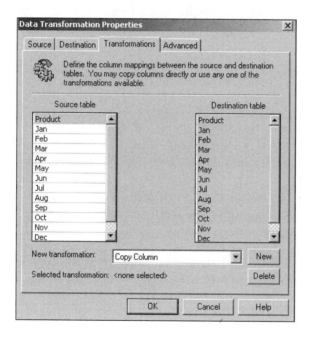

Figure 2.18   SQL Server 7.0 Transformations tab with all the mappings removed.

You get a screen similar to the one for the ActiveX Script Task. You can write any script you want to aid in your manipulation of the data.

11. Insert the product Name to the Destination.

You can reference the source or the destination fields by `DTSDestination("fieldname")` or `DTSSource("fieldname")`, as follows:

```
DTSDestination("Product") = DTSSource("Product")
```

Alternatively, you can reference the fields by their ordinal position, as follow (ordinal position uses a base of 1):

```
DTSDestination(1) = DTSSource(1)
```

DTSSource and DTSDestination

DTSSource and DTSDestination are two collections that the scripting can use to assist with the transformations. DTSSource is a collection of fields for one row of source data. This data is read-only information. DTSDestination is also a collection, but of the data destination fields. You can use the values in any source collection to generate and set values in the destination collection. In addition to the actual data value, you can reference the count of data fields, field name, numeric scale, precision, and so on. For more information, please see Chapter 4.

12. Cycle through all the months from 1 to the month number that was extracted from Excel and stored in the global variable "ActualsThroughMonth".

    You can reference global variables with the script DTSGlobalVariables ("variablename").Value. Following is the script for this example:

    ```
    For i = 1 to DTSGlobalVariables("ActualsThroughMonth").Value
    ```

13. Use the DTS Lookup that you created earlier to obtain a particular month's actuals, and store that value in the appropriate destination month.

    This step is where you use the ordinal reference to the destination fields. You will pass in three values, Product Name, Month Number (represented as i), and Current Year.

    To execute the lookup function that you created earlier, use the code DTSLookups("lookupname").Execute(parameter1, parameter2, parameter3, etc). For this example, the function will read as follows:

    ```
    DTSDestination(i+1) =
    DTSLookups("GetActualsCurrentMonth").Execute(DTSSource("Product"),i,
    DTSGlobalVariables("CurrentYear").Value)
    ```

14. Load the Year To Date Actuals, using the year-to-date lookup function, and also pass in the product name, the month number, and the current year from the global variable, as follows:

    ```
    DTSLookups("GetActualsYTD").Execute(DTSSource("Product"),
    DTSGlobalVariables("ActualsThroughMonth").Value),
    DTSGlobalVariables("CurrentYear").Value)
    ```

15. Notify the Transform Data Task that everything is OK and process the data into the destination.

    To do this, set the function called `main` equal to `DTSTransformStat_OK`, as follows:

    ```
    Main = DTSTransformStat_OK
    ```

    You can use many return values to tell the task what to do, from raising errors, to skipping the record to stopping all further processing of the package. For more information on return values, please see Chapter 4.

Listing 2.1 shows how the complete transform data script should read.

Listing 2.1   **Using the Transform Data Task, Global Variables, and the Lookup Query to Summarize and Populate Data into an Excel Spreadsheet**

```
Function Main()
    Dim i

    DTSDestination("Product") = DTSSource("Product")

    'Load Actuals for each month
    For i = 1 to DTSGlobalVariables("ActualsThroughMonth").Value
DTSDestination(i+1) = _ DTSLookups("GetActualsCurrentMonth")
➡.Execute(DTSSource("Product"),i, DTSGlobalVariables("CurrentYear").Value)
    Next
DTSDestination("Full Year") = _ DTSLookups("GetActualsYTD")
➡.Execute(DTSSource("Product"), DTSGlobalVariables("ActualsThroughMonth").Value),
➡DTSGlobalVariables("CurrentYear").Value)
    Main = DTSTransformStat_OK
End Function
```

To verify that the code is syntactically correct, click Parse. If your code parses correctly, click OK twice to return to the main Transform Data Task Properties dialog box (see Figure 2.19).

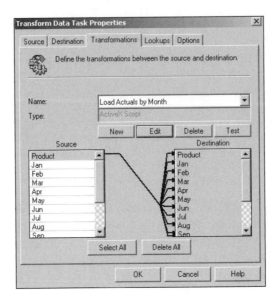

Figure 2.19   SQL Server 2000 Data Transformation mapping.

Figure 2.20 shows the main Transform Data Task Properties dialog box for SQL Server 7.0 after the scripting is complete.

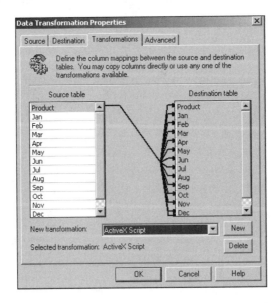

Figure 2.20   SQL Server 7.0 Data Transformation mapping.

Now you will see field mappings from Product to all the destination fields.

Step 6: Load Variance Report Data

Now create a second transform task between the Shipping Budget and Shipping Reports connections.

1. Double-click the newly created Transform Task arrow, and again set the source data to Budget.

> SQL Server 7.0 users will need to select the source and destination before selecting the Transform Data Task.

2. Set the Destination Table name to Actuals Variance.

    This report has Current Month Actuals, Current Month Better/Worse to Budget, YTD Actuals, and YTD Better/Worse to Budget. You need exactly the same lookup you used in the earlier transformation (`GetActualsCurrentMonth`, `GetActualsYTD`). Unfortunately, you will need to rebuild the lookups completely. At this time, DTS doesn't share the lookups between tasks.

3. Go back to the Transformations tab, select Delete All, and then choose Select All.

4. Click New. From the Create New Transformation dialog box, select ActiveX Script in the list of options.

5. For the name, type **Create Variance Report**.

6. Select Properties so that you can write the appropriate VBScript.

    As you did earlier, you will use the global variables, lookup functions, and source and destination field names.

    The first five lines of code is a simple data check on the global variable `ActualsThroughMonth`.

7. If the value is zero, initialize the global variable `ErrorMessage` with the string `"Actuals month value of"` and concatenate the string with the variable `ActualsThroughMonth` and the string `"is invalid"`.

    If the value of the global variable `ActualsThroughMonth` is zero, you will get the message `Actuals month value of 0 is invalid`. It then tells the data pump engine that the transformation step has an error (which will stop the processing of the data) with `Main = DTSTransformStat_Error`, as follows:

    ```
    If DTSGlobalVariables("ActualsThroughMonth").Value = 0 Then
        DTSGlobalVariables("ErrorMessage").Value = "Actuals month value of " &
        DTSGlobalVariables("ActualsThroughMonth").Value & " is invalid."
        Main = DTSTransformStat_Error
    Else
    ```

    If the variable is not zero, the script will process the record.

8. As you did for the first Transform Data Task, add the product name to the destination, as follows:

```
DTSDestination("Product") = DTSSource("Product")
```

9. Save the current-month actuals and YTD actuals for the current product, as follows:

```
CurrentMonthActl =
DTSLookups("GetActualsCurrentMonth").Execute(DTSSource("Product"),
DTSGlobalVariables("ActualsThroughMonth").Value,
DTSGlobalVariables("CurrentYear").Value)
YTDActl = DTSLookups("GetActualsYTD").Execute(DTSSource("Product"),
DTSGlobalVariables("ActualsThroughMonth").Value,
DTSGlobalVariables("CurrentYear").Value)
'Save Current Month actuals and YTD actuals for Product
DTSDestination("Current Month Actuals") = CurrentMonthActl
DTSDestination("YTD Actuals") = YTDActl
```

10. Cumulate the YTD budget, as follows:

```
For i = 1 to DTSGlobalVariables("ActualsThroughMonth").Value
    YTDBud = YTDBud + DTSSource(i+1)
Next
```

11. Calculate the difference between actuals and budget, and save that value to the destination, as follows:

```
DTSDestination("Current Month B/W Budget") = CurrentMonthActl -
DTSSource(DTSGlobalVariables("ActualsThroughMonth").Value+1)
DTSDestination("YTD B/W Budget") = YTDActl - YTDBud
```

12. If all has gone well, commit the changes to the destination, as follows:

```
Main = DTSTransformStat_OK
```

When complete, the entire script will look like Listing 2.2.

Listing 2.2 **Using the Transform Data Task, Global Variables, and the Lookup Query to Create an Actuals Versus Budget Report in Excel**

```
Function Main()

Dim CurrentMonthActl
Dim YTDActl
Dim i
Dim YTDBud


If DTSGlobalVariables("ActualsThroughMonth").Value = 0 Then
    DTSGlobalVariables("ErrorMessage").Value = "Actuals month value of " &
```

```
        DTSGlobalVariables("ActualsThroughMonth").Value & " is invalid."
        Main = DTSTransformStat_Error
    Else
        'Save Product Name to Report
        DTSDestination("Product") = DTSSource("Product")

    'Lookup Current Month actuals and YTD actuals for Product
        CurrentMonthActl =
        DTSLookups("GetActualsCurrentMonth").Execute(DTSSource("Product"),
        DTSGlobalVariables("ActualsThroughMonth").Value,
        DTSGlobalVariables("CurrentYear").Value)
        YTDActl = DTSLookups("GetActualsYTD").Execute(DTSSource("Product"),
        DTSGlobalVariables("ActualsThroughMonth").Value,
        DTSGlobalVariables("CurrentYear").Value)

    'Save Current Month actuals and YTD actuals for Product
        DTSDestination("Current Month Actuals") = CurrentMonthActl
        DTSDestination("YTD Actuals") = YTDActl

        'Cumulate YTD Budget
        For i = 1 to DTSGlobalVariables("ActualsThroughMonth").Value
            YTDBud = YTDBud + DTSSource(i+1)
        Next

        'Calculate the difference between actuals and budget and save
        DTSDestination("Current Month B/W Budget") = CurrentMonthActl -
        DTSSource(DTSGlobalVariables("ActualsThroughMonth").Value+1)
        DTSDestination("YTD B/W Budget") = YTDActl - YTDBud

        'Commit Changes to Destination
        Main = DTSTransformStat_OK
    End If

End Function
```

13. Test the code by clicking Parse.

14. If everything is fine, click OK twice to return to the main Transformations tab, which should look like Figure 2.21.

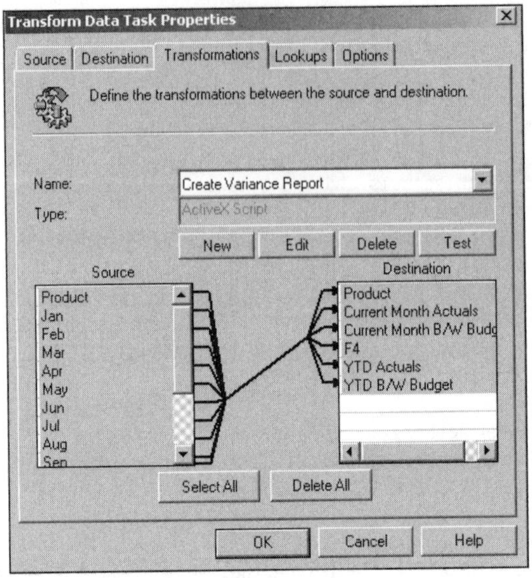

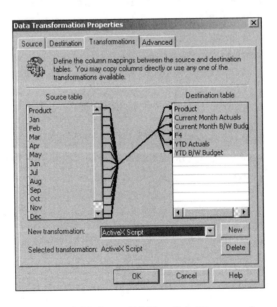

Figure 2.21 SQL Server 2000 Transform Data mappings.

The main Transformations tab will look like Figure 2.22 in SQL Server 7.0.

Figure 2.22 SQL Server 7.0 Transform Data mappings.

Step 7: Create Error Message

The final task is to create an error message if the package encounters a problem. With DTS, you have numerous options for notifying administrators of problems, such as e-mail messages, logs, or raising errors. For this example, you can use a VBScript message box. Normally, using this method is not a good idea, because it requires someone to be nearby to respond to it, but it is useful for this situation.

Create a script task that will display a dialog box if any task fails. The dialog box will display the text of the error message that has been stored in the global variable ErrorMessage. This new script task will have the following code:

```
MsgBox "We have an Error" & vbcrlf & DTSGlobalVariables("ErrorMessage").Value
    Main = DTSTaskExecResult_Success
```

Now you are ready to put your tasks together into a workflow.

Step 8: Add Workflow

All you need to do now is to specify the order in which the tasks are to be executed. Workflow specifies that order. For your reports for Bob, you want to make sure all tasks succeed before moving on to the next task. Figure 2.23 shows the package up to this point in SQL Server 2000.

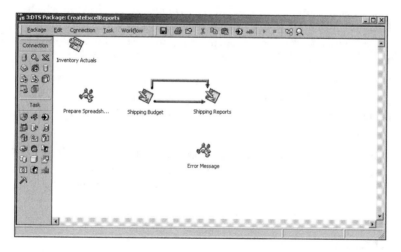

Figure 2.23   Partially completed package.

To add workflow, follow these steps

1. Hold down the Ctrl key, select the "from task" (Get Year), and select the "to task" (Shipping Budget).

2. Click the Workflow menu, and select On Success.

3. To specify an order of task execution between the two Transform Data Tasks, right-click the Load Actuals task to display the shortcut menu, and choose the workflow properties.

   In this case, you will wait until the Load Variance Report Task completes successfully.

4. Click OK to return to the DTS Designer window.

5. To place the error-handler workflow between Shipping Reports and Error Message.

   To do this, select Shipping Reports, hold down the Ctrl key, and select the Error Message Task that you created earlier. Then click the Workflow menu and select On Failure.

6. To review what the Designer built, double-click the red workflow line that was added.

   The Designer automatically added both Transformation Tasks in which Shipping Reports participates. If you want one centrally stationed error handler, you could always add as many precedence constraints as you need. But be careful—add too many and your graphical map becomes difficult to read.

7. Save and run the package.

   To do so, click the Package menu and select Execute to process the package. A process list of the tasks to be executed displays and lets you know whether the tasks were processed successfully.

If you want to see the error message from your script task, open the Shipping Reports spreadsheet, and change the value of cell B2 in Sheet Meta Data from 2 to 0. Save the spreadsheet, close Excel, and rerun your package. Now the package will fail, and the Script Task will display a small message dialog box.

Summary

This chapter is just the tip of the iceberg. You can add a little VBA script in Bob's spreadsheet that will run the package and update itself whenever Bob wants new data. This procedure is covered in Chapter 10, "Interacting with a Package Using Visual Basic." You can even have the package create the Excel spreadsheet locally and then email a copy of the file to a list of recipients. The options are endless.

The remaining chapters in Part I, "Data Transformation Services," will describe in detail the features of each connection, step, and task that comes with DTS, as well as all the properties and settings for the package, including package storage options, versioning, transaction, and performance capabilities. Part I will close by extending the example started in this chapter, showing you how to take advantage of some of those more advanced DTS features.

3

Connections

Microsoft SQL Server provides several connections for data transformation services right out of the box. DTS is able to use ODBC drivers and OLE DB providers to connect to database management systems, file system databases, applications, and text files. The following is the list of built-in connections that come with SQL Server 2000:

- Microsoft OLE DB Provider for SQL Server
- Microsoft ODBC Driver for Oracle
- Microsoft OLE DB Provider for DB2 (see the sidebar "DB2 Connection")
- Microsoft Access
- dBase 5
- Paradox 5.x
- Microsoft Excel 97–2000
- Text File (Source)
- Text File (Destination)
- HTML File (Source)
- Microsoft Data Link
- Other Connection

DB2 Connection

The connection for DB2 will be a connection-type option only if you have installed the driver for Microsoft OLE DB Provider for DB2. If you have not installed this driver, the DB2 connection will not be displayed in your toolbar or menus.

All these connections can be accessed from the DTS Designer window. To use any connection within a DTS package, click one of the connection icons in the tool palette in the DTS Designer window (see Figure 3.1). You can also select a connection from the Connection drop-down menu.

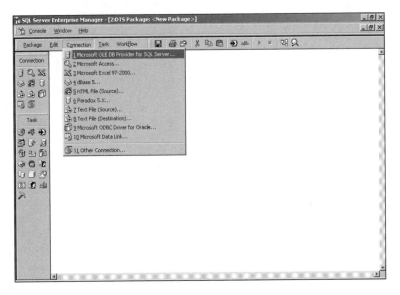

Figure 3.1   The DTS Designer window, showing the Connection tool palette. Connections are also listed in the Connection drop-down menu.

Finally, if you have special needs that none of these connections can meet, SQL Server supports the use of custom OLE DB providers created in Visual C++, Borland C++ Builder, and Delphi. (OLE DB providers created in Visual Basic are not compatible with DTS.) You can access these providers with the Other Connection option in the DTS Designer window.

When SQL Server 7.0 first came out with DTS, it did not include the HTML File option as a built-in connection.

When you select a particular connection, a dialog box pops up, prompting you for information necessary to set up the connection. These dialog boxes are organized according to the type of drivers being used: ODBC or OLE DB. Although most of the ODBC drivers have the same dialog box (Oracle being the exception), the dialog boxes used by the OLE DB providers vary based on how these providers are set up. Some connections require the setup or installation of other components to operate (Oracle client, for example).

Every connection, however, has certain common properties that need to be set. These properties are located at the top of the dialog box as option buttons and a drop-down menu (see Figure 3.2).

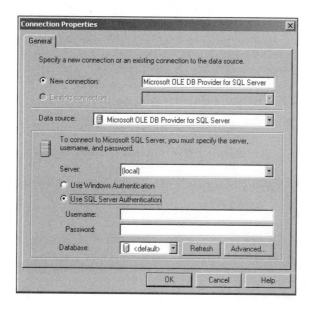

Figure 3.2   The New Connection, Existing Connection, and Data Source options are common properties for every connection.

First, you must select a new connection or existing connection at the top of the Connection Properties dialog box. If you select a new connection, you need to specify a name for the connection. This name must be unique within the current package.

If you select an existing connection, a drop-down menu allows you to select a connection you set up previously. You would use this option if you want to use more than one instance of the connection. One reason to use the Existing Connection option is to maintain the connection properties across the package. Any time you change the properties in one instance, those changes are applied to all instances of that connection (connections with the same names). SQL Server Books Online (BOL), however, recommends that you always create a new connection to support lookups for performance reasons.

When you are deciding whether to use an existing connection or create a new connection, you need to consider what the greater needs of the package will be. Will you need to have high performance? If so, you probably should use multiple connections, as each new connection will garner its own resources. Will your package be high-maintenance and need to be touched often? If so, consider using the existing connection to simplify package design and maintenance.

Connections and Execution

When you are creating a package, it is possible to use many connections that refer to the same data source. When you have many tasks that use the same data sources, you have a couple of options, each of which affects the execution of a package. At first glance, it might seem logical to reuse an existing connection many times. You need to keep in mind, however, that reusing a connection can result in slower performance. DTS can use only one connection at a time during the execution of a package, so tasks using the same connection will be executed in serial. If you create multiple connections to the same data source, however, the tasks can be executed in parallel. You will need to determine how many tasks you want to execute in parallel versus how many connections you want to maintain. Used effectively, this procedure will increase performance without complicating package maintenance.

The final common property for you to set is the data source. The Data Source drop-down menu lists the available ODBC drivers and OLE DB drivers installed on the server.

The following sections discuss the various properties necessary to establish specific connections.

Database Management System Connections

Database management systems are generally server-based systems, such as Oracle and Microsoft SQL Server. In both cases, you will need to provide the server name, a username, and a password.

Microsoft OLE DB Provider for SQL Server

Microsoft OLE DB Provider for SQL Server (refer to Figure 3.2) allows both Windows authentication and SQL Server login and password. If you choose to use Windows authentication, it is important to know that whoever is logged into the server will be the Windows user that the connection will try to authenticate to SQL Server.

The SQL servers that are available on the Windows network are listed in the drop-down Server menu. After you have selected the server and *successfully* authenticated to the server, the Database drop-down menu will be populated with the available databases in that server. You can use the Refresh button to reset the list of databases available on this server.

Advanced Properties

In the Connection Properties dialog box for SQL Server, you will see an Advanced button. If the OLE DB provider supports additional properties—such as Connection Timeout, General Timeout, Current Language, Network Library, and Network Address—you can view and edit those properties in the Connections Properties dialog box. Before using these properties, check the help or support files that come with the OLE DB provider for more details. One of the key properties exposed is Persist Security Info, which determines whether to persist the security information (username and password) with the package.

Microsoft ODBC Driver for Oracle

When using the Oracle connection, you must install an Oracle client, version 7.3 or later. Without this client, you will be unable to use this connection.

After you have installed the Oracle client successfully, you will need to set up the remaining properties. The server property is the global database name of the Oracle instance to which you are trying to connect. Then you will need to provide a valid Oracle username and password (see Figure 3.3).

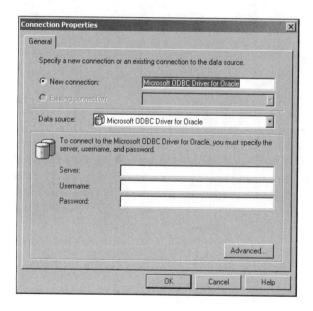

Figure 3.3   Microsoft ODBC Driver for Oracle.

File System Database Connections

The parameters for file system databases are the same for Paradox 5.x, dBase 5, and Microsoft Access (see Figure 3.4). For all these connections, you will need to enter or browse for the filename (UNC names are valid). You will also need to provide a valid username and password for the database.

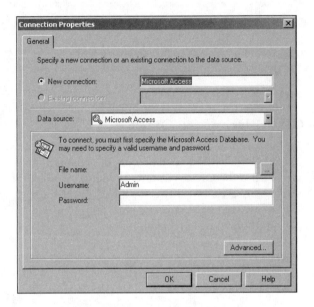

Figure 3.4   Microsoft Access.

Microsoft Access System Database

When using the Microsoft Access connection, you need to consider carefully the impact of using a secured Access database. If you need to access a secure database, you will need to obtain the name and location of the system database. This information will need to be entered in the advanced properties of the connection. By default, the connection is set up to read your default system database and log in the Admin user with an empty password. In a secured database, however, you will need to have a valid username, password, and system database.

Application Connections

By default, the Microsoft Excel connection is the only application connection in DTS. This connection has one property: the filename. You can enter the full path directly or browse for it (see Figure 3.5).

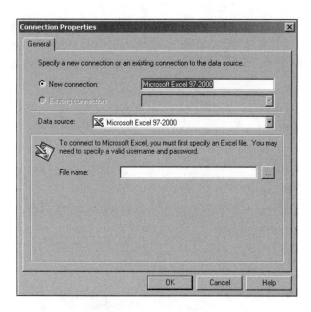

Figure 3.5 Microsoft Excel 97–2000.

Text File Connections

You can set up delimited and fixed-width text files as data sources or destinations. You can also use tables in HTML files as data sources.

Text File (Source and Destination)

The text file connections are direction-specific. One connection is used as the source, and the other is used as the destination. Two connection types are needed because the properties of a destination file connection are different from those of a source file connection. You will need to use the Properties button to define the file specifications for either delimited or fixed-width text files.

You will need to set the following properties for both fixed-width and delimited text files: File Type, Row Delimiter, and number of rows to skip (Skip Rows). You can also let DTS know that the first row is column names (see Figure 3.6).

When you select Fixed Field, you will be able to select the positions of the lengths of the fields (see Figure 3.7).

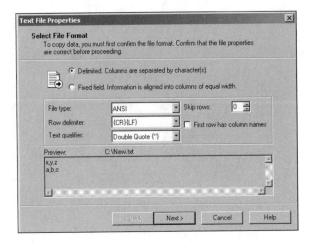

Figure 3.6 Text File Properties dialog box, Select File Format screen.

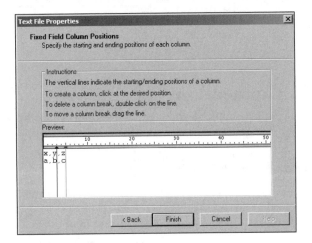

Figure 3.7 The Fixed Field Column Positions screen.

When you select the Delimited file type, you will be able to set a text qualifier on the main properties page. After you set the common properties, click Next. The next screen will let you specify the delimiter, and you will be able to see a sample result of the data using your selection (see Figure 3.8).

HTML File (Source)

You can also use an HTML file as a data source. (As yet, an HTML File destination connection is not supported by the connection type.) The properties available for this connection are the filename, which you can type in the text box or browse for (see

Figure 3.9). Because this connection uses the Jet Engine (like Microsoft Access), you can also specify a username and password. The advanced properties available with this connection are also based on the Jet OLE DB provider. See the advanced properties for Microsoft Access for further information.

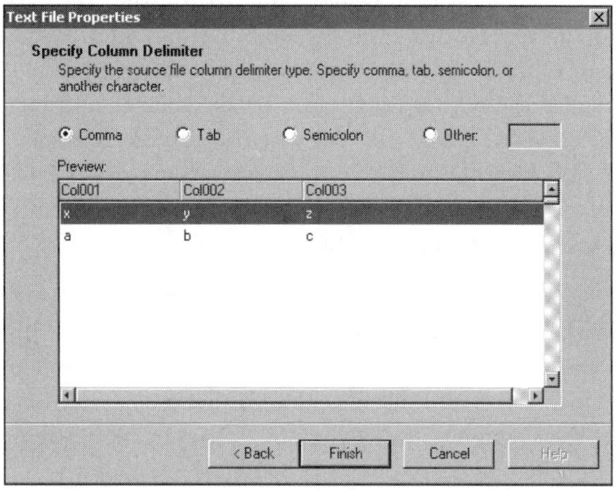

Figure 3.8   Specify Column Delimiter screen.

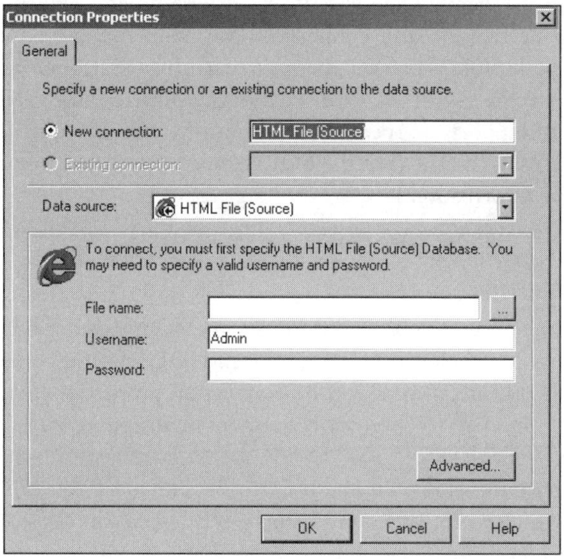

Figure 3.9   HTML File (Source) screen.

Microsoft Data Links

You can use Microsoft Universal Data Links to create a valid DTS connection. Data links are a great way to create connections that are resolved at run time. You can create a connection and store the connection information in a file that can be edited without being resolved by DTS. The data link allows you to edit the connection information (username, server name, password, even the OLE DB provider) without editing the connection properties in the package. Some of these changes can break the package, however. In particular, the package will often break when the provider is changed.

Data links are Universal Data Link files that you can create before setting up the connection or the package through Windows 2000, Windows NT 4, Windows 98, or Windows ME. (Refer to the help topic "Using Data Link" in the operating system for detailed help on creating a data link outside DTS.)

SQL 7.0 Data-Link Limitations

Unlike SQL Server 2000, SQL Server 7.0 does not support run-time resolution of Microsoft Universal Data Link files, so SQL Server 7.0 needs to resolve the connection before saving the package. In SQL Server 2000, you create or edit the UDL without having to resolve it in DTS, which allows you to create or edit a UDL with references to data sources that are not currently available. (In other words, you do not have access to the database, but you can still create the UDL with the correct data access information.) Sometimes, however, it is advantageous to use the data link, because it will expose other connection properties that might be needed for your connection. You will need to be cautious when using UDLs with SQL Server 7.0, because performance issues might arise. These issues are due to the use of the OLE DB Service Provider for session handling and the lack of support for `IrowsetFastLoad` in MDAC 2.1 and MDAC 2.5 when you are using UDLs. (See the SQL Server BOL Data Link Connection topic for more information.)

UDL Link Name

At this point, you can type or browse for the name of an existing UDL file (see Figure 3.10). If you select Always Read Properties From UDL File, the connection will always refer to the file at run time for the connection properties. If you do not select this option, the properties for the connection will be stored in the DTS package and can be changed only in DTS.

Microsoft Data Link works only with OLE DB providers. You can use the OLE DB Provider for ODBC to work with many ODBC data sources that do not have a specific OLE DB provider. (See "Other Connections" later in this chapter for more information on using the OLE DB Provider for ODBC.)

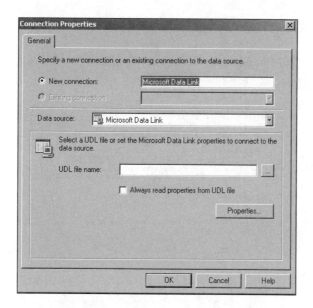

Figure 3.10   Microsoft Data Link connection.

Data Link Properties

Click the Properties button to display the Data Link Properties dialog box, where you can edit the properties of an existing file or set up the properties for a new UDL file. The dialog box has four tabs (see Figure 3.11), which are described in detail in the following list (not all of these tabs are available for every provider):

- **Provider**—Select the provider in the list, and click Next.
- **Connection**—This tab lists the provider-specific connection properties. For detailed information on a specific provider, see the section in this chapter that discusses the provider you want to use. You may also refer to any help documentation that the provider includes.
- **Advanced**—This tab allows you to set some advanced properties. In particular, the Network Settings and Other section includes connection timeout and access permissions.
- **All**—If you go directly to the All tab, you can see and edit all the values set in the other tabs. This tab also includes any OLE DB provider properties not shown in the other tabs.

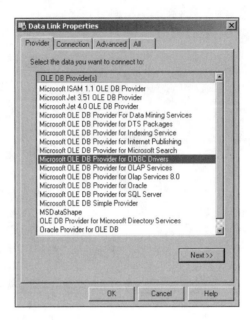

Figure 3.11   Data Link Properties dialog box.

Other Connections

If DTS does not include the provider you need, you can use the Other Connection
option to access ODBC data sources. To use this connection, you will need to select
or create a data source name (DSN) for the driver you have selected. DTS allows you
to use all the DSN types: user, system, and file. From DTS, you can create a new data
source by clicking the New button in the Connection Properties dialog box located
adjacent to the User/System field.

Lotus Notes is a good example of a data source that has an ODBC driver available
on its Web site; you can download this driver and use it with DTS. As always, it is
important to follow carefully the instructions provided with any third-party driver.

You can also create a custom OLE DB provider by using the Visual Studio tool
Visual C++. Refer to `http://msdn.microsoft.com` for more information.

Editing Connections

If you want to edit the properties of a connection, be aware that DTS will try to validate the new properties when trying to save the new settings. If you choose a server that does not exist or is currently unavailable, for example, DTS will not save the changes. (You can work around this by using Disconnected Edit to modify the properties. Disconnected Edit is discussed in detail in Chapter 7, "Package.") If you connect to the data source successfully, using the changes you have implemented, you will be prompted to delete or leave the connection properties of any data-transformation tasks that use the connection.

To rename a connection, right-click the connection you want to rename, and choose Properties from the shortcut menu (refer to Figure 3.2). Select the New Connection option. Then enter the new name for the connection, and click OK. Once again, you will be prompted to delete or leave any data-transformation tasks associated with the connection. If you need to change the name of other connections to this name, open the Properties dialog box for each connection to be changed, and select the new name from the Existing Connections drop-down menu.

Summary

This chapter covered the basics of setting up and editing connections. Using the variety of connections available, you can access and use most data repositories. If the connection is not available by default, remember that you can use a third-party OLE DB or ODBC connection.

4

DTS Tasks

ASKS DEFINE THE WORK UNITS THAT are performed within a DTS package. They are the means by which you specify what you want to happen when the package executes.

Microsoft SQL Server provides several predefined tasks right out of the box. These tasks enable you to copy and manage data, copy and manage SQL Server databases as well as database objects, execute SQL statements and scripts, send mail, and more.

Table 4.1 lists the built-in tasks that come with SQL Server 2000. Note how the tasks are grouped, starting with the data-movement tasks, whose primary functions are to move and transform data. The Transform Data Task is a high-speed tool for accessing, transforming, and writing data. By contrast, the Data Driven Query Task offers more flexibility in terms of processing but takes a performance hit as a result. The Bulk Insert Task specializes exclusively in high-performance loading of text into SQL Server tables.

Table 4.1 **DTS Tasks**

Icon	Built-In Task
	Transform Data Task
	Data Driven Query Task
	Bulk Insert Task
	Execute SQL Task
	ActiveX Script Task
	Execute Process Task
	Execute Package Task
	Dynamic Properties Task
	Send Mail Task
	File Transfer Protocol Task
	Message Queue Task
	Transfer SQL Server Objects Task (now called Copy SQL Server Objects Task)
	Transfer Databases Task
	Transfer Logins Task
	Transfer Master Stored Procedures Task
	Transfer Jobs Task
	Transfer Error Messages Task
	Analysis Services Processing Task
	Data Mining Task

Following the data-movement tasks are the programming tasks, whose purpose is to give you more flexibility in defining how the work is to be done in a DTS package. If you're dealing with data that is already in database tables and views, Execute SQL Task allows you to perform virtually any SQL-based processing on the data. The ultimate flexibility, however, is provided by the ActiveX Script Task, which allows you to program your custom processes by using one of several available scripting languages. The Execute Package Task now provides full support for multiple package execution. In SQL 7.0, you either run a batch file from the Execute Process Task (as mentioned next), or use an ActiveX Script Task. The Execute Process Task provides support for running batch files and EXEs. The Dynamic Properties Task enables packages to obtain run-time parameters for execution.

Next are the group of tasks that focus on specialized processes such as sending email, receiving text and binary files, and handling asynchronous messages. The Send Mail Task enables packages to send email as part of its processing. The File Transfer Protocol Task supports the downloading of files from within and outside the local network. (You can also upload, but only within the network.) The Message Queue Task enables packages to deal with asynchronous messaging capabilities, in which the sender and the recipient of messages don't have to be physically connected to the network at the same time.

These tasks are followed by the database-maintenance tasks, which help you move SQL objects in and out of SQL Server databases.

When you install SQL Server's Analysis Services option, you get the two OLAP or data-warehousing tasks. The Analysis Services Task assists in automating some of the processing of cubes and other objects contained in Microsoft SQL Server 2000 Analysis Services. The Data Mining Task is used for running prediction queries in data mining models (again, within SQL Server 2000 Analysis Services).

Finally, if you have special needs that none of these tasks can meet, SQL Server allows you to create your own custom tasks. Chapter 16, "Creating Your Own Custom Task," shows you how to create one by using any programming language that supports COM (such as Visual Basic). It also shows you how to create a user interface complete with its own icon so that you can access your custom task from the DTS Designer window just like any of the built-in tasks.

Table 4.2 lists the original set of tasks available with SQL Server 7.0. The built-in set of tasks in SQL Server 2000 have been expanded significantly.

Table 4.2   **Built-In Tasks Available with SQL Server 7.0**

Icon	Built-In Task
	Transform Data Task
	Data Driven Query Task
	Bulk Insert Task
	Execute SQL Task
	ActiveX Script Task
	Execute Process Task
	Transfer SQL Server Objects Task (now called Copy SQL Server Objects Task)
	Send Mail Task

As the new .NET servers are launched, you will find DTS playing an even bigger role. Just with Commerce Server 2000 (CS2000) alone, the number of DTS tasks will double. This chapter examines the built-in tasks and explores what they have to offer.

Using DTS Tasks

To use a built-in task within a DTS package, click one of the task icons in the tool palette on the left side of the DTS Designer window (see Figure 4.1). You can also choose a task from the Task drop-down menu.

When you choose a task, an appropriate form pops up that prompts you for information necessary for the proper execution of that task. In some instances, a wizard walks you through the various sets of information needed by the task. Other tasks require you to define a connection first or to configure certain services (such as the MAPI messaging service).

The following sections discuss the data-movement tasks in detail and show you how to use them to support your extraction, transformation, and loading (ETL) processing needs. As you go through these first few tasks, you will notice that you are being introduced to some DTS features that are used elsewhere—in other tasks as well as other areas of DTS. This book will cover each feature thoroughly; keep in mind that you may meet them again as you move on to the rest of the book.

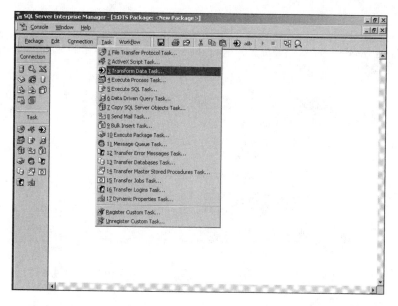

Figure 4.1   The DTS Designer window, showing tasks in the tool palette. Tasks are also listed in the Task drop-down menu.

Using the Transform Data Task

All functions that move and transform data in DTS reside in a DTS component called the *data pump*. As a COM object, the data pump exposes several interfaces that support high-speed movement of data, specialized and custom transformations of data, and use of scripting to perform and control such transformations. The Transform Data Task is the most fundamental implementation of this data-pump engine. This task supports various types of data sources and data destinations. The most important feature of this task is that it is optimized for inserting data rows into the specified destination. In addition, as it moves the data row by row, the task can apply transformations that you can optionally define on one or more columns.

To use the Transform Data Task, you must have two data connections already defined. You will be asked to click on the source connection first and the destination connection next.

Preselect Your Source Connection

If you happen to have one data connection selected (which is often the case because you most likely will have just created your destination connection), DTS assumes that the connection is your *source* connection and simply asks you to click on the destination connection. Make sure that the source connection is selected and that none of the data connections are selected before you create the task.

When you click the destination connection, an arrow will be displayed that points from the source to the destination. This arrow *is* the Transform Data Task. Right-click on the arrow and choose Properties from the shortcut menu to display the Transform Data Task Properties dialog box (see Figure 4.2).

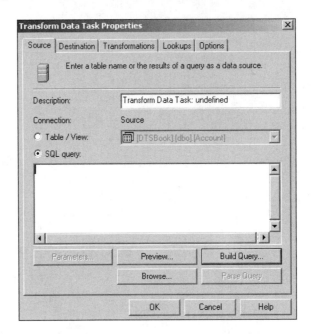

Figure 4.2   Using the Transform Data Task.

The Transform Data Task Properties dialog box has five tabs that require information to make the task run properly. These tabs are Source, Destination, Transformations, Lookups, and Options.

> In SQL 7.0, the Transform Data Task Properties dialog box has only four tabs: Source, Destination, Transformations, and Advanced. The Advanced tab is essentially the same as the Options tab in SQL 2000, except that it contains a Lookup button for defining lookup queries. In SQL 2000, a separate tab, Lookups, has been added.

Setting up the Source Data

In the Source tab, you can choose to use a table or a view that exists in your source data connection. You can take a peek at a portion of the actual data by clicking the Preview button. This procedure is a good way to verify that you are accessing the correct data.

If your source connection supports it, you can use a query instead. You can load an existing query from a file by clicking the Browse button. Query files (with the extension .sql) usually are created and saved from an SQL editor such as SQL 2000's Query Analyzer. If you want to create a new query, you can type it in directly or you can use the Query Designer as discussed in the following section. When the query is ready, you can click the Parse Query button to validate the query's SQL statement.

Using the Query Designer

About the Query Designer

The Query Designer is one of the common features that is used in various places within DTS. You can use it for building source queries and for building lookup queries, as discussed in the "Performing Lookups" section later in this chapter.

The Query Designer allows you to build your SQL query in a graphical manner. It is similar in many ways to the query builders that you see in many desktop database products, including Microsoft Access and Visual Basic. To use the Query Designer, click the Build Query button to bring up the Query Designer window (see Figure 4.3).

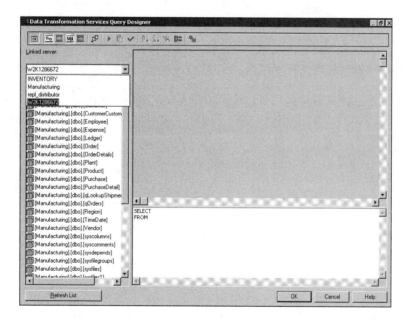

Figure 4.3   The Query Designer window.

In the left pane, the Linked Server drop-down menu defaults to the server specified by the connection you selected for the query. If you have other linked servers defined that give you access to some other remote servers, you will see those in the drop-down menu as well. Note that even if you defined multiple data source connections in the package, only the server associated with the connection that you selected for the query is listed in the drop-down menu.

> **About Linked Servers**
>
> The Linked Server drop-down menu option is available only when using a Microsoft SQL Server data source connection. For more detailed information on linked servers, see SQL Server Books Online (BOL).

After selecting the server, you see a list of available tables and views that you can use in your query. Drag one of these to the top-right window; the object is displayed with all its available columns. When you click the check boxes that correspond to the column, those columns appear in the SELECT statement in the bottom window.

Because the query is based on a SELECT statement, you are not limited to just one table or view. You can drag one or more tables in and join these tables together. You can even specify if these joins are inner or outer joins. This ability to define a complex query is very important because it potentially can offer higher performance than using lookup queries (see the "Performing Lookups" section later in this chapter).

The graphical drag-and-drop capability really takes away the stress of having to learn or understand the complexities of SQL without limiting the power of the queries that are produced.

Using Parameters in the Query

Another benefit of using an SQL query is that it allows you to use dynamic data to selectively build the rows in your data source. In SQL, if the OLE DB service provider supports it, you can use question marks (?) as placeholders within a SQL statement, as in this example:

```
SELECT Customer.CompanyName, Order.OrderID FROM Customer
INNER JOIN Order ON Customer.CustomerID = Order.CustomerID
WHERE Order.ShippedDate > ?
```

The query expects input data to be provided for these placeholders at the time it executes.

In SQL Server 2000, when you build a query with one or more placeholders in the Query Designer window, DTS creates a Parameters collection and then parses the SQL statement from left to right, inserting an item in the collection for each placeholder. It is essential for you to know that DTS then maps your global variables as input to these parameters. *You must ensure that the correct input variable is mapped properly to each parameter so that the proper input data is made available at run time.* To do this, close the Query Designer to return to the Source tab of the Transform Data Task Properties dialog box; then click the Parameters button to bring up the Parameter Mapping dialog box (see Figure 4.4).

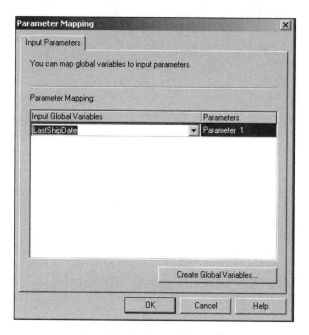

Figure 4.4   The Parameter Mapping dialog box.

The input variables that the parameters get mapped to are *global* variables. Global variables belong to the DTS package, not the task, and can be accessed from anywhere within the package. This arrangement makes sense in that it allows you to set the value of these variables outside the current task before its execution, in much the same way that you would set a variable before passing it as a parameter into a function or procedure.

You can choose the variable to map to each parameter from the corresponding drop-down menu. If you want to create a new global variable, click the Create Global Variables button to bring up the Global Variables dialog box (see Figure 4.5).

This dialog box is very similar to the Global Variables tab of the DTS Package Properties dialog box, where you can create and manage all global variables used in the DTS package (see Chapter 7, "Package").

In SQL Server 7.0, you can use SQL queries in specifying your data source, but you have no easy way to use parameters in the query. SQL Server 2000 exposes the parameters, making it very easy to use dynamic queries for your data source.

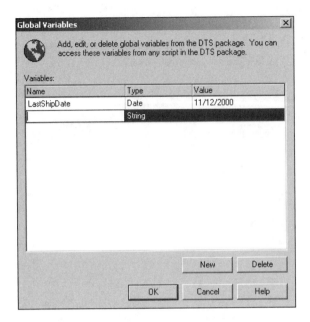

Figure 4.5 The Global Variables dialog box.

Setting up the Destination Table

The Destination tab is where you specify the table into which the source rows will be inserted (see Figure 4.6). If the destination table does not exist, DTS offers to create the table for you (assuming that the underlying data source connection supports it). You need to be careful because DTS will create the table as soon as you click the OK button. You can customize the new table by modifying the creation script that DTS offers. If you canceled out of DTS's initial table-creation offer, you can invoke it again by clicking the Create button. When the table is created, the columns are listed in read-only fashion, meaning that you cannot alter the attributes of the table.

It is important to note that in a Transform Data Task, the destination table is where the data actually ends up.

Transformations

Transformations specify how each source column is processed and which destination column (if any) such processing will affect. You create and manage transformations in the Transformations tab (see Figure 4.7). Transformations are powerful because they provide you with a wide array of methods for customizing how your data is processed.

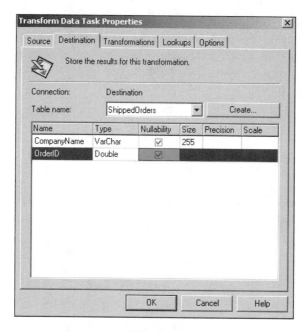

Figure 4.6   The Destination tab.

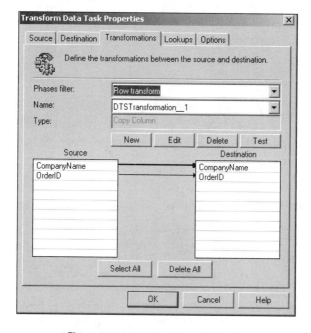

Figure 4.7   The Transformations tab.

The first time you bring up the Transformations tab in a Transform Data Task, you will see that each column is pre-assigned the default transformation Copy Column. Using the task "as is" provides a great and simple way to copy data from one container to another. However, if you need to do more than just copy a column's data, you can delete the default transformation and define a new one by choosing from the built-in DTS transformation types.

Understanding the Built-In Transformation Types

When SQL 7.0 first came out, the only transformations available were Copy Column and ActiveX Script. SQL 2000 has nine built-in transformation types. To create a new transformation, select the source and destination columns, and click New. This will bring up the Create New Transformation dialog box (see Figure 4.8), which lists all the available transformation types.

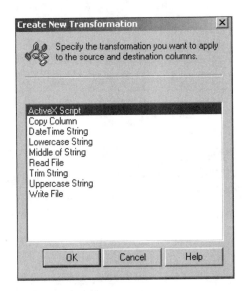

Figure 4.8   The available transformation types.

Table 4.3 lists each of these transformation types and explains their general usage.

Table 4.3   **Transformation Types**

Transformation	**Description**
ActiveX Script	Allows you to write scripts to define column-level transformations.
Copy Column	Copies the data from source to destination. You must map source columns to destination columns. You can map multiple source columns to multiple destination

Transformation	Description
	columns. If you specify no columns, DTS performs a sequential One-to-One mapping of all the columns. When text is truncated, no error or notification is reported.
DateTime String	Allows you to define how date and time values are converted to strings and other formats. You must specify one source column and one destination column, both of which must be compatible with the `datetime` data type.
Lowercase String	Converts strings to lowercase. You must specify the same number of source and destination columns, each of which must be of the `string` data type.
Middle of String	Extracts parts of a string; optionally, converts its case and trims trailing spaces. You must specify the same number of source and destination columns, each of which must be of the `string` data type.
Read File	Copies into the destination column data from a file specified by the source column. You must specify one source column with the string data type. You also must specify a destination column with either a `string` or `binary` data type.
Trim String	Trims leading and trailing spaces; optionally, converts its case. You must specify the same number of source and destination columns, each of which must be of the `string` data type.
Uppercase String	Converts strings to uppercase. You must specify the same number of source and destination columns, each of which must be of the `string` data type.
Write File	Writes data from a source column to a file specified by a second source column. You must specify one source column with the `string` data type. You also must specify a second source column with either a `string` or `binary` data type. You should not specify a destination column.

Most of the transformation types listed in Table 4.3 are self-explanatory and perform relatively simple tasks. However, two of these new transformation types deserve special consideration: Read File and Write File.

If a source column specifies a filename, you can use the Read File transformation to specify the location of this file and copy its contents into the destination column. This transformation can be useful when you are receiving multiple files from different locations, for example, and when you need to load their contents into SQL Server. Save the files in one directory, and list the names of the files in a text file that becomes your data source. When the transformation executes, it opens the file specified by the source column and loads the file's contents into the destination column.

The Write File transformation, on the other hand, will take data from a source column and write it out to a file specified in a second source column. This can be useful when you need to distribute location-specific data to different locations. Set up your data source so that it has at least two columns: a data column and a filename column. When this transformation executes, data contained in the data column will be written to a file specified in the filename column.

> In SQL Server 7.0, the only built-in transformations available are Copy Column and ActiveX Script.

Understanding the Transformation Flags

Each transformation that is created can be customized without writing any code by simply using transformation flags. Transformation flags signal DTS to follow certain predefined rules when the transformation is performed. To set a flag for a transformation, use the Transformations tab of the Transform Data Task Properties dialog box. This tab graphically displays all the column mappings between the source and destination that are used in the task.

Right-click on the line representing the column transformation; then click on Flags to bring up the Transformation Flags dialog box (see Figure 4.9).

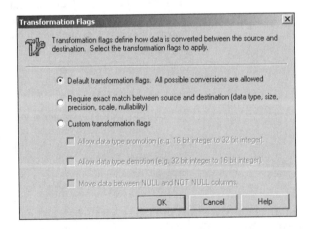

Figure 4.9 Setting transformation flags.

The Default Transformation Flag is the least restrictive option. It allows all possible data conversions to occur. The Require Exact Match Between Source and Destination Flag enforces data type matching between source and destination columns. The Custom Transformation Flag allows you to customize the rules using any combination of three suboptions:

- **Allow Data Type Promotion**—Allows the transformation to convert 16-bit integers to 32-bit integers.

- **Allow Data Type Demotion**—Allows the transformation to convert 32-bit integers to 16-bit integers.

- **Move Data Between NULL and NOT NULL Columns**—Allows the transformation to proceed in case it involves a source that allows nulls and a destination that does not. When a NULL does come through, an exception is reported.

In the data pump, these options are implemented using `DTSTransformFlags` constants. You can set the data pump's `TransformFlags` property programmatically by using these constants. Table 4.4 lists all the possible transformation flags available. As you can see, you can have even tighter control of how the flags are set.

Table 4.4   **Transformation Types**[1]

Flag	Description
DTSTransformFlag_AllowDemotion	Allows the transfer to proceed even if there are potential overflows. Overflows that actually occur during transformation cause the row to be exceptioned. You can specify this value when the source values are all (or mostly) within the range of the destination column.
DTSTransformFlag_AllowLosslessConversion	Allows all conversions for which a lossless conversion is possible (for example, Promotion, non-NULLable -> NULLable, unsigned -> signed with field size increase).
DTSTransformFlag_AllowNullChange	Allows the transfer to proceed even if the source column allows NULL values and the destination column does not. Any row actually containing NULL is exceptioned, however.
DTSTransformFlag_AllowNumericTruncation	Allows the transfer to proceed even when numeric truncation is possible, such as when the source is a floating-point or numeric/decimal type and the destination is an integral type. Loss of significance occurs without error, but integer overflow still causes an error.
DTSTransformFlag_AllowPromotion	Allows the transfer to proceed when promotion in the data range occurs when moving from the source to the destination types, such as I2->I4 or I4->float/double.

continues

Table 4.4 **Continued**

Flag	Description
DTSTransformFlag_AllowSignChange	Allows the transfer to proceed even in the event that the source and destination have a signed versus unsigned mismatch. As with DTSTransformFlag_AllowDemotion, errors may occur during a transform.
DTSTransformFlag_AllowStringTruncation	Allows column (w)char or byte data to be truncated silently (for example, when moving data from a char(60) to a char(40) column).
DTSTransformFlag_Default	Includes the default flag combination of DTSTransformFlag_AllowDemotion, DTSTransformFlag_AllowNullChange, DTSTransformFlag_AllowNumericTruncation, DTSTransformFlag_AllowPromotion, DTSTransformFlag_AllowSignChange, and DTSTransformFlag_AllowStringTruncation.
DTSTransformFlag_ForceConvert	Allows the conversion to proceed at all times, even when the source and destination types are fundamentally different; does a bitwise copy when no other conversion is appropriate.
DTSTransformFlag_PreserveDestRows	Causes the data pump to not clear the destination row storage at the end of row processing. This allows the destination row values to be reused by the next transformation.
DTSTransformFlag_RequireExactType	Requires that the data type of the destination column be exactly the same as the data type of the source column (including length or precision and scale, fixed versus variable length, sign, and nullability).
DTSTransformFlag_Strict	Specifies no flags. The conversion must be between exact types, although conversions between string and nonstring data types is allowed and may cause errors. This value may be overridden by DTSTransformFlag_RequireExactType, which is even stricter.

1. *This table was copied from Microsoft SQL Server 2000 Version 8.00.000 BOL. This information is available on the SQL Server installation CD.*

The ActiveX Script Property Window

Perhaps the most powerful transformation available to you is the ActiveX Script transformation. This section examines that transformation in more detail. You must use an ActiveX Script transformation if you need to perform special calculations or more complex processing on a column. Right-click on the line representing the column transformation; then click on Properties to bring up the ActiveX Script Transformation Properties dialog box (see Figure 4.10).

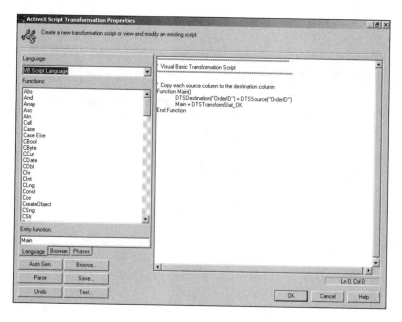

Figure 4.10 ActiveX Script Transformation Properties dialog box.

ActiveX Script's Multiple Uses

The ActiveX Script Transformation Properties dialog box is another common feature used throughout DTS. ActiveX scripts are used in transformations as explained here, as well as in customizing workflows (see Chapter 6, "DTS Workflows"). These scripts also may be used on a stand-alone basis in an ActiveX Script Task (see Chapter 5, "More DTS Tasks").

Click the Language tab to select your scripting language. Microsoft VBScript and JScript are available by default, but any other scripting language you install on your machine should show up here, too. The corresponding language elements are displayed in the left pane.

Installing Third-Party Scripting Languages

You can install a third-party scripting language and use it in an ActiveX script, but you must ensure that the scripting language is installed on the PCs that execute the DTS package. (DTS packages can be run on remote PCs as well as on the server.)

New in SQL 2000 is the Browser tab (see Figure 4.11). In this tab, you can choose constants, columns, and global variables, as well as source and destination columns, and then have DTS insert the corresponding code into the scripting pane on the right side of the dialog box, which is a great help when writing script.

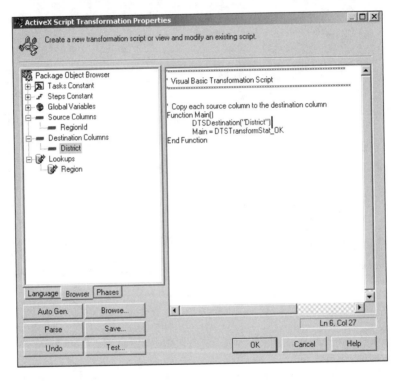

Figure 4.11   The Browser tab.

For example, double-clicking the District object under Destination Columns in the Browser pane generates the code `DTSDestination("VariableCost") =` `DTSSource("state")` and inserts it at the cursor location on the scripting pane.

Using the scripting language of your choice, you can write script that performs significantly complex processing in your transformation. Remember, however, that the processing that you define in each transformation will occur for *each* row. Try not to overload transformations if you don't want performance to suffer.

Performance Hit Posed By Complex Scripts

An important thing to remember is that all the script specified in an ActiveX script transformation gets executed for *each* row that is processed. This may potentially impact the performance of the task.

ActiveX scripts are used in transformations as explained in this chapter as well as in Chapter 6. You also can use these scripts on a stand-alone basis in an ActiveX Script Task. Wherever ActiveX script is used, you will notice that the default script initially presented to you is in this general format:

```
Function Main()
    (Optional) {DestinationSpec} = {SourceSpec}
    Main = {Some DTS status constant}
End Function
```

Functions, as you know, allow the return of a value to the calling program. To return a value from a function, you usually set the name of the function to that value, as in the following code snippet:

```
Main = {Some DTS status constant}
```

Depending on the context in which the ActiveX script is used, the return status code may have a particular effect on the processing being performed.

The following section examines a particular set of return values associated with DTS transformations.

Transform Status Codes

ActiveX script defined within DTS transformations returns transform status codes (see Table 4.5). Note that some of the status codes are specific to Transform Data Tasks and that others are specific to Data Driven Query Tasks.

Table 4.5 **Transform Status Codes**[2]

Return Value	Description	Transform Data Task	Data Driven Query Task
DTSTransformStat_ AbortPump	Terminates all processing at the current row.	Y	Y
DTSTransformStat_ DeleteQuery	Executes the query that is marked as Delete in the Queries tab, using values from the currently transformed binding row.		Y
DTSTransformStat_ DestDataNotSet	If all transformations return this value, the current row is not written to the destination.	Y	Y

continues

Table 4.5 **Continued**

Return Value	Description	Transform Data Task	Data Driven Query Task
DTSTransformStat_Error	The current transformation encountered an error.	Y	Y
DTSTransformStat_ErrorSkipRow	Terminates further processing of this row; reports the error but does not write the row to the exception file.	Y	Y
DTSTransformStat_ExceptionRow	Terminates further processing of this row; reports the error and writes the row to the exception file.	Y	Y
DTSTransformStat_Info	The transformation succeeded with additional information that the application can process further.	Y	Y
DTSTransformStat_InsertQuery	Executes the query that is marked as Insert in the Queries tab, using values from the currently transformed binding row.		Y
DTSTransformStat_NoMoreRows	Indicates that the current row is the last to be processed. No error is raised.	Y	Y
DTSTransformStat_OK	The transformation succeeded. Writes the row to the destination if specified. No error is raised.	Y	Y
DTSTransformStat_OKInfo	The transformation succeeded. Writes the row to the destination if specified. Reports the additional information to the error handler.	Y	Y
DTSTransformStat_SkipFetch	Restarts processing of the current source and destination rows by executing all transformations again. No rows are fetched.	Y	Y

Return Value	Description	Transform Data Task	Data Driven Query Task
DTSTransformStat_ SkipInsert	Does not write the current row to the destination.	Y	Y
DTSTransformStat_ SkipRow	Terminates further processing of this row.	Y	Y
DTSTransformStat_ SkipRowInfo	Terminates further processing of this row; reports additional information to the error handler.	Y	Y
DTSTransformStat_ UpdateQuery	Executes the query that is marked as Update in the Queries tab, using values from the currently transformed binding row.		Y
DTSTransformStat_ UserQuery	Executes the query that is marked as Select in the Queries tab, using values from the currently transformed binding row.		Y

2. *This table was copied from Microsoft SQL Server 2000 Version 8.00.000 BOL. This information is available on the SQL Server installation CD.*

An ActiveX Script transformation, for example, may have the following script:

```
Function Main()
    DTSDestination("column_name") = DTSSource("column_name")
    Main = DTSTransformStat_OK
End Function
```

This indicates to the data pump that the transformation succeeded and that the row should be written to the destination table. If, for example, you expect some errors to occur, add error-handling code and return the appropriate status code instead.

Mapping Transformation Columns

Generally, each arrow in the Transformations tab represents a transformation. However, you can configure the mapping of your transformations in several ways.

Use *One-to-One column mapping* when a transformation requires one source column and one destination column. In a Transform Data Task, this mapping is the default mapping used to generate the Copy Column transformations. When you use this procedure, DTS tries to match columns by name. Thereafter, it maps the first unmatched source column to the first available destination column, regardless of their data types, and repeats this process until all columns have been mapped in one rowset; it ignores any remaining columns in the other rowset. You can apply this type of mapping to the following transformations:

- Copy Column
- Trim String
- Date Time String
- Middle of String
- Read File
- ActiveX Script

Use *N-to-N column mapping* when a transformation requires multiple source columns and matching destination columns. In a Data Driven Query Task, this mapping is the default mapping used to generate the single ActiveX Script transformation (see Figure 4.12).

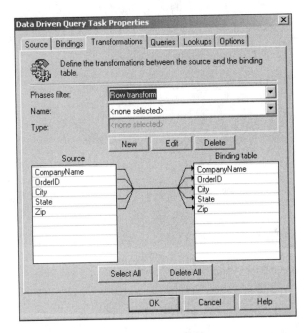

Figure 4.12   Default transformation with N-to-N mapping.

This method works best when the source and destination columns have the same name and they are lined up properly starting from the top. DTS simply starts from the top, maps each pair until it finds no more pairs to map, and it ignores any columns that may remain on either side. Note that no name or data type matching is performed—just a straightforward source column(n)–to–destination column(n) pairing. You can apply this type of mapping to the following types of transformations:

- Copy Column
- Uppercase String

- Lowercase String
- ActiveX Script

Use *N-to-Zero mapping* when a transformation requires one or more source columns and no destination column (see Figure 4.13). Only the ActiveX Script and Write File transformations make sense in this method.

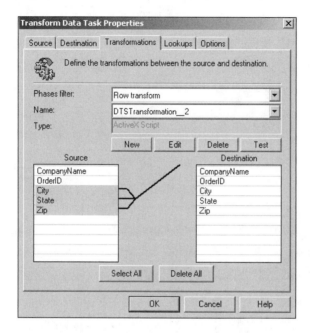

Figure 4.13   ActiveX Script transformation with N-to-Zero mapping.

To set up N-to-Zero mapping, select the source column(s) you want to use; then make sure that no destination column is selected (click on an empty row to be sure). Click the New button, and choose ActiveX Script or Write File to generate the transformation.

Use *Zero-to-N mapping* when a transformation requires one or more destination columns and no source column (see Figure 4.14). This mapping can be applied only to an ActiveX Script transformation because all the other transformation types require at least one source column to be defined.

To set up Zero-to-N mapping, select the destination column(s) you want to use; then make sure that no source column is selected (click on an empty row to be sure). Click the New button, and choose ActiveX Script to create the transformation.

Use *Zero-to-Zero mapping* when a transformation requires neither a source nor a destination column (see Figure 4.15). Because it requires neither a source column nor a destination column, an ActiveX Script transformation is the only one that can have this type of mapping.

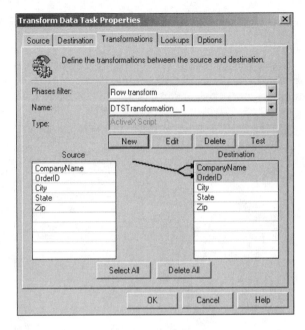

Figure 4.14   ActiveX Script transformation with Zero-to-N mapping.

Figure 4.15   ActiveX Script transformation with Zero-to-Zero mapping.

To set up Zero-to-Zero mapping, make sure that no source or destination column is selected (click on an empty row on both sides to be sure). Click the New button, and choose ActiveX Script to create the transformation. Note that only one line is used to indicate that one or more transformations with this type of mapping have been created in the task.

You need to be aware of a special case of Zero-to-Zero mapping. If you create a Copy Column transformation by using this mapping type, DTS performs a sequential One-to-One mapping of all columns. In fact, you can create multiple instances of this transformation. But why would you want to copy the columns repeatedly without making any changes?

Finally, you can have *N-to-M* and *M-to-N mappings*, in which you have an unequal number of columns between source and destination. A common situation that requires Two-to-One mapping is when you have to populate the destination Full Name field by concatenating First Name with Last Name. This kind of mapping is most appropriate for the ActiveX Script and Copy Column transformations.

To set up N-to-M or M-to-N mapping, select the source column(s); then select the destination column(s). Click the New button, and choose ActiveX Script or Copy Column from the pop-up dialog box to create the transformation. You must ensure that each source column is mapped to a destination column. In an ActiveX Script transformation, the graphical procedures described above are replaced by code. With the Copy Column transformation, some columns may initially be mapped to a column labeled <Ignore>. You must map those columns to specific source or destination columns as appropriate.

Obtaining Higher Performance with Many-to-Many Transformations

You will gain much higher performance if you use Many-to-Many transformation mappings. This is because the data pump invokes fewer transformations as a result.

Lookups

One of the most common transformations performed on data involves converting codes into labels or descriptions that are more meaningful. You will recognize this as the process of "performing a lookup". In DTS, you can achieve this by using an ActiveX Script transformation, as described earlier in this chapter, and writing script that executes a query against a data source. The script would involve establishing a connection to the data source, setting up the query, executing it, and then disconnecting from the data source. Execute all of that for each row, and you can see how much this approach can hurt the performance of the task.

DTS lookups offer a far more efficient way to do this. First, a lookup uses one of the connections that you define in the package; therefore, it doesn't have to connect/ disconnect for each row. Second, a lookup can cache the lookup data, making it available instantly without further database access.

In this section, you build a lookup query and use it in one of the columns being transformed. You add one or more lookups to your task in the Lookups tab (see Figure 4.16).

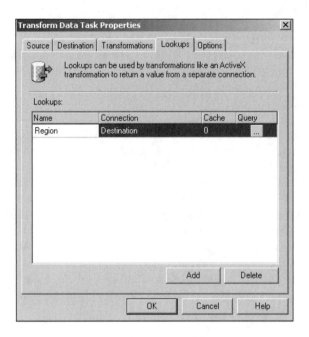

Figure 4.16 The Lookups tab.

In this tab, you can specify the name of the lookup, which connection to use for the lookup, and how many rows of the lookup table to cache. Click the button below the Query column to bring up the Query Designer window (see Figure 4.17).

You will be performing a lookup against a table named Region, which you can see in the list on the left side of Figure 4.17. Drag the table to the pane on the right side of the window, and click the check box next to the column named District to add District to the SELECT statement in the pane at the bottom of the window. The last thing you need to do is specify the WHERE clause; in this case, WHERE (RegionID = ?). The question mark is a placeholder for the parameter that will be passed in when the lookup fires.

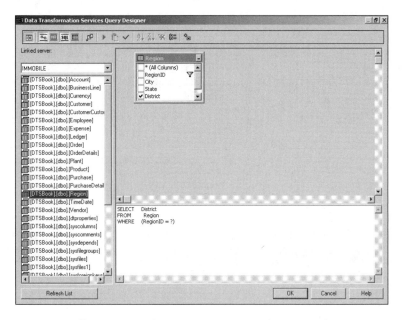

Figure 4.17   The Query Designer window revisited.

Considerations for Building Lookup Queries

When you build lookup queries, keep in mind the following considerations:

- A SQL join with the lookup table in the source data connection is far more efficient than a lookup query.

- If possible, use a data connection other than the source and destination connections in the package.

- This data connection must be an OLE DB service provider. (Specifically, it must support the OLE DB command interface.) You cannot look up values from a text file.

- If the data connection does not support transactions, updates made by the lookup query could remain committed even if the package rolls back the transaction.

- If a lookup query fails, no further processing occurs for the row that was last read from the source connection. The failure counts as one error toward the maximum errors count for the task.

To use the lookup query in a task, create a new transformation, and choose the ActiveX Script transformation type. Do this for the source column Account. In the ActiveX Script Transformation Properties dialog box, you can see that the Browser tab now displays the lookup query that was just created (see Figure 4.18).

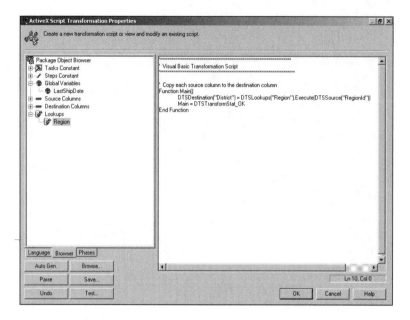

Figure 4.18 Using the lookup query in script.

The default script in the script window simply copies the source column to the destination column and will have something like the following:

```
DTSDestination("District") = DTSSource("RegionID")
```

You want to assign to the destination column the values returned by the lookup query. So, you should change the right side of the equation. The new line should look like this instead:

```
DTSDestination("District") = DTSLookups("Region").Execute(DTSSource("RegionID"))
```

Note that the `Execute` method of the `DTSLookups` collection accepts as a parameter the value of the source column. Because the `Execute` method is a parameter, you can pass any appropriate value to it, including hard-coded values and global variables.

Speaking of global variables, if you define one in the package, it also shows up in the Browser tab. (We created one and named it `LastShipDate`.) The following code fragments demonstrate how to use a global variable in your script:

```
DTSDestination("ShippedDate") = DTSGlobalVariables("LastShipDate").Value

DTSDestination("OrderID") =
➥DTSLookups("Orders").Execute(DTSGlobalVariables("LastShipDate").Value)
```

The first code fragment shows you how to assign the value of the global variable directly to the destination column. The second example shows you how to pass the value of a global variable to the lookup query.

The term *lookup* is not exactly accurate because you can do more than just perform a lookup. You can actually have any valid SQL statement in your query, including INSERT, UPDATE, DELETE, and even EXECUTE (a stored procedure). Following is an example of an update query named UpdateEmployee and its corresponding use in an ActiveX script:

- SQL query:

```
UPDATE Employee SET HasTakenVacation = 1 WHERE EmployeeID = ?
```

- ActiveX script:

```
DTSLookups("UpdateEmployee").Execute(DTSSource("EmployeeID"))
```

As you can see, DTS makes using lookup queries easy. Keep in mind, however, that the more complex your code is, the bigger the penalty in terms of performance. One way to avoid this performance degradation in lookups is to use a join instead. As mentioned earlier in this chapter, when you create the source connection, you can use a SQL query instead of specifying a table. Join your source table with the lookup table, and you won't have to perform lookups on each row.

Transform Data Task Properties Options

The Options tab has several options that provide additional flexibility and enhance the performance of the task (see Figure 4.19).

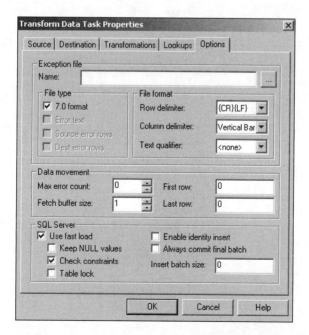

Figure 4.19   The Transform Data Task Properties – Options tab.

Many of these options are used by other built-in DTS tasks. One reason is that all these tasks share the same basic data-pump engine. However, each task has a unique set of options.

The Options tab is a very busy tab, and you will feel overwhelmed when you first bring it up. However, it is actually organized into sections. So, all you need to do is focus on one section at a time.

Table 4.6 lists the options related to error handling and the use of exception files.

Table 4.6   **Exception File Options**

Option	Description
Name	The name of the file where exception records will be written. If the file does not exist when the package executes, the file will be created.
FILE TYPE	
7.0 Format	Specifies to save the exception file in SQL 7.0 format.
Error Text	Specifies that any errors encountered during the task execution be recorded. Information such as the package name, execution start and completion times, and other data are entered in the exception log.
Source Error Rows	Specifies that a separate exception file be created to contain all the rows from the source data that did not get written to the destination. The filename is the same the one specified in the Name field but with the extension "Source" appended to the filename.
Destination Error Rows	Specifies that a separate exception file be created to contain records rejected from the destination file. The filename is the same as the one specified in the Name field but with the extension Dest appended to the filename.
FILE FORMAT	
Row Delimiter	Specifies the delimiter used to separate rows of data in the exception files. A carriage return/line feed {CR}{LF} is used by default.
Column Delimiter	Specifies the delimiter used to separate the columns of data in the exception files. A vertical bar is used by default.
Text Qualifier	Specifies the character used to qualify text in the exception files. The choices are Double Quote {"} Single Quote {'}, and <none>. You can also type a character to use as the text qualifier.

Table 4.7 lists the options that provide some control of how data is read and handled.

Table 4.7   **Data Movement Options**

Option	Description
Max Error Count	Sets a limit for the number of errors allowed before processing for the task is terminated. When the SQL Server fast-load option is selected, each error corresponds either to a row-level failure detected by the Transform Data Task, or to a batch failure. The value of Max Error Count includes the number of row-level errors detected by the Transform Data Task plus batch failures. When the Max Error Count value is exceeded, task execution is terminated. The default is zero, which means that the task will terminate upon the first error.
Fetch Buffer Size	Sets the number of rows of data being fetched at the source during data movement. Generally, you should not need to adjust this value unless it is necessary to optimize the characteristics of the data provider.
First Row	Specifies the first row of data to be moved. This option is useful if the first row consists of column headings or if the first part of a data source has been copied. You can set this value to the row number where processing stopped in an earlier data-pump operation.
Last Row	Specifies the last row of data to move.

Table 4.8 lists the options that affect SQL Server processing.

Table 4.8   **SQL Server Options**

Option	Description
Use Fast Load	Specifies that you want to use high-speed, bulk-copy processing. You can use the fast-load option only when the destination connection is the Microsoft OLE DB Provider for SQL Server. When you enable this option, the data pump can accept batches of transformed data. Batch sizes are controlled by the Insert Batch Size option.
THE FOLLOWING OPTIONS ARE AVAILABLE ONLY IF YOU ENABLE THE USE FAST LOAD OPTION.	
Enable Identity Insert	Allows explicit values to be inserted into the identity column of a table (SQL Server only). This option is available only if an identity column is detected.
Keep NULL Values	Specifies that you want to keep the NULL value in the destination column even if the destination table was created with a default value designated for the column.

continues

Table 4.8 **Continued**

Option	Description
THE FOLLOWING OPTIONS ARE AVAILABLE ONLY IF YOU ENABLE THE USE FAST LOAD OPTION.	
Check Constraints	Specifies whether constraints on the destination table are checked during the load. By default, constraints are ignored. This setting improves the performance, but it also allows data that violates existing constraints to be inserted into the table.
Table Lock	Specifies to lock the whole table when the task executes. Otherwise, row-level locking is used, which reduces performance.
Always Commit Final Batch	Specifies to commit all rows in the final batch that were processed successfully before an error occurs. This property applies when a transformation or insert error occurs during processing of the final batch, so that all rows in the batch prior to the error do not have to be processed again. The setting is useful for large batch sizes.
Insert Batch Size	Specifies the number of rows in a batch.

Value	Action
0 (Default)	The data is loaded in one batch. The first row that fails causes the entire load to be canceled, and the step fails.
1	The data is loaded a single row at a time. Each row that fails is counted as a batch failure, and the value of Max Error Count is incremented by 1. Previously loaded rows are committed or, if the step has joined the package transaction, retained in the transaction subject to later commit or rollback.
>1	The data is loaded one batch at a time. The first row that fails in a batch fails that entire batch. Loading stops, and the step fails. Rows in previously loaded batches are committed or, if the step has joined the package transaction, retained in the transaction subject to later commit or rollback.

Data Driven Query Task

The Data Driven Query Task derives its name from the fact that it relies on parameterized queries to perform the actual modifications of the data. Like the Transform Data Task, it is based on the DTS data-pump engine but is far more flexible. In addition to INSERT, the task supports other Transact SQL statements (including UPDATE, DELETE, and SELECT) as well as most other SQL statements.

This flexibility comes at a price because this task is significantly slower than the Transform Data Task (described earlier in this chapter) and the Bulk Insert Task (discussed in the "Using the Bulk Insert Task" section later in this chapter).

Using Higher-Performance Tasks
If you can accomplish the same thing using Transform Data Task or Bulk Insert Task, use those instead.

When you open the Data Driven Query Task Properties dialog box, the first thing you will notice is that the Bindings tab sits next to the Source tab instead of the Destination tab (see Figure 4.20). This change is a very important but subtle one from the setup in the Transform Data Task. It is worthwhile to take the time to understand the significance of this change if you want to use this task efficiently.

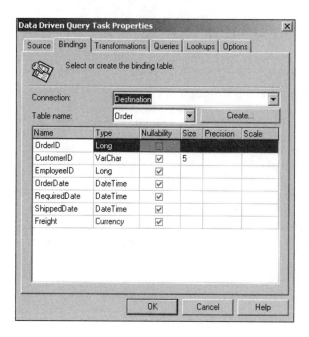

Figure 4.20   The Bindings tab.

Understanding the Role of the Binding Table

To understand the role of the Bindings tab and how it differs from the Destination tab, follow the flow of data in a Data Driven Query Task as it executes:

1. Using the definition in the Source tab, DTS retrieves a row from the source data connection.

2. By default, DTS defines ActiveX Script transformations in the Transformations tab that copy each column in the source row to a matching or appropriate column in the rowset specified by the binding table.

    Optionally, you can transform a column by using lookup queries and ActiveX script calculations. Even though data has moved from the source table to the binding table, at this point no modifications to data have occurred (except for the transformations in memory). More important, no changes have been written to any destination.

3. By default, the ActiveX Script transformation generated by DTS returns the status code, DTSTransformstat_InsertQuery.

    This status code tells DTS that the query to be executed is the Insert query defined in the Queries tab.

4. Knowing which query to execute, DTS now maps appropriate values in the binding table to the parameters of the selected query.

    Note that a set of parameter mappings is defined for each query that is built in the Queries tab.

5. Finally, using the values passed in through its parameters from the binding table, the query performs the actual data modifications in the destination table.

As you can see, no direct movement of data from source to destination occurs. The final destination of the data may or may not be the destination specified in the Binding tab. The result depends on how the query is set up.

About the Binding Table

The important thing to remember is that the Binding table may not necessarily be the Destination table. The Binding table provides the data that is mapped into the parameters for the query that is to be executed. The query itself could be targeted to update a completely different table.

In the Data Driven Query Task Properties dialog box, the Source, Transformations, and Lookups tabs are similar to those in the Transform Data Task Properties dialog box, and you use them in exactly the same way. When you use ActiveX scripting in the Transformations tab, however, return values have an added significant meaning because of the way it affects the behavior of the task through queries. In the next section, you will be shown how to build the data-driven queries, and you will see how to use the transform status return values to specify which query is executed.

The Driven Queries

You build the queries for a Data Driven Query Task by using the Queries tab (see Figure 4.21). The Query Type drop-down menu gives you four choices: Insert, Update, Delete, and Select. However, DTS does not enforce these types on the actual query that you build. You can select an Insert type and then build a Delete statement (however, we suggest you keep the two in sync). This means you can create up to four queries of the same type or any combination, depending on what your task needs to accomplish.

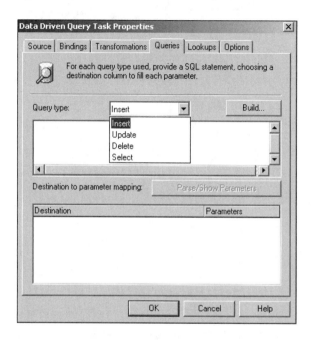

Figure 4.21   The Queries tab.

You use the query (or queries) by writing some code in an ActiveX Script transformation, just as you did with the lookup query for the Transform Data Task. For example, assuming an appropriate query has been set up for each of the four query types, the following code fragment shows how a query is selected and fired:

```
Select Case Trim(DTSSource("ChangeCode"))
  Case "New"
   Main = DTSTransformStat_InsertQuery
  Case "Change"
   Main = DTSTransformStat_UpdateQuery
  Case "Delete"
   Main = DTSTransformStat_DeleteQuery
  Case Else
   Main = DTSTransformStat_SkipRow
End Select
```

Based on the value of the source column "ChangeCode", the script returns one of four possible DTSTransformStat constants (see Table 4.9, a subset of the transform status codes discussed earlier in this chapter). Returning DTSTransformStat_InsertQuery causes the query associated with the query type Insert to be executed, returning DTSTransformStat_UpdateQuery causes the query associated with the query type Update to be executed, and so on.

Table 4.9   **Transform Status Codes**

Return Value	Description	Transform Driven Data Task	Data Query Task
DTSTransformStat_ DeleteQuery	Executes the query that is marked as Delete in the Queries tab, using values from the currently trans-formed binding row.		Y
DTSTransformStat_ InsertQuery	Executes the query that is marked as Insert in the Queries tab, using values from the currently trans-formed binding row.		Y
DTSTransformStat_ UpdateQuery	Executes the query that is marked as Update in the Queries tab, using values from the currently trans-formed binding row.		Y
DTSTransformStat_ UserQuery	Executes the query that is marked as Select in the Queries tab, using values from the currently trans-formed binding row.		Y

In some instances, you may need to execute more than one of these queries. For example, you may need to delete some rows first and then insert new rows. To do this, you need to return multiple return codes that are combined together using a logical OR, as in the following example:

```
Main = DTSTransformStat_DeleteQuery OR DTSTransformStat_InsertQuery
```

When the transformation executes, the two queries indicated in the function's return value are performed.

Avoid a Performance Hit

To avoid a performance hit, use only one ActiveX Script transformation to perform the query selection for a Data Driven Query Task.

Data Driven Query Task Options

The Options tab of the Data Driven Query Task Properties dialog box is very similar to the Options tab of the Transform Data Task Properties dialog box. The main difference is that the Data Driven Query Task Properties dialog box does not have the section on SQL Server options. So, you can't choose Use Fast Load and its ancillary options (see Figure 4.22). This is all because speed is not the primary focus in this task—functional flexibility is instead.

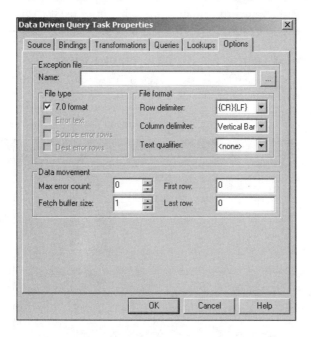

Figure 4.22   The Options tab.

The options are similar to those of the Transform Data Task because the two tasks rely on the same data-pump engine. Tables 4.4 and 4.5 earlier in this chapter explain these options in greater detail.

The Multiphase Data Pump

As developers, we are always wishing we had more control over our applications. That is certainly true with DTS applications as well. After we discovered how we could use ActiveX Script and status codes in DTS transformations, we soon learned how difficult it was to control the process of looping through the rows. We also learned how it often forced us to use two sometimes three or more tasks to accomplish what could very well be done with one task.

When you add ActiveX script to a transformation, you are actually customizing the behavior of the DTS data pump and taking control of at least part of its processing. More specifically, you are customizing the data pump's row transform phase. In SQL

7.0, it was all that was available. Now with SQL 2000, more hooks into the data pump have been exposed allowing much more control of its processing.

> In SQL 7.0, the row transform phase was the only phase you could gain an entry point into in order to customize the behavior of the data-pump engine.

Gaining Access to the Multiphase Data Pump

To gain access to these new hooks, right-click on the Data Transformation Services folder in Enterprise Manager, and click on Properties to open the Package Properties dialog box (see Figure 4.23).

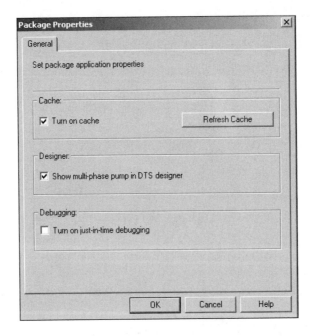

Figure 4.23   The Package Properties dialog box.

By default, the check box labeled Show Multi-phase Pump in DTS Designer (in the Designer section) is unchecked, thus limiting you to the transformation phase. Check this check box to expose the additional phases.

Now whenever you work with transformations, you will see an additional tab labeled Phases (see Figure 4.24).

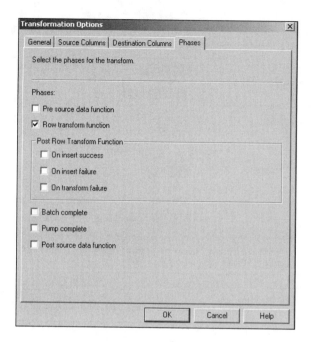

Figure 4.24 The Phases tab.

By default, the only option checked in this tab is Row Transform Function, which calls the default Main function just as in SQL 7.0's ActiveX Script transformations. In spite of being limited then to just that one scripting option, we were able to do a lot with it. It is not so difficult to see how much more powerful SQL 2000 DTS is with seven new entry points to connect into the data pump.

Adding script and hooking it into the data pump is easy. Simply write the function script in the ActiveX Script Transformation Properties dialog box. Then enable the entry point at which you want that script to execute by clicking on the Phases tab. The tab is located in the lower left adjacent to the Language and Browser tabs. Check the appropriate check box, and type the name of the function you just wrote in the associated text box.

When the transformation fires, the DTS data pump uses this information to execute your function(s) in the proper sequence.

Understanding the Data Pump Phases

As you might expect, each of the seven new entry points corresponds to a particular phase in the data pump's process flow. Figure 4.25 provides an overview of these phases and shows how the data pump's processes flow through these phases.

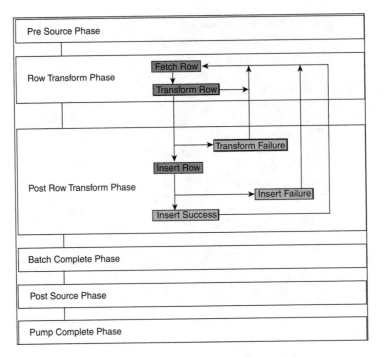

Figure 4.25   The data-pump process flow and phases.

Processing starts by fetching a row from the source data connection. If any transformations have been specified, these are applied to the incoming row. Then the data pump attempts to insert the updated row into the destination rowset. Next, the data pump processes any exceptions that may have occurred, including any special return codes you included in your functions. If a batch size greater than one has been specified, the rowset is saved in a batch buffer, and a new source row is fetched. When the batch size is complete, the batch is written to the destination table, and a new batch is started. The task ends when all batches have been processed.

In Figure 4.25, you can see all the phases and all the entry points for your custom scripts. The *pre source phase* executes before any source row is fetched. This phase allows you to perform any one-time processing, such as writing header rows or performing initialization that may be necessary. You do not have access to the source row in this phase, but you do have access to the destination row and can write preliminary information to it.

This is the default data pump phase. The Main function stub specified in the ActiveX Script Transformation Properties dialog box provides a starting point for adding custom scripting code for this phase. The row transform phase allows read access to source data and meta data and write access to destination data.

The *post row transform phase* occurs after the row transform phase and consists of three subphases:

- **On Transform Failure**—This phase executes whenever an error occurs in the row transform phase; whether it is an implicit error, or your code returns a DTSTransformStat_Error or DTSTransformStat_ExceptionRow status. This error does not count toward the maximum error specified in the Options tab. When the failure occurs, your script can make the necessary changes. Whatever happens in your code, processing will continue, resulting in either a successful or an unsuccessful insertion of the row into the destination buffer. Note that this is exclusive, it is either successful or it is a failure, which means only one of the following phases can occur next.

- **On Insert Success**—This phase executes when the current row is inserted successfully into the destination rowset. At this point, no data has been written to the database.

- **On Insert Failure**—This phase occurs when the insertion of the current row into the destination rowset fails. Again, this error does not count toward the maximum errors specified in the Options tab. Because the insertion fails, the row count for the batch is not incremented either.

The *on batch complete phase* occurs each time the number of rows inserted into the destination buffer equals the batch size specified in the Options tab. It also occurs when all rows have been processed and the destination buffer contains at least one row. When this phase occurs, the rows in the destination buffer are written to the destination table. If an error occurs, it is possible that some or all rows in the buffer are not written out to the table, depending on whether the package is configured to use transactions. You need to remember two important things:

- The phase executes on completion of a batch, whether it is written to the table successfully or not.

- This phase may not execute (when an insert failure occurs for each row, for example).

The *post source data phase* occurs after all the batches have been processed. At this point, you still have access to the destination data. So, you can write out any final information required by your application.

The *on pump complete phase* is the last phase to execute, in spite of the fact that it is not the last phase listed in the Phases tab. You no longer have access to data at this point. However, this is still a full ActiveX Script environment. Therefore, you can still do many things: connect to databases through ADO, work with SQL Server through SQL-DMO, send messages to a pager, and so on.

By working with these phases, you can easily add a great amount of functionality to your DTS package, such as data aggregation, custom error handling, and row-level restartability. One huge benefit of opening all these entry points to the data-pump engine is that it allows you to consolidate more of your script in one place: the DTS package.

Bulk Insert Task

The Bulk Insert Task is a specialized task that focuses on loading data from text files into SQL Server tables and doing it really fast (see Figure 4.26). It is not based on the DTS data-pump engine; instead, it is based on the Transact-SQL BULK INSERT statement. Unlike the Transform Data Task, this task requires only one data connection—to a SQL Server destination table. For the source, it specifically asks for a text data file. Because speed is its primary focus, the Bulk Insert Task does not allow you to perform any transformations on your data. Also, you must ensure that your source data columns are mapped properly to the destination columns.

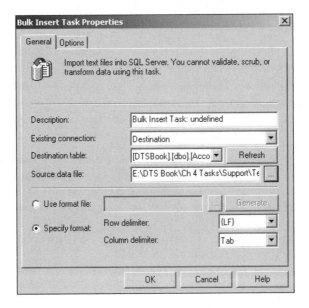

Figure 4.26 Using the Bulk Insert Task.

A common mistake is to have column headings in your data file without specifying a format file. If you have column heading information in the first row of your input data files, choose the Use Format File option and generate the format file or browse to it if one already exists. This format file traces its roots to the BCP (Bulk Copy Program) format file in earlier versions of SQL Server. When you generate a format file, a wizard walks you through the various options. One of these options allows you to specify whether the first row consists of column names (see Figure 4.27). You also can specify format specifications other than the default tab-delimited data format.

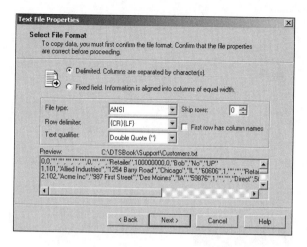

Figure 4.27   Specifying the format file.

Setting Bulk Insert Parameters

Because this task encapsulates the Bulk Insert Transact SQL statement, you are setting the parameters of that statement when you set the options in this task. Any parameter not exposed by the task is set to its default value. If you need to set any of the parameters that are not exposed by the task, you can set them through the BulkInsertTask object by using ActiveX script or through the bcp utility by way of the Execute Process Task (see Chapter 5).

Bulk Insert Task Options

The Options tab of the Bulk Insert Task Properties dialog box has several settings that you need to be aware of, because they can dramatically impact the performance of the task you are building (see Figure 4.28).

Some of these options, you will recall, showed up earlier in Table 4.8, "SQL Server Options" in the section on Transform Data Task. This is because the ultimate processing handler is the SQL Server engine itself.

Table 4.10 lists the basic options for the Bulk Insert Task, including how to handle check constraints, identity inserts, null data, and table locking.

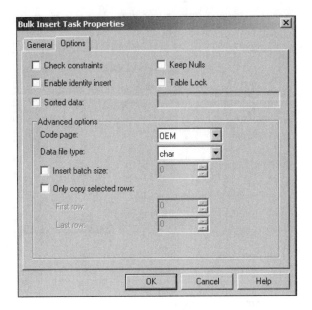

Figure 4.28 The Options tab.

Table 4.10 **Bulk Insert Options**

Option	Description
Check Constraints	By default, constraints defined in the destination table are *not* checked. This means you could end up with some invalid data in your tables. Check this option if you want the constraints to be enforced.
Enable Identity Insert	If you have an Identity column in your table, SQL Server generates its values automatically, which means that it normally will not allow a row to be inserted if the row has a non-null value in this column. Check this option if you have values in your data file for the Identity column of your table.
Keep Nulls	If you have default constraints defined for certain columns in your table, those columns will contain the default values if the row being inserted contains nulls. Check this option if you want to override the default values and insert the nulls instead.
Sorted Data	By default, SQL Server assumes that the data is not sorted. If you have a clustered index defined on your table, and your data file is sorted primarily on the column(s) in the clustered index, check this option to enhance the performance of the Bulk Insert Task's operations. You must specify the valid column(s) on which the data is sorted.

Option	Description
Table Lock	By default, SQL Server uses row-level locks when performing bulk inserts. Performance is improved because the locking operation is performed only once and the copy operations do not have to wait for rows locked by other users. Check this check box to improve the performance of the task.

Table 4.11 lists more advanced options for the Bulk Insert Task. You will recognize most of these options as parameters of bcp. Now you can take advantage of bcp's advanced options without programming or clunky batch commands.

Table 4.11   **Advanced Bulk Insert Options**[3]

Option	Description
Code Page	Specifies the code page of the data in the data file. Code Page is relevant only if the data contains char, varchar, or text columns with character values greater than 127 or less than 32. The possible values for Code Page are: ■ **OEM** (default). Columns of char, varchar, or text data type are converted from the system OEM code page to the SQL Server code page. ■ **ACP**. Columns of char, varchar, or text data type are converted from the ANSI/Microsoft Windows code page (ISO 1252) to the SQL Server code page. ■ **RAW.** No conversion from one code page to another occurs; this option is the fastest one. ■ **nnn** (specific code page). Specific code page number, such as 850.
Data File Type	Specifies the type of data in the data file. The Bulk Insert Task adjusts its copy operations accordingly. The possible values for Data File Type are: ■ **char** (default). Performs the bulk copy operation from a data file containing character data. ■ **native.** Performs the bulk copy operation by using the native (database) data types. The data file to load is created by bulk-copying data from SQL Server via the bcp utility. ■ **wide char.** Performs the bulk copy operation from a data file containing Unicode characters. ■ **widenative.** Performs the same bulk copy operation as native, except that char, varchar, and text columns are stored as Unicode in the data file. The data file to be loaded was created by bulk-copying data from SQL Server via the bcp utility. This option offers a higher-performance alternative to the widechar option and is

Table 4.11 **Continued**

Option	Description
	intended for transferring data from one computer running SQL Server to another by using a data file. Use this option when you are transferring data that contains ANSI extended characters to take advantage of native mode performance.
Insert Batch Size	Specifies the number of rows in a batch. The Bulk Insert Task adjusts its copy operations accordingly. The possible values are: ■ **0** (default). The data is loaded in a single batch. The first row that fails causes the entire load to be canceled, and the step fails. ■ **1.** The data is loaded one row at a time. Each row that fails is counted as one row failure. Previously loaded rows are committed or, if the step has joined the package transaction, retained provisionally in the transaction, subject to later commitment or rollback. ■ **>1.** The data is loaded one batch at a time. Any row that fails in a batch fails that entire batch; loading stops, and the step fails. Rows in previously loaded batches are committed or, if the step has joined the package transaction, retained provisionally in the transaction, subject to later commitment or rollback.
Only Copy Selected Rows	Allows you to specify a contiguous range of rows to be copied, starting at the physical row specified by First Row and ending at the physical row specified by Last Row.

3. This table was copied from Microsoft SQL Server 2000 Version 8.00.000 BOL. This information is available on the SQL Server installation CD.

Summary

This chapter introduced the built-in DTS tasks and showed you how to use them in a DTS package. You got a glimpse of the engine underlying the core data-transformation tasks, called the data-pump engine. The chapter discussed the two DTS tasks that represent the two main implementations of that engine, including the Transform Data Task and the Data Driven Query Task. You learned how to use ActiveX script to customize the behavior of the various phases of the data pump. Finally, the chapter introduced a third data-movement task, the Bulk Insert Task, which is not based on the data pump. Chapter 5 covers the other built-in DTS tasks.

5

More DTS Tasks

THIS CHAPTER COVERS THE REST of the DTS tasks that were listed in Chapter 4, "DTS Tasks." These additional tasks are listed in Table 5.1.

Table 5.1 **Additional DTS Tasks**

Icon	Description
	Execute SQL Task
	ActiveX Script Task
	Execute Process Task
	Execute Package Task
	Dynamic Properties Task
	Send Mail Task
	File Transfer Protocol Task

continues

Table 5.1   **Continued**

Icon	Description
	Message Queue Task
	Transfer SQL Server Objects Task (now called Copy SQL Server Objects Task)
	Transfer Databases Task
	Transfer Logins Task
	Transfer Master Stored Procedures Task
	Transfer Jobs Task
	Transfer Error Messages Task
	Analysis Services Processing Task
	Data Mining Task

The group of tasks that allow you to control various processes within a DTS package are explained first. These tasks are the *programming tasks*. These include Execute SQL Task, which allows you to use SQL and have direct access to SQL databases; the ActiveX Script Task, which allows you to use scripting languages to handle more complex processes; the Execute Process Task, which enables you to invoke batch commands and external executables; and the Execute Package Task and Dynamic Properties Task, which round out the programming group and facilitate the execution of tasks within a package.

Next, the chapter will cover the *messaging tasks*, which allow you to send emails and download files, as well as send and receive queued messages.

The *database management tasks* help you move databases and database objects between SQL Server instances will also be discussed. When you use these tasks, it is important to set up your SQL Server installation so that it starts up with the appropriate network account. In some cases, using the local system account will prevent the tasks from copying objects over the network.

Finally, the chapter touches on the tasks specific to the Analysis Server. Analysis Services is a server product included with SQL Server 2000 that lets you implement Online Analytical Processing (OLAP). The Analysis Services Processing Task and the Data Mining Task help automate some of the processes required to maintain data warehouses and to mine the data for useful information.

Execute SQL Task

The Execute SQL Task allows you to do just what the name says—execute an SQL statement. In SQL 7.0, this was all that you could do with this task. Furthermore, it was difficult to pass parameters in. You had to resort to modifying the text of the SQL statement from outside this task before executing it. Using its result set directly was equally difficult unless it was saved into a temporary table that a later task could access. In SQL 2000, the addition of the Parameters feature changes all of that (see Figure 5.1).

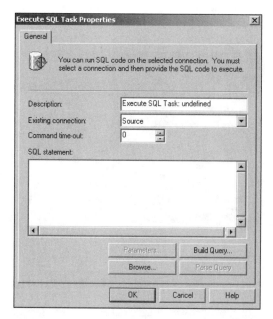

Figure 5.1   The Execute SQL Task Properties dialog box, showing the new Parameters button.

Chapter 4 showed you how to use parameters in a query when building a Transform Data Task (see Figure 4.4). The same concepts apply when you work with SQL code that expects values to be passed in during execution.

When you execute SQL code, however, a result set is usually returned, and you most likely would want to gain access to this result set. Both the Transform Data Task and the Data Driven Query Task use the result automatically. By design, the Execute SQL Task does not do anything with any result set; its purpose is simply to execute the SQL code that you give it. However, SQL 2000 now allows you access to the result set.

> ***Limitations of SQL 7.0's Execute SQL Task***
> The only thing that the original Execute SQL Task in SQL 7.0 did was execute the SQL code. It did not allow any parameter to be passed in, nor did it enable access to the result set if the SQL code returned one.

Using the SQL Result Sets

Click on the Parameters button to display the Parameter Mapping dialog box. You will see the familiar Input Parameters tab. However, in order to use the result set you will be more interested in the new Output Parameters tab (see Figure 5.2).

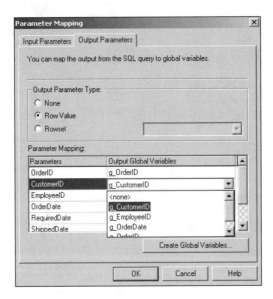

Figure 5.2   The Output Parameters tab.

The Output Parameters tab provides two options. You can either save one row from the result set, or save the whole result set itself.

Saving a Row

To save one row from the result set, click on the option Row Value. This enables the Parameter Mapping window that displays all the columns returned by the SQL code. Then you can map the columns to global variables. Map any column that you don't need to <None>.

You can create global variables by clicking on the Create Global Variables button. Again, you will recall that this brings up the Global Variables dialog box that was introduced in Chapter 4.

When the task executes, DTS saves the appropriate columns of the *first* row to the corresponding global variables as defined in the Parameter Mapping window.

Multiple Rows Become One Row

When a result set returns multiple rows, only the columns of the *first* row are saved to the global variables.

Saving an Entire Result Set

If you want to save more than one row, you can save the whole result set instead. To do this, click on the option Rowset. Then, from the drop-down menu on the right side of the dialog box, select the particular global variable where you want the result set to be saved (see Figure 5.3). The global variable must have a type of <Other>.

Figure 5.3   Saving a rowset to a global variable.

When the task executes, the result set is saved to the variable you selected. Then you can use ActiveX Data Objects (ADO) to access this data using an ADO recordset. Because the global variable's value (in this case, the result set) can be saved with the package, and because you don't have to connect to the data source to access the data, what you really have is a disconnected ADO recordset.

Before you go ahead and store gigabytes of SQL results into a global variable, be aware that doing so can severely impair the loading and saving of your DTS package.

After the data (a single row or a whole result set) has been saved to one or more global variables, you can use the ActiveX Script Task to retrieve the data from the global variables collection of the package (see the following section).

> **Data Type Required to Save a Result Set**
>
> When you create a global variable that will store a result set, make sure that you set its data type to
> <Other>.

ActiveX Script Task

Use an ActiveX Script Task whenever you need to perform functions that are not available in any of the other built-in tasks of DTS. With this task, you are limited only by the capabilities of the scripting language that you use.

When you add an ActiveX Script Task to the package, it opens the ActiveX Script Task Properties dialog box (see Figure 5.4). This dialog box is exactly the same one that you saw in Chapter 4. But this time, it is saved as a complete task, not just a property of another task type.

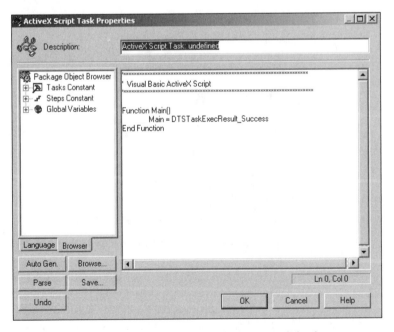

Figure 5.4   The ActiveX Script Task Properties dialog box.

In the Browser tab, you can see the global variables that have been created. You can access the global variables containing data that were returned in a result set. Listing 5.1 shows an example of script you can use to access the row data stored in multiple global variables.

Listing 5.1 **VBScript Using Global Variables**

```
Function Main()
 Dim OrderID
 Dim CustomerID
 Dim EmployeeID
 Dim OrderDate

 OrderID = DTSGlobalVariables("g_OrderID").value
 CustomerID = DTSGlobalVariables("g_CustomerID").value
 EmployeeID = DTSGlobalVariables("g_EmployeeID").value
 OrderDate = DTSGlobalVariables("g_OrderDate").value

 {other processing}

 Main = DTSTaskExecResult_Success
End Function
```

Listing 5.2 is an example of retrieving the result set using ADO.

Listing 5.2 **Using VBScript to Create an ADO Recordset and Save It in a DTS Global Variable**

```
Function Main()
 Dim oRset

 Dim OrderID
 Dim CustomerID
 Dim EmployeeID
 Dim OrderDate

 Set oRset = CreateObject("ADODB.Recordset")
 Set oRset = DTSGlobalVariables("g_Recordset").value

 If oRset.BOF AND oRset.EOF Then
 'There are no rows in the recordset
 Else
 While NOT oRset.EOF
 OrderID = oRset.Fields("OrderID").value
 CustomerID = oRset.Fields ("CustomerID").value
 EmployeeID = oRset.Fields ("EmployeeID").value
 OrderDate = oRset.Fields ("OrderDate").value
```

continues

Listing 5.2 **Continued**

```
{other processing}

oRset.MoveNext
Wend
End If

Main = DTSTaskExecResult_Success
End Function
```

You may have noticed that the code examples are more involved than previous ActiveX scripts. In an ActiveX Script Task, you can do more without worrying about performance. Unlike a transformation, the code is not executed for each row.

Performance Considerations

The code in an ActiveX Script Task is executed once. Code in a transformation is executed once for each row. Therefore, you incur a smaller penalty for doing more within the script.

The status codes also are different. In an ActiveX Script Task, you can return the following status codes:

- **DTSTaskExecResult_Success**—Indicates that the task executed successfully.
- **DTSTaskExecResult_RetryStep**—Indicates that the task should be restarted.
- **DTSTaskExecResult_Failure**—Indicates that the task execution failed.

Execute Process Task

The Execute Process Task enables you to run programs external to the DTS environment. These programs include executable programs (.exe files) and batch files. For example, it is easier to write Copy File or Delete File commands in a batch file and have it launched by an Execute Process Task than it is to write an ActiveX Script Task. Or perhaps you have a legacy application that needs to run as part of a database-loading procedure. The Execute Process Task allows you to tie disparate programs into a cohesive set of processing procedures.

When you add this task to a package, the Execute Process Task Properties dialog box comes up (see Figure 5.5). This dialog box is relatively simple compared with the ones you have seen earlier in this book.

Specify the .exe or batch file that you want to execute or browse for one if you don't remember its name. If the external program expects parameters to be passed in, you can specify them in the Parameters text box.

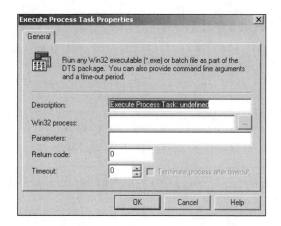

Figure 5.5   The Execute Process Task Properties dialog box.

You can specify a return code for the successful execution of the external process. You can have the task wait until the external process completes or fails by specifying a timeout value of zero. If you choose to specify a timeout value greater than zero, you have the option of having DTS terminate the process when the timeout period expires. If you don't check the Terminate Process After Timeout check box, the task will fail after the timeout period, but the external process will continue to execute.

The one important issue in this task that you should be aware of is the context in which the external process is executed. Essentially, it follows the permissions required for executing SQL Server's xp_cmdshell stored procedure. If the user invoking the task is a member of the sysadmin role in SQL Server, the external process is executed in the context of the account used to run SQL Server. Otherwise, the process is run in the context of a proxy account for SQL Server Agent. Either way, the executable or batch file must be in the PATH environment of the executing account, and the account must have NT execute permissions for that file.

If you are executing the DTS package from the Designer (in Enterprise Manager) or from the command line using DTSRun, especially if you are on a machine other than the server itself, the authentication requirements may be different. The bottom line is that you need to make sure that package execution occurs with the proper authentication and permissions.

Accounts and Permissions

When setting up Execute Process Tasks, be sure that you understand which user account the process will be executed with. Because account permissions tend to change or expire, you need to check these tasks periodically to ensure that they are still executing properly.

Execute Package Task

When you have several DTS packages that you want to execute together or in a particular sequence, you probably would want to have one main package that executes all these packages.

For example, multiple reports may require different types of preprocessing of data. You can develop a DTS package for each report. Although each package can be scheduled to execute individually, more likely they will need to be executed in a coordinated manner.

In SQL 7.0, you had to use the ActiveX Script Task to control the execution of one or more packages. Listing 5.3 is an example of how that was done. For non-programmers, the more common method was to use the Execute Process Task to invoke DTSRun (the command-line executable for launching a DTS package).

Listing 5.3 **VBScript Used in an ActiveX Script Task to Control the Execution of Another DTS Package**

```
Function Main()
 Dim oPkg

 Set oPkg = CreateObject(DTS.Package)
 oPkg.LoadFromSQLServer "ServerName", "UserName", "Password",
 DTSReposFlag_UseTrustedConnection, "", "", "", "PackageName"
 oPkg.Execute
 Set oPkg = Nothing
 Main = DTSTaskExecResult_Success
End Function
```

This task executes just one other package after loading. But, you can have an array of package names; loop through it to load and execute multiple packages.

With SQL 2000, you no longer need to write code to handle the execution of multiple packages because DTS has a built-in task that does the job for you (see Figure 5.6).

By default, when the Execute Package Task Properties dialog box comes up, the Location field is set to SQL Server. This means that the package to be executed will be loaded from the SQL Server that you specify in the box below (see Figure 5.6). However, you can also load packages saved to SQL Server's Meta Data Services or packages saved as a structured storage file (see Chapter 7, "Package").

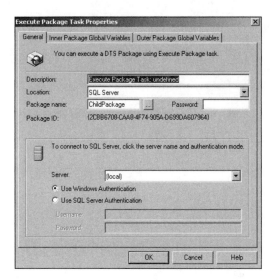

Figure 5.6 The Execute Package Task Properties dialog box.

In addition to simplified package execution, the Execute Package Task makes it easy to pass variables to other packages. You can pass two categories of variables: package variables and task variables. *Package variables* are global variables defined in the parent package's `GlobalVariables` collection. *Task variables* are defined in the Execute Package Task's `GlobalVariables` collection.

Inner Package Global Variables

You can pass task variables by using the Inner Package Global Variables tab (see Figure 5.7). Specify the name of the task variable, data type, and value in the Variables window.

The important thing to remember is that these variables are not added to the global-variables collection of the package in which the Execute Package Task is defined. Instead, they are stored within the task and passed to the child package when the task executes.

The New button at the bottom of the Inner Package Global Variables tab does not create new global variables for the DTS package; it adds the variable to the task's global-variables collection. This collection is listed in the Variables window of the tab.

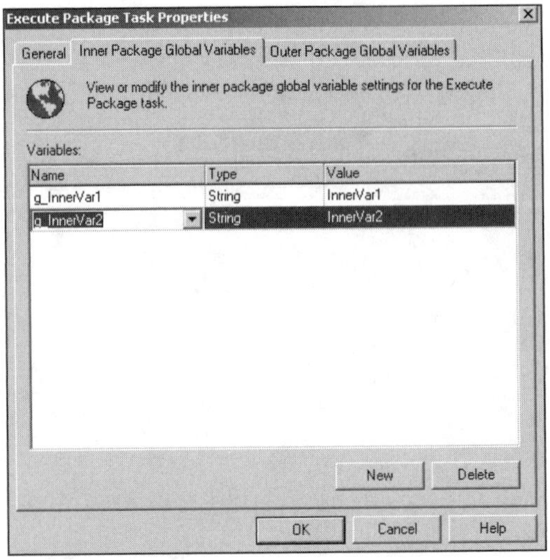

Figure 5.7   The Inner Package Global Variables tab.

Inner-Package Variables Are Task Variables

Variables defined in the Inner Package Global Variables tab are task variables and therefore are stored within the task's global-variables collection, not at the parent-package level. A corresponding variable in the child package must exist for each of these variables, or the task will fail.

Outer Package Global Variables

You can pass package variables by using the Outer Package Global Variables tab (see Figure 5.8). You can select variables only from the list of existing global variables currently defined in the parent package.

Note that you have to create the global variable in the Package Properties dialog box (at the package level). Just as with the Inner Package Global Variables tab, the New button in this tab does not create new global variables. The name of the global variable you want to pass is actually added to the InputGlobalVariables collection of the Execute Package Task. This collection is listed in the Variables window of this tab. At run time, this list is referenced to determine which package variables need to be passed.

A List of Package Variables to Pass

When you add variables in this tab, you essentially are creating a list of package variables that you want to pass to the child package at run time. If the child package does not have these variables in its global-variables collection, those variables are created at run time.

Figure 5.8   The Outer Package Global Variables tab.

When the parent package executes, it first appends the package variables to the child package's global-variables collection (if they don't exist yet). Then the package passes the current values of those package variables to the corresponding child global variables. Next, the package passes the current values of all the task variables to corresponding variables in the child package's global variables.

The task variables are essentially static. You set their values at design time, and these are the values that get passed each time the task executes. Package variables, on the other hand, pass their *current* value when the Execute Package Task executes. If the task is called within a loop, and the value of the package variable changes between calls, the new values are passed to the child package. Understanding package and task variables and how they are passed will enable you to create highly functional groups of DTS packages that work well together.

Dynamic Properties Task

Another great addition to DTS is the Dynamic Properties Task. Use it to modify values of virtually any property within a DTS package at run time. The Dynamic Properties Task Properties dialog box (yes, the Properties dialog box for the Dynamic Properties Task) lists the properties you specify to be set dynamically when the task executes (see Figure 5.9).

Figure 5.9   The Dynamic Properties Task Properties dialog box.

Click on the Add button to bring up the Package Properties dialog box (see Figure 5.10). By default, this dialog box displays the package properties, but you can select other objects in the package and set their properties as well. You can click on a data connection to set `UserID` and `Password`, for example. You also can click on Global Variables to set the value of one or more global variables.

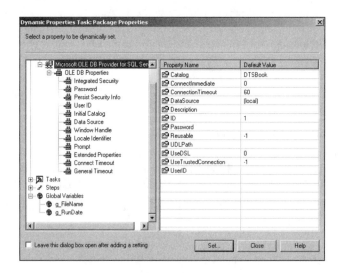

Figure 5.10   The Package Properties dialog box.

It's amazing enough that DTS exposes as many properties as it does with the Dynamic Properties Task. Equally amazing is the number of options it gives you when it comes to choosing the source of the value that you want a property to be set to. Suppose that you need to set dynamically the value of a global variable named g_FileName. Click on the variable to display its properties; then click on the Value property. Now click the Set button to display the Add/Edit Assignment dialog box (see Figure 5.11).

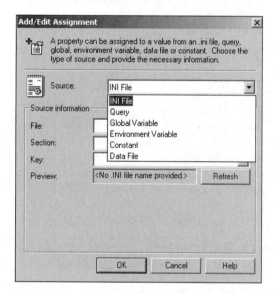

Figure 5.11   The Add/Edit Assignment dialog box.

You can choose among six different source types. Depending on the source you choose, the Source Information items will change to prompt you for the information needed:

- **INI File**—With an INI file, you can specify the filename, the section, and key to identify the value to be used in setting the property value.

- **Query**—With a query, you can specify the data connection; then you can either enter the query directly or browse to a previously saved query and load it. DTS will use the value in the first column of the first row to set the property value.

- **Global Variable**—This option lets you select a variable from the global-variables collection of the package. As you saw earlier in this chapter, the Create Global Variable button enables you to add global variables if necessary.

- **Environment Variable**—This option provides a drop-down menu of all the environment variables available on your development machine. You must make sure that the same environment variable exists on the machine where this package will run.

- **Constant**—This option allows you to enter a specific constant that will be used to set the property value.
- **Data File**—This option allows you to browse for a file containing one or more lines of data. (Yes, it will use multiple lines when needed.)

This section ends the discussion of the programming tasks: the Execute SQL Task, ActiveX Script Task, Execute Package Task, Execute Process Task, and Dynamic Properties Task. Without doubt, you can do a great deal with this set of built-in tasks.

The next three sections discuss the messaging tasks: Send Mail, FTP, and Microsoft's Message Queue Service (MSMQ).

Send Mail Task

The Send Mail Task was introduced in the initial release of DTS. It enables you to send an email message as part of the processing performed within a DTS package. To use a Send Mail Task, you must have messaging services configured properly on the SQL Server machine. You won't be able to create or open a Send Mail Task if the server does not have messaging services installed. Later in this section, you will learn how to integrate mail services with SQL Server.

Sending Mail

Assume for now that messaging has been configured properly on the server. You can click on the Send Mail Task icon on the toolbar to bring up the Send Mail Task Properties dialog box (see Figure 5.12).

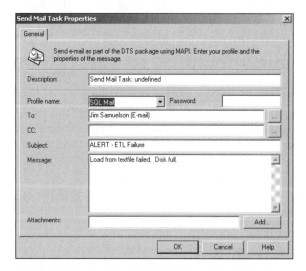

Figure 5.12   The Send Mail Task Properties dialog box.

The Send Mail Task uses one of the mail profiles existing on the server machine. Choose an appropriate mail profile from the Profile Name drop-down menu. Specify the recipients of the email message by typing their email addresses, or click the ellipsis (...) buttons to bring up the Address Book dialog box (see Figure 5.13).

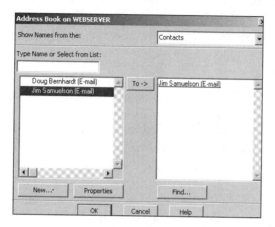

Figure 5.13 The Address Book dialog box.

The Address Book dialog box lets you choose one or more recipients of an email message. You can click on the New button to create a new entry in the Address Book. You also can click on the Properties button to edit the entry for the currently highlighted contact in the list on the left window. After prompting you whether you want to create a new contact or a new distribution list, it brings up the entry screen for creating new contacts in Microsoft Outlook (see Figure 5.14).

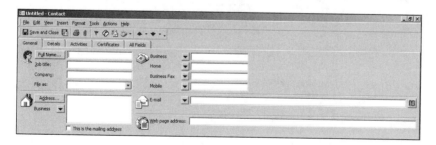

Figure 5.14 Creating new contacts.

You can specify that an attachment be sent with the email. Type the path and name of the file to attach or click the Add button to browse for one.

Configuring Mail Services for SQL Server

If you will recall, SQL Server consists of two main services:

- The SQL Server engine itself, which is called MS SQL Server
- The scheduling engine, which is called SQLServerAgent

Each of these services uses its own corresponding mail services. MS SQL Server uses the SQL Mail service, whereas SQLServerAgent uses its own mail service, called SQL Agent Mail. For the purposes of this section, you are particularly interested in the SQL Mail service.

Essentially, the server on which SQL Server is running must be configured as a mail client. The user account used to start MS SQL Server needs a mail profile.

Numerous versions of mail services and mail clients are available; discussing mail implementation and configuration is beyond the scope of this book. However, here is an example of how it would be done in the context of Windows 2000:

1. Log on to the server machine, using the account you used to start SQL Server.

   To successfully implement SQL Server and mail integration the following is required: on SQL Server 7.0 install MS Outlook 97 or higher, and on SQL Server 2000 install MS Outlook 2000 or higher.

2. Open the Control Panel, and start the Mail applet.

   The Mail dialog box appears, allowing you to add profiles (see Figure 5.15). Note that if a default profile is already specified for the currently logged-in account, that profile will be displayed.

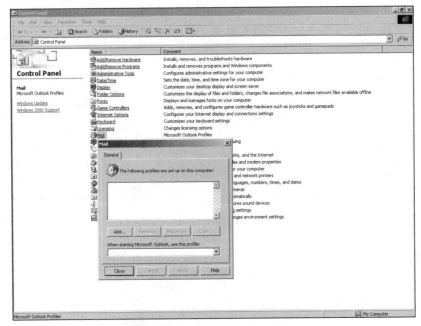

Figure 5.15 The Mail dialog box.

3. Click on the Add button to add a mail profile.

   The Microsoft Outlook Setup Wizard opens (see Figure 5.16). By default, the Use the Following Information Services option is selected. This option creates a default profile called MS Exchange Settings.

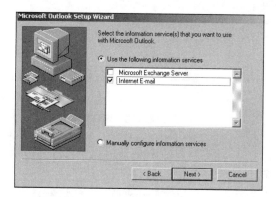

Figure 5.16 The Microsoft Outlook Setup Wizard.

4. Select the second option, Manually Configure Information Services, and click Next.

   This allows you to specify a name for your new profile. Call it SQL Mail (see Figure 5.17). When you click Next, you are prompted to set up the mail account.

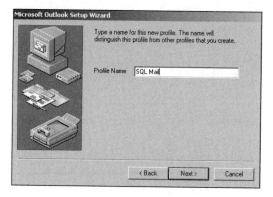

Figure 5.17 Specifying a name for a new mail profile.

5. Set up the mail account.

The SQL Mail Properties dialog box opens (see Figure 5.18). Note that SQL Mail is the name of the profile you are configuring.

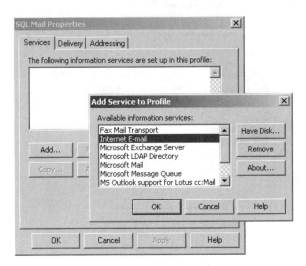

Figure 5.18 The SQL Mail Properties dialog box.

6. Click on the Add button in the Services tab.

The Add Service to Profile dialog box opens, allowing you to choose the messaging service that you need for the mail account (see Figure 5.18). This example uses the Internet email service, but you can use other services. More than likely, Exchange Server will be available in your environment. Select the desired service, and click OK to bring up the Mail Account Properties dialog box.

7. In the SQL Mail Account Properties dialog box, you will be asked to configure the mail account (see Figure 5.19).

Note that the mail account is named SQL Mail Account.

8. Click on the Servers tab to specify the particular mail servers that SQL Server will be contacting (see Figure 5.20).

If you happen to have Internet Information Server (IIS) installed, chances are that you have an SMTP configured for that server as well. You could set SQL Server to send out mail through that SMTP server and not burden the main mail server that serves the users of your enterprise.

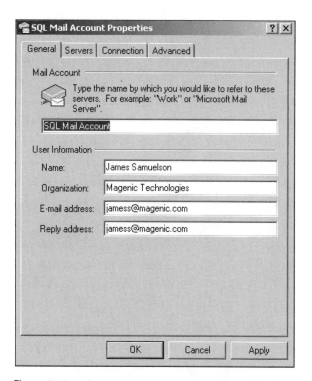

Figure 5.19   The SQL Mail Account Properties dialog box.

9. When completed, you are brought back to the SQL Mail Properties dialog box. Click on the Add button to bring up the Add Service to Profile dialog box. Select the Outlook Address Book service. After the selection, you will be returned to the SQL Mail Properties dialog box. Click on Add again, and select Personal Folders from the Add Service to Profile dialog box. Click OK and the Create/Open Personal Folders File dialog box will appear. Provide a location and name for the file to be created in the File Name field. Click Open, and the Create Microsoft Personal Folders dialog box will pop up. Accept the default values, click OK, and you are brought back to the SQL Mail Properties dialog box. You should see the Mail Service, Outlook Address Book, and Personal Folders services listed in the "The following information services are set up in this profile:" field (see Figure 5.21).

   Now you can configure SQL Server to use the SQL Mail service.

10. Start SQL Enterprise Manager, right-click the server where you want SQL Mail to be configured, and choose Properties from the shortcut menu.

   The SQL Server Properties (Configure) dialog box opens (see Figure 5.22).

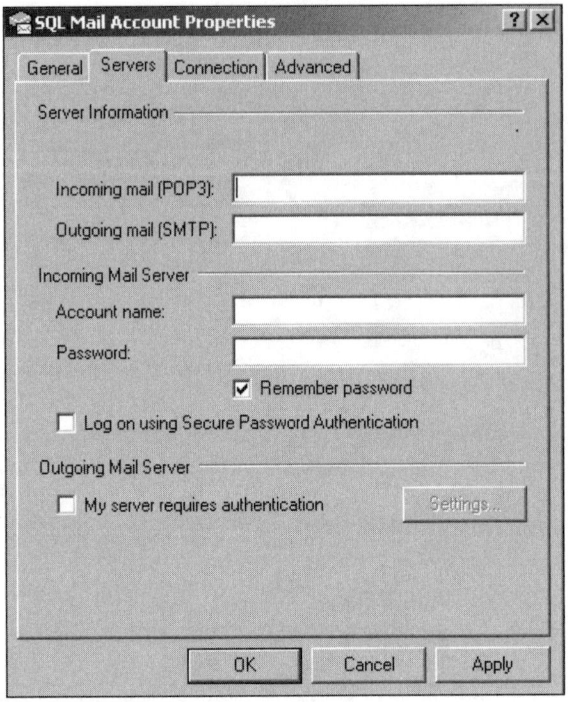

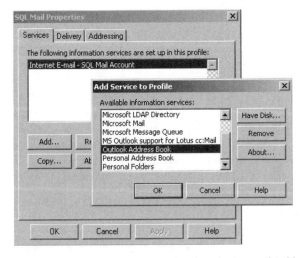

Figure 5.20   Configuring the mail servers that SQL Server will contact.

Figure 5.21   Configuring an Address Book and a Personal Folder.

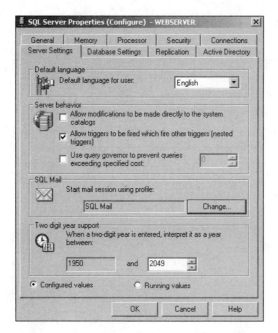

Figure 5.22   The SQL Server Properties (Configure) dialog box.

11. Click on the Server Settings tab; then click on the Change button in the SQL Mail section.

    The SQL Mail Configuration dialog box opens (see Figure 5.23).

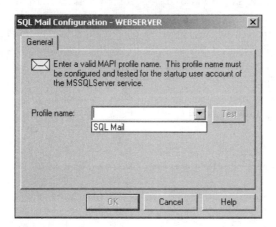

Figure 5.23   The SQL Mail Configuration dialog box.

12. Choose the mail profile (which you named SQL Mail in Step 4) from the drop-down menu.

    To set up SQL Mail from Enterprise Manager, double-click the Support Services folder to expand it. Right-click the SQL Mail object and select Properties from the menu.

13. Click the Test button to see whether the profile was configured properly.

    If so, you should see a message saying that a mail session was started and stopped successfully (see Figure 5.24). If you get an error instead, try stopping and starting SQL Server first. In some installations, you may have an option to auto-start SQL Mail with SQL Server. This option should start the mail session for the SQL Server account properly.

Figure 5.24   SQL Mail configured successfully.

File Transfer Protocol Task

The File Transfer Protocol Task is a limited implementation of an FTP client. It lets you get files from an Internet FTP site or from a directory and save it in a destination directory. Right-click on the File Transfer Protocol Task object in the DTS Designer main panel and select Properties from the object menu (see Figure 5.25).

In the Location tab, you must specify a correct site and the proper login information at design time because DTS attempts to connect right away. You also need to specify the destination directory. A Browse button (...) is available to make locating this directory easier.

Select Directory from the Source drop-down menu to transfer files from a directory. Click on the Browse button (...) to bring up the Browse for Folder dialog box (see Figure 5.26).

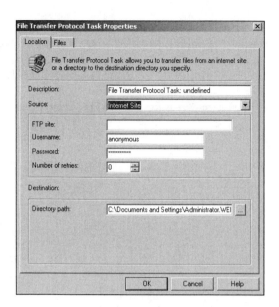

Figure 5.25 The File Transfer Protocol Task Properties dialog box.

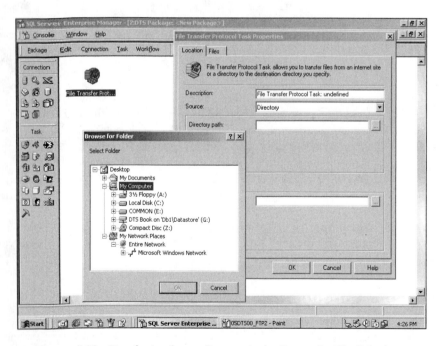

Figure 5.26 Transferring from a directory in the Browse for File dialog box.

Selecting a directory on a local drive will return a path in the format [drive]:[directory path]. Selecting a directory on the network will return a path in UNC format (\\servername\directory_path). Click OK to close the dialog box.

Click the Files tab to see the source and destination directories (see Figure 5.27).

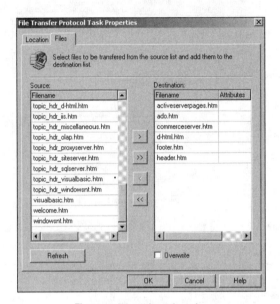

Figure 5.27   The Files tab.

Aside from making it easy to select the files to download, this tab shows file sizes, which can be critical information that you would want to know when setting up a download. The Source directory shows all available files for downloading, but the Destination directory does not show any existing files at all. The only time the Destination directory will list a file is when you've specified one from the Source directory by double-clicking on it or by clicking on the source file and then clicking on the right-arrow button (>). In other words, it only shows the files that you intend to download.

If you are waiting for a file to arrive at the source directory, the Refresh button is a great help because it gets the latest list of files and refreshes the display every time you click on it.

Message Queue Task

One of the biggest additions to SQL Server 2000 DTS is support for Microsoft's Message Queue Service (MSMQ). MSMQ enables an application architecture where two distinct applications or two instances of the same application can communicate with each other without a direct connection. Each application instance can execute at a different time, and yet the communication between the two is still bridged by way of MSMQ.

In simple terms, a message is sent by one application to a queue that is managed by an MSMQ server. The second application can retrieve this message at its own pleasure.

In Windows 2000, MSMQ is included as a configurable component of the server. In Windows NT 4, you can install MSMQ from the Windows NT 4.0 Option Pack. You need at least the MSMQ client services for the MSMQ task to work properly.

You can use the Message Queue Task to either send or receive MSMQ messages (see Figure 5.28).

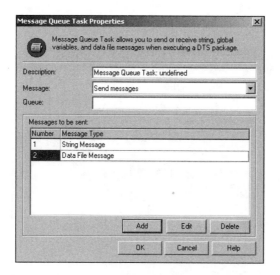

Figure 5.28   The Message Queue Task Properties dialog box.

You have to specify a queue where you want to send or receive your message. Specifying the correct queue is important; otherwise, the task will fail at run-time. To specify a queue, use the following format:

```
computer_name\queue_type$\queue_name
```

This format is broken down as follows:

- `computer_name` is the server running the MSMQ service.
- `queue_type` is Outgoing, Public, Private, or System.
- `queue_name` is the name of the server's queue.

MSMQ supports three types of messages, and DTS allows you to send and receive all three types. These message types include:

- String message
- Data-file message
- Global-variable message

Within a Message Queue Task, DTS allows you to send or receive, but not both. If you choose to send, you can create multiple messages and send them all out when the task executes. DTS lists the message number and type of each message that you add. Note that you are limited to 4MB for each message.

Sending Messages

To send a message, choose Send Messages from the Message drop-down menu and click the Add button. The Message Queue Message Properties dialog box opens (see Figure 5.29).

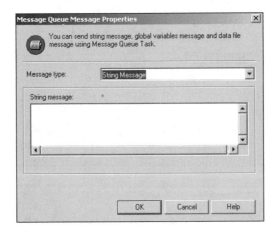

Figure 5.29   The Message Queue Message Properties dialog box .

By default, this dialog box lets you build a string message to send. Type the message in the String Message text box; then click on the OK button. The message is added to the main list of messages to be sent out.

To send a global-variables message, select Global Variables Message from the Message Type drop-down menu. The options in the Message Type menu change to a list of global variables (see Figure 5.30). Click the New button to add an item to the list. Then you can choose a global variable from the drop-down menu below the Name column. You can send multiple global variables in one message as long as the collection does not exceed 4MB. Click on the Create Global Variables button to add global variables to the package.

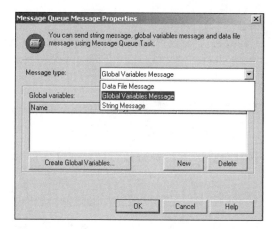

Figure 5.30   Sending a global-variables message.

To send a data-file message, choose Data File Message from the Message Type drop-down menu. Then enter the filename of the data file you want to send or browse to it by clicking the ellipsis (...) button (see Figure 5.31). DTS adds this message to its list without validating that the file exists. You must ensure that the file exists at the time the task executes to keep it from failing.

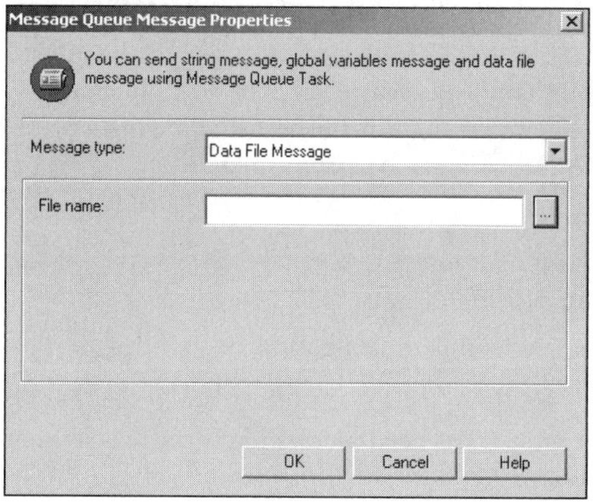

Figure 5.31   Sending a data-file message.

Receiving Messages

To receive a message, choose Receive Messages from the Message Type drop-down menu. The menu options change to those appropriate for receiving a string message (see Figure 5.32).

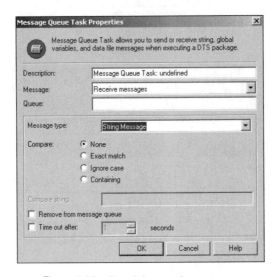

Figure 5.32   Receiving a string message.

Using the Compare options, you can receive any string message without any constraints, or you can enter a compare string and set up a filter by using the following rules:

- **Exact Match**—String message must match the compare string, including case.
- **Ignore Case**—A case-insensitive match must occur between the message and the compare string.
- **Containing**—The compare string must be found within the message string.

Check the Remove from Message Queue check box to tell DTS to delete the message from the queue after it has been received. You can specify how long the task will wait to receive a message.

To receive a global-variables message, choose the appropriate option from the Message drop-down menu. The dialog box displays options appropriate for receiving a global-variables message (see Figure 5.33).

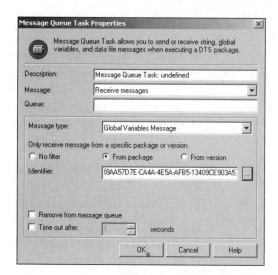

Figure 5.33   Receiving a global-variables message.

You can receive a global-variables message without restriction, or you can choose to limit its source. When limiting the source, you can specify a specific source package or, better yet, a specific version of a source package. DTS will ask for an identifier, which is a GUID. If you can remember the GUID of your source package, you are welcome to type it in the Identifier text box, but DTS does not expect you to do so. You can click the ellipsis button (…) instead to find the package from the appropriate server (see Figure 5.34). You must have the proper login account to access packages from the server.

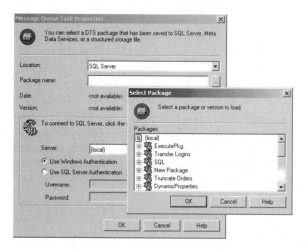

Figure 5.34   Specifying the source package/version.

Note that the package can also come from SQL Server's Meta Data Services or a Structured Storage File because DTS can save packages to these storage destinations. Just as you do for receiving a string message, you can elect to receive the global-variables message from the queue when it arrives or specify how long DTS will wait to receive the message.

To receive a data-file message, choose the appropriate option from the Message drop-down menu. The dialog box displays options appropriate for receiving a data-file message (see Figure 5.35).

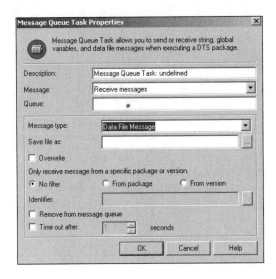

Figure 5.35   Receiving a data-file message.

Specify the filename to save the incoming file into or browse to it by clicking the browse button (...). If the destination file contains data, you can specify to overwrite it by checking the Overwrite check box.

You can receive a data-file message without restriction, or you can choose to limit its source by specifying a source package or a specific version of a package. Again, DTS will help you seek out this package if necessary. You have the option of deleting the message after it is received or specifying how long DTS will wait for the message.

Message queuing has seen little use in the real world—at least, not the widespread use that Microsoft Transaction Server and SQL Server have enjoyed. By adding the Message Queue Task to DTS, Microsoft made it easier to use MSMQ. More message-based application architectures might appear in the future.

Copy SQL Server Objects Task

The Copy SQL Server Objects Task is the renamed Transfer SQL Server Objects Task that was introduced in SQL 7.0 (see Figure 5.36). Aside from the name change, the task itself has had a few meaningful changes. With this task, you can copy SQL Server objects between SQL 7.0 servers, between SQL 2000 servers, and from a SQL 7.0 server to a SQL 2000 server. In the third scenario, you effectively can create SQL 2000 versions of your existing SQL 7.0 database objects.

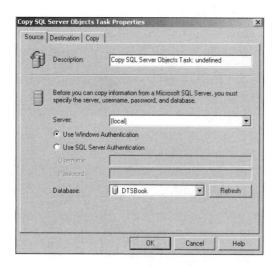

Figure 5.36 The Copy SQL Server Objects Task Properties dialog box.

To copy SQL Server objects, you need to specify a source and destination. You will notice that the Source and Destination tabs of the Properties dialog box are quite similar. In SQL 2000, however, you can create a new database as the destination on the target server by selecting <new>. Doing so brings up the Create Database dialog box (see Figure 5.37).

DTS prompts you for the basic information needed to create a database but does not actually create it until you execute the task.

By default, DTS copies all objects in the source database. If you deselect this option, you can click on the Select Objects button to bring up the Select Objects dialog box, where you can specify the objects you want to copy (see Figure 5.38).

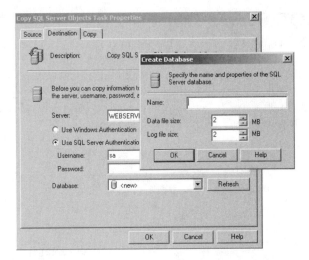

Figure 5.37 The Destination tab and the Create Database dialog box.

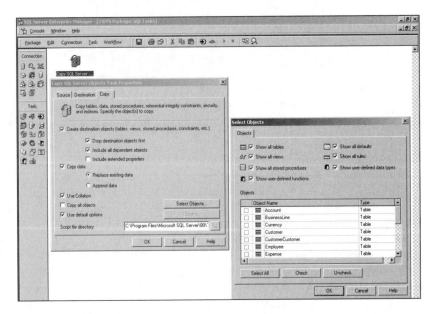

Figure 5.38 The Copy tab and the Select Objects dialog box.

You must remember two important things about the Copy SQL Server Objects Task:

- If you have foreign keys defined for the table(s) you intend to copy, DTS will copy the related tables and views as well.
- If you are copying between SQL 7.0 databases, and the source database is upgraded to SQL 2000, the task will fail. You cannot copy from a SQL 2000

database to a SQL 7.0 database. You will have to reconfigure the task to make sure that the source and destination databases are appropriate.

Although the Copy SQL Server Objects Task deals with objects specific to a database, at times you may need to copy objects specific to the server instead. To do so, you use the five tasks discussed in the following sections: Transfer Databases, Transfer Logins, Transfer Master Stored Procedures, Transfer Jobs, and Transfer Error Messages.

Transfer Databases Task

The Transfer Databases Task lets you move or copy databases to a SQL 2000 server. Yes, that's right—only to a SQL 2000 server. You cannot copy even between two SQL 7.0 servers. Note that this is true for all the tasks that transfer database objects between servers.

Just as with the Copy SQL Server Objects Task, the Source and Destination tabs of the Properties dialog box are similar. The basic option, however, is limited to choosing the name of the server involved and specifying the login account to use (see Figure 5.39).

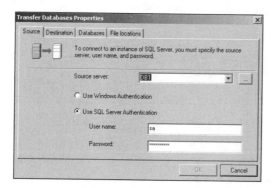

Figure 5.39   The Transfer Databases Properties dialog box.

After you specify the source and destination information, DTS will enumerate the databases on both sides and show you which ones can be moved or copied (see Figure 5.40). DTS will provide check boxes only for those databases that qualify, preventing you from specifying the wrong databases. In addition, DTS will not allow you to move or copy any of the built-in master, msdb, model, or tempdb databases.

The File Locations tab shows the default locations where DTS will copy the associated files of the database(s) you specified (see Figure 5.41). If you accept this default setting, all the files for all the databases will be copied to the same location.

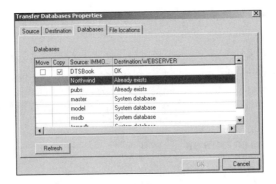

Figure 5.40   The Databases tab.

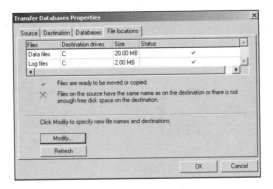

Figure 5.41   The File Locations tab.

Click on the Modify button to bring up the Database Files dialog box. This dialog box allows you to specify locations for each individual file that will be copied. Click on the ellipsis button (…) to bring up the CDW dialog box (see Figure 5.42). This dialog box lets you browse to the folder on the destination server where you want the file to be copied. Unfortunately, SQL Server will not let you create the destination folder on the fly.

About the Copy Database Wizard

You may be wondering what the title of the dialog box, CDW, means. The title refers to the Copy Database Wizard, which uses the same COM objects that implement this task. You can invoke this wizard by right-clicking the Databases folder in Enterprise Manager, choosing All Tasks from the shortcut menu, and then clicking the Copy Database Wizard option. The wizard walks you through the steps for copying a database from one server to another.

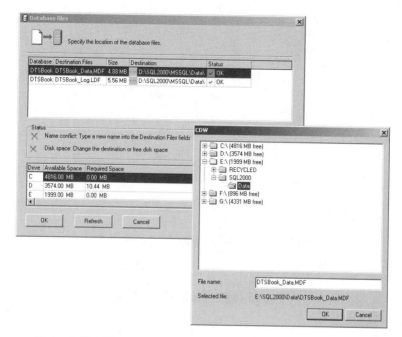

Figure 5.42   The Database Files dialog box and the CDW dialog box.

When DTS enumerates the files to be copied, it does some significant checking in terms of disk-space availability as well as names conflicts. DTS shows both the required and the available disk space, and it shows whether an existing file of the same name already exists on the server. These checks help prevent the task from failing when the package is executed.

Transfer Logins Task

The Transfer Logins Task lets you transfer logins from a SQL 7.0 or SQL 2000 server to a SQL 2000 server. As in the preceding task, the Source and Destination tabs of the Properties dialog box are similar (see Figure 5.43). Both tabs ask for the server name and login information.

By default, the task copies all logins detected at the source server when the task is executed. In the Logins tab, you have the option to copy only the logins from selected databases (see Figure 5.44).

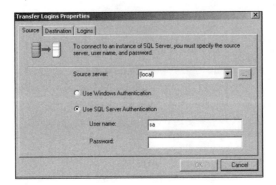

Figure 5.43 The Transfer Logins Properties dialog box.

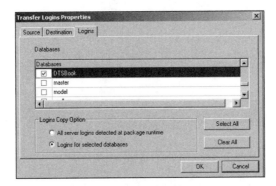

Figure 5.44 The Logins tab.

Veteran DBAs probably will smile upon discovering this task in DTS. The task simplifies two of the most mundane activities performed in a database-server environment: extracting user logins and creating (or re-creating) logins. DBAs have spent countless man-hours scripting just these two activities.

Transfer Master Stored Procedures Task

This task is used to copy stored procedures that you have added to the master database. Again, you can copy from both SQL 7.0 and SQL 2000 servers, but the destination will have to be a SQL 2000 server. The Properties dialog box for this task (see Figure 5.45) is very similar to the one for the preceding task.

Instead of the Logins tab, however, this dialog box has a Stored Procedures tab (see Figure 5.46). By default, the task copies all your stored procedures from the source master database at the time of execution. The Stored Procedures tab, however, gives you the option to select particular stored procedures to be copied.

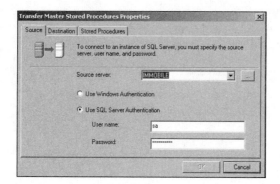

Figure 5.45   The Transfer Master Stored Procedures Properties dialog box.

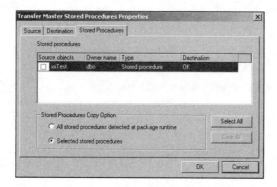

Figure 5.46   The Stored Procedures tab.

This task provides a quick way to restore your custom master stored procedures from a duplicate database; it also allows you to upgrade your SQL 7.0 custom master stored procedures to SQL 2000.

Transfer Jobs Task

The Transfer Jobs Task allows you to copy jobs from a SQL 7.0 or SQL 2000 server. Again, the destination needs to be a SQL 2000 server. *Jobs* are units of work to be performed by SQL Server. Jobs are managed and scheduled by the SQL Server Agent service. Each SQL Server stores all its job information in the msdb database, which explains why the Properties dialog box for this task is called Transfer Msdb Jobs Properties (see Figure 5.47).

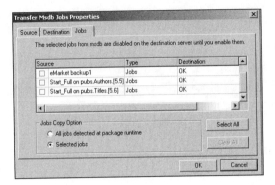

Figure 5.47 The Transfer Msdb Jobs Properties dialog box.

By default, the task copies all the jobs it finds at the source server at the time of execution. As usual, you have the option to specify which jobs to copy.

Transfer Error Messages Task

The Transfer Error Messages Task lets you copy error messages that you have added by using the `sp_addmessage` stored procedure. The task will copy from a SQL 7.0 or SQL 2000 server to—you guessed it—only a SQL 2000 server. This situation may sound like a broken record, but taking note of it is important.

The Properties dialog box for this task looks the same as those for the preceding tasks. The dialog box has Source and Destination tabs, as well as the Error Messages tab.

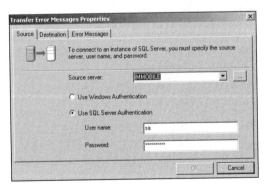

Figure 5.48 The Transfer Error Messages Properties dialog box.

By default, the task copies all your custom error messages from the source server's master database at the time of execution. The Error Messages tab, however, gives you the option to select particular error messages to be copied (see Figure 5.49).

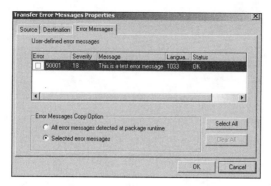

Figure 5.49 The Error Messages tab.

Just as you can with your custom stored procedures, this task provides a quick way to restore your custom error messages from a duplicate database. The task also allows you to upgrade your SQL 7.0 custom error messages to SQL 2000.

This section ends the discussion of the database management tasks. The following two sections discuss the tasks added to DTS by the installation of Analysis Services.

Analysis Services Processing Task

The Analysis Services Processing Task is one of two add-on tasks that are enabled with the installation of Microsoft Analysis Services. As you probably are aware, Analysis Services is the renamed Microsoft OLAP Services. OLAP is short for On Line Analytical Processing, the alter ego of On Line Transactional Processing (OLTP). With OLAP, data needs to be in a format that lends itself to easy reporting through aggregation as well as drill-down. Because relational data is not well structured for these purposes, the data needs to be transformed to a storage format that is optimized for OLAP. This data storage, otherwise known as an OLAP database, commonly includes such structures as cubes, partitions, dimensions, and mining models. Analysis Services provides the platform for building and maintaining OLAP databases.

In Analysis Services, the Analysis Server provides the services for extracting data from relational sources and for building and populating cubes and dimensions in an OLAP database. The Analysis Manager is the administrative tool for interacting with the Analysis Server. This tool provides the cube editor and the dimension editor, which you use to specify how the cubes and dimensions will look.

If you are unfamiliar with these terms, see the Analysis Services documentation included with SQL Server.

After the OLAP database structures have been built, certain processing has to occur to keep them updated. Such processing can be a complete rebuild or an incremental update. The Analysis Services Task helps automate this processing.

To use the Analysis Services Task, click the yellow cube in the Task toolbar to bring up the Analysis Services Processing Task dialog box (see Figure 5.50).

Figure 5.50 The Analysis Services Processing Task dialog box.

The basic steps required to configure this task are:

1. Select the object to process.
2. Select the processing options.
3. Click OK.

You select the object to process in the tree view on the left side of the dialog box. Depending on the type of object you select, processing options are enabled on the right side of the dialog box, allowing you to select them.

Default Repository for Analysis Services

When you install the Analysis Services component from the SQL Server 2000 CD, you might think that the OLAP databases would reside on SQL Server. On the contrary, the default installation uses a Microsoft Access database to open the application beyond the users of SQL Server. As a result, when you build your Analysis Services Task, only the server where you installed Analysis Services shows up in the tree view. Analysis Manager provides an option to migrate the repository to SQL Server.

Processing Options

Just as in Analysis Manager, the processing options include the following:

- Full process
- Refresh data
- Incremental update

Table 5.2 lists the options for each object type that can be selected for processing.

Table 5.2 **Analysis Services Processing Options** [1]

Icon	Object	Option	Processing Value	Description
	Database	Full Process	0	Completely processes all cubes, partitions, and dimensions in the database.
	Cubes folder	Full Process	0	Completely processes all cubes in the folder.
		Refresh Data	1	For each cube in the folder, performs a refresh data operation if possible; otherwise, completely processes the cube.
	Cube with single partition	Full Process	0	Completely processes the cube, including structural changes. This option is the most thorough type of cube processing.
		Refresh Data	1	Reloads cube data and recalculates aggregations. This option processes changes to existing source data but not the addition of source data. This option does not process structural cube changes, such as new dimensions, levels, or measures.
		Incremental Update	2	Adds new data to cube and updates aggregations. This option processes the addition of source data. This option does not process changes to the cube's structure or existing source data.

continues

Table 5.2   **Continued**

Icon	Processing Object	Option	Value	Description
	Cube with multiple partitions	Full Process	0	Completely processes the cube, including structural changes. This option is more thorough than the Refresh Data option.
		Refresh Data	1	Reloads cube data and recalculates aggregations. This option processes changes to existing source data but not the addition of source data. This option does not process structural cube changes, such as new dimensions, levels, or measures.
	Partition, including remote partitions	Full Process	0	Reloads partition data and recalculates aggregations. This option processes changes to existing source data but not the addition of source data. This option does not process structural changes to the parent cube, such as new dimensions, levels, or measures.
		Incremental Update	2	Adds new data to a partition and updates aggregations. This option processes the addition of source data. This option does not process changes to the structure of the parent cube or existing source data of the partition.
	Linked cube	Full Process	0	Completely processes the linked cube.
	Virtual cube	Full Process	0	Completely processes the virtual cube.
	Dimensions folder	Full Process	0	Completely processes all dimensions in the folder.

Table 5.2 **Continued**

Icon	Processing Object	Option	Value	Description
		Incremental Update	2	For each dimension in the folder, performs an incremental update operation if possible; otherwise, completely processes the dimension.
	Shared dimension	Full Process	0	Completely processes the dimension, including structural changes, and rebuilds the dimension structure. This option is more thorough than the Incremental Update option.
		Incremental Update	2	Processes the addition of members (that is, rows) to the dimension table. This method does not process changes to the structure of the dimension or relationships among members.
	Virtual dimension	Full Process	0	Completely processes the virtual dimension and rebuilds the dimension structure.
	Mining Models folder	Full Process	0	Completely processes mining models in the folder.
		Refresh Data	1	For each mining model in the folder, performs a refresh data operation if possible; otherwise, completely processes the mining model.
	Relational Mining model	Full Process	0	Completely processes the mining model.

continues

Table 5.2 **Continued**

Icon	Processing Object	Option	Value	Description
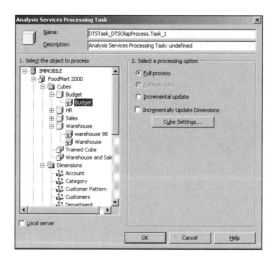	OLAP Mining Model	Refresh Data	1	Adds new data to the source data of the mining model and updates nodes. This option does not process changes to the structure of the mining model or existing source data.

1. This table was copied from Microsoft SQL Server 2000 Version 8.00 Books Online (BOL). This information is available on the SQL Server installation CD.

Selecting a database object enables only the Full Process option, which means that all the cubes, dimensions, and partitions in the database are processed. Selecting any other object within the database, however, may enable other options (see Figure 5.51).

Figure 5.51 Processing options for a cube.

Processing Cubes

For cubes and partitions, you can configure additional options. Click on the Cube Settings button to bring up the Cube/Partition Settings dialog box (see Figure 5.52).

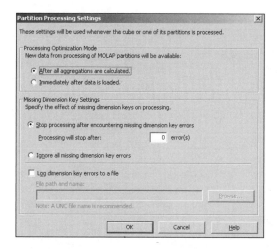

Figure 5.52   The Cube/Partition Settings dialog box.

You can enhance the performance of the task (or at least give the impression that it is fast) by not waiting to make the data available until processing is complete. To do so, select the Immediately After Data Is Loaded option in the Processing Optimization Mode section. At times, however, you must complete all processing before making the data available. In those cases, select the After All Aggregations Are Calculated option.

As you know, transforming data from OLTP and other sources does not always run smoothly. Sometimes, certain data is not available. When this data happens to be dimension key values, you can select the Stop Processing After Encountering Missing Dimension Key Errors option. You can specify the number of errors at which point processing will stop. Alternatively, you can select the Ignore All Missing Dimension Key Errors option to allow processing to continue even if errors are encountered. When you have incomplete dimension keys, some of the details in the fact table will not be reflected in the resulting cube.

The last option for cube/partition processing allows you to log the dimension-key errors. You can browse to an existing file, or you can specify the path and filename where errors will be logged.

Processing Mining Models

When you select a mining–model object for processing, you have the option to specify a training query (see Figure 5.53).

Figure 5.53   Processing options for mining models.

Click on the ellipsis button (…) to open the Training Query dialog box (see Figure 5.54). This dialog box allows you to enter a training query that is used in processing the mining model.

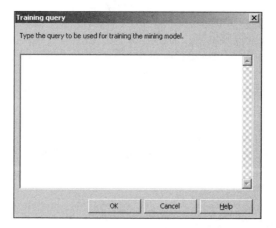

Figure 5.54   Specifying training queries for mining models.

Training queries must conform to the OLE DB for OLAP specification. You can use the Multidimensional Expressions query language to create your training query because MDX is part of the OLE DB for OLAP specification.

Data Mining Task

The Data Mining Task is the second add-on task introduced by Microsoft's Analysis Services. To use the Data Mining Task, you must have an existing data mining model defined in an Analysis Services database.

A *data mining model* is a representation of data in terms of rules and patterns. Using statistical information gleaned from the data itself, you can derive certain predictive information. Given such customer information as (a) number of children at home, (b) annual income, and education, for example, a mining model can predict which credit-card type fits that customer. This section uses the sample FoodMart database that comes with Analysis Services to explore this task.

To create the Data Mining Task, click on the pickaxe icon on the task toolbar. The Data Mining Prediction Query Task dialog box opens (see Figure 5.55).

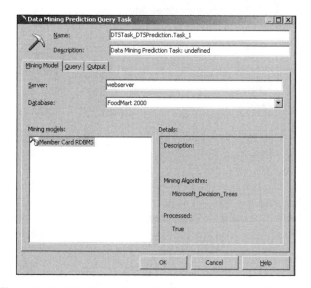

Figure 5.55   The Data Mining Prediction Query Task dialog box.

In the Mining Model tab, specify the name of the server where Analysis Services is installed. If DTS finds this server, it lists all available Analysis Services databases in the Database drop-down menu. After you select a database, DTS displays all the available mining models on the Mining Models window on the left side of the dialog box. Click on a particular mining model, and its details are displayed in the Details list. The example in this section uses the Member Card mining model.

Click on the Query tab to specify the prediction query that you want to process. In the Input Data Source text box, type a connection string that points to a data source containing the input data to be processed. Alternatively, you can click the ellipsis button (…) to open the Data Link Properties dialog box (see Figure 5.56).

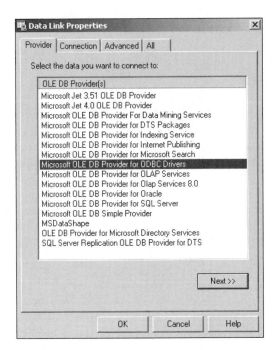

Figure 5.56 The Data Link Properties dialog box.

In the Provider tab, select the OLE DB provider for the data source you want to use. Your choice most likely will be dictated by how the mining model was created and where the Analysis Services database is stored.

Click the Connection tab to configure your connection to the data source (see Figure 5.57). This tab will vary depending on the provider you selected. In this example, a data source called FoodMart 2000 (created as part of the Analysis Services installation) is available. Specify whatever connection information is appropriate for your selected data source. Then click on the Test Connection button to see whether you can connect to the data source.

Back in the Query tab, you can type or paste in the query that you want to use. This query must have syntax conforming to the OLE DB for Data Mining specification. Fortunately, DTS provides a Query Builder to help build such a query. Click the New Query button to bring up the Prediction Query Builder dialog box (see Figure 5.58).

Earlier in this chapter, you learned that you need an existing mining model to create the Data Mining Task. The mining model specifies (among other things) a case table, a case key, input columns, and the prediction column. These elements are the basis for building the query.

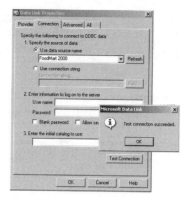

Figure 5.57 The Connection tab.

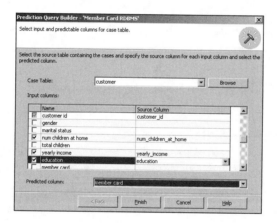

Figure 5.58 The Prediction Query Builder dialog box.

For this example, the mining model uses the Customer table as the case table, so choose it from the Case Table drop-down menu.

In the Input Columns window, specify the names of the columns you want to use for this particular query by checking the check boxes corresponding to the names. Deselect the check boxes for column names that you don't want to include in the query. Because a case key is needed to identify individual cases in the result set, the designated key column is selected automatically, and its check box is grayed out to keep you from deselecting it. The other input columns that you want to include are the [num children at home], [yearly income], and [education] columns. For each of

the input-column names you've checked, you need to specify the source columns
containing the data to be processed. Click the cell to the right of a name you have
selected, and a drop-down menu appears. Choose the appropriate column from that
menu.

Finally, from the Predicted Column drop-down menu, choose the column that you
want to predict in this task. (A mining model can have multiple prediction columns.)
Click the Finish button to display the actual query (see Figure 5.59).

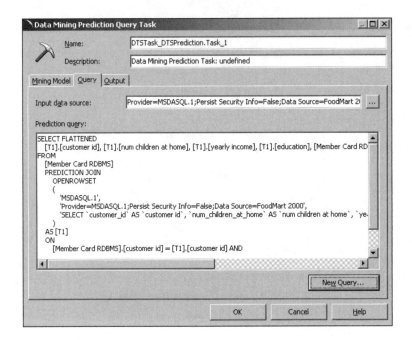

Figure 5.59 The prediction query.

The last step in building the Data Mining Task is specifying where the result set will
be stored. You use the Data Link Properties dialog box for this purpose. You can store
the result set in the same data source where your Analysis database resides or in any
other database that suits your needs. In Figure 5.60, the result set is saved in a SQL
Server table.

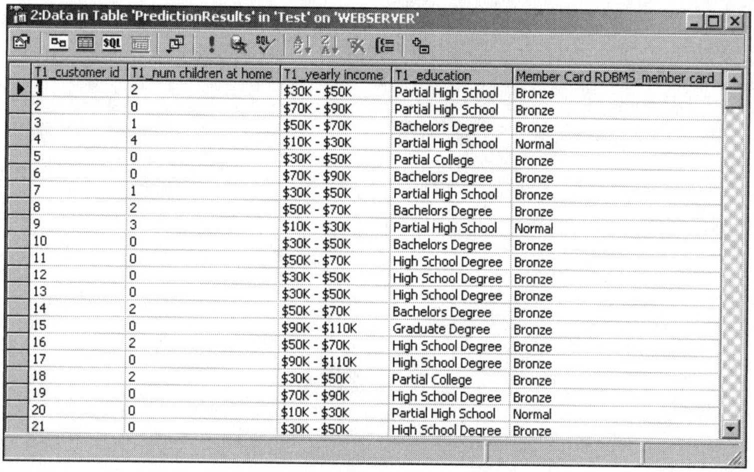

T1_customer id	T1_num children at home	T1_yearly income	T1_education	Member Card RDBMS_member card
1	2	$30K - $50K	Partial High School	Bronze
2	0	$70K - $90K	Partial High School	Bronze
3	1	$50K - $70K	Bachelors Degree	Bronze
4	4	$10K - $30K	Partial High School	Normal
5	0	$30K - $50K	Partial College	Bronze
6	0	$70K - $90K	Bachelors Degree	Bronze
7	1	$30K - $50K	Partial High School	Bronze
8	2	$50K - $70K	Bachelors Degree	Bronze
9	3	$10K - $30K	Partial High School	Normal
10	0	$30K - $50K	Bachelors Degree	Bronze
11	0	$50K - $70K	High School Degree	Bronze
12	0	$30K - $50K	High School Degree	Bronze
13	0	$30K - $50K	High School Degree	Bronze
14	2	$50K - $70K	Bachelors Degree	Bronze
15	0	$90K - $110K	Graduate Degree	Bronze
16	2	$50K - $70K	High School Degree	Bronze
17	0	$90K - $110K	High School Degree	Bronze
18	2	$30K - $50K	Partial College	Bronze
19	0	$70K - $90K	High School Degree	Bronze
20	0	$10K - $30K	Partial High School	Normal
21	0	$30K - $50K	High School Degree	Bronze

Figure 5.60 Result set in a SQL Server table.

Summary

This chapter discussed the additional DTS tasks. Although these tasks do not perform the core ETL functions per se, they lend support to the main data-movement tasks introduced in Chapter 4, "DTS Tasks."

The chapter covered the programming tasks—Execute SQL, ActiveX Script, Execute Process, and Execute Package—as well as the Dynamic Properties Task. These tasks enable you to control the processing in many ways. You've learned that you can pass parameters to and use the result set returned by the Execute SQL Task. The Execute Package Task makes it easier to coordinate the execution of multiple packages. Also, the Dynamic Properties Task makes it much easier to pass parameters to a package or to modify its properties at run time.

The chapter explained that the messaging tasks make it easy to send mail, download from FTP sites and directories, and send and receive MSMQ messages. The chapter also discussed how to use the database-management tasks to copy databases and database objects to SQL 2000 servers. Finally, the chapter introduced the OLAP tasks that help you automate the processing in an Analysis Services database.

Chapter 6, "DTS Workflows," explains how two or more tasks can be hooked together inside a DTS package so that they can execute in a controlled manner.

6

DTS Workflows

PRECEDENCE CONSTRAINTS AND STEPS ARE USED to define the workflow in the DTS packages. Microsoft SQL Server provides three precedence constraints for use in designing the package workflow. Table 6.1 gives the types of constraints and the colors used to designate them in the DTS Designer window.

Table 6.1 **DTS Precedence Constraints**

Precedence Constraint	Arrow Color
On Completion	Blue
On Success	Green
On Failure	Red

How to Use DTS Workflows

To use the workflows within a DTS package, you should select two tasks in the DTS Designer and then select the precedence constraint you need from the Workflow menu or from the shortcut menu by right-clicking one of the tasks.

> **About the Order of the Tasks**
>
> When you create workflows, the order in which you select the tasks is important. First, you need to make sure that you select the source task and then the destination task to get the precedence restraint in the correct direction. You also must be aware that the order in which you set the tasks can affect the actual order in which the steps are executed.

After selecting the tasks, you will be able to select one of the three precedence-constraint options: On Completion, On Success, and On Failure (see Figure 6.1).

When you select a particular constraint, DTS inserts a line that has a color specific to the type of precedence, with an arrow signifying the direction of the workflow (refer to Table 6.1 earlier in this section).

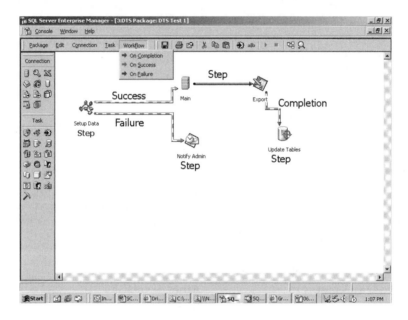

Figure 6.1 The DTS Designer window, showing workflows in the Workflow drop-down menu.

Precedence Properties

If you right-click the workflow arrow, you can change the precedence properties of the workflow (see Figure 6.2).

Workflow precedence constraints have very few properties. You can change the Source Step, Precedence, and Destination Step settings. The source and destination steps are applied to the DTS tasks in the package. You can change the order of the workflow by switching the source and destination steps.

Figure 6.2   The Precedence tab of the Workflow Properties dialog box.

The other property that you can change is the precedence. You can choose among the three precedence constraints described in the following sections.

On Completion

You use this precedence constraint if you want to progress from step to step unconditionally. When you use this constraint, whether the source step succeeds or fails, the next step will execute when the source step completes.

On Success

You use this precedence constraint to execute the destination step only if the source step returns success. If the source step fails, all steps after the success constraint will not be executed. The On Success constraint allows you to establish steps that are required to be executed in a specific order.

Unexecuted Steps

In the progress dialog box, any steps that are not executed are represented by a black cross in a circle. Also note that these steps will not be recorded in the package log. (See Chapter 7, "Package," for more information about the package log.)

On Failure

You use this precedence constraint to execute the destination step only if the source step fails. A good example of this use is when a step fails to send an email to the appropriate person. If a step fails, the email task would be executed.

Workflow Properties

You can access workflow properties by right-clicking a task and choosing Workflow Properties from the shortcut menu. This option is available for any task. The Precedence-tab properties were discussed earlier in this chapter. The precedence restraints that are displayed in the dialog box, however, are the ones that precede the selected step. You access the workflow properties in the Options tab (see Figure 6.3).

Transaction Properties

Some options for using transactions in your package can be defined in the steps. First, you can have a step join a DTS transaction if a transaction is available.

Enabling Transactions

Transactions must be enabled on the package for the workflow to join the transaction. Chapter 7 has more detailed information on enabling and using transactions in DTS.

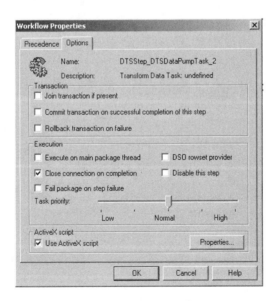

Figure 6.3   The Options tab of the Workflow Properties dialog box.

Second, you can have the workflow cause all the transactions to commit on success or to roll back on failure by selecting the appropriate check boxes. These options affect the current package transaction and will commit or roll back all the pending steps to this point. If neither of these options is selected, the transaction will continue until the commit or rollback is called. For more information on transactions in a DTS package, see Chapter 7.

Transaction Commit Order

On commit, all steps will be executed in the order in which they were executed in the package.

Execution Properties

Several properties affect the execution of steps. Some of them affect the execution of the package as well, including how the step will be executed (threading instructions). Other properties are helpful in debugging a package. The following sections describe these properties.

Execute on Main Thread

You should use this option if you are using a data provider or executing objects that are not free-threaded. Examples of providers that are not free-threaded are Microsoft's OLE DB Provider for Jet and most file-based data stores (such as Microsoft Excel, dBase, and HTML).

Warning from SQL BOL

Microsoft's SQL Server Books Online (BOL) warns that serious errors will occur if you try to use parallel execution with Microsoft's OLE DB Provider for Jet and most file-based data stores without setting Execute on Main Thread to TRUE.

Close Connection on Completion

When a package is executed, the connection will remain open, or when accessing a file, the Win32 file system will retain the file lock until the package has completed its execution. You can use this option to close connections or release file locks when the step has completed instead of waiting for the package to finish. You might want to use this option if you transfer data to a file (destination connection) and need to email it after you complete the data dump. In that case, you would want to close the connection, freeing the file lock to send it in the email message.

Some data providers benefit from closed connections. Also, some data providers perform better with fewer connections. Much of the time, however, the performance of a package is affected adversely when you close and open connections. You should refer to the documentation on the data provider to establish the best circumstances for using this option.

Fail Package on Step Failure

You use this option if you want to stop the entire package explicitly if this specific step fails. This property was introduced in SQL Server 2000. With its addition, you can use On Failure to branch the package workflow. If you are running multiple steps in parallel, this option also could be useful for stopping the entire package.

> When SQL Server 7.0 first came out with DTS, the Fail Package on Step Failure option was not available.

DSO Rowset Provider

This option, if selected, will expose OLE DB rowset data to external data consumers, such as the Query Analyzer (see Figure 6.4). When you use this option, the transformed data is returned to the calling program, not to the destination. Then you can use this feature to debug the transform before sending the data to the actual destination.

This option also might be helpful if you have a transform that you need to use in an application many times. Each time the call is made, the transform allows the data-transformation capabilities of the Transform Data Task to be used in many other programs.

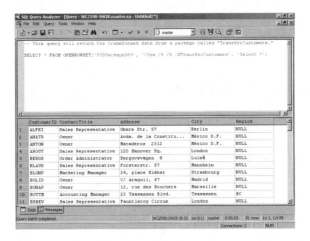

Figure 6.4 The Query Analyzer, retrieving data from the Transform Data Task when the DSO Rowset Provider option is turned on.

You can access this data in two ways: querying the data by using the Transact SQL statement OPENROWSET, and joining to the package data by setting up the package as a linked server.

When you use the DSO Rowset Provider, be aware of the following:

- The package from which the data is being queried must be executed from the calling program. The package cannot execute and send the data to a requesting consumer.

- You can access data only from a step that is associated with a Transform Data Task.

- You must be able to bind to destination columns, which means the destination cannot be a text file.

Enable this property only if you plan to use it. After the property is enabled, the Transform Data Task for which it is set will not run when the package is executed normally. Only OPENROWSET can access the data pump task while the DSO Rowset Provider property is enabled.

Querying Package Data

You can access data from Transform Data Tasks in a package in two ways, as described in the following sections.

Using OPENROWSET to Query Package Data

You can use the following syntax in Query Analyzer to query package data from a package stored in a file:

```
SELECT * FROM OPENROWSET('DTSPackageDSO','/F<pathname>','<query>')
```

This syntax works with a package saved to SQL Server:

```
SELECT * FROM OPENROWSET('DTSPackageDSO', '/Usa /P /S
➥/N<package name>','Select * ')
```

The parameters used with OPENROWSET are as follows:

- **Provider name**—DTSPackageDSO. DTSPackageDSO is the DTS OLE DB Provider, and it is always used here.

- **Provider string**—/F<pathname> for files and /U<username> /P<password> /S<servername> /N<package name [/V<version>] for SQL Server packages. If you leave the server name blank, the local server is used. If you do not include a version, the last saved version will be used. The switches used here are the ones used with the dtsrun.exe utility. (See Table 7.4 in Chapter 7 for a complete list of parameters.)

- **Query**—Select *. This parameter is used to pass through the rowset data.

Using Distributed Queries to Query Package Data

First, you need to set up the package as a linked server. as follows:

```
sp_addlinkedserver
➡'<servername>','<packagename>','DTSPackageDSO','<provider string>)
```

The parameters are as follows:

- **Server name**—The name you choose for the linked server.
- **Package name**—In this context, anything you want to use, including a null string.
- **Provider name**—DTSPackageDSO. DTSPackageDSO is the DTS OLE DB Provider, and it is always used here.

After you set up the linked server, you can use it in a distributed query like the following:

```
SELECT i.ItemID, i.ItemName, w.Location
FROM Inventory AS i, dtsLinkedServerName…WarehousePackageStep as w
WHERE i.ItemID = w.ItemID
```

For more information, search for OPENROWSET in SQL Server BOL and MSDN Online.

Disable This Step

You use this option to disable this workflow step when the package is executed. This property is extremely helpful when you are trying to debug a package.

Task Priority

You can set the thread priority in Windows for this step. The default is normal while low and high priorities are available.

ActiveX Script

You can use ActiveX scripting in the workflow to exercise greater control over the execution of the steps in a package. Although ActiveX scripting in the workflow allows you to stop, restart, and even loop package execution, its primary goals are initialization and preventing a step from executing. Several constants are available to help you program the execution or disabling of steps (see Table 6.2).

Table 6.2   **ActiveX Script Constants for DTS Workflows[1]**

Constant	Value	Description
DTS STEP SCRIPT RESULT CONSTANT	NA	These constants are the possible results that can be returned to the step via the ActiveX script. The DTS Step Script Result constants should be used only in DTS workflow scripts, not in scripts associated with an `ActiveXScriptTask` object or `DataPumpTransformScript` or `DTSTransformScriptProperties2` transformations.
`DTSStepScriptResult_ DontExecuteTask`	1	When used in scripting, this constant will not run the task associated with this step. In the status window for the package, the task will be shown as Not Run. Please note that any step not run will not be logged in the package log, because DTS does not log steps that are not executed.
`DTSStepScriptResult_ ExecuteTask`	0	This constant causes the step to execute immediately.
`DTSStepScriptResult_ RetryLater`	2	This constant tries to execute the step later.
DTS STEP EXECUTION STATUS CONSTANTS	NA	You can set or return the status of the task associated with the step here.
`DTSStepExecStat_ Completed`	4	The step has been executed and is marked as complete.
`DTSStepExecStat_ Inactive`	3	The step is inactive and will not be run.
`DTSStepExecStat_ InProgress`	2	The step is in the process of being executed. This constant can be useful with steps that take awhile to complete.
`DTSStepExecStat_ Waiting`	1	The step is waiting to execute. It will execute upon its turn in the workflow.
DTS STEP EXECUTION RESULT CONSTANTS	NA	These constants are the return values for completed steps.
`DTSStepExecResult_ Failure`	1	The step failed.
`DTSStepExecResult_ Success`	0	The step succeeded.

1. *Some of the information in this table is from Microsoft SQL Server 2000 Version 8.00 BOL. This information is available on the SQL Server installation CD.*

See SQL Server BOL for more constants for workflow and precedence. These constants would be most useful if you are using Visual Basic to program the package. The constants included in Table 6.2 are the ones most likely to be used in workflow scripting.

The following sections describe the scripting options.

Setting up the Sample Package

This package is simple, because the goal is to illustrate how workflow scripting is set up and how it reacts in some situations. Although the package is simple, you should be able to apply the principles to any package in which you need to have added control of workflows.

Create a new package, and add three ActiveX script tasks. Name these tasks Step 1, Step 2, and Step 3 (see Figure 6.5).

Listings 6.1, 6.2, and 6.3 show the code for these tasks.

Listing 6.1 **Step 1 Code**

```
Function Main()
    msgbox "Step 1 Running"
    DTSGlobalVariables("attempts").Value = 0
    Main = DTSTaskExecResult_Success
End Function
```

Listing 6.2 **Step 2 Code**

```
Function Main()
    msgbox"Step 2 Running"
    Main = DTSTaskExecResult_Success
End Function
```

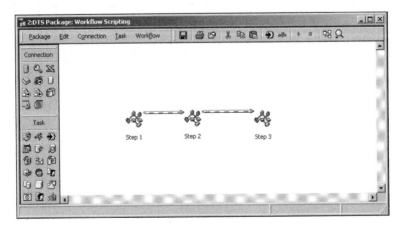

Figure 6.5 The workflow scripting package.

Listing 6.3   **Step 3 Code**

```
Function Main()
    msgbox "Step 3 Running"
    Main = DTSTaskExecResult_Success
End Function
```

Now that the package is set up, you can begin working with the ActiveX scripts in the steps' workflow properties.

Stopping Execution

A natural use of workflow scripting is to verify whether a file exists before the Transform Data Task loads it. The VBScript in Listing 6.4 verifies that a file called Manufacturing.mdb exists in the C:\DTS2000\Data\ directory [2] before it lets the step to which it is tied execute, thus allowing the rest of the package to execute.

Listing 6.4   **VB Script in Workflow That Checks to See Whether a File Exists Before Letting the Task Execute**

```
Function Main()
    Dim fso
    Set fso = CreateObject("Scripting.FileSystemObject")
    If (fso.FileExists("C:\DTS2000\Data\Manufacturing.mdb")) Then
        Main = DTSStepScriptResult_ExecuteTask
    Else
        Main = DTSStepScriptResult_DontExecuteTask
    End If
End Function
```

This code uses the File System object to verify that the Access database exists where it is supposed to exist. If this database does exist, the step executes. Otherwise, the code tells the step not to execute, and all other steps are not executed. If you have other independent workflows running, they will continue to run as expected.

This method would allow you to transform from multiple data sources without causing the package to fail if one is incorrect. To test this method, add the code in the following section to the workflow properties ActiveX script for Step 1.

Restarting Execution

Sometimes during a package execution, you need to pause until a certain condition becomes true before you can continue. The script in Listing 6.5 polls for a file, pauses five seconds, and tries again. After five attempts to find the file, the script fails. To demonstrate that fact, the file in this example does not exist.

2. All data files and scripts used in this book are available to be downloaded from http://www.magenic.com/publications or http://www.newriders.com. The self-extracting ZIP file will create a directory structure starting with DTS2000. You can extract the files to any drive or directory, but all file references in this book will be based on C:\DTS2000\.

To try this example, remove the script from the workflow properties ActiveX script in Step 1, and add the script in Listing 6.5 to the workflow properties ActiveX script in Step 2.

Listing 6.5 **VBScript in Workflow to Restart a Package After a Specified Time Delay and Several Retries**

```
Function Main()
Function Main()
      Dim oPackage
      Dim CurrentTime
      Dim NextTime
      Dim fso

      Set fso = CreateObject("Scripting.FileSystemObject")

      DTSGlobalVariables("attempts").Value = DTSGlobalVariables
➡("attempts").Value + 1
      CurrentTime = Now()
      NextTime = dateadd("s", 5, Now())

      Set oPackage = DTSGlobalVariables.Parent
      msgbox "Initial Value #" & DTSGlobalVariables("attempts").value

      'Test to see if the file exists
If (fso.FileExists("C:\MyFile")) Then
            'If it does, execute the package
            msgbox "Execute Package"
            Main = DTSStepScriptResult_ExecuteTask
      Else
            'If it doesn't, retry in increments of 5 seconds 5 times
            If DTSGlobalVariables("attempts").Value < 6 Then
                  do until (CurrentTime > NextTime)
                        CurrentTime = Now()
                  loop
                  msgbox "Retry #" & DTSGlobalVariables("attempts").value
                  Main = DTSStepScriptResult_RetryLater
            Else
                  'Stop execution once retries = 5
                  msgbox "Execution Stopped at 5 retries"
                  DTSGlobalVariables("attempts").Value = 0
                  Main = DTSStepScriptResult_DontExecuteTask
            End If
      End If
End Function
```

As you read through the code, you will see that it uses two global variables. If the variables don't exist, DTS will create them when they are first used.

Looping Execution

This section illustrates how to create a loop condition in the workflow. By adding the script in Listing 6.6 to the workflow properties ActiveX script for Step 3, you will see how a loop can include more steps than the ones directly related to the calling step. (Be sure to deselect the workflow properties ActiveX script option in Step 2 before running this example.) Similar to the restart script, the loop script uses a global variable to hold an integer for counting. If the counter has not reached 5, Step 3 is not executed, and Step 1 is set to waiting, which causes Steps 1 and 2 to be executed again. (Step 2 is executed because it comes between Step 1 and Step 3 in the workflow.) The workflow will continue to loop until the counter reaches 5.

Listing 6.6 **VBScript in Workflow That Loops a Package Five Times**

```
Function Main()
    Dim oPkg
    DTSGlobalVariables("counter").Value = DTSGlobalVariables("counter").Value + 1
    If DTSGlobalVariables("counter").Value < 5 Then
        Msgbox "Counter" & DTSGlobalVariables("counter").Value
        Set oPkg = DTSGlobalVariables.Parent
        'Set step 1 status to waiting.
        oPkg.Steps("DTSStep_DTSActiveScriptTask_1").ExecutionStatus =
            DTSStepExecStat_Waiting
        'Do not execute task 3, step 1 will restart.
        Main = DTSStepScriptResult_DontExecuteTask
    Else
        'Execute task 3
        Main = DTSStepScriptResult_ExecuteTask
    End If
End Function
```

For another example of looping, see Chapter 15, "Managing Distributed Databases with DTS and Message Queues."

Looping in the Workflow

Although many people use the workflow for looping, as illustrated in this section, you need to be careful when implementing it. The implementation of looping in the workflow ActiveX script can have side effects. If possible, you should use an ActiveX Script Task or Dynamic Properties Task to implement looping in a DTS package. See Chapter 12, "Building a Data Warehouse with DTS and Analysis Services," for an example of both tasks.

Workflow Scripting Tips

The following are a couple of tips to keep in mind when you are working with workflows:

- Workflow properties are available for any step in a package.

- Although the Data Transformation Task is represented by a line and arrow, it is not considered to be a workflow by itself; it is a step in the workflow. You still can assign it precedence, however, when you use a single connection for the destination in one step and the source in the next step. This procedure changes the color of the line used to represent the Data Transformation Task accordingly.

By using workflow scripting, you can exercise greater control of the execution of steps in a package, which allows you to validate and even prepare data for use in the tasks being executed by the steps.

Summary

This chapter explained the components of the DTS workflow, along with steps and precedence constraints. You saw how the precedence constraints could be used to maintain data integrity, validate data, and notify users if necessary. You also saw how the workflow can be used to set up and participate in transactions. In addition, you saw how to use ActiveX scripts to control the workflows you are using, including stopping, restarting, and looping through workflows. When you understand how the workflow and its components function, you will have greater control of the execution of your package.

7

Package

THIS CHAPTER DISCUSSES MANY OF THE package-level properties and methods, including transactions, execution methods, properties, and storage locations. Some of these properties enable or change the implementation of properties in connections, tasks, or workflows.

You can use the properties of the package to affect package execution, package transactions, and package logging. The properties are package-specific in that they affect the entire package. Some of the properties of tasks and workflows are dependant on properties set up in the package (see "Transactions" later in this chapter). To access these properties, choose Properties from the Package menu, or right-click an unoccupied area of the workspace and choose Package Properties from the shortcut menu. Either action opens the Package Properties dialog box.

The Package Properties dialog box has four tabs: General, Global Variables, Logging, and Advanced (see Figure 7.1). Each of the options on these tabs will be discussed in detail the following sections.

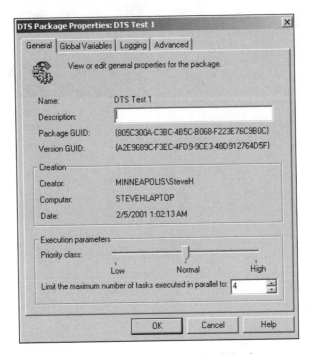

Figure 7.1 The Package Properties dialog box.

General Properties

The General tab has three sections of properties. Most of the properties on this tab are read-only; some of them can be set in other areas of the package. The first section contains the descriptors for the package, including the Name, Description, Package GUID, and Version GUID. The name is set when you save the package (see "Package Storage Locations" later in this chapter). You can add or edit the description of the package in this tab. The two GUIDs are used to identify the package and its current version. (You can store multiple versions in SQL Server Local Packages, Meta Data Services Packages, and the Structured Storage file.) The version GUID will be the same as the package GUID if it is the first and only version.

The next section is the Creation area, where you can find the creator of the package. The creator is stored in Windows networking domain\username format. The next field is the Win32 computer name of the machine on which the package was created. After that, you can find the date and time the package was created.

The Execution Parameters section allows you to set the Windows process priority. The default is Normal, but you can set it for High or Low. You also can set the maximum number of tasks to be executed in parallel. The number you use here can increase or decrease the efficiency of the package, depending on how the steps are set up. If you set this number too high and have a high number of steps being executed in parallel, it will significantly slow the execution of the package. If you set the value too low, it will negatively impact a package that has a number of steps set up for simultaneous execution.

In SQL Server 7.0, the Package Properties dialog box has only three tabs: General, Global Variables, and Advanced (see Figure 7.2). The logging features available in the Logging frame of the Logging tab in SQL Server 2000 are not available in SQL Server 7.0. (These features include package logging.) Error handling is on the General tab in SQL Server 7.0, whereas it is located on the Logging tab in SQL Server 2000. Another difference is the Auto Commit Transaction property on the Advanced tab in SQL Server 7.0. When this check box is checked, the SQL Server handles each SQL command in the package as a separate transaction. When the check box is cleared, an implicit transaction is assumed to include all the tasks until a commit or rollback from a workflow. If more steps occur after the commit or rollback, a new implicit transaction begins. (The workflow transaction properties are the same for both versions of SQL Server.) One other limitation of SQL Server 7.0 is the inability of DTS to support more than one simultaneous transaction.

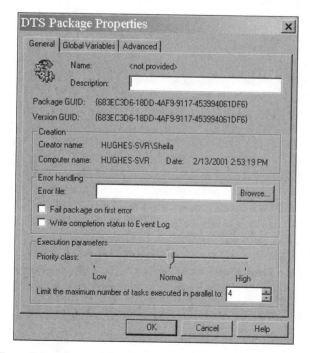

Figure 7.2 The Package Properties dialog box in SQL Server 7.0.

Global Variables

The Global Variables tab has a table that allows you to change the names, types, and initial values of these global variables. You can use these variables many places in the package. (See Chapter 4, "DTS Tasks," specifically the section on the ActiveX task, for some of the types of usage available) The values that you set in this tab are saved with the package. This is also true if the value is changed during the execution of the package. If the value is changed, the new value will show up in this dialog box after the package has run.

You can use this attribute to set and recover values that have been used in the execution of the package. These variables are in scope for the duration of the execution of the package. This tab also allows you to enforce explicit declaration of all variables in all scripts in the package (similar to the Option Explicit declaration in Visual Basic).

Logging

You set package-logging properties in the Logging tab of the Package Properties dialog box. The DTS package log can be used to track down any problems or errors that occurred during the execution of a package. The log tracks the execution or lack of execution of individual steps in the package. You can see whether any given step succeeded, failed, or did not run. (Although steps that do not run are not listed in the log, their absence from the log shows that they did not run.) This information is stored in msdb tables in SQL Server (package information in the sysdtspackagelog table, step information in the sysdtssteplog table) or in SQL Server Meta Data Services (package information in Package Tab in the DTS Meta Data node of Enterprise Manager).

You can save the log in any instance of SQL Server 2000. You can use the properties to specify which server instance you will use and how you will access the server (Windows Authentication or SQL Server Authentication, username and password). In this frame you can also choose to fail the package on a log error. You might want to use this option if your process requires that the package be logged.

You can view the log by right-clicking the package in the detail of the Local Packages or Meta Data Services Packages in Enterprise Manager and choosing Package Logs from the shortcut menu. This brings up the DTS Packages Logs dialog box, which allows you to select and open any package log available in this location (see Figure 7.3). You can then view the log (see Figure 7.4), which displays the step details and allows you to view more information (if available) and the error information on steps that failed due to errors. Any step that is executed is displayed with a red cross for failure or a green check for success. Steps that are not run will not be included in the log.

Custom Task and ActiveX Script Task Logging

The PackageLog object allows you to log custom tasks in the sysdtstasklog table. (See Chapter 16, "Creating Your Own Custom Task," for more information on creating a custom task.) When you create a custom task, the package log is included in CustomTask_Execute as a parameter, as follows:

```
Private Sub CustomTask_Execute(ByVal pPackage As Object, _
    ByVal pPackageEvents As Object, ByVal pPackageLog As Object, _
    pTaskResult As DTS.DTSTaskExecResult)
...
pPackageLog.WriteStringToLog "Task Successful"
...
```

The DTSPackageLog scripting object provides a way for ActiveX scripts to add log entries into the sysdtstasklog table by using script, as follows:

```
Dim objLog
Set ObjLog = DTSPackageLog
ObjLog.WriteStringToLog "Task Successful"
```

In both cases, you can view the log data by clicking the More Info button in the Log Data dialog box.

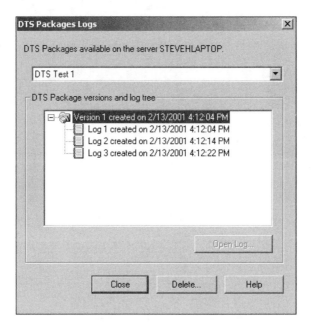

Figure 7.3 List of available logs.

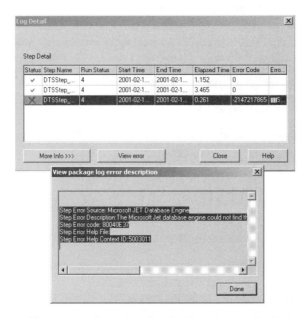

Figure 7.4   The package log details with error details showing.

Table 7.1 defines the values in the Run Status column. The remaining columns add further detail about the step as it was executed (times, step names, and error information).

Table 7.1   **Run Status Codes in the Package Log**

Run Status	Description
1	Step Waiting
2	Step In Progress
3	Step Inactive
4	Step Completed

SQL Server 7.0 does not support DTS package logging.

Error Handling

The Error Handling properties are located in the Logging tab of the Package Properties dialog box. You can set three properties. First, you can set the location of the error file.

Sample of Error File

Notice in this example log file, the executed package wrote information to the package log about all steps in the package, whether or not an individual step ran. If a step ran, it will retain start and end times, and the step execution time. For steps that did not run, the log lists the steps and notes that the step was not executed.

The execution of the following DTS package succeeded:

```
Package Name: DTS Test 1
Package Description: (null)
Package ID: {805C300A-C3BC-4B5C-B068-F223E76C9B0C}
Package Version: {A2E9689C-F3EC-4FD9-9CE3-48D912764D5F}
Package Execution Lineage: {24890402-01BC-4F62-BEDC-CF8B3ACF667C}
Executed On: STEVEHLAPTOP
Executed By: SteveH
Execution Started: 2/13/2001 11:14:18 AM
Execution Completed: 2/13/2001 11:14:25 AM
Total Execution Time: 7.03 seconds

Package Steps execution information:


Step 'DTSStep_DTSDataPumpTask_2' succeeded
Step Execution Started: 2/13/2001 11:14:18 AM
Step Execution Completed: 2/13/2001 11:14:24 AM
Total Step Execution Time: 5.888 seconds
Progress count in Step: 1

Step 'DTSStep_DTSActiveScriptTask_1' succeeded
Step Execution Started: 2/13/2001 11:14:18 AM
Step Execution Completed: 2/13/2001 11:14:18 AM
Total Step Execution Time: 0.631 seconds
Progress count in Step: 0

Step 'DTSStep_DTSSendMailTask_1' was not executed

Step 'DTSStep_DTSExecuteSQLTask_1' failed

Step Error Source: Microsoft JET Database Engine
Step Error Description:The Microsoft Jet database engine could not find the object
'test'. Make sure the object exists and that you spell its name and the path name
correctly.
Step Error code: 80040E37
Step Error Help File:
Step Error Help Context ID:5003011

Step Execution Started: 2/13/2001 11:14:24 AM
Step Execution Completed: 2/13/2001 11:14:25 AM
Total Step Execution Time: 0.33 seconds
Progress count in Step: 0
*******************************************************************************
```

Second, you can set the package to fail on the first error. When this option is selected, the package will result in failure if an error occurs in any step. This option is important if you are tracking the successful completion of the package for any reason. If you do not select this option, the package can have steps fail but will result in the successful completion of the package.

When this happens, a package that is using Execute Package tasks with precedence constraints may not work as expected. The Execute Package tasks will receive the success notice from the executed package even if steps in the package fail. This could also affect you if you are executing dependent steps that are running in parallel. To stop the parallel processes, you should fail the package when any step fails. You can also use this property to help manage transactions, as discussed in the following section.

Finally, you can set the package to write the completion status of the package to the application event log in Windows NT or Windows 2000 (see Figure 7.5).

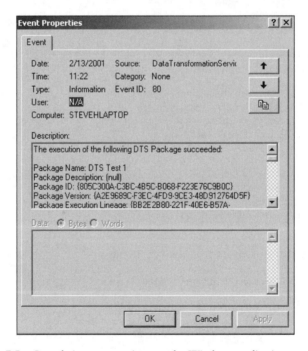

Figure 7.5 Completion status written to the Windows application event log.

Full Text in Event Log

Recording package execution status to the Windows application log can be beneficial if you want to leverage existing enterprise monitoring tools that use the Windows application log for their source data. To view the Windows application log, go to the Start menu and point to Programs/Administrative Tools, and then click Event Viewer. Click Application on the Log menu. Microsoft SQL Server events are identified by the entry MSSQLSERVER in the Source column. SQL Server Agent events are identified by the entry SQLSERVERAGENT. You can also create a filtered view on SQL Server events by pointing to the View menu, clicking Filter Events, and in the Source list, selecting MSSQLSERVER and or SQLSERVERAGENT. To view more information about a specific event, double-click the event. The code that follows is the full text in event log:

```
Event Type:    Information
Event Source:   DataTransformationServices
Event Category:    None
Event ID:    80
Date:    2/13/2001
Time:    11:22:07 AM
User:    N/A
Computer:    STEVEHLAPTOP
Description:
The execution of the following DTS Package succeeded:

Package Name: DTS Test 1
Package Description: (null)
Package ID: {805C300A-C3BC-4B5C-B068-F223E76C9B0C}
Package Version: {A2E9689C-F3EC-4FD9-9CE3-48D912764D5F}
Package Execution Lineage: {BB2E2B80-221F-40E6-B57A-8B4AC931698B}
Executed On: STEVEHLAPTOP
Executed By: SteveH
Execution Started: 2/13/2001 11:22:04 AM
Execution Completed: 2/13/2001 11:22:07 AM
Total Execution Time: 3.365 seconds

Package Steps execution information:


Step 'DTSStep_DTSDataPumpTask_2' succeeded
Step Execution Started: 2/13/2001 11:22:04 AM
Step Execution Completed: 2/13/2001 11:22:07 AM
Total Step Execution Time: 2.804 seconds
Progress count in Step: 1

Step 'DTSStep_DTSActiveScriptTask_1' succeeded
Step Execution Started: 2/13/2001 11:22:04 AM
Step Execution Completed: 2/13/2001 11:22:04 AM
Total Step Execution Time: 0.391 seconds
Progress count in Step: 0
```

continues

continued

```
Step 'DTSStep_DTSSendMailTask_1' was not executed

Step 'DTSStep_DTSExecuteSQLTask_1' failed

Step Error Source: Microsoft JET Database Engine
Step Error Description:The Microsoft Jet database engine could not find the object
'test'. Make sure the object exists and that you spell its name and the path name
correctly.
Step Error code: 80040E37
Step Error Help File:
Step Error Help Context ID:5003011

Step Execution Started: 2/13/2001 11:22:07 AM
Step Execution Completed: 2/13/2001 11:22:07 AM
Total Step Execution Time: 0.05 seconds
Progress count in Step: 0
```

Transactions

DTS has the capability to use transactions with the packages. You can use transactions to keep data in multiple servers consistent, to incorporate multiple tasks or steps into a single unit, to put multiple transactions in a single package, or to control errors in a asynchronous environment. Transactions are not available for all tasks or connection types (see the sidebar "Supported Connection and Task Types" in this section), and for transactions to work, MS DTC must be running on the computer on which the package is to be executed. Many reasons for using transactions exist, but several properties need to be set up in the workflows and in the package for them to work correctly. When you use transactions, carefully analyze how you are setting up your packages and transaction properties to prevent many of the anomalies that can occur.

Supported Connection and Task Types

The connection types are as follows:

- **Microsoft OLE DB Provider for SQL Server.** This is the standard OLE DB provider for SQL Server, which implements transactions.

- **ODBC data source.** The ODBC driver must support the attribute SQL_ATT_ENLIST_IN_DTC, and this attribute must be set. See the ODBC driver documentation for more information.

- **Microsoft Data Link.** The data link can access any OLE DB driver. The driver must implement the ItransactionJoin interface if you want it to join a distributed transaction. See the OLE DB driver documentation for more information.

If you need to establish more than one transaction in the package, you need to establish a new connection for each transaction. A connection can participate in only one connection at a time.

Following are the task types. These tasks can join package transactions:

- Bulk Insert task

- Data Driven Query task

- Transform Data task

- Execute Package task

- Execute SQL task

These tasks support their own local or distributed transactions but cannot join package transactions.

These transactions are created in code and not supported by DTS directly:

- Microsoft ActiveX Script task

- Execute Process task

These tasks do not support transactions because when they are completed, they cannot be rolled back:

- File Transfer Protocol task

- Dynamic Properties task

- Send Mail task

- Copy SQL Server Objects task

- Message Queue task

All these tasks can commit or roll back transactions. At this time, however, custom tasks cannot participate in transactions.

Uses for DTS Transactions

The uses for DTS transactions are:

- To collect data from multiple tasks and apply them to the data destination in a single transaction. This method is especially helpful for data that is related but handled in separate tasks, such as uploading shipments and new inventory counts.

- To update different servers consistently. By setting up transactions for updates to each data destination, you will be able to keep the data on multiple servers consistent.

- To control errors in an asynchronous environment by using Message Queue tasks. When you use transactions, you can resend the message if some portion of the task fails and roll back any database changes that depend on the Message Queue task. For more information on the Message Queue, see Chapter 15, "Managing Distributed Databases with DTS and Message Queues."

Use Execute Package tasks to control multiple transactions. By setting up transactions in each of the packages, you will be able to control the sequence of transactions via the main package.

The Transactions section of the Advanced tab of the Package Properties dialog box has three properties that you need to set to use transactions in the package.

To activate transactions in the package, check the Use Transactions check box. Checking this option enables the other options in this section and enables the use of transactions in the workflows. If this option is not checked, any requests from the workflows to join a transaction will be ignored.

The next property to set is Commit on Successful Package Completion. When you choose this property, all open transactions will commit when the package completes if either of the following statements is true:

- No steps have failed.
- The Fail Package on First Error check box is cleared.

The last property to set on the Advanced tab is Transaction Isolation Level. This property determines the locking level used in the transactions to isolate the user from dirty reads, nonrepeatable reads, and phantom data. Table 7.2 shows the isolation levels with increasing degrees of protection, from Chaos to Serializable. The default in SQL Server including DTS is Read Committed. Refer to the isolation levels section of SQL Server Books On Line (BOL) for more information.

Table 7.2   **Transaction Isolation Levels   (from Least to Greatest)**

Transaction Isolation Level	**Description**
Chaos	Anything goes; no protection.
Read Uncommitted	Updates can be lost. Only physically corrupt data will not be read.
Read Committed	Lowest level; does not lose updates. Does not accept dirty reads.
Repeatable Read	No dirty or nonrepeatable reads.
Serializable	Transactions are completely isolated. No dirty or nonrepeatable reads; no phantom data.

On the Advanced tab of the Package Properties dialog box, you should set the Fail Package on First Error option when you are using transactions. By selecting this option, you force a package to return an error on a failed step; therefore, it will correctly roll back the transaction. (Refer to "Error Handling" earlier in this chapter for more details.)

You also can set properties that affect transactions on workflows. By using the workflow properties, you can have steps join a transaction, roll back the transaction on step failure, and commit the transaction on successful completion of the step. See Chapter 6, "DTS Workflows," for more information.

Transaction Scenarios

When you use transactions in DTS, you must be aware that different combinations of steps and workflows affect how the transaction will be initiated and committed. Sometimes, you need many steps participating in the same transactions; at other times, you need to use many transactions. Each situation has a different setup to keep you from getting anomalous data. Please understand that much care is necessary to set up transactions in DTS packages successfully.

Sequential Tasks

First, you should try to organize the package steps sequentially. This layout is the simplest one to use with transactions (see Figure 7.6). By using precedence constraints, you can establish that all tasks must succeed to commit the transaction. Set the package property to use transactions. Then set all the steps to join a transaction, if present, and to roll back the transaction on the step failure. In the final step, set the property to commit the transaction on the successful completion of the step.

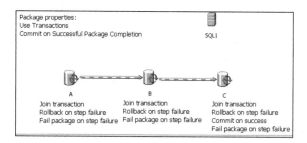

Figure 7.6   Sequential tasks in a transaction.

Parallel Tasks

Sometimes, you may find it necessary to execute steps in parallel. If you need to have these steps be part of the same transaction, you need to plan the layout carefully to prevent anomalous results. First, use DTS package failure to roll back the transaction in the case of any step failure. Next, carefully consider whether you need more than one connection. If you need only one connection, SQL Server will serialize the execution of the steps in spite of the parallel configuration, which means that the precedence relationship will be enforced, but not the order of execution. If you need two connections, and these connections are on different data sources (in particular, different SQL Server instances), the tasks configured in parallel will execute as expected: in parallel. If the connections refer to the same data source—in this case, the same SQL Server instance—you can set the Execute on Main Package Thread workflow property or use precedence constraints to ensure that the package does not fail when the tasks try to join the transaction.

You need to manage the package carefully to prevent unexpected and undesirable results. Suppose that you have three tasks, A, B, and C. Two of these tasks execute from one connection, SQL1, and one executes from the second connection, SQL2 (see Figure 7.7).

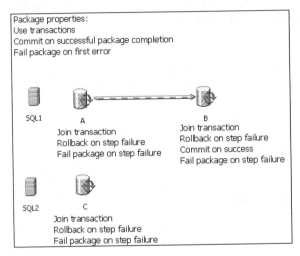

Figure 7.7   Parallel tasks using transactions.

If tasks A and C execute simultaneously and task C fails, task A continues to successful completion. Task C's failure causes the transaction to roll back, so the work from A and C is rolled back. However, because task A completed successfully, task B will start, joining a new transaction, and then will commit the transaction if the package property Commit on Successful Package Completion is set. For this reason, you must set Fail Package on First Error for the package. This property causes all steps that haven't started not to execute; then the rollback occurs as expected on all tasks currently participating in the transaction.

Branching Workflows

If you find it necessary to initiate certain tasks based on the success or failure of a series of parallel steps, you will want to branch your processes based on the success or failure of the transaction. In the previous example, we had three tasks that were part of a transaction in a package that would fail on the first error. To branch the process, use the Execute Package task and precedence to determine the next step (see Figure 7.8). For this package, clear the Fail Package on First Error check box so that the failure of the Execute Package step will be returned and precedence followed. You also need to check Use Transactions for the package.

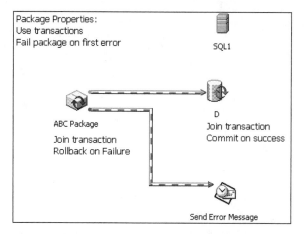

Figure 7.8   Branching transactions using an Execute Package task.

In Figure 7.8, you see that if the ABC package fails, an email task is executed, but on success, task D will execute. Table 7.3 shows the various properties you can set to have the tasks use transactions in different ways.

Table 7.3   **Branching Transactions: Step Properties to Be Set**

	Join Transaction	**Commit Transaction**	**Rollback Transaction**
Tasks A, B, C, D in same transaction	PackageABC Task D	PackageABC Task D	PackageABC Task D
Tasks A, B, C, in different transaction than task D	Task D	Task D	Task D

Checkpointing for Multiple Transactions

At times, you might be able to divide the work in a package logically into separate transactions. In that case, you would want to use a method of checkpointing to handle the transactions (see Figure 7.9). You set up the steps to participate in the first transaction and then, using precedence relationships, step to an ActiveX Script task. No code needs to be placed in this task, because it is only a placeholder. You set the workflow properties on the task to join the transaction and to commit the transaction upon the successful completion of this step. By doing so, you can insulate the transactions and have better control of the process. When the ActiveX Script task completes successfully, the next steps can continue, joining a new transaction if necessary.

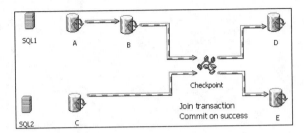

Figure 7.9   Using ActiveX Script tasks as checkpoints.

Inheriting Transactions

In DTS, you can use the Execute Package task to inherit transactions. You do so by creating packages that use transactions and then running them in a parent package with the Execute Package task. By enabling the Join Transaction If Present feature in the Options tab of the Workflow Properties dialog box, a package can inherit the parent package's transaction if the package is part of an Execute Package Task that has joined the transaction (Join Transaction If Present). When this situation occurs, all the steps in the subpackages that have joined the transactions are included in the transaction.

Using inherited transactions changes the way transactions are handled in the subpackages. Steps in the child package join the parent package transaction so that no new package transaction is created. The properties that call for committing the transaction on the successful completion of the step or package are ignored. No rollback will occur when the package completes even if an error occurs. However, if you set the workflow to rollback the transaction on step failure, it will rollback the parent transaction. Be sure to set the Fail Package on First Error property for the subpackages. This property prevents the Execute Package Task from returning success when a step in a subpackage fails.

For more information on DTS transactions, search for *DTS transactions* in Microsoft SQL Server BOL.

Miscellaneous Properties

The remaining properties in the Advanced tab of the Package Properties dialog box are Lineage, Scanning Options, and OLE DB. The Lineage and Scanning Options are closely related to the Meta Data Repository, which is covered in Chapter 18, "Data Lineage." The OLE DB property determines how OLE DB data objects are instantiated.

Lineage

The first option is Show Lineage As a Source Column. This option adds global data-lineage variables to the package but does not write them to Meta Data Services until the Write Lineage to Repository option is selected. Just showing the lineage allows you to create a custom task that can work with the lineage tracking and auditing information. Only when the write option is selected will the lineage be saved to the repository each time the package is saved. The lineage data is used to implement row- and column-level logging, which is discussed in more detail in Chapter 18.

Scanning Options

The Scanning Options dialog box provides several properties related to how the DTS package's meta data is scanned for the repository. These options are discussed in detail in Chapter 18 in the "Scanning Options" section.

OLE DB

The only option that you can implement here is Use OLE DB Service Components. When this option is selected (which is the default), the package instantiates the OLE DB data-source objects by using the OLE DB service components, which can increase both the functionality and the performance of the OLE DB data provider. (Refer to the OLE DB provider documentation for provider-specific information.)

Some data providers support only forward-only scrolling, for example. By using the service components, you can enable the consumer to scroll within the data set by using the client cursor engine. (The client cursor engine also supports the use of Find in the data set.)

You also can enable session pooling by using the service components, which can improve the performance of the package. (You can learn more about the OLE DB service components at `http://msdn.microsoft.com/library/psdk/dasdk/oled0cs7.htm`.) The DTS providers (`PackageDSO`, `RowQueue`, and `FlatFile`) and the Microsoft OLE DB Provider for SQL Server ignore this setting. If the check box is cleared, the data-source objects are instantiated directly with `CoCreateInstance`; thus, the services are not available.

Disconnected Edit

In DTS Designer, right-click the design sheet, and then click Disconnected Edit to bring up the Edit All Package Properties dialog box. The Edit All Properties dialog consists of two parts: The layout of the package appears in the left pane, and the properties related to the selected component in the component appear in the right pane (see Figure 7.10).

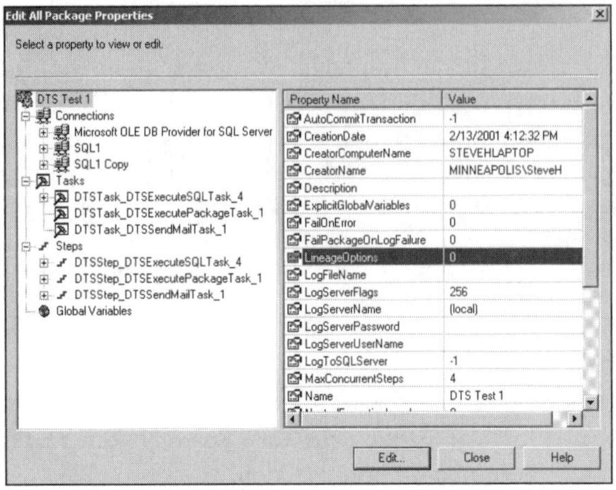

Figure 7.10   Edit All Properties.

Some of the properties in this Edit All Properties dialog box (such as task, step, and connection names) are not available in the Properties dialog boxes of the objects themselves. You can use Disconnected Edit to change the properties of a package when the source or destination is not available. DTS tries to connect to the data sources or destinations to validate the connection information; Disconnected Edit allows you to bypass this protection feature.

Using Disconnected Edit is dangerous because you can edit many properties in the package without DTS validating the changes. If you edit them here, there is no guarantee that the changes will work when the package is executed. Use Disconnected Edit only if you are very comfortable with most of the components of DTS and if this tool is the only way to edit the properties you need to modify.

Package Storage Locations

You can save a package in a number of ways. Each storage location has certain advantages, which are discussed later in this chapter. When you save the package initially, or use the Save As option, the Save DTS Package dialog box allows you to save to different locations via the Location drop-down menu (see Figure 7.11). You need to understand that each time you choose Save As from the File menu, the package GUID will change, not just the version GUID.

Locations Supported by SQL Server 7.0
Not all storage locations are available in SQL Server 7.0. The location list in version 7.0 includes DTS COM-Structured Storage File, SQL Server Storage, and Repository.

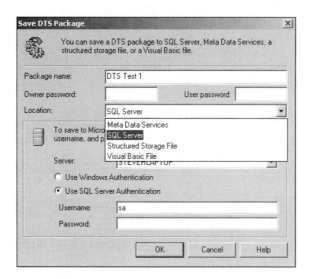

Figure 7.11 Package storage locations.

SQL Server

You can use SQL Server to save the package to the sysdtspackages table (see the "Sample Record from sysdtspackages" sidebar in this section) in the msdb database on the selected server instance. When you save the package here, it will appear in the Enterprise Manager tree below the Data Transformation\Local Packages node.

When you save in SQL Server, versions are established each time the package is saved. The first time the package is saved, the package GUID and the version GUID (visible in the General tab of the Package Properties dialog box; refer to Figure 7.1) are the same GUID. When the package is edited and resaved, the version GUID changes. You will not be prompted to save the new version if the package has already been saved, because SQL Server will save the package as a new version by default. This allows you to keep a record of the changes made in a package and also allows you to specify which version to run so that you can continue development while allowing the production package (such as an earlier version) to execute. This location is by far the most convenient and simplest way to save and maintain versions.

Sample Record from sysdtspackages

The actual packages that are stored in SQL Server are located in the msdb database in SQL Server. Following is a sample package record from the sysdtspackages table in msdb:

```
name        DTS Test 1
id          805C300A-C3BC-4B5C-B068-F223E76C9B0C
versionid   2896CDE1-47C8-4FB0-9A93-965B119AE15A
```

continues

continued

```
description    Test package
categoryid     B8C30002-A282-11D1-B7D9-00C04FB6EFD5
createdate     2000-12-05 01:11:05.003
owner          MINNEAPOLIS\SteveH
packagedata    {Image}
owner_sid      0x01
packagetype    0
```

Meta Data Services

This option saves the package in the Meta Data Repository of any valid SQL Server 2000 instance (in SQL Server 7.0 this was called SQL Server Repository). For more detailed information on using Meta Data Services with DTS packages, see Chapter 18. You can open a package saved as meta data in the Data Transformation\Meta Data Services Packages node of Enterprise Manager.

Structured Storage File

You can use this option to save the DTS package to a .dts file. The Structured Storage File is the most portable of the various storage options, because you can copy and transfer the file quite easily. The file is called a *structured file* because it uses COM-structured storage. If you are doing a great deal of package editing and then saving the package to the same file, the file can become quite large because each version is saved. When you save the package in a structured storage file, you are prompted for a file-name. If you create a new file, the package has only one version: the current one. If you choose an existing filename, you will be prompted to add the current package to the existing file, creating a new version of the file. In the SQL Server Enterprise Manager console tree, right-click on the Data Transformation Services folder. Then click Open Package from the context menu. In the Select File dialog box, click the file you want, and then click Open. If multiple versions of the DTS Package were created, the Select Package dialog box appears where you can click the package or package version you want to open (see Figure 7.12).

Visual Basic File

SQL Server 2000 also allows you to save the package to a .bas file. You can open this file in Visual Basic and edit it in the Visual Studio development environment. When the package has been stored to Visual Basic, it cannot be edited with SQL Server. The package can be executed only programmatically through Visual Basic or its compiled program. By saving the package to this location, you are also able to see the syntax of the DTS objects that can be programmed.

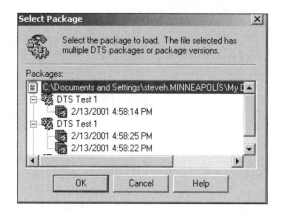

Figure 7.12 Opening a package stored in a structured storage file

---

Saving a Package to Visual Basic in SQL Server 7.0
Although SQL Server 2000 can save a package directly to a Visual Basic file via
the Save As dialog box, you need to use a separate utility to save the package to
a Visual Basic file in SQL Server 7.0. The source code for the scriptpkg.exe utility is located in the compressed file dtsdemo.exe in the \DevTools\Samples\
DTS folder on the SQL Server 7.0 installation CD-ROM.

Package Security

When you save a package to SQL Server or a structured storage file, you can secure it
beyond the Windows authentication or SQL server authentication levels. When you
save the package, you can assign owner and user passwords. When you assign an owner
password, you need to use this password to edit or run the package. To assign a user
password, you need to assign an owner password. Using both passwords allows a user
to run the package, but the user will not have permission to edit or to open the package. Microsoft recommends that you apply this security option to further secure both
the package and the database, especially if you are not using Windows authentication
for data access.

Connection Security

Some security issues are specifically related to the connection objects in DTS. First, if you use Microsoft Data Link files (.udl), you should use Windows Authentication for database access. The reason is that Data Links require you to enter the SQL Server username and password when you use SQL Server Authentication. This information is stored in unsecured form in the file. The level of access that the SQL Server user has determines how much of a security breach exists. However, if you use Windows Authentication, it sets a flag in the UDL file, making the access information secure.

Second, when you use SQL Server connection objects, DTS persists the authentication details with the package. If you still need to prevent persisted security details, you can turn off the Persist Security Info option in the Advanced Connection Properties dialog box for the SQL Server connection. Please be aware that this option is available only for a SQL Server connection; setting it to False can cause other problems when you are working in secure environments. To prevent problems with persisted security information, you should use Windows NT Authentication, because no usernames or passwords are persisted with the package.

Package Execution

You can execute a package from three locations: Enterprise Manager, a DTS tool, and the command line. In Enterprise Manager, you can execute local and Meta Data Services packages by right-clicking on the selected package located in the details pane of the Enterprise Manager Console tree and selecting Execute from the context menu.

You can execute a package from the two primary DTS tools: the DTS Designer and DTS Import/Export Wizard. From an open package, you can execute the package from one of three locations in the DTS Designer. First, you can click the Execute button on the toolbar. Second, you can choose Execute from the Package menu. Third, you can execute the package by right-clicking a blank space on the DTS Designer window and choosing Execute from the shortcut menu. You also can execute a package at the end of the DTS Import/Export Wizard by selecting the Run Immediately option and clicking Finish.

Microsoft provides two utilities for executing the package from a command line. The DTS Run utility can be accessed by typing **dtsrunui** without any command switches. This will bring up the DTS Run dialog box (see Figure 7.13), which allows you to select the location of the package, the package name and version, and the location details. After the package has been selected you can Run or Select a scheduled task to run. (The Run and Schedule buttons remain disabled until a valid package version is selected.)

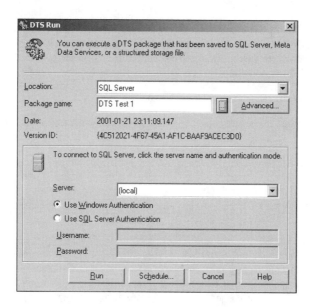

Figure 7.13   DTS Run dialog box.

Clicking the Advanced button gives you access to global variables, logging information, and command-line information. You can edit the global variables temporarily by adding new ones or editing existing ones. These global-variable changes are valid only for the current DTS Run session and are not saved when the session is closed.

You also can select the log file and specify whether to write the completion status of the package to the event log. For the command line, you can choose to encrypt the command for use in the next utility, dtsrun.exe. In addition, you can have the line generated in SQL Server 7.0 format. When you click the Generate button, the utility will create a command line for dtsrun.exe that has the selected properties applied. You can use this generated command line in the next utility described by copying and pasting it into a command line.

Command-Line Execution in SQL Server 7.0
SQL Server 7.0 supports only one command-line utility: dtsrun. It does not support dtsrunui. Also, SQL Server 7.0 does not support all the command-line options listed in Table 7.4. The following switches are not supported:

- /A, global variables

- /L, log filename

- /W, Windows event log

- /Z, SQL Server 2000 encryption

Command-Line Formats Generated from DTS Run

When you generate a command line from the DTS Run utility (dtsrunui.exe) to execute a DTS package using dtsrun.exe, you are presented with different options that determine the format of the command line.

This command line is created when you select no options:

```
DTSRun /S "(local)" /N "DTS Test 1" /V "{A2E9689C-F3EC-4FD9-9CE3-48D912764D5F}" /W
"0" /E
```

This command line is created when you select SQL Server 7.0 Format only:

```
DTSRun /S "(local)" /N "DTS Test 1" /V "{A2E9689C-F3EC-4FD9-9CE3-48D912764D5F}" /E
```

This command line is created when you select Encrypt the Command only:

```
DTSRun
/~Z0x4050833D40908D31188F436727E340111E360047CC10CBD59BC560636ABBED22B630673340E95
049A1FC69CE0D3AD96854F2101F3C3C763B24F05A0E779B2C395BE7D572B60289D3ED997FF2B3ECD0F
5EF0C89358B354DFF1B6A21189C3114774E283B4486379A18A06195C5FDB5C4E52E2C498359EF43DA4
20D288956D4DC2FBA62214FC8696EDAC8B08F2E09E860768DA74C59A4210AC1CB09714F7194E7CC12D
9C563C2536029F25662CD72DA508B5098CC8CA960FAA083CC96
```

This command line is created when you select Encrypt the Command and SQL Server 7.0 Format together:

```
DTSRun /~S 0xBD02B5BE90E2B90926828A12F24175AA /~N
0x64C9C49314125FB980EC63C075EACCD8FCBD1CF0E8A295B5 /~V
0xD751BE59BF32E3D7BB500A00CE73B349219F0597C886C9C9FFAD32B71BC6C02648EF197C56B976B2
92871661BA8FA7A2089F804E9D9A58EB66C920CE6F82CC21008194D41AB757A2CF6A2662FFDB60E9
/E
```

The other utility is dtsrun.exe. This utility has no graphic components and several switches (see Table 7.4) that give you more control over the execution of the package. You can generate the command line with switches by using the dtsrun utility as mentioned in the previous paragraph. From this utility, you can execute packages stored in the SQL Server msdb, structured storage files, and SQL Server Meta Data Services.

Table 7.4 **dtsrun Utility Command-Line Switches**

Switch	Value to Enter	Description
/?		Displays the command-line options.
~		Specifies that the value following the switch is encrypted. Valid with /S, /U, /P, /N, /G, /V, /M, /F, and /R.

Switch	Value to Enter	Description
/S	server_name [\instance_name]	Specifies the server to use. If you includeonly server_name, the default instance will be used. To use another instance, use this format: server_name\instance_ name.
/U	user_name	SQL Server login used to connect to SQL Server.
/P	Password	SQL Server password used with the login to connect to SQL Server.
/E		Use trusted connection (Windows Authentication).
/N	package_name	Name of the package to be run.
/G	package_guid_string	Package ID assigned to the package when it was saved.
/V	package_version_ guid_string	Version ID assigned to the package when it was saved.
/M	package_password	Either the owner or user password assigned to the package.
/F	Filename	Name of the structured storage file being executed. If a server_name is also given, the SQL Server package is executed and then added to the structured storage file.
/R	repository_database_ name	Name of the repository database to use. If no name is given, the default database is used.
/A	global_variable_ name: typeid=value	Use this option to create and set multiple global variables in the package if you have Owner permission. Refer to BOL for valid type identifiers.
/L	log_file_name	Name of the package log file if it is to be different from the one stored in the package.
/W	Windows_Event_Log	True = Use event log. False = Do not use event log.
/Z		Specifies that the command line has been encrypted with SQL Server 2000 encryption.
/!X		Prevents the package from being executed. You can use this option when you want to create an encrypted command line but do not want to execute the package.

continues

Table 7.4 **Continued**

Switch	Value to Enter	Description
/ ! D		Deletes a package from an instance of SQL Server.
/ ! Y		Displays the encrypted command line for executing the package without executing the package.
/ ! C		Copies the command line to Microsoft Windows Clipboard.

Notes on dtsrun Command-Line Switches

You can use encrypted options by adding a tilde (~) after the slash and before the option switch.

The switch for global variables (/A) is the option that allows multiple values. For all other options, the last value will be the one used by the utility.

Any spaces between the switch and the values are optional and will be ignored. If the values contain embedded spaces, the values need to be embedded between double quotation marks.

All the execution methods described in this section return various levels of detail about the success or failure of the package that is being executed. When you are executing a package from the DTS tools, the Enterprise Manager, or the DTS Run utility (dtsrunui.exe, not dtsrun.exe), a dialog box opens when the package runs. The Executing DTS Package dialog box (see Figure 7.14) shows each step in the package and the status, start time, finish time, and execution time for each step. (The status text varies according to the task being executed.)

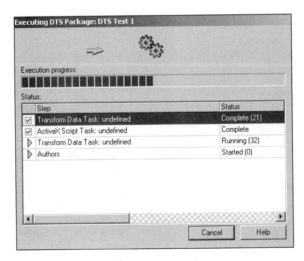

Figure 7.14   Executing DTS Package dialog box.

If the package has Execute Package Tasks, this dialog box does not display the steps from each Execute Package Task. Some information from the steps is displayed as the tasks execute in the status line above the progress bar. From this dialog box, you can cancel the package. The package does not quit running immediately, however; it waits until any steps that do not support canceling complete. To view this information later, you need to refer to the package log.

If an error is encountered when you use the dtsrun utility from the command line, the package will stop executing and display error information and usage instructions. No dialog box is displayed when you use this utility. This is very helpful when you are trying to execute the package by using batch files or scheduled tasks in Windows and do not want any graphical interfaces involved.

Package Scheduling

You can schedule packages to run at specific times and in specific patterns. If you need to run a package nightly, monthly, or even hourly, you can do so by setting up a SQL Server Job. The easiest way to do this is by right-clicking on the package in the detail pane of the Local Packages or Meta Data Services Packages folder in the SQL Server Enterprise Manager console tree. If the SQL Server Agent is not running when you try to schedule it, you will receive a warning; then you can proceed to set up the schedule (see Figure 7.15). You can set a Recurring Job Schedule the same way that you would set up a recurring job in SQL Server.

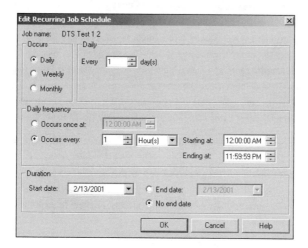

Figure 7.15   Scheduling a package.

After you set up a job, you can edit it in the Management/SQL Server Agent/Jobs section of Enterprise Manager. You also can view the Job History here. However, editing the actual job step is difficult because the wizard uses the encrypted dtsrun command line. On the other hand, you can create the job manually in the Jobs section of the Enterprise Manager by creating an Operating System Command (CmdExec) step that uses the dtsrun utility. You can find details on the various formats and syntaxes used with dtsrun.exe in "Package Execution" earlier in this chapter. (Remember that you can use the DTS Run utility, dtsrunui.exe, to generate the command line.)

To create and execute this SQL Server job successfully, the SQL Server agent must have the security permissions to run operating-system commands from within SQL Server (via CmdExec or xp_cmdshell). If you need to schedule your package but cannot grant the necessary permissions to the agent, see the sidebar "Alternative to SQL Server Jobs for Scheduled Packages."

SQL Server jobs also have logging available. The first level of job logging is displayed in the detail view of the job listing in the Jobs detail of the Enterprise Manager. You can see the details of the last job, run as well as details on the current and future status of the job, including whether the job is enabled, runnable, or scheduled and when it is scheduled to run again. The next level of logging allows you to view the job history, which contains the detailed history of the job. Here you can look for specifics about why a job fails. Checking the job history for errors before troubleshooting your package is important. If you were able to execute the package from Enterprise Manager but not through the scheduler, you are most likely to find the problem in the job history. For more information about SQL Server jobs, refer to the BOL topic "Creating Jobs."

Alternative to SQL Server Jobs for Scheduled Packages

Sometimes, you need to secure the SQL Server Agent to the point that you will not be able to execute packages in scheduled jobs. A workaround is to create a Windows Scheduled Task and use the dtsrun command-line utility to execute the package. Launch the Scheduled Task wizard by double-clicking Scheduled Tasks in Control Panel, and then double-clicking Add Scheduled Tasks. You can schedule a task to run daily, weekly, or monthly, change the schedule for a task, and customize how a task runs at a scheduled time. The first step in the Scheduled Task wizard is to click on Browse and select the dtsrun executable using the following pathname: [SQL Server Folder]\80\Tools\Binn\dtsrun.exe).

Next, add a name, select the frequency of the task, choose the start time and date, and add the username and password to run the task. When these properties are entered, check the Advanced Properties check box, and click Finish. The Properties dialog box for the task opens. At this point, you need to edit the Run text to include all the appropriate command switches and parameters. Now that you have scheduled the package successfully, you can track its success or failure through the package logs in SQL Server Data Transformation Services.

Package Deletion

Deleting a package is fairly simple. To delete the entire package from SQL Server or Meta Data Services, right-click the package and choose Delete from the shortcut menu. You need to be the owner or a member of the sysadmin fixed server role to delete the package or a version of the package. You can delete any version of a package that has been saved to SQL Server. You can delete the most recent package only if it is stored in Meta Data Services. To delete versions, right-click the package and choose Versions from the shortcut menu. When the DTS Package Versions dialog box opens, select the package version and click Delete. You cannot delete individual versions from packages stored in a structured storage file or a Visual Basic file.

Summary

Using the information provided in this chapter, you should be able to make good decisions on which package properties are necessary to fulfill your needs. Whether the package needs to be portable (storage locations), needs to implement transactions, or needs to be executed on a schedule, you should be able to choose the options necessary to get the desired result. For information on advanced logging of packages, see Chapter 14, "Custom Error Logging with DTS," and Chapter 18, "Data Lineage."

8

Putting It All Together—An Extended DTS Example

Chapter 1, "DTS in the ETL World", introduced Sparks Electronics, an electronics manufacturer and distributor with offices in several states. Chapter 2, "DTS—An Overview," examined basic package components, and you saw how easy it is to create a stand-alone package that could be run on demand. Chapters 3 through 7 took a more in-depth look at DTS package components.

In this chapter, you get a chance to put all this knowledge together and build an automated system to collect and distribute reporting data for Sparks Electronics. In addition to building the package, you will examine issues that affect DTS performance. The example used in this chapter is not particularly difficult. Although you might use other tools to achieve the same purpose, the example proves a suitable platform to demonstrate the use of DTS. Working through the exercise will provide experience and insights that you need to tackle more complicated problems.

Setting the Scenario

As you recall from Chapter 1, Sparks Electronics has its headquarters and one operating facility in Minneapolis and two operating facilities in California. All sites use the same administrative software, which is hosted on SQL 2000. See C:\DTS2000\Data.[1]

In addition to the data maintained by each site, the Minneapolis office maintains a Sites table; see C:\DTS2000\Data\DTS2000Mfg_Config.mdb.[2]

In an effort to control costs, you have been asked to consolidate the expense ledger from each location into a single reporting database. Summarized data must be made available via Excel for analysis by HQ accounting staff.

Sparks does not want to implement a fully blown data warehouse at this time. However, managers at all sites would like to have a summary of expenses by plant and sales by warehouse. For now, HTML reports are acceptable. Your solution should be robust and require little or no intervention during day-to-day operations.

All too often, reporting systems fail with little or no indication. In the event of failure, appropriate reports should be generated. It is important to keep the end user informed of the system's status.

Solution

In this chapter, you will use the knowledge gained in the preceding chapters to build a robust production-based system. Begin by building a central reporting database to hold and report on consolidated data. Then you can build a package that runs daily to extract data from each remote site and load it into the reporting database.

On successful load, produce and distribute a .csv file for accounting and HTML reports for plant managers. On failure, inform operations.

When developing a solution, divide and conquer. Package workflow can be complex; break it down into more modular packages. Individual packages are smaller, and each package is more focused, more readable, and easier to debug.

To implement this solution, you need to complete the following tasks:

1. Develop packages to copy source data to tempdb on the target host.

2. Develop scripts to merge data from tempdb into the final target tables. Integrate these scripts with your package(s).

3. Build a package to export the consolidated data to Excel.

---

1. All data files and scripts used in the book are available to be downloaded from http://www.magenic.com/publications or http://www.newriders.com. The self-extracting zip file will create a directory structure starting with DTS2000. You can extract the files to any drive or directory, but all file references in this book will be based on C:\DTS2000\.

2. If you want to follow along here, all data files and scripts used in the book are available to be downloaded from http://www.magenic.com/publications or http://www.newriders.com.

4. Use SQL's `sp_MakeWebTask` to produce a simple HTML report for managers.

5. Use SQL's `sp_MakeWebTask` to produce a HTML job-status report.

6. Build a master package to execute the other packages and scripts.

7. Schedule a daily job to process the extraction and reporting.

Development Environment

Chapter 7, "Package," examines options for package storage. These options include:

- Microsoft SQL Server 2000 Meta Data Services
- Local package on your reporting database
- DTS structured files
- Visual Basic .bas files

Microsoft SQL Server 2000 Meta Data Services stores package versions, meta data, and data lineage information. It should be reserved for package releases and is not a suitable environment for developing and testing packages.

Local packages, stored in the msdb database, can be listed, edited, and run from Enterprise Manager or DTS Designer. In addition, scheduling execution of local packages is a simple matter via SQL Server Agent.

You can use Windows Explorer to list DTS-structured storage files, and with a little effort, you can edit and run them using DTS Designer or from Enterprise Manager. Although you can schedule execution via the Windows NT AT command and dtsrun utility, doing so is awkward.

VB files can be listed via Windows Explorer. They must be edited and compiled in VB and scheduled via the Windows NT AT command.

Working with local packages in Enterprise Manager provides the best development environment. If you want to, moving the packages into Meta Data Services later is simple.

Global, Local Configuration, and Transactional Data

To develop a viable solution, you need to consider the nature of the data to be consolidated. Specifically, you need to consider the following:

- Global configuration data
- Local configuration data
- Transactional data

Global configuration data should be the same for all sites and database instances. Examples include country codes, state codes, corporate locations, and currency exchange information. Essentially, you want a snapshot of the data at every location.

If the data is not subject to Data Referential Integrity (DRI), SQL's snapshot replication is an attractive solution. SQL's transactional or merge replication can work around DRI constraints, but those methods can be complex to set up and monitor. A simple DTS package with a Delete/Update/Insert script may be the preferred solution.

Local configuration data is maintained at each remote site or database instance. Examples include local employees and customers. When you integrate information from two or more sources, you need to find a way to identify data from each source uniquely. You may need to modify or upgrade data that references that information.

If you have a hand in developing the remote databases, you could divide up the primary key, using a different identity range for each database instance. Although this solution is relatively simple to implement and requires little overhead for two or three databases, it can become problematic if you need to manage many more databases—a separate instance for each store in a nationwide retail chain, for example. You could use GUIDs to keep things separate. This method will increase the size of the primary key from 4 to 16 bytes, which could have an adverse effect on size and performance of larger databases.

Unfortunately, neither option is available for Sparks Electronics. You will need to build a compound key based on the originating database and original key. As you will see, this method will involve significant additional effort.

When the data you need to integrate contains a large number of transactions, copying and merging it all each day is difficult. Tracking changes is better.

When the data is indexed on an identity column and only new data can be added, tracking new rows is a simple matter. If existing records can change, using an index on a SQL timestamp allows you to track both new and updated records. To track data deletes, you need to take a lesson from merge replication and use triggers to log the deletes to a separate table.

In cases where you are trying to collect data from various sources without manipulation or summarization, transaction or merge replication may be a viable option. However, replication will not work if you need to do significant data transformation or if you only want to propagate summary data. In addition, replication can require a higher level of understanding to set up, and it can be difficult to recover in the event of an error.

Replication versus DTS is not always a simple answer. What works well in one situation may not work well in another. The scope of this book is not to cover replication but to show you what is involved in a DTS-based implementation so that you might be better able to make your own determination.

Building the Reporting Database and Creating Data Extract Packages

Begin implementing your solution by building the reporting database and developing packages to copy source data from each site to tempdb on the reporting server. For illustration purposes, we cover the loading of data from only two sites: Minneapolis and San Jose.

Building the Reporting Database

You can build a reporting database in many ways. If the sample database was hosted on SQL Server, you could use Enterprise Manager's Data Import Wizard to simply copy the database schema.

Given that the sample data is hosted in Access, the DTS Import Data Wizard cannot simply copy the schema. However, it can create a database and import the Access tables and data. Although you don't need the data, it's a simple matter to write a SQL script to truncate the data.

To create a database to hold global configuration and reporting data, follow these steps:

1. In the Enterprise Manager console, bring up the DTS Import/Export Wizard by double-clicking on the databases folder to expand it. Then right-click on the desired database object and point to All Tasks; then click Import Data.

2. Fill out the Choose Data Source screen as follows:
   - Data Source: Microsoft Access
   - File Name: C:\DTS2000\Data\Dts2000MFG_Minneapolis.mdb [3]

3. Fill out the Choose a Destination screen as follows:
   - Destination: Microsoft OLE DB provider for SQL Server
   - Server: your reporting server
   - Authentication Type: Choose Windows or SQL Authentication, as appropriate
   - Database: <new>

4. Fill out the Create Database screen as follows:
   - Name: `DTS2000Mfg_Rpt`
   - Accept the defaults for other options

5. In the Specify Table Copy or Query screen, choose Copy Tables and Views.

6. In the Select Tables or Views screen, select all the tables.

   The Import Wizard will ignore Access system tables.

---

3. If you want to follow along, all data files and scripts used in the book are available to be downloaded from `http://www.magenic.com/publications` or `http://www.newriders.com`.

7. In the Save, Schedule and Replicate Package screen, choose Run Immediately. Normally, you might want to save the package for future reference. In this example, however, you are creating a test database, so we are selecting Run Immediately.

8. In the Execute DTS Package screen, choose Finish.

At this point, all tables *and* data will be copied to the new Dts2000Mfg_Rpt database. Before the data can be used for reporting, you need to remove it. In Enterprise Manager, choose Query Analyzer from the Tools menu and run the script shown in Listing 8.1, or run C:\DTS2000\Packages\SQLServer2000\DTS2000 – Truncate Tables.sql. [4]

Listing 8.1 **T-SQL to Truncate All the Tables in a Database**

```
Use DTS2000Mfg_Rpt
Go
Declare tCursor insensitive cursor for Select Name from sysobjects
  where type = 'u'
Declare @Table sysname
open tCursor
Fetch tCursor into @Table
While @@Fetch_Status = 0
Begin
  Print @TABLE
  Declare @Sql Varchar(2048)
  Select @SQL = 'Truncate Table [' + @Table + ']'
  Execute (@SQL)
  Fetch tCursor into @Table
End
Close tCursor
Deallocate tCursor
```

Building a Package to Import Configuration Data to tempdb

You need to build two packages to load data to tempdb on your reporting server: one to load configuration data and a second to load remote-site data.

You could use the DTS Package Designer to develop the entire package, but it's a lot less work to use DTS Import Wizard to get started and then do final modifications using Package Designer.

---

4. If you want to follow along, all data files and scripts used in the book are available to be downloaded from http://www.magenic.com/publications or http://www.newriders.com.

To create the package to import configuration data, follow these steps:

1. In the Enterprise Manager console, bring up the DTS Import/Export Wizard by double-clicking on the databases folder to expand it.

2. Right-click on the tempdb database object and point to All Tasks, and then click Import Data.

3. The next screen you see is the Choose Data Source dialog box where you provide the following values:

    - Data Source: Microsoft Access
    - File Name: C:\DTS2000\Data\DTS2000MFG_Config.mdb

4. Click Next to move to the Choose a Destination dialog box where you provide the following values:

    - Destination: Microsoft OLE DB provider for SQL Server
    - Server: your reporting server
    - Authentication Type: Choose Windows or SQL Authentication, as appropriate
    - Database: tempdb

5. On the Specify Table Copy or Query screen, select Copy Tables and Views.

6. On the Select Tables or Views screen, select Site.

7. Fill out the Save, Schedule and Replicate Package screen as follows:

    - Select Run Immediately.
    - Save the package on the local server as `DTS2000Mfg_Import_Config`.

8. On the Execute DTS Package screen, select Finish.

The package shown in Figure 8.1 is rather simple and will be easy to test.

As designed, the package attempts to create a new table each time, causing errors on subsequent runs.

You can add a SQL task to delete tables, or you can modify the table create tasks to do so. If you use the SQL task, you will also need to make the table create task dependant on the success of the table delete step.

You can modify the table create task to delete an existing Site table. Open the package by double-clicking on it in Enterprise Manager. Then double-click on Table Create and add the code shown in Listing 8.2 at the top of the script.

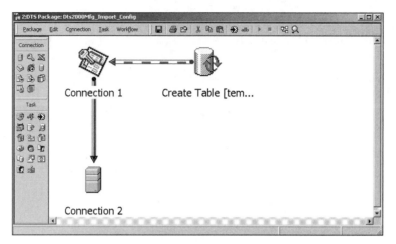

Figure 8.1 DTS2000Mfg_Import_ConfigData package.

Listing 8.2 **Site Table Delete**

```
if exists ( select * from tempdb..sysobjects where
id=object_id('[tempdb].[dbo].[site]'))
  drop table [tempdb].[dbo].[site]
```

Building a Package to Import Site Data to tempdb

You have multiple sites to load. Rather than build a package for each, create a package to load a single site and then modify it to use global variables to control the site loaded.

To create a package to load Minneapolis data, follow these steps:

1. In Enterprise Manager console tree, double-click on the reporting server object to expand it.

2. Double-click on the databases folder to expand it and right-click on the tempdb object, point to All Tasks, and then click on Import Data.

3. This brings up the Choose Data Source dialog box. Provide the following values:

   - Data Source: Microsoft Access
   - File Name: C:\Dts2000\Data\DTS2000Mfg_Minneapolis.mdb

4. Fill out the Choose a Destination screen as follows:

   - Destination: Microsoft OLE DB provider for SQL Server

   - Server: your reporting server

   - Authentication Type: Choose Windows or SQL Authentication, as appropriate

   - Database: tempdb

5. On the Specify Table Copy or Query screen, select Copy Tables and Views.

6. On the Select Tables or Views screen, select Plant and Expense.

7. Fill out the Save, Schedule and Replicate Package screen as follows:

   - Select Run Immediately.

   - Save the package on the local server as `DTS2000Mfg_Import_SiteData`.

8. On the Execute DTS Package screen, select Finish.

As designed, the package attempts to create a new table each time.

Open the package by double-clicking on it in Enterprise Manager. Inside the DTS Designer main panel, double-click on the Create Table Task object associated with the Plant table. Insert the code shown in Listing 8.3 at the beginning of the SQL Statement window in the Execute SQL Task properties dialog box.

Listing 8.3 **Site Table Delete**

```
if exists ( select * from tempdb..sysobjects where
id=object_id('[tempdb].[dbo].[plant]'))
  drop table [tempdb].[dbo].[plant]
```

You need to make similar modifications to the Create Expense Task. At this point, the package can import data only from Minneapolis.

To modify the package to use a global variable that controls the source database and allows data from any site to be loaded, follow these steps:

1. Open the package by double-clicking it in Enterprise Manager.

2. Point to Package and click on Properties from the toolbar menu in the DTS Designer main panel.

3. Click on the Global Variables tab and add Variable Data Source. String set as C:\DTS2000\Data\Dts2000MFG_Minneapolis.mdb. Click on the Global Variables tab and do the following:

   - Create an ActiveX Script Task that includes the code from Listing 8.4.

Listing 8.4   **Using Global Variables to Set Connections**

```
Function Main()
    DtsGlobalVariables.Parent.Connections("Connection 1").DataSource = _
        DtsGlobalVariables.Item("Data Source").Value
    DtsGlobalVariables.Parent.Connections("Connection 3").DataSource = _
        DtsGlobalVariables.Item("Data Source").Value
    Main = DTSTaskExecResult_Success
End Function
```

- Make the Plant Access connection dependent on the script as follows:
    - Click on the new ActiveX Script Task.
    - Shift-click on Connection 2 (SQL Plant table).
    - Select Workflow \Success from the toolbar.
4. Make the Expense Access connection dependent on the script as follows:
    - Click on the new ActiveX Script Task.
    - Shift-click on Connection 4 (SQL Ledger table).
    - Select Workflow \Success from the toolbar.

Figure 8.2 shows the Import Site Data package using global variables.

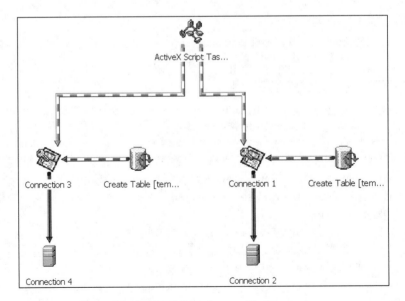

Figure 8.2   DTS2000Mfg_Import_SiteData package.

Moving Data from tempdb into the Reporting Database

With a copy of Site, Plant, and Expense data loaded into tempdb, you need to develop scripts to integrate the information into your reporting database.

The data presents some interesting challenges. In the following section, you will investigate each table and create scripts to manipulate and merge the data developed.

Manipulating Global Configuration Data

The reporting database was based on one of the site databases, which contained a Site table. In Enterprise Manager, choose Query Analyzer from the Tools menu to run the script shown in Listing 8.5, and add a Site table.

Listing 8.5   **Creating the Site Table**

```
if not exists (
  select * from DTS2000Mfg_Rpt..sysobjects where ID =
object_id('DTS2000Mfg_Rpt..Site')
  ) select * into DTS2000Mfg_Rpt..Site from tempdb..Site
```

To synchronize the tables, you need to remove obsolete records that are no longer required, update records that have changes, and add new records. You can perform these tasks in any order, but it usually is more efficient to do the deletion, followed by the update and then the insertion.

In most cases, it's best not to remove obsolete Global Configuration because it makes it difficult to produce historic reports. A better solution is to mark the record in the source table so that it is considered to be inactive and then propagate the change. If you insist on deletion, Listing 8.6 shows you how to use a left join between DTS2000Mfg..Site and tempdb..Site to identify and delete the records.

Listing 8.6   **Deleting Obsolete Site Records**

```
Delete DTS2000Mfg_Rpt..Site
Where SiteId in
  (select
    t.SiteId
  from
    DTS2000Mfg_Rpt..Site t
  left join
    tempdb..Site s
    on s.SiteId = t.SiteId
  where
    s.SiteId is Null
  )
```

Listing 8.7 shows the format used to update existing records. In addition to predicates used to join the tables on key fields, the listing shows unequal predicates used to limit changes in records with differences.

Listing 8.7 **Updating Existing Site Records**

```
Update
  DTS2000Mfg_Rpt..Site Set
    --t.SiteID=s.SiteID,
    SiteName=s.SiteName,
    SiteLocation=s.SiteLocation
  from
    tempdb..Site s
  where
    DTS2000Mfg_Rpt..Site.SiteID=s.SiteID and
    (
      DTS2000Mfg_Rpt..Site.SiteName<>s.SiteName or
      DTS2000Mfg_Rpt..Site.SiteLocation<>s.SiteLocation
    )
```

For larger tables that contain many fields, creating an update script can be tedious. The script shown in Listing 8.8 can be used to automate much of the work. See C:\DTS2000\Packages\SQLServer2000\DTS2000 – Create Update Script.sql.

Listing 8.8 **Automating Assignments and Predicates**

```
use DTS2000Mfg_Rpt
set nocount on
set quoted_identifier off
go
declare @Table sysname
declare @SQL varchar(1024)
set @table = 'Site'
print '    Update ' + @Table + ' Set '
select @sql = "
  select '            ' + c.name + '=s.' + c.name + ','
    from sysobjects s
    join syscolumns c on s.id =c.id
    where s.name='" + @Table + "' order by colid "
 Exec( @sql)
print '    From Tempdb..' + @Table + 's where '
print '('
select @sql = "
  select '          DTS2000Mfg_Rpt.." + @Table + "." + c.name + '<>s.' + c.name + '
or'
    from sysobjects s
    join syscolumns c on s.id =c.id
    where s.name='" + @Table + "' order by colid "
  Exec (@sql)
print "    )"
```

Run the script, cut the results, and paste them into a new query window. In most cases, all you need to do is comment out key-field assignments, remove the comma at the end of the last filed assignment, change the or in the key fields to and, and move them outside the parentheses.

Listing 8.9 shows the use of a left join between `tempdb..Site` and `DTS2000Mfg..Site` to identify and insert new records.

Listing 8.9 **Inserting New Site Records**

```
insert into DTS2000Mfg_Rpt..Site
select
  s.*
from
  tempdb..Site s
left join
  DTS2000Mfg_Rpt..Site t
  on s.SiteId = t.SiteId
where
  t.SiteId is Null
```

To include these scripts as part of the `DTS2000Mfg_Import _Config` package, follow these steps:

1. Double-click on the package in Enterprise Manger.

2. Choose Execute from the Task menu, and set the properties as follows:

   - Description: Manipulate Site Config Data
   - Existing Connection: Connection 2

   By default, when the package was created, the Site Access source connection was labeled Connection 1, and the SQL target table was labeled Connection 2.

   - SQL Statement: Enter the scripts from Listings 8.5, 8.6, 8.7, and 8.9.

   See C:\DTS2000\Packages\SQLServer2000\DTS2000 – Manipulate Global Site Config Data.sql.

3. Make the Manipulate Site Config Data Task dependent on the Site Data Import Task, as follows:

   - Click on Connection 2 (SQL Site table).
   - Shift-click on the Manipulate Site Config Data Task.
   - Choose Success from the Workflow menu.

The final Import Config package should be similar to Figure 8.3.

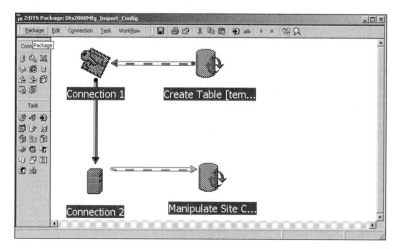

Figure 8.3   DTS2000Mfg_Import_ConfigData package (final).

Manipulating Local Configuration Data

You need to integrate local plant configuration data from two or more sources. If the data was segmented by a primary key range or used GUIDs, integrating the data could be handled similarly to the global configuration data in the previous section. However, you do not have control over how the data is segmented, and you need to find a way to differentiate among sources. Combining `SiteId` with `PlantId` is a viable composite key.

Before you begin, add a `SiteId` field to the Reporting database's Plant table. The simplest way to do this is to right-click on the table in Enterprise Manager, select Design Table, and add the field as shown in Figure 8.4.

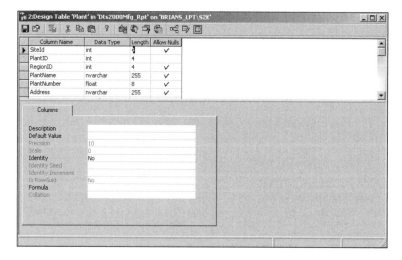

Figure 8.4   Adding global key SiteId to Plant table.

When you are loading data from multiple sites, you need to be able to distinguish the site you are currently working on. Although this will eventually need to be done programmatically, for test purposes, you can hard-code the value for Minneapolis.

Deleting configuration data can make historical reports difficult to produce. But if necessary, you can use the code in Listing 8.10, which shows a left join between `DTS2000Mfg..Plant` and `tempdb..Plant` to identify and delete expired records.

Listing 8.10 **Deleting Expired Local Plant Configuration Records**

```
Use DTS2000mfg_Rpt
Declare @SiteId int
Select @SiteId = SiteId from Site where SiteLocation =
    'C:\DTS2000\Data\DTS2000MFG_Minneapolis.mdb'
Delete from DTS2000Mfg_rpt..Plant
where SiteId = @SiteId
    and PlantId in
     (select
        t.PlantId
    from
        DTS2000Mfg_rpt..Plant t
    left join
        tempdb..Plant s
        on t.PlantId = s.PlantId
    where
        t.SiteId = @SiteId
        and
        s.Plantid is Null
    )
```

Listing 8.11 shows the format used to update existing records. In addition to predicates used to join records on key fields, the listing shows unequal predicates used to limit changes to records with differences. Again, the script shown in Listing 8.8 can automate much of the work.

Listing 8.11 **Updating Existing Local Plant Configuration Records**

```
Declare @SiteId int
Select @SiteId = SiteId from Site where SiteName ='Minneapolis' --Siteid =1
Update Plant Set
    --SiteId=s.SiteId,
    --PlantID=s.PlantID,
    RegionID=s.RegionID,
    PlantName=s.PlantName,
    PlantNumber=s.PlantNumber,
    Address=s.Address,
    City=s.City,
    State=s.State,
    Zip=s.Zip,
    Phone=s.Phone,
    Fax=s.Fax,
    SQFT=s.SQFT,
```

continues

Listing 8.11   **Continued**

```
    PlantBuiltDate=s.PlantBuiltDate,
    FixedWorkingCapital=s.FixedWorkingCapital,
    MonthlyCapacity=s.MonthlyCapacity,
    FixedMonthlyCost=s.FixedMonthlyCost
From Tempdb..Plant s where
  DTS2000Mfg_Rpt..Plant.SiteId=@SiteId and
  DTS2000Mfg_Rpt..Plant.PlantID=s.PlantID and
(
    DTS2000Mfg_Rpt..Plant.RegionID<>s.RegionID or
    DTS2000Mfg_Rpt..Plant.PlantName<>s.PlantName or
    DTS2000Mfg_Rpt..Plant.PlantNumber<>s.PlantNumber or
    DTS2000Mfg_Rpt..Plant.Address<>s.Address or
    DTS2000Mfg_Rpt..Plant.City<>s.City or
    DTS2000Mfg_Rpt..Plant.State<>s.State or
    DTS2000Mfg_Rpt..Plant.Zip<>s.Zip or
    DTS2000Mfg_Rpt..Plant.Phone<>s.Phone or
    DTS2000Mfg_Rpt..Plant.Fax<>s.Fax or
    DTS2000Mfg_Rpt..Plant.SQFT<>s.SQFT or
    DTS2000Mfg_Rpt..Plant.PlantBuiltDate<>s.PlantBuiltDate or
    DTS2000Mfg_Rpt..Plant.FixedWorkingCapital<>s.FixedWorkingCapital or
    DTS2000Mfg_Rpt..Plant.MonthlyCapacity<>s.MonthlyCapacity or
    DTS2000Mfg_Rpt..Plant.FixedMonthlyCost<>s.FixedMonthlyCost
)
```

Finally, Listing 8.12 shows a left join between `DTS2000Mfg..Plant` and `tempdb..Plant` to identify and insert new records.

Listing 8.12   **Updating Existing Local Configuration Records**

```
Declare @SiteId int
Select @SiteId = SiteId from Site where SiteName ='Minneapolis'  --Siteid =1
Insert into DTS2000Mfg_rpt..Plant
Select
    @SiteId, s.*
From
    tempdb..Plant s
where PlantId in
    (select
        s.PlantId
    from
        tempdb..Plant s
    left join
        DTS2000Mfg_rpt..Plant t
        on t.SiteId = @SiteId
        and s.PlantId = t.PlantId
    where
        t.Plantid is Null
    )
```

To include these scripts as part of the `DTS2000Mfg_Import _SiteData` package, follow these steps:

1. Double-click on the package in Enterprise Manager.
2. Select Execute SQL Task from the Task menu, and set the properties as follows:
   - Description: Manipulate Plant Config Data
   - Existing Connection: Connection 4

   By default, when the package was created, the Plant Access source connection was labeled Connection 3, and the SQL target table was labeled Connection 4.

   - SQL Statement: Enter the scripts from Listings 8.10, 8.11, and 8.12.

   See C:\DTS2000\Packages\DTS2000 - Manipulate Local Plant Data.sql.

3. Try to make the SQL statement a parameterized Query as follows:
   - Change
     ```
     Select @SiteId = SiteId from Site where SiteName ='Minneapolis'
     ```
     to
     ```
     Select @SiteId = SiteId from Site where SiteLocation = ?
     ```

   If you experienced difficulties, see the sidebar "Homegrown Parameterized Queries."

   - Click on the Parameters button in the Execute SQL Task Properties dialog box, and map the input Parameter 1 to the global variable Data Source.
4. Make the Manipulate Plant Config Data Task dependent on the Plant Data Import Task, as follows:
   - Click on Connection 2 (SQL Plant table).
   - Shift-click on the Manipulate Plant Config Data Task.
   - Choose Success from the Workflow menu.

Homegrown Parameterized Queries

Parameterized queries are SQL statements that can be changed from run to run. These queries contain placeholders that are substituted prior to execution. DTS uses a question mark (?) as a placeholder. Parameterized queries are supported only when they are supported by the connection source. The Execute SQL Task can map parameters to global variables for input or output.

Although SQL documentation recommends using parameterized queries to support dynamically changing queries, these queries can be finicky. You should thoroughly test these queries before placing them into a production environment.

Earlier, you added an ActiveX Task to allow the Import Site Data package to handle different data sources. The script in Listing 8.13 shows how to programmatically parameterize your queries. See C:\DTS2000\Packages\SQLServer2000\DTS2000 - Homegrown Parameterized Query.txt.

continues

Listing 8.13   **Homegrown Parameterized Query**

```
Function Main()
    DtsGlobalVariables.Parent.Connections("Connection 1").DataSource = _
        DtsGlobalVariables.Item("Data Source").Value
  DtsGlobalVariables.Parent.Connections("Connection 3").DataSource = _
        DtsGlobalVariables.Item("Data Source").Value

    Dim xoTask
    Set xoTask = FindTask( "Manipulate Plant Data")
    sEdit xoTask.CustomTask.SqlStatement, "'Location'", _
        "'"+ DtsGlobalVariables.Item("Data Source").Value + "'"

    Set xoTask = FindTask( "Manipulate Expense Data")
    sEdit xoTask.CustomTask.SqlStatement, "'Location'", _
        "'"+ DtsGlobalVariables.Item("Data Source").Value + "'"

    Main = DTSTaskExecResult_Success
End Function

Function FindTask( asTaskDescription)
    Dim xoTask
    for each xoTask in DtsGlobalVariables.Parent.Tasks
        if instr( lcase(xoTask.Description),lcase(asTaskDescription)) then
            set FindTask = xoTask
            exit Function
        end if
    next
End Function

Sub sEdit( asString, asFrom, asTo)
    if instr( asString, asFrom) then
        asString = left( asString, instr( asString, asFrom)-1) _
            + asTo _
            + mid( asString, instr( asString, asFrom)+ len(asFrom))

    end if
End Sub
```

Manipulating Large Data Sets

The ledger table contains a large number of records. This table would be difficult to copy and merge each day. Only new records are added to the ledger. If you can determine the records added, the job is greatly simplified.

You could set up the query to retrieve only records that are less than a day old. Recovering from production errors would be difficult, however.

A better plan is to check and see when the last run was processed. You can use a DTS parameterized query to locate and save the most recent ledger date into a global variable and then modify the site-data selection to reference this value.

Dealing with Datetime Conversion Errors

A parameterized query may have trouble mapping a SQL datetime to an Access datetime. This will require that you convert both to a string or the form yyyymmdd to do comparisons.

Update the local package `DTS2000Mfg_Import_SiteData` to extract only the most recent expense data, as follows:

1. In Enterprise Manager, double-click on the `DTS2000Mfg_Import_SiteData` package to bring up the DTS Designer main panel.

2. Choose Properties from the Package menu. Point to Package on the menu bar and click on Properties.

3. Select the Global Variables tab, add Global Variable 'Last Expense YYYYMMDD' as a string, and set its default value to 19980101.

4. Add an Execute SQL Task to find the most recent ledger data.

   Set the parameters as follows:

   - Description: Find Most Recent Expense
   - Connection: Connection 4 (SQL Expense table)
   - SQL: Enter the T-SQL script shown in Listing 8.14

Listing 8.14   **Find Most Recent Expense**

```
select convert( char(8), dateadd(day,-1,max( expensedate)),112)
LastExpenseYyyyMmDd
from Expense
```

   - Tab to Parameters, and map the output parameter row value `LastExpenseYyyyMmDd` to the global parameter `Last Expense YYYYMMDD`.

5. Click the Expense Data Transformation Task, and update the parameters as follows:

   - Update the source SQL query to include the `WHERE` clause shown in Listing 8.15.

Listing 8.15   **Parameterized Expense Extract**

```
SELECT  PlantID, AccountID, ExpenseDate, TimeID, CategoryID,
CurrencyID, Amount
FROM    Expense
WHERE   Format(ExpenseDate,"yyyymmdd") > ?
```

   - Tab to Parameters, and map Parameter 1 to `Last Expense YYYYMMDD`.

Now that you have ensured that only new information is imported to tempdb, all that remains is to develop a script to merge the data with the reporting data.

When merging data, you cannot attempt to perform deletes. Listing 8.16 shows the form used to update existing records or insert new records. In addition to predicates used to join records on key fields, the listing shows unequal predicates used to limit changes to records with differences.

The script shown in Listing 8.8 can automate much of the work.

Listing 8.16 **Updating the Expense Data Set**

```
Use DTS2000mfg_Rpt
Declare @SiteId int
Select @SiteId = SiteId from Site where SiteLocation =
    'C:\DTS2000\Data\DTS2000MFG_Minneapolis.mdb'
Update Expense Set
    --PlantID=s.PlantID,
    --AccountID=s.AccountID,
    --ExpenseDate=s.ExpenseDate,
    TimeID=s.TimeID,
    CategoryID=s.CategoryID,
    CurrencyID=s.CurrencyID,
    Amount=s.Amount
From Tempdb..Expense s where
  DTS2000Mfg_Rpt..Expense.SiteID=@SiteID and
  DTS2000Mfg_Rpt..Expense.PlantID=s.PlantID and
  DTS2000Mfg_Rpt..Expense.AccountID=s.AccountID and
  DTS2000Mfg_Rpt..Expense.ExpenseDate=s.ExpenseDate and
(
    DTS2000Mfg_Rpt..Expense.TimeID<>s.TimeID or
    DTS2000Mfg_Rpt..Expense.CategoryID<>s.CategoryID or
    DTS2000Mfg_Rpt..Expense.CurrencyID<>s.CurrencyID or
    DTS2000Mfg_Rpt..Expense.Amount<>s.Amount
)
Insert into DTS2000Mfg_rpt..Expense
Select
    @SiteId, s.*
From
    tempdb..Expense s
left join
    DTS2000Mfg_rpt..Expense t
    on t.SiteId = @SiteId
      and t.PlantID=s.PlantID
      and t.AccountID=s.AccountID
      and t.ExpenseDate=s.ExpenseDate
where
    t.SiteId is Null
```

To include these scripts as part of the `DTS2000Mfg_Import _SiteData` package, follow these steps:

1. Double-click on the package in Enterprise Manger.
2. Add an Execute SQL Task, and set the parameters as follows:
   - Description: Manipulate Expense Data
   - Connection: Connection 2 (SQL Expense table)
   - Enter the script shown in Listing 8.16.
     See C:\DTS2000\Packages\ SQLServer2000\DTS2000 – Manipulate Local Expense Data.sql.
   - Make this connection a parameterized query.
     Change
     ```
     Select @SiteId = SiteId from Site
     where SiteName ='Minneapolis'
     ```
     to
     ```
     Select @SiteId = SiteId from Site
     where SiteLocation = ?
     ```

   As before, if you experience problems, use an ActiveX script of the type shown in Listing 8.13.
   - Tab to Parameters, and map the input Parameter 1 to the global variable Data Source.
3. Make the Manipulate Expense Data Task dependent on the Expense Data Import Task, as follows:
   - Click on Connection 2 (SQL Expense table).
   - Shift-click on the Manipulate Plant Config Data Task.
   - Choose Success from the Workflow menu.

The final package should be similar to Figure 8.5.

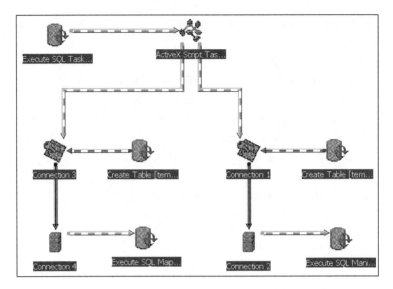

Figure 8.5 DTS2000Mfg_Import_SiteData package (final).

Exporting Data and Generating Reports

With the data consolidated, you need to export expense data to Excel for HQ accounting staff and generate HTML expense reports for plant manages.

Creating an Excel spreadsheet

In this section, you use the DTS Export Wizard to create a package to export data to an Excel spreadsheet, as follows:

1. In Enterprise Manger, right-click on your reporting database.

2. Choose Export Data from the All Tasks menu to bring up the Choose Data Source dialog box.

3. Fill out the Choose Data Source screen as follows:

   - Destination: Microsoft OLE DB provider for SQL Server

   - Server: your reporting server

   - Authentication Type:Choose Windows or SQL Authentication, as appropriate

   - Database: DTS2000MFG_Rpt

4. Fill out the Choose a Destination screen as follows:

   - Destination: Microsoft Excel 8.0

   - File: C:\InetPub\wwwroot\DTS2000MonthlyExpenses.Xls

5. On the Specify Table Copy or Query screen, choose Query.

   Listing 8.17 shows a query that you can use to export the Site, Plant, and Expense data.

Listing 8.17 **Site Plant Expense Query**

```
select
    convert( char(16),SiteName) SitePlant,
    convert( char(16),PlantName) Plant,
    convert( char(7), ExpenseDate, 120) ExpenseMonth,
    convert( Decimal(16,2), Sum (Amount)) MonthlyExpenses
from
    site s
join
    plant p
    on s.SiteId = p.SiteId
join expense e
    on p.SiteId = e.SiteId
    and p.plantid = e.plantid
Group By
    convert( char(16),SiteName),
    convert( char(16),PlantName),
    convert( char(7), ExpenseDate, 120)
Order By
    convert( char(16),SiteName),
    convert( char(16),PlantName),
    convert( char(7), ExpenseDate, 120)
```

6. On the Select Source Tables and Views screen, select the query that you just created.

7. Fill out the Save, Schedule and Replicate Package screen as follows:

   - Select Run Immediately.

   - Save the package on the local Server as `DTS2000Mfg_Rpt_to_Excel`.

8. On the Execute DTS Package screen, select Finish.

As is the case with table creation, DTS has a problem when the file already exists. Add an ActiveX script to delete an existing file as follows:

1. Double-click on the package to open it in Package Designer.

2. Add a new ActiveX script, using the code shown in Listing 8.18.

Listing 8.18 **Using ActiveX Scripting to Delete an Excel Spreadsheet**

```
Function Main()
  Set fso = CreateObject("Scripting.FileSystemObject")
    If fso.FileExists("C:\InetPub\wwwroot\DTS2000MonthlyExpenses.xls") Then _
    fso.DeleteFile ("C:\InetPub\wwwroot\DTS2000MonthlyExpenses.xls ")
  Set fso = Nothing

  Maim = DTSTaskExecResult_Success
End Function
```

3. Make the export dependent on the file delete as follows:

   - Click on the new ActiveX Script Task.
   - Shift-click on Table Create Task.
   - Choose Success from the Workflow menu.

Figure 8.6 shows the complete package.

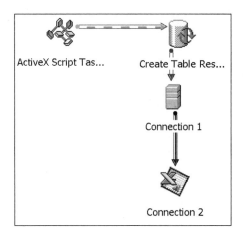

Figure 8.6 DTS2000Mfg_Rpt_to_Excel package.

Simple HTML Report

You can use SQL's `sp_MakeWebTask` to generate simple HTML reports.
`sp_MakeWebTask` is a powerful tool with many options. A discussion of all the permutations and combinations are beyond the scope of this book. You are encouraged to review SQL's BOL for a more complete coverage of this tool.

Listing 8.19 shows you how to use `sp_MakeWebTask` to generate an HTML report. It includes the query required to generate data. Table 8.1 details the parameters used.

Listing 8.19 **Generating a Simple HTML–Based Report**

```
sp_makewebtask
  @dbname = 'DTS2000Mfg_Rpt',
  @outputfile = 'C:\InetPub\wwwroot\DTS2000MonthlyExpenses.HTML',
  @webpagetitle = 'DTS 2000 Monthly Expenses By Plant',
  @lastupdated= 1,
  @resultstitle = ' DTS 2000 Monthly Expenses By Plant ',
  @tabborder = 1,
  @colheaders = 1,
  @Query = '
  select
       convert( char(16),SiteName) SitePlant,
       convert( char(16),PlantName) Plant,
       convert( char(7), ExpenseDate, 120) ExpenseMonth,
       convert( Decimal(16,2), Sum (Amount)) MonthlyExpenses
  from
       site s
  join
     plant p
     on s.SiteId = p.SiteId
  join expense e
     on p.SiteId = e.SiteId
     and p.plantid = e.plantid
  Group By
     convert( char(16),SiteName),
     convert( char(16),PlantName),
     convert( char(7), ExpenseDate, 120)
  Order By
     convert( char(16),SiteName),
     convert( char(16),PlantName),
     convert( char(7), ExpenseDate, 120)
  '
```

Table 8.1   **sp_MakeWebTask Options Used**

Parameter	Values
@dbname	The source database for the report. The default is the current db.
@outputfile	You must provide the report-file location, which may be on the reporting SQL server or a UNC name. In either case, SQL Server Agent must have Window NT file-creation permission to the path.
@webpagetitle	The title of the HTML document. The default is SQL Server Web Assistant. For a blank title, specify two space characters.
@resultstitle	The title displayed above the query results in the HTML document. The default is Query Results.
@lastupdated	If 1, the generated HTML document displays Last updated:. The default is 1.
@tabborder	If 1, a border is placed around the results. The default is 1.
@colheaders	If 1, column headers are displayed. The default is 1.
@query	You must provide a Transact SQL query to produce report data.

Using HTML to Report Job History

Although it's good practice to email exit status to appropriate operations personnel, it is also important that end users be informed of job status.

If you are using a Web-based viewer to provide reporting, you can use sp_MakeWebTask to show job status, as shown in Listing 8.20. In fact, it might be a good idea to make such a page the gateway to the reporting.

Listing 8.20   **Using *sp_MakeWebTask* to Create an HTML-Based DTS Job History**

```
sp_makewebtask
  @dbname = 'DTS2000Mfg_rpt',
  @outputfile = 'C:\InetPub\wwwroot\DTS2000JobHistory.HTML',
  @webpagetitle = 'DTS 2000 Job History',
  @lastupdated= 1,
  @resultstitle = 'DTS 2000 Job History',
  @tabborder = 1,
  @colheaders = 1,
  @Query = '   SELECT
    convert(Char(32), sj.name) JobName,
    sjh.run_date,
    sjh.run_time,
    sjh.run_duration Duration,
    sjh.message
  From
    msdb.dbo.sysjobs_view sj
  Left Outer Join msdb.dbo.sysjobhistory sjh
      ON (sj.job_id = sjh.Job_id)
```

```
Where
    convert(char(36), sj.Job_ID)
      + convert(char(8),Run_Date)
      + convert(char(6),Run_time) in (
    Selest
           max( convert(char(36), sj.Job_ID)
             + convert(char(8),Run_Date)
             + convert(char(6),Run_time))
    From
      msdb.dbo.sysjobs_view sj
    Left Outer Join msdb.dbo.sysjobhistory sjh
        on (sj.job_id = sjh.Job_id)
    Where
           sj.name like ''DTS%''
    Group by
      sj.Job_id
    )
    and step_name = ''(Job outcome) '''
```

Note the use of two single quotes (') to delimit strings in the query.

DTS2000Mfg_Production—Pulling It All Together

Now you have all the pieces. All that remains is to build a single package to control the entire process (see Figure 8.7).

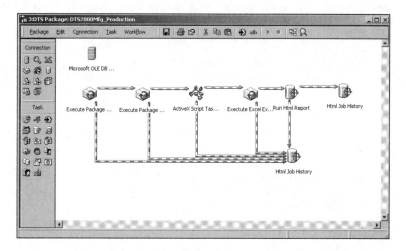

Figure 8.7 DTS2000Mfg_production.

To build the dts2000Mfg_Production package, follow these steps:

1. Right-click on your reporting server Data Transformation Services, then Local Packages, and select New Package.

2. Select Package Save from the DTS Designer main panel menu bar and save the package as `DTS2000Mfg_Production`.

3. Add a connection, using Microsoft OLE DB Provider for SQL, and configure it to access your reporting database.

4. Add an Execute Package Task to execute `DTS2000Mfg_ImportConfig`, and set the options as follows:

   - Description: Execute Package Task: Import Config
   - Package: `DTS2000Mfg_Import_Config`

5. Add an Execute Package Task to execute `DTS2000Mfg_Import_SiteData` for Minneapolis, and set the options as follows:

   - Description: Execute Package Task: Import Minneapolis Data
   - Package: `DTS2000Mfg_Import_SiteData`
   - Map the inner global variable Data Source to C:\DTS2000\Data\ DTS2000Mfg_Minneapolis.mdb.

6. Add an ActiveX Script Task to execute `DTS2000Mfg_ImportSiteData` for San Jose.

   You could use an Execute Package Task to perform this task. DTS 7.0 does not support passing global variables to a package, however. The task shows you how to use VB script for this purpose. Set the options as follows:

   - Description: Execute ActiveX: Import SanJose
   - Enter the script shown in Listing 8.21.

   See C:\DTS2000\Packages\ Dts 2000 - Import SanJose.txt.

Listing 8.21 **Execute Package to Import SanJose ActiveX Script**

```
Function Main()
  Dim oPackage
  Set oPackage = CreateObject("DTS.Package")
  oPackage.LoadFromSQLServer  "Brians_Lpt\s2k", "", "", _
    DTSSQLStgFlag_UseTrustedConnection, _
    "", "", "", _
    "DTS2000Mfg_Import_SiteData"
  oPackage.FailOnError = True
  RunPackage oPackage,_
```

```
    "C:\DTS2000\Data\DTS2000Mfg_SanJose.mdb"
  oPackage.UnInitialize
  Main = DTSTaskExecResult_Success
  exit function
Errored:
  oPackage.UnInitialize
  Main = DTSTaskExecResult_Failed
End Function

Sub RunPackage(oPackage, asSource)
  oPackage.GlobalVariables.Item("Data Source") = asSource
  oPackage.Execute
End Sub
```

7. Add an Execute Package Task to export expense data to Excel, and set the options as follows:

   - Description: Execute Package: Export Excel

   - Package: `DTS2000Mfg_Rpt_To_Excel`

8. Add an Execute SQL Task to generate a HTML expense report, and set the options as follows:

   - Description: Execute SQL: Run HTML Report

   - Connection: Use the connection pointing to `DTS2000Mfg_Rpt`.

   - SQL: Enter the script show earlier in Listing 8.19, or copy C:\DTS2000\ Packages\DTS2000 – Generate Expense HTML Report.sql.

9. Add an Execute SQL Task for HTML Job Report, and set the options as follows:

   - Description: Execute SQL: HTML Job Report

   - Connection: Use the connection pointing to `DTS2000Mfg_Rpt`.

   - SQL: Enter the script shown earlier in Listing 8.20.

   See 'C:\DTS2000\Packages\DTS2000 – Generate JobHistory HTML Report.sql.

10. Add an Execute SQL Task for HTML Job Failed, and set the options as follows:

    - Description: Execute SQL: HTML Job Failed

    - Connection: The one pointing to the Reporting database

    - SQL: Enter the script shown earlier in Listing 8.20.

See 'C:\DTS2000\Packages\DTS2000 – Generate JobHistory HTML Report.sql.

- Modify the script so that

    ```
    @resultstitle = 'DTS 2000 Job History'
    ```

is changed to

```
@resultstitle = 'DTS 2000 Job FAILED'
```

11. Use the options in the Workflow menu to chain each of the following steps together on success:

    - Execute Package Task: Import Config
    - Execute Package: Import_ Minneapolis
    - Execute ActiveX: Import SanJose
    - Execute Package: Export Excel
    - Execute SQL: Run HTML Report
    - Execute SQL: HTML Job Report

12. Use the options in the Workflow menu to have all steps sink to the HTML Job Failed on Failure.

Scheduling the DTS Package

After the package is developed and tested, you can simply run the package when required or schedule it to run periodically.

If you need to run the package often but not regularly, simply right-click on it to execute it when required.

To schedule a package to run on a periodic basis, right-click on it and update its schedule (see Figure 8.8).

For the most part, the Job Scheduler is self-explanatory. You can set when the job is first run, how often, and when it finishes. Note that changing the frequency from Daily to Weekly or Monthly provides additional options.

Tracking Job History

Double-click on the Management folder, then SQL Server Agent, and finally on Jobs. In the details pane, right-click a job, and click View Job History to view the history of a local job.

Click on the Show Step Details check box to display more information. Figure 8.9 shows the status of all jobs by category.

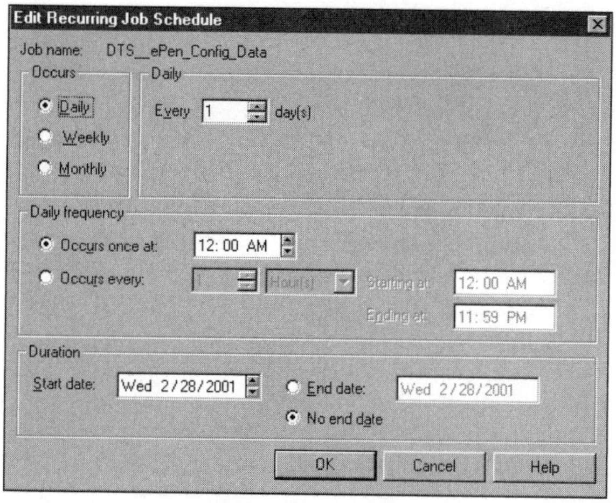

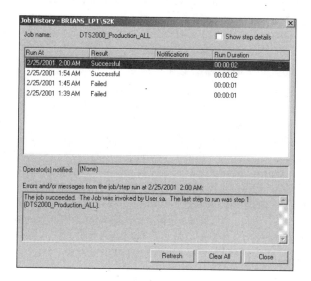

Figure 8.8   DTS job schedule.

Figure 8.9   DTS job history.

When one package executes another, step information for the subordinate jobs is not always written to the job history. In this case, you may need to look at the package logs for complete information. (Package logs are not supported in SQL 7.0)

To view DTS package logs, select Data Transformation Servers for your reporting server in Enterprise manager. Depending on where the package is stored, right-click on Meta Data Services or Local Packages, and select Package Logs.

Controlling Scheduled DTS Jobs

Double-click on a job to edit job properties or change its schedule.

Right-click on the job to do the following:

- Start the job and run it manually.

  Note that if the job is already running, you cannot start another instance until the first job completes.

- Stop a currently running job.

- Delete the job to permanently remove it.

- Disable the job to prevent execution until you enable execution later.

Enhancing Performance

Up to this point, this chapter has said little about the performance of your package. This fact does not imply that performance tuning can be an afterthought. In fact, it is usually best to design performance into the package from the start.

In the following sections, we will take a brief look at some issues that can affect package performance.

General Server Performance

A well-tuned package will not run well if SQL Server is not tuned properly. Use Windows NT Perfmon to monitor CPU, memory, and disk I/O.

If CPU utilization is high, use the SQL Trace and Index Tuning Wizard to ensure that you have the correct indexes to support your package. If you are short on memory or doing excessive paging, consider adding memory.

It is also important to ensure that SQL's files are well laid out. Whenever possible, keep tempdb, data, and logs on separate disks.

Finally, if you are not running DB optimization as part of a regular (weekly) maintenance plan, consider running DBCC ShowConfig and DBCC ReIndex to optimize SQL internal data storage. Should CPU utilization or disk I/O remain high, use SQL Profiler to identify, analyze, and tune your applications.

Avoid Using DTS

As the saying goes, "When you have a hammer, everything looks like a nail." DTS is a very powerful and flexible tool. This power and flexibility come at the cost of additional CPU cycles. In many situations, you should consider other, more efficient options.

When you are moving data with limited transformations between tables, a Transact-SQL query will prove to be significantly more efficient.

Whenever possible, use linked servers and Transact-SQL to move data between two SQL servers. For multiple sources on one or more SQL servers, consider running a distributed query by using SELECT INTO.

Using Bulk Insert and BCP

You can use Bulk Insert, BCP, and DTS copy to import data. BCP and DTS copy are available to export data. Depending on your requirements, the choice of which to use can have a great impact on performance.

When you are importing text data that does not require transformations, use the Bulk Insert Task, which is significantly faster. When minimal transformations are required, consider either BCP or DTS copy operations, which run at approximately the same speed.

To export data that does not require transformations, use BCP, which can be three to six times faster than using DTS.

Avoid *ExecuteOnMainThread*

On multiprocessor systems, to minimize execution time, set `ExecuteOnMainThread` to False. This setting allows DTS to start multiple threads and process steps in parallel.

However, not all tasks and applications called by DTS can support multiple threads, including the following:

- Connection drivers that are not thread-safe
- COM objects called by a package that are single-threaded

In these situations, `ExecuteOnMainThread` must be set to True.

Avoid ActiveX Scripts

Whenever possible, avoid scripts. Copy operations are 25 to 50 percent faster than scripts written in VBScript. Scripts written in VBScript are about 10 percent faster than scripts written in JScript, which are about 10 percent faster than scripts written in PerlScript.

Using column names helps you document your script. For example, use `DTSSource("PlantID")` rather than `DTSSource(1)`. However, if the source or destination has more than 20 columns, using the column Index may be more efficient.

Enhancing Data-Pump Performance

By default, the DTS Import/Export Wizard creates packages with many-to-many column mappings, whereas DTS Designer assigns one-to-one column mappings to transformations to improve readability.

Each mapping is a separate transformation that must separately invoke the script engine. If you have a lot of data or transformations, this can adversely affect performance.

When you are using DTS Designer, and you have a lot of data or many transformations, consider mapping as many transformations as possible to a many-to-many.

Data-Driven Queries

Data-driven queries must process each source row separately. On larger files, the additional processing can add up quickly.

Although it may be more complex, where possible, consider using a BCP or Bulk Insert to load the data followed by an SQL script to process the data as a set.

In addition to making the process more efficient, each task will be simpler to develop and debug.

Summary

In this chapter, you used the knowledge you gained in the previous chapters to build a robust production-based system. You used different techniques wee to move and transform data from source to destination. You created packages to import global configuration data, site configuration data, and transactional data to tempdb. You developed scripts to integrate tempdb data into a Reporting database. You created packages or tasks to export data and produce HTML reports. Finally, you combined all these subordinate packages into a single package that could be run or scheduled as required.

In addition, you learned about various techniques that improve the performance of the DTS processes. Armed with this information, you should have sufficient understanding to build reasonably complex production DTS environments.

II

Automating Data
Transformation Services

9

Building a Package Using Visual Basic

In Chapter 2, "DTS—An Overview," we used DTS Designer to create a sample DTS package. DTS Designer, a simple yet effective tool, provides a graphic interface for manipulating the underlying DTS object model. Although providing ample functionality for most applications, it does not expose all objects, properties, and methods of the model. As a result, it is not the best mechanism for certain situations, such as the following:

- Standalone applications or servers
- GUI applications in which you want to interact with users and allow them to control or monitor DTS progress
- Automated processing, such as:
    - Processing all the files in a directory
    - Processing spreadsheets in an Excel workbook
    - Processing XML input
    - Processing Outlook messages
- Processing events, allowing corrective action at run time

In these cases, it's simpler to use the DTS object model to either create a new package or access and manipulate an existing one from a custom application. Although any language that supports COM automation can be used, we will confine our discussions to Visual Basic (VB) 6.0.

Prior to SQL 2000, developing a package in VB required considerable effort. With SQL 2000, the capability to save a DTS package to a VB .bas file has eliminated most of this work.

The Scenario

As you may recall in Chapter 2, you produced several reports for Bob by using DTS Designer. At the last managers' meeting, other product managers expressed an interest in Bob's new reports. However, each needed to see a different product mix. You have been asked to set up DTS to generate reports based on inventory, such as Bob's Shipping Reports, but to use a Shipping Budget provided by individual managers.

You could copy Bob's package (see Figure 9.1) and modify the location of the budget for each manager. This would be a great deal of work. In addition, if anything were to change, such as the location of the Manufacturing database, each package would require maintenance.

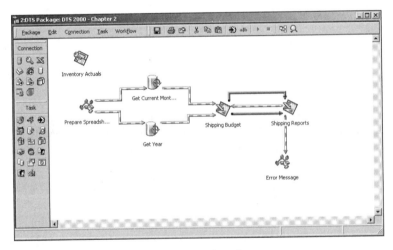

Figure 9.1   DTS package.

One of the nicest features added to SQL 2000 is the capability to develop a package by using DTS Package Wizard or DTS Designer and then save it as a VB .bas file.

In this chapter, you will save the package as a VB .bas file, include it in a VB project, and then add a simple GUI to allow each manager to specify the location for his or her budget and report.

In this scenario, building a package in VB is an attractive solution. To create a report, a manager would do the following:

1. Copy ShippingBudget.xls to his work area and customize it as required.

2. Run the application.

3. When prompted, provide the location for the copy of the ShippingBudget.xls. ShippingReport.xls will be copied to the same directory as the budget. The ShippingReports copy is processed by DTS to produce the desired report.

To build this solution, you do the following:

1. Start the DTS Designer by opening C:\DTS2000\Data\ CreateExcelReports.dts[1] and saving it as a VB .bas file.

2. Create a sample managers directory (C:\Temp\DTS2000Manager).

3. Copy C:\DTS2000\Data\ShippingBudget.xls[2] into this directory.

4. Start VB, and begin a new standard .exe, as follows:

   - Add a reference for the DTS package.

   - Add a file reference to the script generated by DTS.

   - Save the project and compile. (This step is required to ensure that the App.Path works correctly during debugging.)

   - Modify the VB application to prompt for the location of ShippingBudget.xls, copy ShippingReports.xls to the same directory as the budget, and run the DTS package to update the copy of ShippingReports.xls.

   - Run the application, and when prompted for the budget location, specify C:\Temp\DTS2000Manager\ShippingBudget.xls.

5. Use Excel to view the generated report (C:\Temp\DTS2000Manager\ ShippingReports.xls).

Generating a VB DTS Package with SQL 2000 DTS Designer

The first step in implementing your solution is to save the CreateExcelReport package as a VB .bas file by following these steps.

1. Start Enterprise Manager, and select your server.

2. Right-click Data Transformation Services, select Open Package, and load C:\DTS2000\Packages\CreateExcelReport.dts[3].

---

1. All data files and scripts used in the book are available to be downloaded from http:/ /www.magenic.com/publications or http://www.newriders.com. The self-extracting ZIP file will create a directory structure starting with DTS2000. You can extract the files to any drive or directory, but all file references in this book will be based on C:\DTS2000\.

2. If you want to follow along, all data files and scripts used in the book are available to be downloaded from http://www.magenic.com/publications or http://www.newriders.com.

3. If you want to follow along, all data files and scripts used in the book are available to be downloaded from http://www.magenic.com/publications or http://www.newriders.com.

In SQL 7.0 the Open Package command is found below All Tasks.

3. Use the Save As menu option to open the Save DTS Package dialog box (see Figure 9.2).

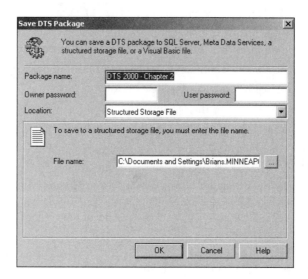

Figure 9.2   The Save DTS Package dialog box.

4. Type **CreateExcelReport** in the Package Name text box.
5. Ignore the password options, because they have no effect on the VB file.
6. From the Location drop-down menu, choose Visual Basic File.
7. Type **C:\DTS2000\Packages\CreateExcelReport** in the File Name text box.
8. Click OK.

The result is a VB .bas file that contains all the code needed to create and execute the DTS package. This file can be included in a new or existing VB application or an ActiveX .dll.

About Saving Packages

After you save a package as a VB file, you can no longer use the DTS Designer to edit the package. If you spend a great deal of time developing a template that you might want to use a basis for other projects, save it first in SQL Server or as a DTS structured (.dts) or DTS template (.dtt) file. Then use the DTS Designer to script the =.bas file.

You can use SQL Server 2000 DTS Designer to edit packages created with the SQL Server 7.0 DTS Designer. Although it can be used to script a VB .bas file, scripts will use the SQL 2000 DTS object model.

Unfortunately, the SQL 7.0 DTS Designer does not provide an option for creating VB .bas files. All is not lost; the SQL 7.0 CD comes with ScriptPkg, a demo program that you can use to automate much of the work. The program can be run against any SQL 7.0 DTS package to produce a VB 6.0 .bas file.

In the \DevTools\Samples\DTS folder on the SQL 7.0 CD, you will find the self-extracting DTSDemo.exe program. Run it, and extract to a convenient location. In the extracted Designer subdirectory, you will find ScriptPkg.vbp. Open the project in VB. Edit ScriptPkg.bas to set the server and the package you want to convert. When you run the program, it will script the package to C:\TEMP\packagename.txt.

This tool is especially useful for data sources for which OLE DB provider properties are not documented, such as the `DTSFlatFile` provider, which is used for importing/exporting text files. It is also helpful for troubleshooting connection-string problems with ODBC drivers and OLE DB providers.

ScriptPkg has two known problems:

- Lookups for a data pump may not be scripted correctly unless you are using the latest service pack.

- The `main` function included most of the package. Larger packages may exceed VB's limitation on the number of lines in one function. If this occurs, you will need to break the script into multiple functions.

Including the DTS Script in a VB Application

To use the generated DTS script, you need to integrate it into a new or existing VB project. The following project types are supported:

- Standard .exe
- ActiveX .exe
- ActiveX .dll
- ActiveX Document .exe

To implement your solution, open a new standard .exe. Choose Add Module from the Project menu to include the C:\DTS2000\Data\CreateExcelReport.bas module.

You will need to add a reference to the DTS object library. Choose References from the Project menu to open the References dialog box, and select Microsoft DTSPackage Object Library (see Figure 9.3).

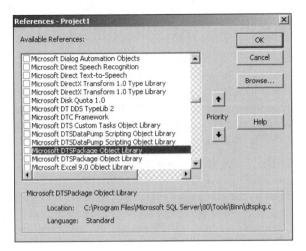

Figure 9.3   VB DTS package-object reference.

If you also have SQL 7.0 client tools installed, be sure that you select the most recent version of the DTS package object model.

DTS Dynamic Link Libraries

SQL 2000's Server or SQL Client Tools installation includes several DTS dynamic link libraries. By default, the files are installed in C:\Program Files\Microsoft SQL Server\80\Tools\Binn\, as follows:

- **Dtspkg.dll.** Implements the Microsoft DTS Package Object Library, DTSPkg, which allows you to create and modify DTS packages.

- **Dtspump.dll.** Implements the Microsoft DTS DataPump Scripting Object Library, DTSPump, which allows you to write directly to the data pump. The Transform Data Task, Data Driven Query, and Parallel Data Driven Query Task use the DTS pump interface.

- **Custtask.dll**—Implements the Microsoft DTS Custom Tasks Object Library, CustTask, which provides the Message Queue Task, the File Transfer Protocol Task, and the Dynamic Properties Task.

Depending on your application and the DTS package requirements, running the application on a machine that is not running SQL Server may require one or all of these .dlls, DMOs, dependent .rlls, and util libraries. Microsoft recommends installing SQL client tools in advance or using the VB Package Wizard, which will take care of the details.

VB Threading Considerations

When executing a package from a program written in Visual Basic and monitoring package or task events, all steps in the package must be configured to execute on the main thread. This is because a limitation in VB prevents it from properly handling multiple simultaneous calls to its events.

Connection Considerations

Take care when you set up your connections. When a package is included in a VB application, it executes on the machine running the program, not on the SQL Server host, as is the case with packages run by SQL Server Agent. Any connections set to local when you designed the package must be updated to include a reference to the server.

Compiling and Running the Package

You can run the package under the debugger or compile it to an executable.

If you hope to run the application on another computer, in addition to the SQL client tools, you will need to ensure that the necessary VB runtime libraries are installed. Once again, the VB Package Wizard will take care of these details.

The DTS Object Model

All interaction with the package occurs through the DTS object model, which provides an extensive set of components designed to extract, cleanse, transform, and load data between data stores. Figure 9.4 provides a high-level map of the DTS object model. This diagram shows an overview of objects that are covered in Chapters 3 through 6.

While working on your VB application, use the diagram and the object browser in VB to familiarize yourself with the DTS object model.

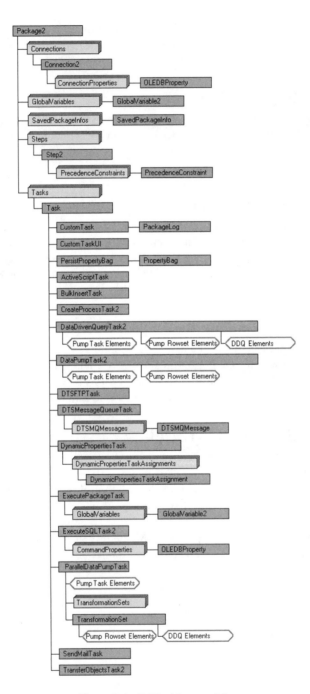

Figure 9.4 DTS object model.

The DTS VB Script

Before implementing your solution, a review of the code generated would be instructive.

The package scripted by DTS Designer is rather large. The code sets all properties for all objects, including properties set to their default values. Even for a simple package, this situation can result in thousands of lines of code.

At first, this code can be intimidating. Analysis shows a simple scripting strategy (see Listing 9.1).

Listing 9.1 **Package Scripting Strategy**

```
'******************************************************************
'Microsoft SQL Server 2000
'Visual Basic file generated for DTS Package
'  . . .
'******************************************************************

Option Explicit
Public goPackageOld As New DTS.Package
Public goPackage As DTS.Package2

Private Sub Main()
    'Set Package Options
    'Define Global Variables
    'Define Connections
    'Define Steps
    'Define Precedents
    'Call Routines to Define Each Task
    'Call Routines to Define Data Transformations
    'Execute or Save Package
End Function 'Main

Subroutines to Define Each Task and Transformation
  ...
```

The same scheme is used to script a package from either DTS 2000 or DTS 7.0. The object models for both versions are similar. In places where new functionality has been included, rather than augmenting the original, a new object has been added that is indicated with the number 2 appended (Package2, Connection2, Step2, and so on). The original objects (Package, Connection, Step, and so on) remain for compatibility.

> *About the Type-Mismatch Error*
> You'll receive a type-mismatch error if you attempt to run a DTS application that uses any of the extended objects on a computer that has SQL Server 7.0 client tools installed.

As mentioned earlier in this chapter, the DTS Designer generates code that sets most, if not all, properties for an object—even default values. You could reduce the amount of code by removing these redundant statements. These statements, however, document what is going on, and if you remove the wrong line, your package will fail (at best) or run and quietly produce garbage (at worst).

Setting Package Options

The first thing scripted is the creation of the package object, which holds the basic information as well as collections for connections, steps, tasks, and so on. You cannot create a new DTS.Package2 directly or declare one by using WithEvents. Instead, you create a standard DTS package and cast it into a Package2, as shown in Listing 9.2.

Listing 9.2 **The Package Object in Visual Basic**

```
Public goPackageOld As New DTS.Packagect

Public goPackage As DTS.Package2
set goPackage = goPackageOld

    goPackage.Name = "CreateExcelReports"
goPackage.WriteCompletionStatusToNTEventLog = False
    goPackage.FailOnError = False
    goPackage.PackagePriorityClass = 2
    goPackage.MaxConcurrentSteps = 4
    goPackage.LineageOptions = 0
    goPackage.UseTransaction = True
    goPackage.TransactionIsolationLevel = 4096
    goPackage.AutoCommitTransaction = True
    goPackage.RepositoryMetadataOptions = 0
    goPackage.UseOLEDBServiceComponents = True
    goPackage.LogToSQLServer = False
    goPackage.LogServerFlags = 0
    goPackage.FailPackageOnLogFailure = False
    goPackage.ExplicitGlobalVariables = False
    goPackage.PackageType = 0
```

> To create a package that is compatible with SQL Server 7.0, you would replace the first few lines as follows:
>
> ```
> Public goPackageAs As DTS.Package
> set goPackage = goPackageOld
> ```

Table 9.1 describes each package option from the preceding code listings.

Table 9.1 **Package Options**

Option	Description
Name and Description	Describe the package.
PackagePriorityClass	Sets the Windows 32 process priority.
MaxConcurrentSteps	Controls the number of steps that can execute concurrently. Each step runs in its own thread.
	However, if the steps are set to execute on the main thread, this number has no effect.
	Usually, a value larger than the number of CPUs will be of little use.
	If you have tasks with long CPU waits (results pending from another server or MSMQ), you can set this option higher.
FailOnError	If True, disables package-error processing and raises a VB error. Great for debugging.
WriteCompletionStatusToNTEventLog	If True, writes the status on completion to the NT application's event log.
LineageOptions and RepositoryMetadataOptions	LineageOptions defines how the package lineage is presented and recorded. RepositoryMetadataOptions defines meta data scanning and resolution options when storing the package in the SQL Server 2000 Meta Data Services.
UseTransaction	If True, runs package steps under a single transaction contingent on the correct transactional setting for steps and providers.
TransactionIsolationLevel	Sets the package transaction's isolation level. The default is Read-Committed.
AutoCommitTransaction	If True, commits pending transactions upon successful completion.
ExplicitGlobalVariables	If True, requires that global variables are declared before use. Similar to Microsoft Visual Basic when you turn on Option Explicit.
LogToSQLServer, LogServerFlags, LogServerName, LogServerPassword, LogServerUserName, and FailPackageOnLogFailure	Enable logging to an instance of SQL Server 2000, identify the server, and provide authentication information.
UseOLEDBServiceComponents	If True, specifies that OLE DB components will be used.
PackageType	Provides information about the application that creates the package.

Defining the Package's *GlobalVariables* Collection

Next, you script the `GlobalVariables` collection. This collection is used to store and share data between steps and ActiveX scripts in the package, and even between packages. You can add, remove, or change the value of `GlobalVariables` objects dynamically during execution. Each `GlobalVariables` object provides a variant data type.

DTS scripts a single global reference that is used to create all the necessary `GlobalVariables` objects and appends them to the package object's `GlobalVariables` collection (see Listing 9.3).

Listing 9.3 **Working with Global Variables in Visual Basic**

```
'...................................................................
' Begin to write package global variables information
'...................................................................
    Dim oGlobal As DTS.GlobalVariable

    Set oGlobal = _
        goPackage.GlobalVariables.New("ActualsThroughMonth")
        oGlobal = 0
    goPackage.GlobalVariables.Add oGlobal
    set oGlobal = Nothing

    Set oGlobal = _
        goPackage.GlobalVariables.New("ErrorMessage")
    oGlobal = ""
    goPackage.GlobalVariables.Add oGlobal
    set oGlobal = Nothing

    Set oGlobal = _
        goPackage.GlobalVariables.New("CurrentYear")
        oGlobal = 0
    goPackage.GlobalVariables.Add oGlobal
    set oGlobal = Nothing
```

Defining Package Connections

The `Connections` collection, which is used to store package OLE DB data provider information, is scripted next. Each `Connection` object describes a single data provider. If the OLE DB provider can support connection pooling, you can reuse these connections across multiple steps or tasks.

DTS scripts a single `Connection` reference, which is used to create all the necessary `Connection` objects and appends them to the package object's `Connections` collection.

For your solution, DTS scripts three connections (see Listing 9.4). The first one represents the Access data source; the second two represent the Excel spreadsheets.

Listing 9.4 **Working with Package Connections in Visual Basic**

```
'-------------------------------------------------------------------
'Create package connection information
'For security purposes, the password is never scripted
'-------------------------------------------------------------------
Dim oConnection as DTS.Connection2

'------------ a new connection defined below.
Set oConnection = _
goPackage.Connections.New("Microsoft.Jet.OLEDB.4.0")
   oConnection.ConnectionProperties("User ID") = "Admin"
   oConnection.ConnectionProperties("Data Source") = _
       "C:\...\Manufacturing.mdb"
   oConnection.Name = "Inventory Actuals"
   oConnection.ID = 1
   oConnection.Reusable = True
   oConnection.ConnectImmediate = False
   oConnection.DataSource = "C:\...\Manufacturing.mdb"
   oConnection.UserID = "Admin"
   oConnection.ConnectionTimeout = 60
   oConnection.UseTrustedConnection = False
   oConnection.UseDSL = False
   'If a password is required, uncomment and add here
   'oConnection.Password = "<put the password here>"
goPackage.Connections.Add oConnection
Set oConnection = Nothing
...
```

In general, connection information depends heavily on the OLE DB provider.

Simple options such as `DataSource`, `UseTrustedConnection`, `UserID`, `Password`, and `Timeout` are self-explanatory. Table 9.2 describes some additional options.

Table 9.2 **Connection Options**

Option	Description
Reusable	If `True`, multiple steps can share the connection.
ConnectImmediate	If `True`, the connection to the data store occurs when the package starts; otherwise, the connection waits until a task using it begins.

Options that define the provider are often poorly documented or difficult to find. In most cases, it is significantly less effort to let DTS Designer do the work.

As you can see, passwords are not scripted. If passwords are required, simply uncomment the appropriate lines and provide the required information.

Defining Package Steps

DTS next scripts the `Steps` collection, which defines task workflow for a package. Each step specifies one or more tasks to be run. A step can execute in parallel with other steps, serially, or conditionally based on their execution.

The DTS Designer creates steps automatically for each task you define. All that remains is for you to define the precedence constraints. In code, steps need to be defined explicitly, and tasks need to be assigned to them. Tasks that are not assigned to a step will not execute.

Tasks and steps can be created in any order. The DTS Designer follows a top-down approach, scripting first the steps, then the precedence, and finally the task details (see Listing 9.5).

Listing 9.5   **Working with Package Steps in Visual Basic**

```
'-----------------------------------------------------------
' Create package steps information
'-----------------------------------------------------------
Dim oStep as DTS.Step2
Dim oPrecConstraint as DTS.PrecedenceConstraint

'------------ a new step defined below
Set oStep = goPackage.Steps.New
   oStep.Name = "DTSStep_DTSActiveScriptTask_1"
   oStep.Description = "Prepare Spreadsheet"
   oStep.ExecutionStatus = 1
   oStep.TaskName = "DTSTask_DTSActiveScriptTask_1"
   oStep.CommitSuccess = False
   oStep.RollbackFailure = False
   oStep.ScriptLanguage = "VBScript"
   oStep.AddGlobalVariables = True
   oStep.RelativePriority = 3
   oStep.CloseConnection = False
   oStep.ExecuteInMainThread = False
   oStep.IsPackageDSORowset = False
   oStep.JoinTransactionIfPresent = False
   oStep.DisableStep = False
   oStep.FailPackageOnError = False
goPackage.Steps.Add oStep
Set oStep = Nothing
...
```

Table 9.3 describes each package step option.

Table 9.3   **Package Step Options**

Option	Description
AddGlobalVariables	If True, allows the step to access global variables.
CloseConnection	If True, closes the connection when the step finishes.

Option	Description
IsPackageDSORowset	Must be `True` if the Transform Data Task returns a rowset.
DisableStep	Enables or disables a step.
FailPackage	If `True`, aborts the package if the step fails.
JoinTransactionIfPresent	If `True`, executes the task within the scope of the transaction when the package is using transactions.
CommitSuccess	If `True`, commits data on step success.
RollbackFailure	If `True`, performs a rollback on step failure.
ExecuteInMainThread	Must be set to `True` if you are using a COM language, such as VB, that does not support free threading Write Custom Tasks or Execute Package Tasks while hooking into events. Also must be `True` if a step or task uses ActiveX script code to call, via `CreateObject`, a COM object that is not free-threaded or if you are using an OLE DB provider that is not free-threaded.
Relative Priority	Determines the step priority relative to the rest of the package. If `ExecuteInMainThread` is `True`, the parameter is not used.

Defining Package Constraints

Unless otherwise constrained, package steps run in parallel, up to the limit specified by the package's `MaxConcurrentSteps` property. To order execution, Precedence Constraints are added to a particular step. Precedence Constraints define conditions to be met before step execution. If a step has more than one Precedence Constraint, it will not begin until all its Precedence Constraints are satisfied.

For your package, DTS scripts Precedence Constraints as shown in Listing 9.6.

Listing 9.6 **Working with Package Constraints in Visual Basic**

```
'------------ a precedence constraint for steps defined below
Set oStep = goPackage.Steps("DTSStep_DTSDataPumpTask_1")
Set oPrecConstraint = _
oStep.PrecedenceConstraints.New("DTSStep_DTSActiveScriptTask_1")
   oPrecConstraint.StepName = "DTSStep_DTSActiveScriptTask_1"
   oPrecConstraint.PrecedenceBasis = 0
   oPrecConstraint.Value = 0
oStep.precedenceConstraints.Add oPrecConstraint
Set oPrecConstraint = Nothing
...
```

Table 9.4 describes some package constraint options.

Table 9.4 **Package Constraint Options**

Option	Description
PrecedenceBas	If 1, precedence is determined by the value returned by the step. If 0, precedence is based on step success or failure.
Value	Determines the conditions to be met:
	4—Completion. Step executes after preceding step, regardless of status.
	1—Success. Step executes only when the preceding step succeeds.
	0—Failure. Step executes only when the preceding step fails.

Defining Package Tasks

The DTS Designer places the code that defines tasks and transformations in separate subroutines titled Task_Sub1, Task_Sub2, and Task_Sub3.

At this point the routines are executed to define the tasks transformations and add them to the appropriate steps (see Listing 9.7).

Listing 9.7 **Working with Tasks in Visual Basic**

```
'...............................................................
' Create package tasks information
'...............................................................

'Task_Sub1
'    task DTSTask_DTSActiveScriptTask_1
'    (Prepare Spreadsheet)
Call Task_Sub1( goPackage)

'Task_Sub2
'    task DTSTask_DTSDataPumpTask_1
'    (Load Variance Report)
Call Task_Sub2( goPackage)
...
```

Executing the Package

Finally, DTS scripts the package execution as shown in Listing 9.8.

Listing 9.8 **Executing the Package in Visual Basic**

```
'................................................................
' Save or execute package
'................................................................

'goPackage.SaveToSQLServer "(local)", "sa", ""
goPackage.Execute

goPackage.Uninitialize
set goPackage = Nothing
set goPackageOld = Nothing

End Sub
```

Uninitialize cleans up the package and releases all memory references.

If you want to save the package to the local SQL Server, uncomment the SaveToSQLServer line and provide the required login information.

Adding an *ExecuteSQLTask*

After the main procedure, DTS scripts package tasks. Each task is scripted as a separate subroutine. The Tasks collection defines package tasks. Each task defines a unit of work to be performed. Any task described in Chapter 4, "DTS Tasks," and Chapter 5, "More DTS Tasks," can be used. The CreateExcelReports package uses an ActiveScriptTask and a DataPumpTask.

Adding an *ActiveScriptTask*

Listing 9.9 shows the code DTS scripts to define the ActiveScriptTask used in your solution.

Listing 9.9 **Working with *ActiveScriptTask* in Visual Basic**

```
'Task_Sub2
'    DTSTask_DTSActiveScriptTask_1 (Prepare Spreadsheet)
Public Sub Task_Sub2(ByVal goPackage As Object)

Dim oTask As DTS.Task
Dim oLookup As DTS.Lookup

Dim oCustomTask2 As DTS.ActiveScriptTask
Set oTask = goPackage.Tasks.New("DTSActiveScriptTask")
Set oCustomTask2 = oTask.CustomTask

    oCustomTask2.Name = "DTSTask_DTSActiveScriptTask_1"
    oCustomTask2.Description = "Prepare Spreadsheet"
```

continues

Listing 9.9 **Continued**

```
oCustomTask2.ActiveXScript = _
  "'********************************" & vbCrLf & _
  "' Visual Basic ActiveX Script" & vbCrLf & _
  "'*******************************" & vbCrLf & _
  "Function Main()" & vbCrLf & _&_
  " Dim xlApp"& vbCrLf &_
  " Set xlApp = & vbCrLf &_
  " CreateObject(""Excel.Application"")" & vbCrLf & _
  " xlApp.Workbooks.Open " & vbCrLf & _
  "   ""C:\..\Shipping Reports.xls""" & vbCrLf & _
  " xlApp.Run (""ResetReports"")" & vbCrLf & _
  " For each c in xlApp.Range(""ActualsMetaData"")" & vbCrLf &
  " If c.Value = ""ActualsThroughMonth"" or c.Value = ""CurrentYear""
  ➥Then" & vbCrLf &
  "   "DTSGlobalVariables(c.Value).Value = c.offset(0,1).Value" & vbCrLf &
  " End If" vbCrLf &
  " Next " vbCrLf &
  " xlApp.ActiveWorkbook.Close True" & vbCrLf & _
  " xlApp.Quit" & vbCrLf & _
  " Set xlApp = Nothing" & vbCrLf & _
  " Main = DTSTaskExecResult_Success" & vbCrLf & _
  "End Function"
oCustomTask2.FunctionName = "Main"
oCustomTask2.ScriptLanguage = "VBScript"
oCustomTask2.AddGlobalVariables = True

goPackage.Tasks.Add oTask
Set oCustomTask2 = Nothing
Set oTask = Nothing

End Sub
```

This procedure is not complicated. Create a task, set its task properties, and append the task to the package's `Tasks` collection. The `Lookup` reference is scripted, but it is not used for this task. Steps and precedences have already been defined to execute the task, so no further work is required.

Table 9.5 describes some active script task options.

Table 9.5 **Active Script Task Options**

Option	Description
`ScriptLanguage`, `FunctionName`, and `ActiveXScript`	Define the task.
`AddGlobalVariables`	Allows the script to access the package's global variables.

Adding a *DataPumpTask*

The `DataPumpTask` scripted for your solution defines an instance of the Transform Data Task that implements a data pump object to transform data as it is moved from source to destination.

This task is more complex, consisting of the following steps:

1. Define the `DataPumpTask` options.
2. Define the task's transformation script.
3. Define the task's transformation script columns.
4. Define the task's ActiveX script.
5. Define the task's transformation script lookup.
6. Add the DataPumpTask to the package tasks object.

Defining the *DataPumpTask* Options

Listing 9.10 shows the code that defines the `DataPumpTask` options.

Listing 9.10 **Working with the *DataPumpTask* in Visual Basic**

```
'Task_Sub3
'   DTSTask_DTSDataPumpTask_1 (Load Actuals)
Public Sub Task_Sub3(ByVal goPackage As Object)

Dim oTask As DTS.Task
Dim oLookup As DTS.Lookup

Dim oCustomTask3 As DTS.DataPumpTask2
Set oTask = goPackage.Tasks.New("DTSDataPumpTask")
Set oCustomTask3 = oTask.CustomTask

    oCustomTask3.Name = "DTSTask_DTSDataPumpTask_1"
    oCustomTask3.Description = "Load Actuals"
    oCustomTask3.SourceConnectionID = 2
    oCustomTask3.SourceObjectName = "Budget"
    oCustomTask3.DestinationConnectionID = 3
    oCustomTask3.DestinationObjectName = "Actuals"
    oCustomTask3.ProgressRowCount = 1000
    oCustomTask3.MaximumErrorCount = 0
    oCustomTask3.FetchBufferSize = 1
    oCustomTask3.UseFastLoad = True
    oCustomTask3.InsertCommitSize = 0
    oCustomTask3.ExceptionFileColumnDelimiter = "|"
    oCustomTask3.ExceptionFileRowDelimiter = vbCrLf
    oCustomTask3.AllowIdentityInserts = False
    oCustomTask3.FirstRow = "0"
    oCustomTask3.LastRow = "0"
    oCustomTask3.FastLoadOptions = 2
    oCustomTask3.ExceptionFileOptions = 1
    oCustomTask3.DataPumpOptions = 0
```

Table 9.6 describes the `DataPumpTask` options.

Table 9.6 **DataPumpTask Options**

Option	Description
`SourceConnectionId` and `SourceObjectName`	Identify the source table. `SourceSQLStatement` can be used instead of `SourceObjectName` when you want to use a SQL statement against the source.
`DestinationConnectionId` and `DestinationObjectName`	Identify the destination table.
`ProgressRowCount`	Sets the number of rows between event notifications.
`MaximumErrorCount`	Sets the number of errors the task can tolerate before giving up. The default, 0, causes termination after the first error.
`FetchBufferSize`	Sets the number of rows the data provider will return each fetch when retrieving nonbinary data, and adjusts the size to balance memory and the overhead that calls incur. The default value, `100`, works well in most cases.
`InsertCommitSize`	Similar to bcp `batch size`; sets rows processed between each commit.
`UseFastLoad`	If `True`, DTS will use the OLE DB interface `IrowsetFastLoad`. The data path inside SQL Server will be the same as when you are using bcp and bulk insert.
`AllowIdentityIinserts`	If `True`, allows you to insert user-provided values for identity columns.
`FirstRow` and `LastRow`	Allows processing of a subset of the source. `FirstRow=11` would exclude the first 10 rows, and `LastRow=99` would stop at row 99. Use `0, 0` to process all rows.
`ExceptionFileName`	If you allow errors, trapped rows are logged to this file, using the delimiters specified by `ExceptionFileRowDelimiter` and `ExceptionFileColumnDelimiter`.

Defining the *DataPumpTask*'s **Transformation Script**

After the task is initialized, DTS scripts the transformations to perform. Each transformation is scripted in a separate subroutine (see Listing 9.11).

Listing 9.11 **Adding a Transformation Script to the *DataPumpTask* from Visual Basic**

```
Dim oTransformation As DTS.Transformation2
    Dim oTransProps as DTS.Properties
    Dim oColumn As DTS.Column
    Set oTransformation = _
    oCustomTask3.Transformations.New("DTSPump.DataPumpTransformScript")
```

```
oTransformation.Name = "Copy Actuals"
oTransformation.TransformFlags = 63
oTransformation.ForceSourceBlobsBuffered = 0
oTransformation.ForceBlobsInMemory = False
oTransformation.InMemoryBlobSize = 1048576
oTransformation.TransformPhases = 4
```

In general, the default transformation options will work. Discussion of specific options is beyond the scope of this book. See Books on Line (BOL) if you require further clarification.

Defining the *DataPumpTask*'s Transformation Script Columns

Although a task can access the source and destination rowsets, the transformation can access columns only you assign. Next, DTS scripts the source and destination for any column processed. Listing 9.12 shows the code for the Product column.

Listing 9.12 **Working with Transformation Script Column Definitions for the Product Data Field in Visual Basic**

```
'Define Source Columns
Set oColumn = _
oTransformation.SourceColumns.New("Product" , 1)
    oColumn.Name = "Product"
    oColumn.Ordinal = 1
    oColumn.Flags = 102
    oColumn.Size = 255
    oColumn.DataType = 130
    oColumn.Precision = 0
    oColumn.NumericScale = 0
    oColumn.Nullable = True
    oTransformation.SourceColumns.Add oColumn
    Set oColumn = Nothing
...
'Define Destination Columns
Set oColumn =
oTransformation.DestinationColumns.New("Product" , 1)
    oColumn.Name = "Product"
    oColumn.Ordinal = 1
    oColumn.Flags = 102
    oColumn.Size = 255
    oColumn.DataType = 130
    oColumn.Precision = 0
    oColumn.NumericScale = 0
    oColumn.Nullable = True
    oTransformation.DestinationColumns.Add oColumn
    Set oColumn = Nothing
...
```

Table 9.7 describes column options.

Table 9.7   **Column Options**

Option	Description
`Name`	Defines the column name.
`Ordinal`	Sets the column number.
`DataType` and `Flags`	Correspond to the OLE DB data type (DBTYPE) and column flags (DBCOLUMNFLAGS).
`Size`	Sets the maximum length.
`Precision` and `NumericScale`	Defines decimal and numeric data types.
`Nullable`	If `True`, allows the column to accept null values.

Defining the *DataPumpTask*'s Transformation Script ActiveX Script

Next, DTS scripts an ActiveX script to process and transform the data (see Listing 9.13).

Listing 9.13   **Using Visual Basic to Add the Transformation Script's ActiveX Script**

```
Set oTransProps = oTransformation.TransformServerProperties
oTransProps("Text") = _
    "'****************************************" & _
    "' Visual Basic Transformation Script" & _
    "'****************************************" & _
    "' Copy each source to the destination "& _
    "Function Main()" & _
    "   Dim I, CMActuals "& vbCrLf & _
    "   DTSDestination(""Product"") = " & _
    "       DTSSource(""Product"")" & vbCrLf &
    "   'Load Actuals for each month" & _ vbCrLf &
    "   For i = 1 to DTSGlobalVariables(" & _
    """ActualsThroughMonth"").Value" & _ vbCrLf &
    "      DTSDestination(i+1) = " & _
    "      DTSLookups(" & _
    "   ""GetActualsCurrentMonth"").Execute (" & _
    "         DTSSource(""Product""),) " &
    " DTSGlobalVariables(""CurrentYear"").Value,i) " _& vbCrLf &
    "   Next" & vbCrLf & _
    "   DTSDestination(""Full Year"") = " & _
    "   DTSLookups(""GetActualsYTD"").Execute(" & _
    "   DTSSource(""Product""), " & _
    "   DTSGlobalVariables(
    "      ""CurrentYear"").Value), " &
    "  DTSGlobalVariables(
    "      ""ActualsThroughMonth"").Value) " & vbCrLf &_
    "   Main = DTSTransformStat_OK " & _ vbCrLf &
    "End Function"
```

```
oTransProps("Language") = "VBScript"
oTransProps("FunctionEntry") = "Main"

Set oTransProps = Nothing

oCustomTask3.Transformations.Add oTransformation
   Set oTransformation = Nothing
```

Note that lookups, which are yet to be defined, have been forward-referenced.

Defining the *DataPumpTask*'s Transformation Script Lookup

The DataPumpTask, like the DataDrivenQueryTask, supports Select statements and lookups, which you can use to perform parameterized queries. The Lookup feature lets a transformation retrieve data from locations other than the immediate source or destination row being transformed. Listing 9.14 shows sample code.

Listing 9.14 **Using Visual Basic to Script the *Lookup* Query Used in a *DataPumpTask***

```
'------- A Lookup is defined here
Set oLookup = oCustomTask3.Lookups.New("GetActualCurrentMonth")
  oLookup.Name = "GetActualCurrentMonth"
  oLookup.ConnectionID = 1
  oLookup.Query = _
"SELECT SUM([OrderDetails].[Quantity]) AS CumTotal" &
"FROM ([Order] INNER JOIN " &
"  OrderDetails ON [Order].[OrderID] = " &
"  [OrderDetails].[OrderID]) INNER JOIN " &
"    Product ON [OrderDetails].[ProductID] = " &
"  [Product].[ProductID] " &
" WHERE ([Product].[ProdName] = ?) AND " &
"  (YEAR([Order].[ShippedDate]) = ?) AND " &
"  (MONTH([Order].[ShippedDate]) = ?) ";
  oLookup.MaxCacheRows = 0

  oCustomTask3.Lookups.Add oLookup
  Set oLookup = Nothing
```

About Lookups

Lookups are associated with a particular task and can't be shared.

Table 9.8 describes the lookup options.

Table 9.8 **Lookup Options**

Option	Description
ConnectionId and Query	Define the actual lookup. Any question marks in the query are replaced with parameters when the lookup is performed.
MaxCacheRows	Improves lookup performance. Lookups can use a cache to store values from previous executions. Use 0 for no caching. The default, 100, works well in most cases.

Saving the *DataPumpTask* to the Package's *Tasks* Collection

Finally, the task is appended to the package's Tasks collection (see Listing 9.15).

Listing 9.15 **Scripted *DataPumpTask* Append**

```
goPackage.Tasks.Add oTask
Set oCustomTask3 = Nothing
Set oTask = Nothing


End Sub
```

ExecuteSQLTask

ExecuteSQLTask is another common task used in many DTS packages. This task is very straightforward and is much like ActiveScriptTask. Listing 9.16 shows the code scripted by DTS to define the ExecuteSQLTask.

Listing 9.16 **Working with the *ExecuteSQLTask* in Visual Basic**

```
'Task_Sub1
'   DTSTask_DTSExecuteSQLTask_1 (Reports Get ActualsThroughMonth)
Public Sub Task_Sub1(ByVal goPackage As Object)

Dim oTask As DTS.Task
Dim oLookup As DTS.Lookup

Dim oCustomTask1 As DTS.ExecuteSQLTask2
Set oTask = goPackage.Tasks.New("DTSExecuteSQLTask")
Set oCustomTask1 = oTask.CustomTask

    oCustomTask1.Name = "DTSTask_DTSExecuteSQLTask_1"
    oCustomTask1.Description = "Reports Get ActualsThroughMonth"
    oCustomTask1.SQLStatement = _
      "SELECT  Value" & vbCrLf & _
      "FROM    ActualsMetaData" & vbCrLf & _
      "WHERE  (VariableName " & vbCrLf & _
      "      = 'ActualsThroughMonth')"
```

```
oCustomTask1.ConnectionID = 3
oCustomTask1.CommandTimeout = 0
oCustomTask1.InputGlobalVariableNames = """"""
oCustomTask1.OutputGlobalVariableNames = _
    """ActualsThroughMonth"""
oCustomTask1.OutputAsRecordset = False

goPackage.Tasks.Add oTask
Set oCustomTask1 = Nothing
Set oTask = Nothing

End Sub
```

This code is not very complicated. Create a task, set its properties, and append it to the package's Tasks collection. The Lookup reference is scripted, but it is not used for this task.

Table 9.9 describes some task options.

Table 9.9 **Task Options**

Option	Description
ConnectionID, CommandTimeout, and SQLStatement	Define the data source and statement to run.
InputGlobalVariableNames and OutputGlobalVariableNames	Map statement parameters to global variables.
OutputAsRecordSet	Must be True if the task returns a recordset.

Building Your Solution

Now that you understand how the package is scripted, you can begin to build a solution.

At this point, you should have already done the following:

1. Started the DTS Designer.
2. Opened C:\DTS2000\Data\CreateExcelReport.dts[4].
3. Saved the .dts file as a VB script (C:\DTS2000\Data\CreateExcelReport.bas).
4. Created a sample managers' directory, C:\Temp\DTS2000Manager.
5. Copied C:\DTS2000\Data\ShippingBudget.xls into this directory.
6. Started VB and begun a new standard .exe.
7. Added a reference for the DTS package object.

4. If you want to follow along, all data files and scripts used in the book are available to be downloaded from http://www.magenic.com/publications or http://www.newriders.com.

8. Added a file reference to the script generated by DTS (C:\DTS2000\ Data\CreateExcelReport.bas).

9. Saved the project (C:\DTS2000\Data\CreateExcelReport.vbp) and compiled it. This step is required to ensure that the `App.Path` works correctly during debugging.

To complete the solution, you must do the following:

1. Modify the VB application to prompt for the location of ShippingBudget.xls, copy ShippingReports.xls to the same directory as the budget, and run the DTS package to update the copy of ShippingReports.xls.

2. Run the application, and when prompted for the budget location, specify C:\Temp\DTS2000Manager\ShippingBudget.xls.

3. Use Excel to view the generated report (C:\Temp\DTS2000Manager\ ShippingReports.xls).

Modifying the VB Application

Next, you modify the beginning of the DTS script to prompt for the location of ShippingBudget.xls, copy ShippingReports.xls to the same directory as the budget, and run the DTS package to update the copy of ShippingReports.xls. Listing 9.17 shows the final changes.

Listing 9.17   **Application Customizations**

```
Option Explicit
Public goPackageOld As New DTS.Package
Public goPackage As DTS.Package2

'File References
Dim msInventory As String
Dim msReports As String
Dim msBudget As String
Dim msPath

Private Sub Main()
    'Find Inventory
    msInventory = App.Path + "\Manufacturing.mdb"

    'Prompt for Budget
    msBudget = InputBox("Enter", "Budget File", _
        App.Path + "\" + "Shipping Budget.xls")

    'Copy Report (if required)
    msPath = msBudget
    While Len(msPath) > 1 And Right(msPath, 1) <> "\" _
      And Right(msPath, 1) <> ":"
        msPath = Left(msPath, Len(msPath) - 1)
    Wend
```

```
msReports = msPath + "Shipping Reports.xls"
If msPath + "Shipping Reports.xls" <> App.Path + "\Shipping Reports.xls" _
   And Dir(msPath + "Shipping Reports.xls") Then
      FileCopy App.Path + "\Shipping Reports.xls", _
         msPath + "Shipping Reports.xls"
End If
```

DTS explicitly scripts file locations in property assignments or property statements. The way this script is written makes it impossible to change them programmatically at run time. You must use the VB editor to make replacements, as follows:

1. Replace C:\DTS2000\Data\Inventory.mdb with " + msInventory + ".

2. Replace C:\DTS2000\Data\ShippingReports.xls with " + msReports + ".

3. Replace C:\DTS2000\Data\ShippingBudget.xls with " + msBudget+ ".

4. Compile and test.

Running the Application

Use VB's Run command to start the application. When prompted for the location of your budget as shown in Figure 9.5, specify C:\Temp\DTS2000Manager\ShippingBudget.xls.

Figure 9.5   VB DTS budget location.

Viewing the Output

The application will have copied C:\DTS2000\DATA\ \ShippingReports. xls[5] to C:\Temp\DTS2000Manager\ShippingReports.xls and run the DTS package to merge it with C:\Temp\DTS2000Manager\ ShippingBudget.xls.

Use Excel to view the generated reports (C:\Temp\DTS2000Manager\ShippingReports.xls).

5. If you want to follow along, all data files and scripts used in the book are available to be downloaded from http://www.magenic.com/publications or http://www.newriders.com.

Summary

In this chapter, you saw that in some situations, the DTS Wizard or the DTS Designer does not provide the functionality needed.

For one such problem, you examined a quick and efficient solution using VB. You designed a package using DTS Wizard, saved it to a VB script, and then include the script in a VB project where you could provide a solution that extended and complemented the DTS engine.

Chapter 10, "Interacting with a Package Using Visual Basic," builds on this topic, covering more complex and interesting problems.

10

Interacting with a Package Using Visual Basic

I N CHAPTER 9, "BUILDING A PACKAGE Using Visual Basic," you saw that in some situations the DTS Designer might not be the best tool to implement your solution. You then created a VB program that used the DTS object model to transform and load data into a SQL database. In this chapter, you will build on this knowledge and investigate some best practices. You will learn about the following:[1]

- Executing DTS packages from Visual Basic
- Making best-practice modifications to DTS VB .bas files
- Loading and saving packages
- Event Handling
- Error Handling

1. All data, scripts, and programs used in this chapter are available for download from http://www.magenic.com/publications or http://www.newriders.com. The self-extracting ZIP file will create a directory structure based on DTS2000. The Visual Basic programs discussed in this chapter are available in \DTS2000\VBProjects\BestPractices. You can extract the files to any drive or directory, but all file references in this book are based on C:\DTS2000\.

Armed with this knowledge, we will investigate DTS solutions to various real-world problems. Although DTS provides tasks to deal with most common data transformation problems, in some situations you will want to complement DTS with a programming language such as Visual Basic. Usually, these situations are not due to technical limitations of DTS, but due to business or user requirements.

You can use Visual Basic to do the following:

- Create a simplified DTS package scheduler for users to manage when and how often packages are being run.
- Process the data before doing DTS work, such as converting the data to a .csv file.
- On a predetermined schedule, download files from the Web; log successes and failures; and notify the administrator of failures, completions, and their associated processing time.
- Perform file-management tasks prior to DTS importing the data. Such tasks can include copying; deleting; renaming; comparing two files; and checking file properties, such as date and size. Then you can have DTS process only those files that are valid.
- Create a custom FTP task that extracts data from a remote system and then kick off DTS to populate a data warehouse.

In this chapter, we will build Visual Basic/DTS packages that will:

- Process all files in a directory
- Process spreadsheets in an Excel workbook
- Process XML input
- Process Outlook messages

Although all examples were developed using SQL 2000, the basic principles will work with little or no modifications against a SQL 7.0 Server.

Executing DTS Packages in Visual Basic

To execute your DTS package in Visual Basic, perform the following steps:

1. Create a new standard .exe project.
2. Depending on your requirements, add references to the following:
   - Microsoft DTSDataPump Scripting Object Library
   - Microsoft DTSPackage Object Library
   - Microsoft DTS Custom Tasks Object Library

3. Dimension a package object.
4. Load the package.

5. Execute the package.

6. Uninitialize the package.

VB is not limited to defining and running packages. It is also possible to load and execute a previously defined package.

When you finish with the `Package` or `Package2` object, you should release references to all DTS objects except the `Package` and call the `UnInitialize` method. When you release package references, include object variables that you declared `WithEvents` to handle package events.

DTS client applications can respond to the events raised by DTS. DTS raises events to communicate the status of work being done, thereby allowing you to control the execution of the package, task, or step. The execution status can show successful completion or an error; both are a type of execution status. Chapters 4 and 5 provide the full list of execution-status values for a task C. Chapter 6, "DTS Workflows," provides the full list of execution-status values for packages.

By default, when you run a project, you get no indication of completion or errors. Adding completion notification and error handling is recommended.

Making Best-Practice Upgrades to the VB .bas Files

In most cases it is easier to use VB to manipulate an existing DTS package. When you want to script and edit a package, consider modifying the VB code to create and return a `Package` object as follows:

1. Name the file *PackageName*.bas.

2. Change Sub Main to Function Package.

3. Do not execute the Uninitialize method.

4. Return the package created.

This process will allow you to manipulate the existing and scripted packages separately from the rest of your code.

The changes can be seen in Listing 10.1.

Listing 10.1 **Recommended Changes to the Package .bas File**

```
Option Explicit
Public goPackageOld As New DTS.Package
Public goPackage As DTS.Package2

Public Function Package() As DTS.Package2
  '~~Private Sub Main()
  Set goPackage = goPackageOld
  ...
' Save or execute package
```

continues

Listing 10.1 **Continued**

```
'goPackage.SaveToSQLServer "(local)", "sa", ""
'~~goPackage.Execute
'~~goPackage.Uninitialize
 Set Package = goPackage
 Set goPackage = Nothing
 Set goPackageOld = Nothing
End Function
```

To include *PackageName*.bas in your project, call the package as shown in Listing 10.2.

Listing 10.2 **Calling the Package from VB**

```
' DTS 2000 - Best Practices
Private moPackage As DTS.Package2
Option Explicit

Private Sub Form_Load()
  Set moPackage = PackageName.Package
  moPackage.Execute
End Sub
```

Loading and Saving Packages in Visual Basic

VB is not limited to defining and running packages. Both the `Package` and `Package2` objects provide methods to load, save, or execute a previously defined package.

To load a package, create a `Package` or `Package2` object and then invoke one of the following object methods:

- LoadFromSQLServer
- LoadFromRepository
- LoadFromStorageFile

To save a package, create a `Package` or `Package2` object and then invoke one of the following object methods:

- SaveToSQLServer
- SaveToSQLServerAs
- SaveToRepository
- SaveToRepositoryAs
- SaveToStorageFile
- SaveToStorageFileAs

If the package is run before being saved, you must call the `UnInitialize` method first.

To save a VB .bas file scripted by DTS Designer or ScriptPkg to a SQL Server package, follow these steps:

1. At the end of Sub Main, uncomment this line:

   ```
   'objPackage.SaveToSQLServer ...
   ```

2. Comment out the following line:

   ```
   objPackage.Execute
   ```

3. Run the project.

Package Load and Save Repository Methods

The Package and Package2 objects provide the LoadFromRepository method to load a DTS package from a Microsoft Meta Data Services Repository and the SaveToRepository and SaveToRepositoryAs methods to save a DTS package to a Microsoft Meta Data Services Repository. Listing 10.3 shows the method syntax.

Listing 10.3 **Package Load and Save Repository Methods**

```
Package.LoadFromRepository _
  RepositoryServerName, RepositoryDatabaseName, _
  RepositoryUserNaem, RepositgoryUserPassword,

  PackageGUID, [VersionGUID], [PackageName], _
  [Flags], [pVarPersistStgOfHost]

Package.SaveToRepository _
  RepositoryServerName, RepositoryDatabaseName, _
  RepositoryUserName, RepositoryUserPassword, _
  [Flags], [CategoryID], [pVarPersistStgOfHost]

Package.SaveToRepositoryAS _
  NewName, _
  RepositoryServerName, RepositoryDatabaseName, _
  RepositoryUserName, RepositoryUserPassword, _
  [Flags], [CategoryID], [pVarPersistStgOfHost]
```

Table 10.1 shows parameter use.

Table 10.1 **Repository Load and Save Parameters**

Parameter	Description
RepositoryServerName	Meta Data Services server name.
	If empty or NULL, RepositoryDatabaseName is evaluated as an ODBC DSN; otherwise, RepositoryServerName and RepositoryDatabaseName are used to create a connection without a DSN.

continues

Table 10.1 **Continued**

Parameter	Description
RepositoryDatabaseName	Meta Data Services database name or data source name (DSN).
RepositoryUserName	Meta Data Services username.
RepositoryUserPassword	Meta Data Services user password.
PackageGUID	Package identifier GUID string.
VersionGUID	Version identifier GUID string.
PackageName	Name of package to be loaded.
Flags	Value from the DTSRepositoryStorageFlags constants, indicating user authentication type: ■ DTSReposFlag_Default—Use Nnme and password provided. ■ DTSReposFlag_UseTrustedConnection—NT authentication
PvarPersistStgOfHost	Screen layout information associated with a package (used only by DTS Designer)

Listing 10.4 shows how to load and save a package to Microsoft Data Services Repository.

Listing 10.4 **VB Code to Load and Save a Package to a Repository**

```
Private moPackage As DTS.Package2
Set moPackage = New DTS.Package2

'Load Repository Package
moPackage.LoadFromRepository _
    "Brians_LPT\S2K", "", "", "", _
    "", "", "LoadMftCustomersToTempDB", _
    DTSReposFlag_UseTrustedConnection

'Save Repository Package
moPackage.SaveToRepositoryAs _
    "NewPackage", _
    "Brians_LPT\S2K", "", "", "", _
```

Package Load and Save SQL Server Methods

The Package and Package2 objects provide the LoadFromSQLServer method to load a DTS package from SQL Server local packages and the SaveToSQLServer and SaveToSQLServerAs methods to save a DTS package to SQL Server local packages. Listing 10.5 shows the method syntax.

Listing 10.5   **Package Load and Save to SQL Server Methods**

```
Package.LoadFromSqlServer _
  ServerName, [ServerUserName], [ServerPassword], [Flags], _
  [PackageOwnerPassword], [PackageOperatorPassword], _
  [PackageCategoryID], _
  [pVarPersistStgOfHost], _
  [bReusePasswords]

Package.SaveToSqlServer _
  ServerName, [ServerUserName], [ServerPassword], [Flags], _
  [PackageOwnerPassword], [PackageOperatorPassword], _
  [PackageCategoryID], _
  [pVarPersistStgOfHost], _
  [bReusePasswords]

Package.SaveToSqlServer _
  NewName, _
  ServerName, [ServerUserName], [ServerPassword], [Flags], _
  [PackageOwnerPassword], [PackageOperatorPassword], _
  [PackageCategoryID], _
  [pVarPersistStgOfHost], _
  [bReusePasswords]
```

Table 10.2 shows parameter use.

Table 10.2   **SQL Server Load and Save Parameters**

Parameter	Description
ServerName	Server name
ServerUserName	Server username
ServerPassword	Server user password
Flags	Value from the DTSSQLServerStorageFlags constants indicating user authentication type:
	■ DTSSQLStgFlag_Default—Use name and password provided
	■ DTSSQLStgFlag_UseTrustedConnection—NT authentication
PackagePassword	Package password if the package is encrypted

continues

Table 10.2 **Continued**

PackageGUID	Package identifier GUID string
PackageVersionGUID	Version identifier GUID string
PackageName	Package name
PvarPersistStgOfHost	Screen layout information associated with a package (used only by Package Designer)

The code in Listing 10.6 shows you how to load and save a package to a SQL server.

Listing 10.6 **VB Code to Load and Save a Package to SQL Server**

```
Private moPackage As DTS.Package2
Set moPackage = New DTS.Package

 'Load SQL Package
moPackage.LoadFromSQLServer _
  "Brians_LPT\S2K", _
  "", "", DTSSQLStgFlag_UseTrustedConnection, _
  "", "", "", "LoadMftCustomersToTempDB"

'Save SQL Package
moPackage.SaveToSQLServerAs _
  "NewName", _
  "Brians_LPT\S2K", _
  "", "", DTSSQLStgFlag_UseTrustedConnection, _
  "", "", ""
```

Package Load and Save Storage File Methods

The Package and Package2 objects provide the LoadFromStorageFile method to load a DTS package from a .dts file and the SaveToStorageFile and SaveToStorageFileAs methods to save a .dts file. Listing 10.7 shows method syntax.

Listing 10.7 **Package Load and Save to Storage File Methods**

```
Package.LoadFomStorageFile _
  UNCFile, _
  Password, [PackageGUID], [VersionGUID], [Name], _
  [pVarPersistStgOfHost]

Package.SaveToStorageFile _
  [UNCFile], [OwnerPassword], [OperatorPassword], _
  [pVarPersistStgOfHost], _
  [bReusePasswords]
```

```
Package.SaveToStorageFileAs _
  NewName, _
  [UNCFile], [OwnerPassword], [OperatorPassword], _
  [pVarPersistStgOfHost], _
  [bReusePasswords]
```

Table 10.3 shows parameter use.

Table 10.3 **Storage File Load and Save Parameters**

Parameter	Description
UNCFile	File specification of DTS package storage file
Password	Package password if the package is encrypted
PackageGUID	Package identifier GUID string
VersionGUID	Version identifier GUID string
Name	Package name
PvarPersistStgOfHost	Screen layout information associated with a package (used only by Package Designer)

The code in Listing 10.8 shows loading and saving a package to a DTS storage file.

Listing 10.8 **VB Code to Load and Save a Package to a DTS Storage File**

```
Private moPackage As DTS.Package2
Set moPackage = New DTS.Package2

moPackage.LoadFromStorageFile _
  "C:\DTS2000\Data\LoadMftCustomersToTempDB.dts", "

moPackage.SaveToStorageFile _
  "C:\DTS2000\Data\LoadMftCustomersToTempDB_2.dts"
```

Handling DTS Package Events in Visual Basic

The DTS package can raise various status and control events during package execution. If you want to receive these events, you must declare a package WithEvents and provide event handlers in either a form or class module.

A Package2 object may not be declared WithEvents. If you require Package2 functionality, it is a simple matter to create a Package object and assign it to a Package2 object. Use the Package2 object to access Package2 functionality while the Package event handlers respond to events.

After you declare a package WithEvents, you must provide event handlers for all the package events. If you fail to do so, you will receive an access violation error when an unhandled event is raised. If a particular event is not of interest, provide a minimal handler consisting of the public Sub and End Sub statements.

DTS supports multiple threads that allow concurrent processing of package steps. Visual Basic, however, does not support multiple threads. To use event handlers, it is important that you set the ExecuteInMainThread property to True for each step object in the package.

Table 10.4 describes DTS package events and the information returned when specified conditions occur.

Table 10.4 **DTS Package Events**

Event	Condition	Information Returned
OnStart	A step has started.	Step name
OnFinish	A step has completed.	Step name
OnProgress	This event occurs periodically during step execution.	Step name, progress count (which is rowcount), percentage complete, and description
OnQueryCancel	This event gives the application a chance to cancel a step.	Step name
OnError	A DTS error occurred during package execution.	Step name, error code and description, help file and context, and interface ID

The flow of DTS package events is as follows:

1. OnStart once at the beginning of each step.

2. OnQueryCancel if it is safe to terminate the step.

3. During step execution:

   - OnProgress may occur one or more times to provide progress information.

   - OnQueryCancel may occur at times when it is safe to terminate the step.

4. OnFinish once at the end of each step.

5. OnQueryCancel if it is safe to terminate the step.

   OnError may occur at any time.

Listing 10.9 shows how to set up package execution to respond to events. Code for the actual event handlers is included with the event descriptions.

Listing 10.9 **Code to Have a VB Component Respond to Package Events**

```
Private moPackageOld as DTS.Package
Private moPackage As DTS.Package2
Public moPackageEventHandler WithEvents as DTSPackage

Private Sub form_Load()
 ' Establish Package and Event Handler
  Set moPackageOld = New DTS.Package
  Set moPackage = moPackageOld
  Set moPackageEventHandler = moPackageOld

 ' All Steps/Tasks MUST run on VB Main Thread
  Dim oStep As DTS.Step
  For Each oStep In moPackage.Steps
    oStep.ExecuteInMainThread = True
  Next

 ' Execute
  moPackage.Execute

  'Cleanup
  moPackage.UnInitialize
Exit Sub
```

OnStart Event

The package raises an OnStart event at the beginning of each DTS task and step. To handle the event, you must provide a handler of the form shown in Listing 10.10.

Listing 10.10 **Using the DTS Package *OnStart* Event**

```
Private Sub moPackageEventHandler _OnStart(ByVal EventSource As String)
  MsgBox EventSource + " - " + "OnStart"
End Sub
```

In this event and all package events, moPackageEventHandler is the name of the package declared WithEvents. For all package events, tasks defined by DTS return the step name for EventSource. Custom tasks may return whatever they want.

OnFinish Event

The package raises an OnFinish event at the end of each DTS task and step. To handle the event, you must provide a handler of the form shown in Listing 10.11.

Listing 10.11 **Using the DTS Package *OnFinish* Event**

```
Private Sub moPackageEventHandler _OnFinish(ByVal EventSource As String)
  MsgBox EventSource + " - " + "OnFinish"
End Sub
```

OnProgress Event

The package raises an OnProgress event from time to time to provide task-progress information.

The ProgressRowCount property of the DataDriveQuery Task or a DataPump Task can be used to configure the number of rows processed between events.

To handle the event, you must provide a handler of the form shown in Listing 10.12.

Listing 10.12 **Code to Respond to the DTS Package *OnProgress* Event**

```
Private Sub moPackageEventHandler_OnProgress( _
  ByVal EventSource As String, _
  ByVal ProgressDescription As String, _
  ByVal PercentComplete As Long, _
  ByVal ProgressCountLow As Long, _
  ByVal ProgressCountHigh As Long)

  MessageBox ("" & _
    "ProgressDescription: " & ProgressDescription & vbCrLf & _
    "PercentComplete:     " & PercentComplete & vbCrLf & _
    "ProgressCountLow:    " & ProgressCountLow & vbCrLf & _
    "ProgressCountHigh: " & ProgressCountHigh, _
    EventSource )
End Sub
```

Table 10.5 defines OnProgress event parameters.

Table 10.5 *OnProgress* Event Parameters

Parameter	Description
EventSource	Source of event being executed. Tasks defined by DTS return the step name for EventSource. Custom tasks may return whatever they want.
ProgressDescription	Description of task progress.
PercentComplete	Percentage of task completed. If the percentage completed cannot be reported, 0 is returned.
ProgressCountLow	Low 32 bits of units (such as rows) completed.
ProgressCountHigh	High 32 bits of units (such as rows) completed.

OnQueryCancel Event

The package raises an OnQueryCancel event only when it is safe to stop execution of the task. Use this event to terminate package execution gracefully.

To handle the event, you must provide a handler of the form shown in Listing 10.13.

Listing 10.13 Code to Interact with the DTS Package *OnQueryCancel* Event

```
Private Sub moPackageEventHandler_OnQueryCancel( _
  ByVal EventSource As String, _
  pbCancel As Boolean)

  if MsgBox ("Continue to Execute",vbOKCancel) = OK then
    pbCancel = False
  Else
    pbCancel = True
  End If
End Sub
```

If pbCancel is set to True by the event handler, DTS stops task execution and fails with an error. If a task completes quickly, the event may not occur.

About pbCancel

The value of pbCancel may be True or False when the event is raised.

It is important to explicitly set pbCancel to False if you do not want to cancel execution!

OnError Event

The package raises an OnError event to indicate and provide information about an error. The event also allows the event handler to cancel task execution. A step does not terminate after an error unless the MaximumErrorCount is exceeded or the event handler explicitly sets pbCancel to True.

To handle the event, you must provide a handler of the form shown in Listing 10.14.

Listing 10.14 Code to Respond to the DTS Package *OnError* Event

```
Private Sub moPackageEventHandler_OnError( _
  ByVal EventSource As String, _
  ByVal ErrorCode As Long, _
  ByVal Source As String, _
  ByVal Description As String, _
  ByVal HelpFile As String, _
  ByVal HelpContext As Long, _
```

continues

Listing 10.14 **Continued**

```
ByVal IDofInterfaceWithError As String, _
pbCancel As Boolean)

If MsgBox ( _
  "ErrorCode:     " & ErrorCode & vbCrLf & _
  "Source:      " & Source & vbCrLf & _
  "Description:  " & Description & vbCrLf & _
  "HelpFile:     " & HelpFile & vbCrLf & _
  "IDofIFWErr:  " & IdofInterfaceWithError, _
  EventSource, _
  VbOkCancel) <> vbOK then
  pbCancel = False
Else
  pbCancel = True
End If
End Sub
```

Table 10.6 defines OnError event parameters.

Table 10.6 *OnError* **Event Parameters**

Parameter	Description
EventSource	Source of event being executed. Tasks defined by DTS return the step name for EventSource. Custom tasks may return whatever they want.
ErrorCode	Error code of the failure.
Source	Source of error message (an OLE DB provider description, for example).
Description	Description of the error.
HelpFile	Help-file name.
HelpContext	Help context ID.
IDOfInterfaceWithError	ID of the user interface returning the error, a globally unique identifier (GUID).
PbCancel	If pbCancel is set to True by the event handler, DTS stops task execution.

Handling DTS Package Errors in Visual Basic

At the highest level, a DTS object property set, get, or method execution succeeds or fails. Errors that occur while you are creating DTS objects and setting their properties are to be dealt with using standard VB error handling.

The package `FailOnError` property specifies whether package execution halts on any step error. A step `FailPackageOnError` property determines whether package execution halts when an error occurs in that step. Unless one of these properties is set to `True`, errors that occur during `Package` or `Package2` Execute are processed by DTS and are not propagated back to the caller.

When `FailOnError` or `FailPackageOnError` is `True`, the description of the returned error often tells you only that the package failed because a (named) step failed. To determine why a step failed, you query each step's `GetExecutionErrorInfo` for more information. To determine which step(s) raised errors, the `ExecutionStatus` property of the step should be `DTSStepExecStat_Completed`, and the `ExecutionResult` property should have the value `DTSStepExecResult_Failure`.

If `FailOnError` is `True`, an error may have occurred in only one step. Otherwise, depending on package workflow, multiple steps may have failed.

The error handler needs to iterate through all the objects in the Steps collection to find all errors.

The code in Listing 10.15 shows a typical package error handler.

Listing 10.15 **Code to Manage DTS Package Errors**

```
Private Sub RunDTSPackage( )
  Dim xoPackage As New DTS.Package
  On Error GoTo PackageError
  ...
  xoPackage.FailOnError = True
  xoPackage.Execute
  Unload me
  Exit Sub

PackageError:
  MsgBox( "Package Error: " & Err.Number _
    & Err.Description & vbCrLf _
    & PackageErrors(moPackage), _
    vbExclamation, App.EXEName
  Unload Me
  Exit Sub
End Sub

Private Function PackageErrors(ByVal aoPackage As DTS.Package2) As String
  Dim xoStep      As DTS.Step
  Dim xsMessage   As String
  Dim xlErrNum    As Long
  Dim xsDescription As String
  Dim xsSource    As String

  If xoPackage Is Not Nothing Then
    'Find Steps that Failed
    'Steps that did not execute are ignored
```

continues

Listing 10.15 **Continued**

```
    For Each xoStep In aoPackage.Steps
       If oStep.ExecutionStatus = DTSStepExecStat_Completed _
       And oStep.ExecutionResult = DTSStepExecResult_Failure Then
         'Populate Error information
         oStep.GetExecutionErrorInfo xlErrNum, _
           xsSource, xsDescription
         'Build Error Message
         xsMessage = xsMessage & vbCrLf _
           & "Step " & xoStep.Name & " failed, error: " _
           & xlErrNum & vbCrLf _
           & xsDescription
       End If
    Next
    PackageErrors = sMessage
         End If
End Function
```

Processing Multiple Input Files

Now that you have a better understanding of the issues and techniques for accessing the DTS object model in Visual Basic, let's take a look at some real problems.

There are many situations when the data you require is located in many files or directories. DTS has no trouble loading data from a single file or even from all the files in a directory *at the time the package is created*. It is more complicated to set up a package to scan a directory and process all files.

Scenario

Sparks Corporation is attempting to get a better handle on its shipping and receiving. To meet this objective, they purchased handheld scanners for every shipping clerk.

Each package is scanned as it is shipped or received. The scanners, which normally are disconnected from the network, are set in a docking station daily to recharge their batteries and download data to a network drive, C:\DTS2000\Data\Scanner.[2]

Each scanner stores data in a separate file, using the name Scanner_SCANNERID_YYYYMMDD_HHMM.csv. SCANNERID is the scanner's identifier. YYYYMMMDD_HHMM is the year, month, day, hour, and minute of the last entry in the file. Table 10.7 defines the file format.

---

2. All data files and scripts used in the book are available for download from http://www.magenic.com/publications or http://www.newriders.com. The self-extracting ZIP file will create a directory structure starting with DTS2000. You can extract the files to any drive or directory, but all file references in this book are based on C:\DTS2000\.

Table 10.7   **Scanner File Format**

Field	Description
Scanner	Scanner ID
Time	Scanned date and time
Sequence	Scanner independent sequence number, used to ensure that no data is missing
BarCode	The bar code scanned
ShipReceive	'S' for shipments, 'R' for items received

You have been asked to create a program to load the data into SQL Server.

Solution

Build a package that can load a single file. Then use a VB program to scan the directory and call the package once for each file.

First, you create a package that can load a single scanner .csv file. Then use the DTS Import Wizard to create a package as follows:[3]

- Data Source: text file `C:\DTS2000\Data\Scanner\Scanner_hp1234z_ 20010209_1050.csv`.

- File Format: Delimited, Skip=0. First row has column names; accept the default settings for all other fields.

- Column Delimiter: comma.

- Destination: your SQL Server tempdb.

- Select Source Tables: Change `[tempdb].[dbo].[Scanner_....]` to `[tempdb].[dbo].[ScannerData]`.

- Run: Yes.

- Save: To SQL Server package `LoadScannerToTempDb`.

Before running the package again, you need to modify the LoadScannerToTempDb Task so that it does not attempt to create the table if it exists. Follow these steps:

1. Open the package, using DTS Designer.

2. Select the Create Table `[tempdb].[dbo].[ScannerData]`, and insert the following SQL statement before `Create Table`:

3. All data files and scripts used in the book, including this package LoadScannertoTempDB. dts, are available for download from `http://www.magenic.com/publications` or `http:// www.newriders.com`. The self-extracting ZIP file will create a directory structure starting with `DTS2000`. All packages in this book are located in the `Packages` subdirectory of the `\DTS2000` directory.

```
if not exists (select * from tempdb..sysobjects where id =
object_id('[tempdb].[dbo].[ScannerData]'))
```

3. Save the package to C:\DTS2000\WorkSpace\LoadScannerToTempDb.dts.

Now all that remains is to create the VB program to process many files. Follow these steps:

1. Open VB, and begin a standard .exe.

2. Reference the DTS object model.

3. Set up the program to handle DTS package events and errors as described in "Handling DTS Package Events in Visual Basic" and "Handling DTS Package Errors in Visual Basic" earlier in this chapter.

4. Include code to find the scanner data files, load the package, and execute once for each file (see Listing 10.16).

Listing 10.16   **VB Program to Scan a Directory and Call a DTS Package Once for Each File**

```
Private moPackage As DTS.Package2
Private moPackageOld As DTS.Package
Private WithEvents moPackageEventHandler As DTS.Package

Private Sub Form_Load()
  Dim xsDir As String        'Directory to Processes
  Dim xoFiles As New Collection  'List of Files to Process
  Dim xsFile As Variant      'File Name
  Dim xiFile As Integer      'File Handle
Dim xsBuffer As String       'File I/O buffer
  Dim xsTry As String        'Tell ErrorHandler whatz up

  On Error GoTo PackageError

  'Get Directory
  If UBound(Split(Command())) > 1 Then
    xsDir = Split(Command())(1)
  Else
    xsDir = mksScannerDataDir
  End If
  xsDir = xsDir & IIf(Right(xsDir, 1) <> "\", "\", "")

  'Get File List
  xsFile = Dir(xsDir & mksScannerFiles, vbNormal)
  While xsFile <> ""
    xoFiles.Add xsFile
    xsFile = Dir()
  Wend
```

```
'Load DTS Package
Set moPackageOld = New Package
Set moPackage = moPackageOld
Set moPackageOld = Nothing
moPackage.LoadFromStorageFile mksPackageName, ""

'Process Files
For Each xsFile In xoFiles
  'Verify File Format
  '  Could not be done in file load loop
  '  ANY file I/O between dir calls
  '  may cause it to lose it's place
  xiFile = FreeFile()
  Open xsDir & xsFile For Input As xiFile
    Line Input #xiFile, xsBuffer
  Close xiFile
  If UCase(Trim(xsBuffer)) = mksScannerData Then
    'Establish an Event Handler
    Set moPackageEventHandler = moPackage
    'Set DataSource
    moPackage.Connections("Connection 1").DataSource = _
      xsDir & xsFile
    'All Steps/Tasks MUST run on VB Main Thread
    Dim oStep As DTS.Step
    For Each oStep In moPackage.Steps
      oStep.ExecuteInMainThread = True
    Next
    'Let VB see Errors
    moPackage.FailOnError = True
    'Execute
    moPackage.Execute
    txtDTSEvents = txtDTSEvents & vbCrLf & vbCrLf
  Else
    txtDTSEvents = txtDTSEvents & vbCrLf & _
      " Error: Not a Scanner Data File" & vbCrLf & vbCrLf
  End If
Next

'Cleanup
moPackage.UnInitialize
Set moPackage = Nothing
Exit Sub

PackageError:
...
End Sub
```

As you can see, the most complicated part of the job is looking for the files and verifying the format. With that done, it is a simple matter to set the package connection information and execute the package. See C:\DTS2000\VBPackages\ ProcessManyFiles\ ProcessManyFiles.vbp for the complete code.

All that remains is to insert or update records from `tempdb` into the MFT database.

Processing Multiple Spreadsheets

DTS provides an interface for many OLE DB-compliant data sources. Excel is no exception. If you were to point the DTS Wizard at an Excel workbook, it would build a Create Table and Import Task for each spreadsheet.

This would be fine if each spreadsheet contained different data, but the spreadsheets may have similar data and are separated only to make editing and viewing more manageable. In this case, you could use a postload process to combine the data into a single table. However, people like to play with workbooks, so there is a good chance that one spreadsheet will have a slightly different format, making it difficult to postprocess.

Scenario

Sparks Corporation does work in the United States, Mexico, and Canada. It is important that they have up-to-date accurate currency information. The accounting department has been maintaining a currency workbook. Each currency is maintained in its own spreadsheet. Each spreadsheet contains date, currency, and currency exchange information (see C:\DTS2000\Data\Currency.xls).

You have been asked to develop a program to load the data into the MFT database once a month.

Solution

Build a package that can load a single spreadsheet. Then build a VB program to load each spreadsheet.

First, create a package that can load a single Excel spreadsheet. Go to C: \ DTS2000\Packages\SqlServer2000\LoadCurrencyToTempDb.dts. Then use the DTS Import Wizard to create a package as follows:

- Data Source: Excel 97-2000 (see C:\DTS2000\Data\Curency.xls)
- Destination: Your SQL Server tempdb
- Select Source Tables: Select the USD table and set the destination to `[tempdb].[dbo].[Currency]`
- Run: Yes
- Save: To SQL Server package `LoadCurrencyToTempDb`

Before running the package again, you need to modify the LoadScannerToTempDb Task so that it does not attempt to create the table if it exists. Follow these steps:

1. Open the package, using DTS Designer.

2. Select the create table [tempdb].[dbo].[Currency], and insert the following at the top of the SQL statement:

```
if not exists (select * from tempdb..sysobjects where id =
object_id('[tempdb].[dbo].[Currency]'))
```

3. Save the package to C:\DTS2000\WorkSpace\LoadCurrencyToTempDb.dts.

All that remains is to create the VB program to process many files. Follow these steps:

1. Open VB, and begin a standard .exe.

2. Reference the DTS object model.

3. Set up Form1 with the txtDtsEvent, Event, and Error process as shown in Listing 10.16.

4. Include code to find the scanner data files, load the package, and execute once for each file (see Listing 10.17).

Listing 10.17 **VB Program to Find Scanner Data Files in an Excel Spreadsheet, Load a DTS Package, and Execute it Many Times by Changing the Connection**

```
Private moPackage As DTS.Package2
Private moPackageOld As DTS.Package
Private WithEvents moPackageEventHandler As DTS.Package

Const mksPackageName = _
    "C:\DTS2000\Packages\SQLServer2000\LoadCurrencyToTempDb.dts"
Const mksCurrencyFile = "C:\DTS2000\Data\Currency.xls"
Option Explicit

Private Sub Form_Load()
  On Error GoTo PackageError

 'Define Excel Objects
  Dim xoXL As Excel.Application
  Dim xoWB As Excel.Workbook
  Dim xoSheet As Excel.Worksheet
  Dim xoRange As Excel.Range

  Dim xoSheets As New Collection
  Dim xsSheetName As Variant

  Dim xsSql As String

' Start Excel, Get Application Object and Open Workbook
  Set xoXL = CreateObject("Excel.Application")
  xoXL.Visible = False
```

continues

Listing 10.17 **Continued**

```
' Load DTS Package
Set moPackageOld = New Package
Set moPackage = moPackageOld
Set moPackageOld = Nothing
moPackage.LoadFromStorageFile mksPackageName, ""

' Validate SpreadSheets
For Each xoSheet In xoWB.Sheets
  If UCase(xoSheet.Cells(1, 1)) = "DATE" _
  And UCase(xoSheet.Cells(1, 2)) = "CURRENCY" _
  And UCase(xoSheet.Cells(1, 3)) = "CONVERSIONFACTOR" _
  Then
    xoSheets.Add xoSheet.Name
  Else
    Msgbox ("Validate: " & xoSheet.Name & _
      "Not a Currency Spreadsheet"
  End If
Next

' Release Excel Object References prior to Executing Package
Set xoRange = Nothing
Set xoSheet = Nothing
xoWB.Close
Set xoWB = Nothing
xoXL.Visible = False
xoXL.UserControl = False
Set xoXL = Nothing

' Process SpreadSheets
For Each xsSheetName In xoSheets
  'Establish an Event Handler
  Set moPackageEventHandler = moPackage
  'Set DataSource
' Only by Scripting the Package to VB and looking at the code
  ' will you have a hope of knowing where to set this
  ' Beware the Single Quote is a "`" not a "'"
  moPackage.Connections("Connection 1").DataSource = _
    mksCurrencyFile
  If xsSql = "" Then
    xsSql = moPackage.Tasks( _
      "Copy Data from USD$ to [tempdb].[dbo].[Currency] Task"). _
        Properties( "SourceSQLStatement").Value
    xsSql = Left(xsSql, InStr(xsSql, "`USD$`") - 1)
  End If
  moPackage.Tasks( _
    "Copy Data from USD$ to [tempdb].[dbo].[Currency] Task"). _
      Properties("SourceSQLStatement").Value = _
        xsSql & "`" & xsSheetName & "$`"
  'All Steps/Tasks MUST run on VB Main Thread
  Dim oStep As DTS.Step
  For Each oStep In moPackage.Steps
    oStep.ExecuteInMainThread = True
```

```
    Next
    'Execute
    moPackage.Execute
  Next

  'Cleanup
  moPackage.UnInitialize
  Set moPackage = Nothing
Exit Sub
```

Listing 10.17 is a little more complex. First, you create an Excel object and use it to verify spreadsheets.

Processing a spreadsheet requires a little more work. The DTS `DataSource` does not change. Instead, you need to modify the connection `SourceSqlStatement`. OLE DB exposes each spreadsheet in a workbook as `SpreadSheetName$`. To get the package to access a different spreadsheet, you modify the `SourceSQLStatement`, stripping off the `USD$` generated for the original package and replacing it with `SpreadSheet$`. See C:\DTS2000\VBPackages\ProcessManyFiles\ProcessManySpeadSheets.vbp for the complete code.

You could have written code to select only currencies that interest you, but it's less work to exclude them when you copy the data from `tempdb` to the MFT database.

Loading XML via DTS

XML is a powerful platform-independent markup language used to represent data. It is the hottest new technology for moving data among computer applications on the same computer, different computers, or even different operating systems.

Simple XML Document Format

An XML document is created using an eXtensible markup language. In its simplest format, an XML document begins with the XML version tag, followed by a document begin tag (`<DocumentName >`), one or more elements, and a document end tag (`<\DocumentName >`).

Each element consists of a element header (`<ElementTag>`) and one or more `Attribute` = `Value` pairs, terminated by a element termination (`>`), as shown in Listing 10.18.

Listing 10.18   **XML Format**

```
<?xml version="1.0"?>
<DocumentName>
<Element Attribute = Value … >
<Element Attribute = Value … >
...
<\DocumentName>
```

Currently, there is no OLE-DB interface for processing XML documents. As a result, DTS cannot process XML directly. Using VB, however, you can load an XML document and convert it to a .csv file that can be processed in the usual manner.

XML does not limit the number of elements in a document. Smaller documents can be processed without much effort. If the document is large (100,000 elements or more), the parser will attempt to load the entire file. At best, this may take a long time; at worst, it will consume all memory, causing the system to hang.

To deal with large XML documents, you need to read the XML stream and pass it into the parser in smaller chunks.

Scenario

Sparks Corporation does work in the United States, Mexico, and Canada. It is important that they have up-to-date, accurate currency information. Previously, the accounting department maintained a currency workbook, but it recently began to store the information as an XML document, as shown in Listing 10.19 (see C:\DTS2000\Data\Currency.xml).

Listing 10.19   **XML Currency Data**

```
<?xml version="1.0"?>
<Currencies>
<Currency Currency="USD" Date="1998-04-01T00:00:00"
  ConversionFactor="1.0000"/>
<Currency Currency="USD" Date="1998-05-01T00:00:00"
  ConversionFactor="1.0000"/>
...
</Currencies>
```

You have been asked to develop a program to load the XML data into the MFT database once a month.

Solution

Write a VB program to convert the XML document to .csv format. Then use the LoadCurrencyToTempdb package to load the data into SQL Server.

Listing 10.20 shows the code for converting XML to .csv.

Listing 10.20   **VB Program to Convert XML Documents and Then Load Them with DTS**

```
' DTS 2000 - Process Many Files
Const mksCurrencyXmlFile = "C:\DTS2000\Data\Currency.xml"
Const mksCurrency'.CSV'File = "C:\DTS2000\WorkSpace\Currency.'.csv'"
Const mksXMLVersion As String = "<?xml version=""1.0""?>"
Const mksXMLStartTag As String = "<Currencies>"
```

```
Const mksXMLEndTag As String = "</Currencies>"
Const mksXMLTagName As String = "Currency"

Const mksPackageName = _
  "C:\DTS2000\Packages\SQLServer2000\LoadXMLCurrencyToTempDb.dts"

Private moPackage As DTS.Package2
Private moPackageOld As DTS.Package
Private WithEvents moPackageEventHandler As DTS.Package

Option Explicit

Private Sub form_load()
  On Error GoTo PackageError

 ' Load XML and Convert to '.CSV'
  Dim xiXmlFile, xsXmlDoc As String, xsXmlText As String
  Dim xi'.csv'File

  xiXmlFile = FreeFile()
  Open mksCurrencyXmlFile For Input As xiXmlFile

  xi'.csv'File = FreeFile()
  Open mksCurrency'.CSV'File For Output As xi'.csv'File
  Print #xi'.csv'File, "Currency,Date,ConversionFactor"

  xsXmlDoc = ""
  While Not EOF(xiXmlFile)
    Line Input #xiXmlFile, xsXmlText
    'Strip Out XML Version
    'Document Begin and End Tags
    If InStr(xsXmlText, mksXMLVersion) = 0 _
    And InStr(xsXmlText, mksXMLStartTag) = 0 Then
      xsXmlDoc = xsXmlDoc & xsXmlText
    End If
    'When there is no more data
    'Or the chunk is large enough, process
    If EOF(xiXmlFile) or Len(xsXmlDoc) > 4098 Then
      SaveXmlTo'.csv' xi'.csv'File, _
        mksXMLVersion & mksXMLStartTag & _
        xsXmlDoc & mksXMLEndTag
      xsXmlDoc = ""
    End If
  Wend
  Close xiXmlFile
  Close xi'.csv'File

' Load DTS Package
Set moPackageOld = New Package
Set moPackage = moPackageOld
```

continues

Listing 10.20 **Continued**

```
   Set moPackageOld = Nothing
   moPackage.LoadFromStorageFile mksPackageName, ""

   'Process File
   'Point the Source Connection to the .'.csv' File
   moPackage.Connections("Connection 1").DataSource = _
       mksCurrency'.CSV'File
   'All Steps/Tasks MUST run on VB Main Thread
   Dim oStep As DTS.Step
   For Each oStep In moPackage.Steps
     oStep.ExecuteInMainThread = True
   Next
   'Execute
   moPackage.Execute

   'Cleanup
   moPackage.UnInitialize
   Set moPackage = Nothing
   Unload Me
   Exit Sub
End Sub

Private Sub SaveXmlTo'.csv'(ai'.csv'File, asXmlDoc)
   Dim aoXmlDoc As MSXML.DOMDocument
   Dim aoRecords As MSXML.IXMLDOMNodeList
   Dim aoRecord As MSXML.IXMLDOMNode
   Dim ai

   'Declare a XML Document and Load it
   Set aoXmlDoc = New MSXML.DOMDocument
   aoXmlDoc.async = False
   aoXmlDoc.loadXML (asXmlDoc)

   'Step Through XML Nodes and Export as '.CSV'
   Set aoRecords = aoXmlDoc.getElementsByTagName(mksXMLTagName)
   For ai = 0 To (aoRecords.Length - 1)
     Set aoRecord = aoRecords.nextNode
     Print #ai'.csv'File, _
       aoRecord.Attributes.getNamedItem("Currency").Text & "," _
       & aoRecord.Attributes.getNamedItem("Date").Text & "," _
       & aoRecord.Attributes.getNamedItem("ConversionFactor").Text
   Next
   End Sub
```

In the first half of the code, you parse the input XML document and break it into manageable chunks—in this case, 4K, but larger chunks (64K or more) are possible.

While reading the input document, you strip off the XML, Document Start and Document End tags. However, Microsoft's XMP Parser requires properly formatted

XML documents. Prior to giving the chunk to the parser, you must wrap it in each chunk with XML Document Start, and Document End tags.

To process the chunk, set the parser's `async` property to `False` and force synchronous loading. Use `getElementsbyTagName` to retrieve a collection of records. Use `nextNode` to step through every record, and use `Attributes.getNamedItem("AtributeName")` to retrieve field data, which is formatted and written to a .csv file.

When the original file is consumed, you can pass the .csv file to the LoadCurrencyToTempdb DTS package for processing. See C:\DTS2000\ VBPackages\ProcessXml\ProcessXml.vbp for the complete code.

All that remains is to insert or update the records from `tempdb` into your destination database.

XML for SQL Server 2000

As an alternative to the solution discussed in this section, you can use the XML Bulk Load component from Microsoft. The XML Bulk Load component gives you high-speed XML-based data loading directly into SQL Server tables. This component is distributed free from Microsoft at `http://www.microsoft. com/xml`. When it is installed, you can execute from any programming language that can work with ActiveX components, such as Visual Basic, VC++, and even VBScript in DTS.

To load an XML document using XML Bulk Load, you will need to provide a mapping of the XML elements to SQL Server tables and fields; this mapping is called XDR Schema. The XDR (XML Data Reduced) Schema is an XML-like document that describes the structure of an XML document and can contain the relational equivalence for the data. For example, the XML Document in Listing 10.19 will have an XDR Schema similar to the one in Listing 10.21.

Please note that the XDR Schema has a section that contains the XML element's name and associated data type, followed by a section that maps each element to the DBMS `sql:relation` (table in SQL Server) and `sql:field` (field in the referenced SQL Server table). For this example, the data goes into the table Currency and loads data into three fields: Currency, Date, and ConversionFactor.

Listing 10.21 **XDR Document for Listing 10.19**

```
    <?xml version "1.0" ?>
<Schema xmlns="urn:schemas-microsoft-com:xml-data"
    xmlns:dt="urn:schemas-microsoft-com:xml:datatypes"
    xmlns:sql="urn:schmas-microsoft-com:xml-sql">

<ElementType name="Currency" dt:type="string"/>
<ElementType name="Date" dt:type="datetime"/>
<ElementType name="ConversionFactor dt:type="numeric"/>
```

continues

Listing 10.21 **Continued**

```
<ElementType name="Currencies" sql:relation="Currency">
    <element type="Currency" sql:field="Currency"/>
    <element type="Date" sql:field="Date"/>
    <element type="ConversionFactor" sql:field="ConversionFactor"/>
</Element type>
    </Schema>
```

To use the XML Bulk Load component in DTS, you need to use the ActiveX Script Task. First, create an instance of the XML Bulk Load object, connect it to SQL Server by setting the `ConnectionString` property, and then execute it while referencing an XDR Schema and the XML document. Listing 10.22 shows the structure of the code. Please note that the XML Bulk Load has a full object model to support the work, and many more properties are available than the ones discussed in this example. The code in Listing 10.22 sets the `ErrorLog` file location.

Listing 10.22 **ActiveX Script That Loads an XML Document called SampleXMLDocument, Using the SampleXDRSchema.xml for the Data Mappings, and Outputs All Errors into ErrorLog.txt**

```
set oBulkLoad = CreateObject("SQLXMLBulkLoad.SQLXMLBulkLoad")
oBulkLoad.ConnectionString = "provider=SQLOLEDB.1;data
source=ServerName;database=DatabaseName"
oBulkLoad.ErrorLogFile = "c:\ErrorLog.txt"
oBulkLoad.Execute = "c:\SampleXDRSchema.xml", "c:\SampleXMLDocument.XML"
set oBulkLoad = Nothing
```

The XML Bulk Load can load data into either single or multiple tables; you just have to make sure that the correct mappings are in the XDR Schema. For more information on the XML Bulk Load as well as full documentation, visit the XML site at Microsoft.com. For more information on XDR Schemas, see SQL Server Books Online.

Processing Outlook via DTS

Email is pervasive in modern business because it is one of the simplest methods of moving data among different computers or even operating systems. Many programs email data to subscribers automatically. What is missing is an automated method for loading email data into SQL Server.

Scenario

MFT has relocated accounting to an office in another city. Each month, it emails Currency.xml to you. You need to develop a program to scan incoming email and process any messages that contain Currency.xml data.

Solution

The best solution to the preceeding scenario is to develop a program to scan email and feed any Currency.xml documents to the package developed in the previous solution.

    When developing the application, you need an early-bound reference to a Microsoft Outlook-type library. Table 10.8 lists the filenames of the type libraries for the different versions of Microsoft Outlook.

Table 10.8 **Outlook Object References**

Outlook Version	How Type Library Appears in References List	Filename
Outlook 97	Microsoft Outlook 8.0 Object Library	msoutl8.olb
Msoutl8.olb	Microsoft Outlook 98 Object Library	msoutl85.olb
Outlook 2000	Microsoft Outlook 9.0 Object Library	msoutl9.olb

The code in Listing 10.23 shows scanning and processing email.

Listing 10.23 **VB Program to Scan Emails and Process Them with DTS**

```
Private moPackage As DTS.Package2
Private moPackageOld As DTS.Package

Const mksPackageName = _
   "C:\DTS2000\Packages\SQLServer2000\LoadCurrencyToTempDb.dts"
Const mksCurrencyFile = "C:\DTS2000\Data\Currency.xls"
Option Explicit

Private Sub Form_Load()
  Dim xoOutlook As Outlook.Application
  Dim xoNameSpace As Outlook.NameSpace
  Dim xoMail As Outlook.MailItem

  Dim xi'.csv'File
  Dim xsTry As String

  On Error GoTo PackageError

' Start Outlook.
  Set xoOutlook = CreateObject("Outlook.Application")

' Logon. No affect if you are already running and logged on
  Set xoNameSpace = xoOutlook.GetNamespace("MAPI")
  xoNameSpace.Logon

' Open '.csv' File
  xi'.csv'File = FreeFile()
```

continues

Listing 10.23   **Continued**

```
Open mksCurrency'.CSV'File For Output As xi'.csv'File
  Print #xi'.csv'File, "Currency,Date,ConversionFactor"

' Cycle Through Inbox, looking for CurrencyXML Message(s)
For Each xoMail In xoOutlook.Session.Folders( _
  "Mailbox - Brian Sullivan").Folders("inbox").Items
    If UCase(olMail.Subject) = "CURRENCY XML" Then
      SaveXmlTo'.csv' xi'.csv'File, _
        mksXMLVersion & mksXMLStartTag & _
          xoMail.Body & _
          mksXMLEndTag
    End If
Next

' Clean up Outlook
xoNameSpace.Logoff
Set xoNameSpace = Nothing
Set xoMail = Nothing
Set xoOutlook = Nothing

' Close '.CSV' file
Close xi'.csv'File

' Load DTS Package
Set moPackageOld = New Package
Set moPackage = moPackageOld
Set moPackageOld = Nothing
moPackage.LoadFromStorageFile mksPackageName, ""
  ...
End Sub
```

The first portion of Listing 10.23 deals with scanning email and extracting XML data to a .csv file. The rest of the code is similar to previous examples.

Divide and conquer is a powerful tool. Separating data extraction from data loading allows you to use known tools to find the data and then allows DTS to transform and load it quickly. See C:\DTS2000\VBPackages\ProcessOutlook\ProcessOutlook.vbp for the complete code.

Summary

In this chapter we have gone through several situations that showed you how to use Visual Basic to run, control, and respond to DTS packages. We covered event handling, error handling, and executing packages. We have used those basics to make DTS packages participate in a variety of solutions in which an external program can provide assistance. This is by no means all there is about writing applications to interact with DTS, but it is my hope that this chapter will provide you with a framework for many of your Visual Basic and ETL application needs.

DTS and the Business Intelligence Process

11

Introduction to Data Warehousing and Analysis Services

Making BETTER BUSINESS DECISIONS QUICKLY is the key to succeeding in today's competitive marketplace. Organizations seeking to improve their decision-making ability can be overwhelmed by the sheer volume and complexity of data available from their varied operational and production systems. Making this data accessible is one of the most significant challenges for today's information-technology professionals.

In response to this challenge, many organizations choose to build a data warehouse to unlock the information in their operational systems. A *data warehouse* is an integrated store of information collected from other systems that becomes the foundation for decision support and data analysis. Although many types of data warehouses exist, based on different design methodologies and philosophical approaches, they have these common traits:

- Information is organized around the major subjects of the enterprise (such as customers, products, sales, or vendors), reflecting a business-process-driven design.

- Raw data is gathered from nonintegrated operational and legacy applications, cleansed, and then summarized and presented in a way that makes sense to end users.

- Based on feedback from end users and discoveries in the data warehouse, the data warehouse architecture changes over time, reflecting the iterative nature of the process.

Data Warehouse Versus Operational Transaction-Oriented Database

Many organizations feel that they have plenty of data, so why should an organization create and manage a copy of the data? The same organizations also feel that they aren't leveraging the information they already have. The goals of the data warehouse versus the transactional database are as follows:

- The goal of the data warehouse is to store data designed to help managers make better decisions by using a subset of transactional data or integrating data from multiple transactional systems.

- The goal of a transactional database is to store all relevant data of a business unit, down to the granularity of the transaction.

A data warehouse is a collection of data in support of management's decision-making process that is subject-oriented, integrated, time-variant, and nonvolatile. The data warehouse focuses on the concept (such as sales) rather than the process (such as issuing invoices). It contains all relevant information on a concept gathered from multiple processing systems.

The *online transaction database* (OLTP) is designed for speed of operation in processing business transactions, striking a balance between record insertion and report generation. The database is designed with normalized tables. To *normalize* is to minimize the duplications of data in a relational database through effective table design. During the design of a relational database, the core components that define an entity are identified as the columns of the normalized table. Other components of that entity, particularly components that have repeating values, are moved to a separate table known as a *lookup table*. This arrangement allows for faster data processing while minimizing storage requirements. Many production transactional databases perform hundreds of thousands of transactions each day.

Data in the data warehouse can be stored in different ways. Data can be stored as summary information, for example. You may choose to summarize invoice information as one entry for the order, rather than store all the line items. Alternatively, you may choose to have the granularity at the daily level. In this case, you would have just one entry for the day's data.

Data warehousing is aimed at the timely delivery of the right information to the right people in an organization. This process is ongoing, not a one-time solution, and requires a different approach from that required to develop transaction-oriented systems.

Data warehouses are often associated with software tools called Online Analytical Processing (OLAP). OLAP tools enable client applications to access the data warehouse data efficiently. OLAP stores the data in an intuitive multidimensional structure called *cubes*.

The data warehouse requires an architecture that differs from that of an OLTP system because it is designed for rapidly querying decision-support information. Table 11.1 outlines some of the differences.

Table 11.1 **The Major Differences Between OLTP and OLAP**

OLTP	OLAP
Highly normalized	Somewhat denormalized
Allow many users to create, update, and delete information	Allow many users read-only access, although write-back OLAP can allow users to do such things as enter their own variable values for what-if analysis
Many small transactions	Usually a daily or weekly load
Key issues are record locking, transactions, high volume, high user concurrency, and performance	Key issues are data consistency, reporting flexibility, size, and query performance
Users are data-entry personnel	Users are managers, analysts, and other knowledge workers
All business-transaction data	A select subset of data, many times coming from multiple sources
Tuning is for performance of transactions	Tuning involves balancing data-load performance with query performance
Constantly changing	Changes less frequently (loads may be monthly or daily)

Difference Between a Data Warehouse and a Data Mart

A data warehouse often is made up of a set of data marts. A *data mart* is a set of data centered on a particular business process or topic (see "Data Marts" later in this chapter). Sales will have a data mart, manufacturing will have its own mart, and human resources will have one as well. The combination of these data marts, which often are read-only, is a data warehouse.

Dimensional Modeling

The data in a data mart is designed to be queried by users to answer questions about unique aspects of their business. Querying speed will be your primary focus when you design your data warehouse. To accomplish this goal, use a dimensional data model.

The development phase of the data warehousing process often begins with the creation of a dimensional model that describes the important metrics and dimensions of the selected subject area. Unlike online transaction processing systems, which organize data in a highly normalized manner, the data in the data warehouse is organized in a highly denormalized manner to improve query performance when stored in a relational database management system.

Relational databases may use star or snowflake schemas to provide the fastest possible response times to complex queries. *Star schemas* contain a single central fact table for the subject area and multiple dimension tables for information about the subject's dimensions. The fact table can contain millions of rows. Commonly accessed information may be preaggregated and summarized to further improve performance. Figure 11.1 shows an example of a star schema.

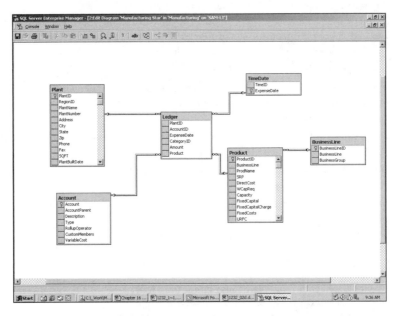

Figure 11.1 Star-schema example.

Although the star schema is considered to be primarily a tool for the database administrator to use to increase performance and simplify data warehouse design, it also represents data warehouse information in a way that makes better sense to end users.

Business Modeling

When you consider what elements to include in your data warehouse, first consider who will be using the data. If you are building the warehouse for a sales department, including manufacturing data may make little sense. Likewise, a manufacturing manager will be more concerned about inventory and production costs than about marketing information. The data warehouse will be broken into subsets of relevant information for differing groups of users. Each subset will be a data mart.

Data Marts

The complete data warehouse will consist of a series of data marts. You may have one for manufacturing information, one for sales information, and one for profit-and-loss information. You will construct your data warehouse one data mart at a time.

When you consider what elements to include in your data mart, you must not only satisfy your core user group, but also consider what information senior management wants. Data marts allow you to implement a large project as a series of smaller, easier-to-manage projects. All the marts together become the data warehouse. (Refer to Figure 11.1 for a diagram of a data mart.)

The Operational Data Store

You will no doubt run across several implementations of operational data stores (ODSs). Within organizations that have several legacy database systems, you may find a separate relational database system that collects data from these legacy systems and stores it in a central location. Then the legacy systems communicate with the ODS when it needs to use information from another legacy system.

Many organizations have a series of modern-generation databases that communicate directly with one another, eliminating the need for a central database used as the ODS.

For every situation you are faced with, you will need to identify a place to acquire your data for your data warehouse. You can use Microsoft's Data Transformation Services to connect to these ODS sources and bring the data into your staging area. If an ODS is not utilized, you can use Microsoft's Data Transformation Services to communicate directly with the transactional database(s).

Staging Area

The next step in the journey to understanding how to implement a data warehouse is becoming familiar with data staging. Data staging can take place in a separate database or a separate set of tables within the data warehouse. The staging is used for intermediary processing tasks, described later. In the perfect world, all of your source data would be consistent, accurate, and unduplicated. But this is not usually the case.

Use the staging area to accomplish several critical missions, such as the following:

- Combine data from multiple sources
- Correct erroneous data
- Transform data into the proper format
- Check for data duplication
- Prepare data for the data warehouse

Figure 11.2 diagrams the processes discussed so far.

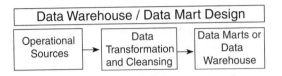

Figure 11.2 Flow chart for data warehouse/data mart design.

Dimensional Modeling of Business Process

The approach that will be used to construct the data warehouse is the dimensional model.

Dimensional models have two components. One component is the dimension tables that hold the text attribute you want to use as column and row headers. You also will be able to put constraints on your dimensions to eliminate part of your data from your query results. This arrangement allows you to see only the data you want to analyze, as well as make comparisons of performance.

The other component is a fact table that you can use to store the information you want to analyze—sales quantities, prices, when the item was sold, who sold it, and so on.

Dimension Table Overview

A *dimension table* is a set of related data organized in a hierarchical manner that assists in viewing data. The hierarchy may contain one or more levels. You must gather all of the information you want to use in your dimension table from your OLTP and bring it into your staging area. For example, the manufacturing Plant dimension table will have the structure that is shown in Figure 11.3.

If the dimension table contained the data in Figure 11.4, you could build a hierarchy that would look like Figure 11.5 in Analysis Services 2000. (Chapter 12, "Building a Data Warehouse with DTS and Analysis Services," shows you how to build this dimension table.) With a hierarchical dimension, it allows your users more flexibility in grouping data or drilling down into data for further detail.

	Column Name	Data Type	Length	Allow Nulls
🔑	PlantID	int	4	
	RegionID	int	4	✓
	PlantName	nvarchar	255	✓
	PlantNumber	float	8	✓
	Address	nvarchar	255	✓
	City	nvarchar	50	✓
	State	nvarchar	50	✓
	Zip	nvarchar	50	✓
	Phone	nvarchar	10	✓
	Fax	nvarchar	10	✓
	SQFT	float	8	✓
	PlantBuiltDate	smalldatetime	4	✓
	FixedWorkingCapital	float	8	✓
	MonthlyCapacity	int	4	✓
	FixedMonthlyCost	float	8	✓
▶				

Figure 11.3   Manufacturing plant dimension table.

PlantID	RegionID	PlantName	PlantNumber	Address	City	State	Zip
0	0	HQ	0	1 Minnesota Place	Minneapolis	MN	55401
1	0	Mankato	1	222 South Front St	Minneapolis	MN	55601
2	1	Chicago	2	1455 Michigan Ave	Chicago	IL	54987

Figure 11.4   Plant dimension table data.

When you build a dimension, you will want to include all the ways you want to slice and dice your data in the warehouse as dimensions. A data warehouse or data mart can have many dimensions, such as the following:

- **Time**—The hierarchy Year, Quarter, Month, Day, Hour, and Minute
- **Customer**—The hierarchy Country, State, City, and Customer Name
- **Product**—The hierarchy Business Group, Business Line, and Product

The tables that supply the data for a dimension can be contained in a single table or in several tables.

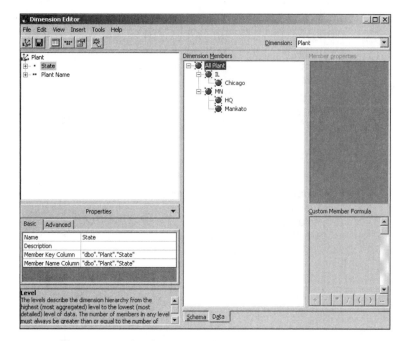

Figure 11.5 Plant hierarchy with RegionID and Plant Name.

A dimension built from a single table is called a *star dimension*, and a dimension built from the relation of two or more tables is called a *snowflake dimension* (see Figure 11.6).

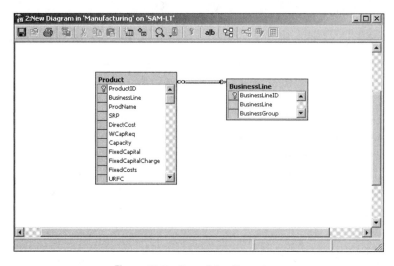

Figure 11.6 Snowflake dimension.

SQL Server Analysis Services dimensions can be classified in two ways:

- **Private dimension**—A private dimension can only be used within the specified cube it is designed for. For example, if a plant-manager dimension that would not be used in any other marts, you could classify it as private.

- **Shared dimension**—A shared dimension can be used in all the data marts that you design. The time dimension is a perfect example. You will not only want to slice sales data by time, but manufacturing data and other data as well. When you build your time dimension, you will surely make it a shared dimension. Cubes with common shared dimensions can be combined and queried as one entity; these combined cubes are *virtual cubes*.

Dimension Granularity

When you build a data warehouse, you must make a decision about the granularity of the data that you want to present. In most cases, you want to record your activity bases on each transaction. In other cases, you may choose to use a daily level of granularity. In this case, you sum the day's daily transactions into one value and record this value in your data warehouse. The drawback to daily granularity is the users will not have the option to drill down to the actual transaction activity. One of the roles Analysis Services fulfills is to allow you to store detailed information for detailed analysis while providing quick access to summarized information.

When you are designing your dimensions, you must make the same decision. In the case of the time dimension, if you have day as your finest level, users will not be able to drill down to transactions by using the time dimension any further than a daily level. If you choose the hour level, your users will be able to analyze trends at an hourly level. When architecting your dimensions, it is important to know the users' requirements for granularity and ensure that you have data at the granularity to meet those requirements.

Slowly Changing Dimensions

Slowly changing dimensions are another issue in designing your dimension. For example, in a customer dimension you may want to track data that is based on marital status. If Liz is single, you will want to lump her data together with all of the other single people. This works until Liz gets married; then you will want to lump all subsequent transactions with married people. But what about previous transactions? If you simply have one field to store marital status and choose to overwrite the old status with the new status, you will not have an accurate depiction of single people's purchases.

This situation is referred to as a slowly changing dimension. There are three ways to handle this, and they are categorized as Type 1, 2, and 3, as follows:

- **Type 1**—Simply overwrite the value of the marital-status field and be satisfied with having inaccurate historical data. If tracking the history of your dimension is not important, you will most likely choose Type 1.

- **Type 2**— Have a second entry for Liz in the dimension table. The first entry would represent all purchases that customer made as a single person, and the second entry would represent all purchases that customer made as a married person. This system allows you to track the history of married and single accurately. However Liz may will look like two people to your end users.

- **Type 3**—Add an additional field to the customer dimension to record the date when the marital status changed. Then overwrite the marital status. This allows you to accurately track your history of married and single, as well as have Liz appear as one person to your end users, but is more difficult to implement.

Fact Table Overview

Fact tables contain two types of data: the facts you want to analyze (sales quantities, sales prices, product cost, and so on) and foreign keys to the dimension tables. To ensure that you know what product was sold, you will have a foreign key in the product dimension. If you want to know when the product was sold, include a foreign key in the time dimension. Include a key for the plant dimension. If you want to track which customers are buying from you, you must include a key that relates back to the customer dimension.

Measures

Quantifiable data contained in the fact table is called a *measure*. A measure can be included that sums the extended price to shows sales volume for various customers or sales volume for each salesperson. If you want to see how many times a customer buys from you, you can include a count of purchase dates. The best data to use for facts is data that can be summed or counted over time.

Dimension Foreign Keys

By the time you start designing your fact table, you should know how your users want to view and slice the data. If you want to track the sales representative who sold the item, build a sales-representative dimension, and include in your fact table data a key that references a person in your sales-representative dimension table. You must include the appropriate key for each fact that refers to a data element in your dimension tables.

You will be porting your data to Microsoft Analysis Services in Chapter 12. Keep in mind one important fact when you design your dimensions: Analysis Services treats the relationship between the fact table and the dimension tables as inner joins. If you include a key in your fact table that is not represented in a dimension table, the data in that row is excluded from all query result sets.

Figure 11.7 shows the typical design of a fact table. The first five elements are foreign keys to dimension tables: product, time, customer, promotion, and store, respectively. The last three fields contain the measure your users will be able to analyze.

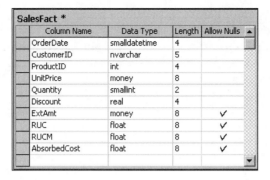

Figure 11.7 Typical fact-table design.

Assembling the Pieces

When diagramming the fact table with the dimension table, you will have a data mart that looks like the diagram in Figure 11.7. Figure 11.1, earlier in this chapter, shows the entire schema of a data mart. The fact table is central to the data mart, with dimension tables joined to the fact table forming a starlike structure.

Populating the Data Mart

Creating the schema is the easiest part of creating the data mart. The bulk of the work in any data mart is cleansing, integrating, and populating the data. Often, up to 80 percent of the time involved in building a data mart involves managing the data-loading process.

Creating the Data Staging Area

You need to create tables and other database objects to support the data extraction, cleansing, and transformation operations required to prepare the data for loading into the data warehouse. You can create a separate database for the data preparation area, or you can create these items in the data warehouse database.

The data preparation area should include tables to contain the incoming data, tables to aid in implementing surrogate keys, and tables to hold transformed data. Other tables may be required for reconciling data from diverse data sources. Such tables may contain cross-reference information to identify common entities, such as customer records from systems that use different keys. A variety of temporary tables may also be needed for intermediate transformations.

The specific design of the data preparation area depends on the diversity of data sources, the degree of transformation necessary to organize the data for data warehouse loading, and the consistency of the incoming data.

The data preparation area should contain the processes that extract the data from the data sources, the processes that transform and cleanse the data, and the processes that load the data into the data warehouse. These processes may be SQL queries, stored procedures, DTS packages, or documents of manual instructions. In developing any database system, the objective is to automate as much of the process as possible and to manage and maintain the automated tools developed. Storing and maintaining the transformation processes in the data preparation area permits you to use standard database backup and restore mechanisms to preserve them.

Regardless of whether a separate database is used, creating the data preparation area involves creating tables, views, indexes, DTS packages, and other elements common to relational databases.

Cleansing and Transforming Data

You can accomplish many data transformations during the process of extracting data from the source systems. However, there are often additional tasks to complete before you can load data into the data warehouse. For example, you must reconcile inconsistent data from heterogeneous data sources after extraction and complete other formatting and cleansing tasks. You also should wait until after the extraction process to incorporate surrogate keys. Some transformations that you might accomplish during the extraction process may interfere with the performance or operation of the online source system; you should defer these tasks until extraction is complete.

After extraction from the source systems, the data should reside in a data preparation area where you can perform the cleansing and transformations before the data is loaded into the data warehouse. The data preparation area can be a separate database or separate tables in the data warehouse database. During the cleansing and transformation phase, you can execute procedures to validate and verify data consistency, transform data into common formats, and incorporate surrogate keys.

You may need to perform manual operations to reconcile data inconsistencies or to resolve ambiguous text-field entries. Each time a manual operation is required, you should try to identify a way to eliminate the manual step in future data transformation operations. In some cases, you may be able to modify the source data systems to eliminate the cause at the source. In other cases, you may be able to establish an automated process that sets aside unresolved data for later manual exception processing so that the bulk of the data can be loaded into the data warehouse without delay for manual intervention.

Typical data transformations include:

- Combining multiple name fields into one field.

- Breaking date fields into separate year, month, and day fields.

- Mapping data from one representation to another, such as TRUE to 1 and FALSE to 0 or postal codes from numeric to text.

- Mapping data from multiple representations to a single representation, such as a common format for telephone numbers or different credit-rating codes to a common "Good, Average, Poor" representation.
- Creating and applying surrogate keys for dimension-table records.

When the data is extracted, cleansed, and integrated into your data warehouse schema, you can use a reporting tool to create reports directly from the star schema, or you can use an OLAP engine like Analysis Services to create the cubes for full multidimensional analysis of the data. The next section provides an overview of Analysis Services, which comes with SQL Server.

Introduction to Analysis Services

OLAP is an increasingly popular technology that can dramatically improve business analysis. Historically, OLAP has been characterized by expensive tools, difficult implementation, and inflexible deployment. Microsoft tackled the OLAP problem and created a solution that makes multidimensional analysis accessible to a broader audience and potentially at a significantly lower cost.

Analysis Services is a fully featured, standalone OLAP product that currently ships with Microsoft SQL 2000. Following are definitions of new terms used in this section:

- **Analysis Services**—Analysis Services refers to the server and client components that ship with SQL Server 2000 that allow for the creation of OLAP applications.
- **Aggregation**—OLTP data records all transaction details. OLAP queries typically need summary data or data aggregated in some fashion. For example, a query to retrieve the monthly sales totals for each product over the past year runs much faster if the database has only summary rows showing the daily or hourly sales for each product than if the query must scan every transaction detail record for the past year.

  The degree to which you aggregate the data in a the Analysis Services OLAP engine depends on a several design factors, such as the speed requirements of your OLAP queries and the level of granularity required for your analysis. For example, if you aggregate sales details into daily summaries instead of hourly summaries, your OLAP queries would run faster, but you could use this arrangement only if you had no need to analyze sales on an hourly basis. Precalculation of summary data is the foundation for the rapid response times of OLAP technology.

- **Calculated member**—A calculated member is a dimension member whose value is calculated at query time by means of an expression that you specify when you define the calculated member. Calculated members typically are measures, such as Sales Price / Quantity = Average Sale Price. Calculated members can also be members of dimensions. You can have a calculated member that converts local time to Greenwich Mean Time, for example.

- **Data staging**—Data to be used in the data warehouse must be extracted from the data sources, cleansed and formatted for consistency, and transformed into the data warehouse schema. The data preparation area, sometimes called the data staging area, is a relational database into which data is extracted from the data sources, transformed into common formats, checked for consistency and referential integrity, and made ready for loading into the data warehouse database.

  The data staging area and the data warehouse database can be combined in some data warehouse implementations as long as the cleansing and transformation operations do not interfere with the performance or operation of serving the end users of the data warehouse data. Performing the preparation operations in source databases is rarely an option because of the diversity of data sources and the processing load that data preparation can impose on online transaction processing systems. The relational database used for data preparation, regardless of where it is performed, must have powerful data manipulation and transformation capabilities, such as those provided by Microsoft SQL Server 2000.

  After the initial load of a data warehouse, the data staging area is used on an ongoing basis to prepare new data for updating the data warehouse. In most data warehouse systems, these operations are performed periodically, often scheduled to minimize the performance impact on the operational data source systems.

- **Dimension Analysis Services dimensions**—These dimensions are a structural attribute of cubes. They are organized hierarchies of categories and (levels) that describe data in the fact table. These categories and levels describe similar sets of members upon which the user wants to base an analysis.

- **Dimensional schema**—Entity-relation modeling is often used to create a single complex model of all the organization's processes. This approach has proved to be effective in creating efficient online transaction processing (OLTP) systems. By contrast, dimensional modeling creates individual models to address discrete business processes. Sales information may go to one model, inventory to another, and customer accounts to yet another. Each model captures facts in a fact table and attributes of those facts in dimension tables linked to the fact table. The schemas produced by these arrangements are called star or snowflake schemas and have been proved to be effective in data warehouse design.

- **Measure**—In a cube, a measure is a value (usually numeric) based on a column in the cube's fact table. In addition, measures are the central values of a cube that are analyzed—that is, the numeric data of primary interest to end users who are browsing a cube. The measures you select depend on the types of information end users request. Some common measures are sales, cost, expenditures, and production count.

- **MDX**—Multidimensional Expressions, the equivalent of using T-SQL to query a SQL Server database, are used to query a multidimensional database.

Analysis Services includes a middle-tier server, Pivot Table Services, which allows users to perform sophisticated analyses of large volumes of data with exceptional performance. Pivot Table Services is responsible for returning the result set from your query, in either a two-dimensional or multidimensional fashion to the calling client. Pivot Table Services also caches results from recently executed queries on the server, resulting in related queries returning results rapidly.

A second feature of Analysis Services is a client cache and calculation engine called PivotTable Service, which helps improve performance and reduce network traffic. PivotTable Service allows users to conduct analyses while they are disconnected from the corporate network by using local cube files.

SQL Server 2000 Analysis Services was originally named OLAP Services in SQL Server 7.0. They both have the same basic architecture using PivotTable Services for the client cache.

OLAP is a key component of the data warehousing process. Analysis Services provides essential OLAP functionality for a wide array of applications, ranging from corporate reporting to advanced decision support. The inclusion of OLAP functionality in the SQL Server product family will help make multidimensional analysis more affordable and will bring the benefits of OLAP to a wider audience—not only smaller organizations, but also groups within larger corporations that have been excluded from the OLAP industry due to the cost and complexity of the products.

Analysis Services Architecture

Microsoft SQL Server Analysis Services was designed from the ground up to help minimize the most significant costs of building and maintaining OLAP applications. Analysis Services consists of server and client (middle-tier) software components. Figure 11.8 shows the architecture of Analysis Services.

On the server side, the Analysis Services server operates as a Microsoft Windows NT or Windows 2000 service and provides the core OLAP and data mining functionality. Programmatic access to administrative functions in the OLAP server is provided through an object model called Decision Support Objects (DSO). Books Online (BOL) has good documentation on DSO.

Analysis Manager, the built-in administrative user interface for Analysis Services, was developed with the DSO object model to manage Analysis Services. It provides a rich user experience without the need for programming. Analysis Manager, like Enterprise Manager, can execute on a computer separate from Analysis Services. It allows the database administrator to design OLAP data models, access information in RDBMS stores, design aggregations, and populate OLAP data stores (among other functions). Like the SQL Enterprise Manager, Analysis Manger is a snap-in for the Microsoft Management Console (MMC).

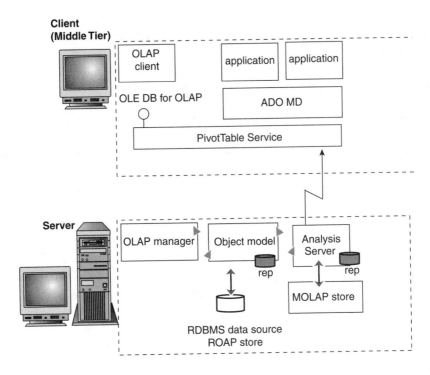

Figure 11.8   Analysis Services architecture.

SQL Server 2000 Analysis Services was originally named OLAP Services in SQL Server 7.0. What is now referred to as the Analysis Manager was the OLAP Manager. Pivot Table Services has retained the same name for the 2000 version.

Analysis Services can access source data in any supported OLE DB data provider—not only SQL Server, but also desktop and server databases including Microsoft Access, Microsoft FoxPro, Oracle, Sybase, and Informix. Any database source that provides an open database connectivity (ODBC) interface is also accessible through a facility in OLE DB that wraps ODBC drivers and exposes them as though they were native OLE DB interfaces. These data sources can also reside on platforms other than the Windows NT operating system, such as Unix, or mainframe systems and databases, such as IBM DB2.

On the client side, OLAP Services includes a component called PivotTable Service. PivotTable Service connects OLAP client applications to the OLAP Services server. All access to data managed by OLAP Services, by custom programs or client tools, is through the OLE DB for OLAP interface provided by PivotTable Service.

OLE DB for OLAP Interface

Due to the industry adoption of OLE DB for OLAP, many third-party products and tools support interaction with Analysis Services. These products provide great flexibility in determining which tools are best for a particular organization. Most of these tools are designed for use by end users to query Analysis Server databases. Where these products differentiate themselves from one to another is how they display the data to users.

Typical data features include:

- Rich chart and graphing capability

- Capability to create additional calculations from base measures in the cube

- Presentation of data on the Web

- Intuitive interfaces

Microsoft Office Pivot Tables are common ways of accessing and querying OLAP data. Microsoft Office Pivot Tables are not synonymous with Pivot Table Services; rather, they are a client interface tool that presents data in a dimensional fashion.

Analysis Services Database

A database is a container for related cubes and the objects they share. These objects include data sources, shared dimensions, mining models, and database roles. If these objects are to be shared among multiple cubes, the objects and cubes must be within the same database.

Cubes

A *cube* is a set of data that is defined by the set of dimensions and measures (see Figure 11.9).

Cubes are the main objects in Analysis Services; it is the vehicle that provides fast access to data in a data warehouse. End users use client applications to connect to an Analysis Services server and query the cubes on the server. An Analysis Services database can contain multiple cubes.

A cube is defined by the measures and dimensions contained within it. The cube that you will build in Chapter 12 includes the measures unit price, quantity, extended amount, and cost, as well as the dimensions customer, plant, product, and time.

After you construct your cube, your users can analyze any of the measures with any combination of the dimensions they want.

Dimensions

Dimensions are organized hierarchies that describe data in the fact table. These hierarchies are arranged in a pyramid-like configuration and the levels within a hierarchy describe similar sets of members upon which the user wants to base an analysis. Although many dimensions are organized in hierarchies, this structure is not necessary.

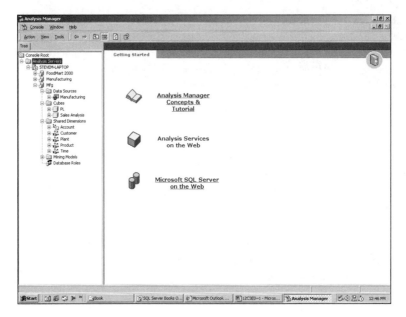

Figure 11.9 Analysis Services MMC interface.

You can create a dimension for use in an individual cube or multiple cubes. A *private dimension* is a dimension created for an individual cube. A *shared dimension* is a dimension that multiple cubes can use.

You can use dimensions to group the data, filter the data, or order the data.

Dimension Levels

Dimension levels describe the hierarchy from the highest (most summarized) level to the lowest (most detailed) level of data. A level exists only within the dimension on which it is based and comes from a column in the dimension table. Each level of the hierarchy contains data associated with the level; this data is called a *member*.

For example, a customer dimension contains the levels state, city, and customer name. Table 11.2 shows the relationship among the levels and members of the customer dimension. In this example, Ames and Des Moines are members of the city level. Judy and Larry are members of the customer level and thus would have the most detailed information associated with them.

Table 11.2 **Customer Dimension**

State	City	Customer
Iowa	Ames	Judy Rathje
Iowa	Ames	Larry Tiegland

State	City	Customer
Iowa	Des Moines	Kim Thomas
Iowa	Marshalltown	Mark Nord
Minnesota	Lakeville	Mark Kells
Minnesota	Burnsville	Matt Mirmak
Wisconsin	Hilltop	Terry Carpenter
Illinois	Rockville	Brent Fear
Illinois	Rockville	Brad Dennis
Illinois	Chicago	Dan Louzek
Illinois	Chicago	Dick Moel

Parent-Child Dimensions

Analysis Services supports parent-child dimensions. A *parent-child dimension* is based on two dimension table columns that together define the lineage relationships among the members of the dimension. One column, called the *member-key column*, identifies each member; the other column, called the *parent-key column*, identifies the parent of each member. This information is used to create parent-child links, which are then used to create a single hierarchy. For example, in Table 11.3, the column that identifies each member is EmployeeID. The column that identifies the manager (the parent in the parent-child relationship) is Manager_EmployeeID.

Table 11.3 **Employee Dimension Table Set up As a Parent-Child Dimension**

EmployeeID	Name	Position	Manager_EmployeeID
1	Julie Thiel	CEO	NULL
2	Rick Walker	CIO	1
3	Renata Miller	New Technology Manager	2
4	Pam Slovack	Database Manager	2
5	Rick Meinecke	Web Manager	2
6	Rodney Ray	Business Intelligence	4

Dimension Members

A *dimension member* is an individual column in the dimension table and is the lowest level of granularity, referred to as a *leaf member*. In Table 11.3, Julie Thiel (the CEO) is a member in the dimension.

Parent-child dimensions are a new feature available for Analysis Services 2000. The parent-child dimension is very useful in circumstances in which the levels may be unbalanced. Table 11.3 shows an example where Rodney is three levels from the CEO and is the only member of the third level. You could add another employee, listing Rodney as the manager, and the dimension would still perform properly with no changes needed in the structure of the dimension.

Member Properties

A *member property* is an attribute of a dimension member. It can provide additional information about a member (such as title in Table 11.3), or it can be used for special calculations in Analysis Services, such as currency translations. Member properties are not required for Analysis Services to work, but they are useful and powerful feature that can improve the overall solution for the end user. You also can create dimensions from member properties to increase the flexibility of your application.

Measures and Aggregations

As data is rolled up, the measures (or facts) that are being viewed are aggregated. Analysis Services provides Sum, Count, Min, Max, and Distinct Count functions. Sum is the most common aggregation for cubes. Count also is useful for seeing population size or calculating average (Sum / Count). The other popular aggregations, Min and Max, help find the top or bottom in the list, such as which salesperson had the lowest sales in January. The Distinct Count aggregation is useful in situations where a full count is misleading, such as when you want to know how many customers purchased a particular product. If Customer A makes three separate purchases of the product, a full count will record as three purchases; a Distinct Count counts all three purchases by Customer A as one purchase.

Calculated Members

One important note regarding calculated members: They enable you to add members and measures to a cube without increasing its size. Although calculated members must be based on data that already exists in the cube, you can create complex expressions by combining this data with arithmetic operators, numbers, and a variety of functions. Analysis Services includes a library of more than 100 functions and allows you to register and use other function libraries.

The syntax for creating calculated members, both simple and complex, is Multidimensional Expressions (MDX). MDX is a specialized syntax designed for working with objects and data of a cube. MDX is not within the scope of this book but is well documented in many other sources and BOL.

Summary

Now that you have learned about the basic concepts and components of data warehousing and SQL Server Analysis Services, you are ready for Chapter 12, "Building a Data Mart with DTS and Analysis Services." In that chapter, you will build a sample DTS package that uses manufacturing data to create a dimensional database that supports a sales analysis cube. Chapter 5, "More DTS Tasks," explains what tools are available within DTS to help manage the data warehouse.

Many books are devoted exclusively to Analysis Services and data warehousing. A good place to start is `http://www.microsoft.com/sql/productinfo/dataware.htm`.

For active newsgroups, go to:

- Microsoft.public.sqlserver.datawarehouse
- Microsoft.public.sqlserver.OLA

12

Building a Data Warehouse with DTS and Analysis Services

CHAPTER 11, "INTRODUCTION TO DATA Warehousing and Analysis Services," discussed the concepts of data warehousing, data marts, cubes, and Analysis Services. This chapter takes you through a sample DTS package that creates a dimensional database; then it walks you through creating a cube using Analysis Services.

In the DTS package created in this chapter, you will make connections to an Excel spreadsheet, an Access database, and a SQL Server database. You will use the Transform Data Task and the SQL Task to prepare your data for the Analysis Services cube.

While creating the cube, you will select an OLE DB provider connection to a SQL Server database. You will define a fact table and measures for your cube through the cube wizard. In addition, you will build several dimension hierarchies, including a time dimension. Finally, you will process and query your cube.

The Data Warehouse Process

The first step in creating the data mart is to create a RDBMS database to hold the dimensional data. In the SQL Server Enterprise Manager, create a database named

ManufacturingStar, and then run the C:\DTS2000\Scripts\ManufacturingStar.sql[1] from Query Analyzer against the ManufacturingStar database. See Figure 12.1 for the Create Database screen.

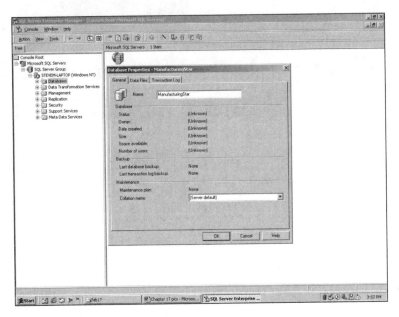

Figure 12.1   Creating the ManufacturingStar database.

This chapter demonstrates building a data warehouse that is intended to accurately reflect the state of business processes over time; you have all the tools discussed in this book at your disposal to aid you in the creation and maintenance of a data warehouse. Some of the issues facing the data warehouse administrator are:

- **Tracking the lineage of the data**—In Chapter 18, "Data Lineage," data lineage tracking is demonstrated. This is an ideal strategy for maintaining the origin and history of data in the warehouse.

- **Adding new fact and dimension data**—Many of the tools demonstrated can be used for adding new data. The SQL Task can be used to INSERT into DataWarehouse (fieldList) SELECT (fieldList) from SourceData. Additionally, the Bulk Insert and Transform Data Task are commonly used to load data.

---

1. All data files and scripts used in the book are available to be downloaded from http://
www.magenic.com/publications or http://www.newriders.com. The self-extracting ZIP file
will create a directory structure starting with DTS2000. You can extract the files to any drive or
directory, but all file references in this book will be based on C:\DTS2000\.

- **Updating dimension data**—One of the most challenging tasks of maintaining a data warehouse is handling changing dimension data. Over a short period of time, dimension data tends to stay the same. An employee who was selling for the Mankato region last week will probably be selling for that same region next week. Over longer periods of time the employee may move to a different region—Chicago, for instance. You want to maintain an accurate warehouse by having the facts be associated with the proper region at the proper time. This is referred to as a *slowly changing dimension (SCD)*. There are three recommended ways to handle SCDs:

  - **Type 1 SCD**—In some cases, you may not care to track the changes of some types of information. If you are not doing advanced analysis on last names, you may choose not to track their name change history. When you detect a change, you may choose simply to update the existing data in the dimension table. In Tables 12.1 and 12.2, it is demonstrated how you would handle a name change of a sales rep using the Type 1 method. The example assumes your sales rep Mary Smith marries Dick Poppins and changes her surname to Poppins.

Table 12.1 **Type 1 SCD Before Update**

SurrogateKey	Dimension Key	RepName
1	1	Mary Smith

Table 12.2 **Type 1 SCD After Mary Marries Dick Poppins**

SurrogateKey	Dimension Key	RepName
1	1	Mary Poppins

  - **Type 2 SCD**—These keep track of history. Whenever you detect that a change occurred in the dimension property value, the existing transactions should continue to be associated with the old values—that is, those that existed before the change. Only new transactions will be associated with the new member.

One of the techniques is to create another entry into the dimension table with the employee's new branch number and an effective date for the entry. Alternatively, you can set a flag for which entry is current. When updating the fact table's key, you can see who the sales representative is and the order date. This will allow you to choose the correct dimension data assigned to the transaction. This method posses difficulties for the sales representative—part of their data is under Mankato and a part under Chicago. This is no problem for the managers of Chicago and Mankato, but come commission time the sales representative will certainly want both sets of data aggregated.

A solution for this situation is to create dimensions for the dimension data that doesn't change. In this case, you could use the employee ID and create an EmployeeID dimension from the Rep dimension table. Since both the Mankato Rep and Chicago Rep have the same EmployeeID, come commission time all sales will be rolled up accurately under the EmployeeID. In Tables 12.3 and 12.4, it is demonstrated how you would handle a name change of a sales rep using the Type 2 method. You will track a new set of records for Mary Poppins after her marriage, but retain the historical information by retaining the dimension record for her prior to marriage.

Table 12.3   **Type 2 SCD Before Update**

SurrogateKey	Dimension Key	RepName
1	1	Mary Smith

Table 12.4   **Type 2 SCD After Update**

SurrogateKey	Dimension Key	RepName	Current
1	1	Mary Smith	0
2	1	Mary Poppins	1

- **Type 3 SCD**—A third way to track changing dimension data is to have another field added to your dimension data that stores the Current Value in one field and Previous Value in another field. This gives you the flexibility to query your data warehouse using either value. In Tables 12.5 and 12.6, it is demonstrated how you would handle a name change of a sales rep using the type 3 method. You will track a new name for Mary Poppins after her marriage in a separate column, but retain the historical information by retaining the dimension record for her prior to marriage.

Table 12.5 **Type 3 Before Update**

SurrogateKey	Dimension Key	RepName	NewRepName
1	1	Mary Smith	

Table 12.6 **Type 3 After Update**

SurrogateKey	Dimension Key	RepName	NewRepName
1	1	Mary Smith	Mary Poppins

Using CRC to Detect Changed Data

One method that you can employ to detect change is a Cyclical Redundancy Checksum (CRC). You can add a field to your dimension table that would hold the value of the CRC. When you are processing new data, you can compare the CRC for a particular member of a dimension with the CRC value you have for that dimension member in your staging area.

If the values do not match, then you have a record that has changes. You can take appropriate action based upon your design for implementing SCDs.

CRC uses an algorithm to generate a value for the text stream that represents all of the fields in the record. Here are some sample values from a CRC algorithm:

9724af39 = "Generated by a CRC algorithm"

Changing the last letter to uppercase gets you a different return value from the CRC:

ac4a8ff1 = "Generated by a CRC algorithM"

- **Log file growth**—When working with a large data set or when performing many operations on a data set, you will find that the log file can grow rapidly. If the log file grows to the point that it has utilized all of the available disk space, you have a problem. One solution is to use an Execute SQL Task to back up and truncate the transaction log, or if you are using the simple recovery model, you can execute a checkpoint at regular intervals.
- **Scheduling regular updates**—Once your data warehouse management DTS package is working properly, you may use the SQL Agent to schedule regular execution of your package.

The next step towards implementing a data mart is to build the DTS package to populate a dimensional schema stored in a RDBMS. The following steps are illustrated for populating a dimensional schema.

Step 1: Create the Connections to the Data Sources

There will be three data connections made in this section.

To begin, right-click the Meta Data Services node under the Data Transformation Service in the SQL Server Enterprise Manager (see Figure 12.2). Select New Package; this will open the package designer window. Save the package as DataMartProcessing.

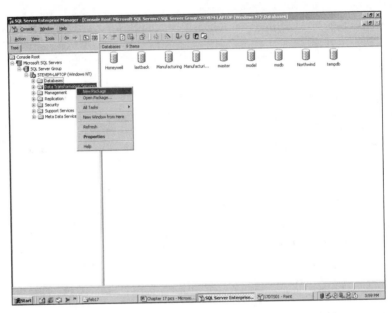

Figure 12.2 Creating a new DTS package from Enterprise Manager.

The first of your three data connections will be to an Excel spreadsheet. Drag the Excel connection task from the Connection Task toolbar to the package designer window. Use the Browse button next to the File Name text box to browse to C:\ DSTS2000\Data\Product.xls[2]. Name the connection Product Excel (see Figure 12.3).

The next step is to connect to the MS Access database that contains the rest of the data for the data mart. Drag the Access connection from the connection task toolbar into the query designer window. Name the connection AccessTransaction. Browse to the C:\DTS2000\Data\Manufacturing.mdb[3].Your connection should look like Figure 12.4.

---

2. If you want to follow along here, all data files and scripts used in the book are available to be downloaded from http://www.magenic.com/publications or http://www.newriders.com.

3. If you want to follow along here, all data files and scripts used in the book are available to be downloaded from http://www.magenic.com/publications or http://www.newriders.com.

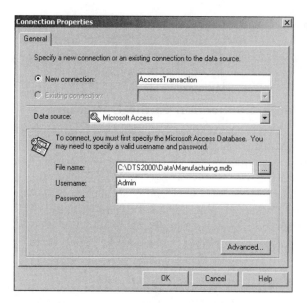

Figure 12.3   Microsoft Excel connection to Product.xls.

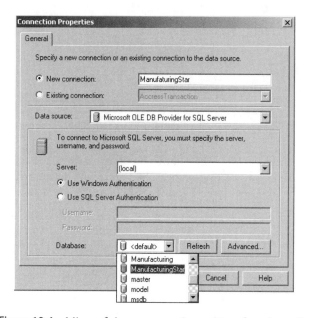

Figure 12.4   Microsoft Access connection to Manufacturing.mdb.

The third connection is made to the destination SQL Server database ManufacturingStar. Choose the Microsoft OLE DB Provider for SQL Server from the Connection Task toolbar. Name the connection ManufacturingStar, and select ManufacturingStar from the drop-down list of available databases.

Step 2: Define a Connection to the Data Mart

Now that all the data connections have been designed, it is time to specify what data to transfer and where the data should be transferred.

The first data transformation task to define is moving the data from Excel into the ManufacturingStar database. In the Package Designer window, first select the Excel Connection. While holding down the Control key, also select the ManufacturingStar connection. With both connections highlighted, right-click, and choose Transform Data Task from the shortcut menu. A graphical connection will be made from the Excel connection to the SQL Server connection (see Figure 12.5).

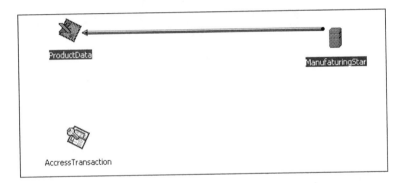

Figure 12.5 The DTS package with a Transform Data Task from Excel to ManufacturingStar.

The next step is to set the properties of the Transform Data Task. Right-click the Transform Data Task and select properties. The Source will default to Table\View and will show the Product page of the Excel Worksheet (see Figure 12.6).

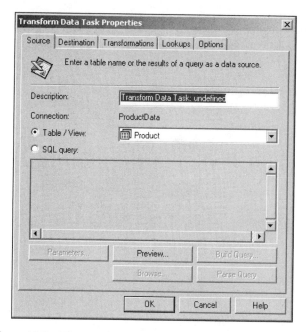

Figure 12.6   The Transform Data properties with the Excel source.

Preview the data to make sure it is there. Select the Destination tabs of the properties dialog box; from the drop-down list, select the Product table from the ManufacturingStar database, as illustrated in Figure 12.7.

The third tab of the Data Transformation dialog box graphically represents the mapping between the source and destination data. DTS has an auto-mapping feature, which will automatically map a copy column from the source to the destination where the field names have the same name (see Figure 12.8). In this case, accept the auto-mappings and select OK to finish this transformation task.

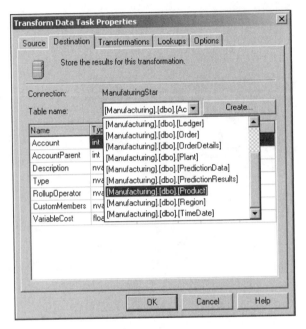

Figure 12.7   The Transform Data properties with the SQL Server Destination, selecting table Products.

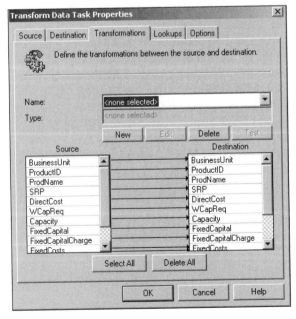

Figure 12.8   The source to destination mappings for products.

For SQL Server 7.0 users, the transformation mappings do not automatically map to fields with the same name. In this example, the source and destination fields' names are in the same order and, therefore, not an issue.

Step 3: Define the Queries to Extract Data from the Sources Previously Defined

The bulk of the data resides in the MS Access database; as a result, we will be making several transformations from Access to SQL Server. To make the package easier to understand, make another instance of your SQL Server connection, and place it in the Designer window next to the Access connection. Select another SQL Server connection from your connection task bar, rather than define the connection over again. Select the existing connection at the top of the dialog box (see Figure 12.9).

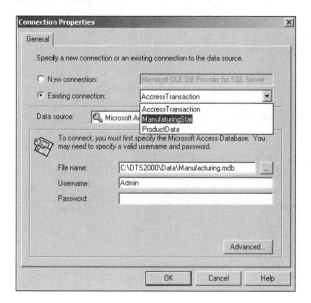

Figure 12.9 Setting a new SQL Server connection object to the existing SQL Server connection.

Your package designer should look something like Figure 12.10.

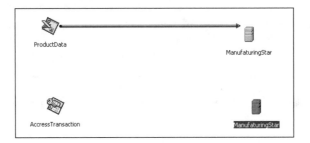

Figure 12.10 DTS package with connections set.

Many Transformations Between Two Connections Versus One Transformation Between Two Connections

It is a matter of personal preference whether you want to make new instances of your connection for each transformation you define or want to have multiple transformations between the two connections. In the example in this chapter, there is a second instance of the SQL Server connection for the MS Access transformations with multiple transformations between the two connections.

Your hardware configuration also plays a role in consideration of multiple connections versus multiple transformations between one connection. If you have a multi-processor server, you may want to have several transformations running in parallel. For a less powerful machine you may want to have multiple connections with one transformation between each connection, running sequentially.

Make a new transformation between the Access Transaction Database and second instance of ManufacturingStar. There are a total of 10 transformation tasks between the Access database and the SQL Server ManufacturingStar. To make the package easier to understand, text annotation will be used to identify what each transformation does.

Text Annotations

To place text annotation in the Designer window, click on the a|b button on the toolbar. A text box will appear in the DTS Designer which will allow you to add text, resize, and move the text annotation box.

Step 4: Define the Transformation and Load Steps

Create a new Transform Data Task for each of the following tables from the Access connection. There is a matching table in ManufacturingStar with identical columns as the source.

- Account
- BusinessLine

- Customer
- CustomerCustomer
- Ledger
- Order
- OrderDetail
- Plant
- Region
- Timedate

Explanation of CustomerCustomer

It may seem strange to have a table named CustomerCustomer; however, we will be using this in Chapter 13, "DTS and Data Mining." One of the services this example company provides is an analysis of the Customers of our Customer. Hence, the table is named CustomerCustomer.

When you have finished the transformation, you should have 10 connections as illustrated in Figure 12.11. Figure 12.11 shows a transformation that will be serialized. This is acceptable with a small data set used in this example. If you have a much larger data set you will want to use more instances of the connection objects, with fewer transformations between them.

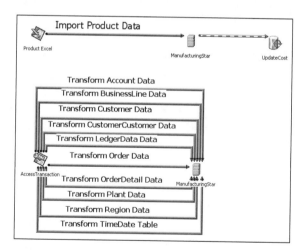

Figure 12.11   DTS package with all the Transform Data Tasks to populate the ManufacturingStar database.

The final task we will perform in this package is to apply an SQL script to the product table we brought in from Excel to update two of the cost fields. It is important that the Excel Transform Data Task has taken place before we apply the update.

From the task toolbar drag the Execute SQL Task near the first instance of the connection to SQL Server. In the description box, type **UpdateCost**. An existing connection must also be specified; this will tell the SQL Task which database to use when executing the SQL script. Type the following SQL statement in the SQL Statement window (see Figure 12.12).

```
update product set URFC = FixedCosts / Capacity
update product set fullyabsorbedcost =
FixedCosts / (select sum(quantity) from orderdetails
where orderdetails.productid = product.productid) + directcost
```

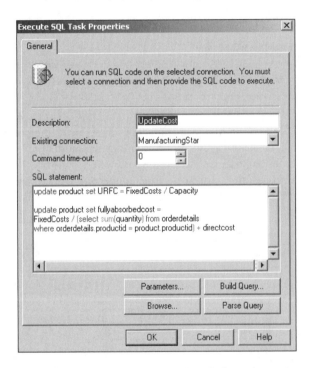

Figure 12.12 The Execute SQL Task with the update script.

Then choose the Parse Query button to ensure there are no errors in the SQL statement. If you do receive an error, make sure your existing connection is ManufacturingStar and that you have typed the SQL statement properly.

The last step is to specify the workflow property to ensure the SQL script runs *after* the product data has been loaded. Click on the ManufacturingStar connection, hold down the Control key, and click on the SQL task. Right-click, and select Workflow, On Success.

You are now done with your package; it should look similar to Figure 12.13.

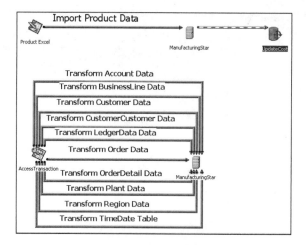

Figure 12.13 Completed DTS package.

Save your package and execute it to populate your data mart. You are now ready to open Analysis Services to begin building the cube.

Building a Cube with Analysis Services

Now that the data mart is populated with data, you can create a cube that will support the analysis. To launch the Analysis Manager, click the Start menu and go to Program Files, Microsoft SQL Server, Analysis Services, Analysis Manager (see Figure 12.14). When the Analysis Manager is visible, click the Analysis Servers node. The node will expand, and the local computer will be listed as an Analysis Server. Expand the Analysis Server node, and you will see the sample Foodmart 2000 Database listed, which was installed when you installed Analysis Services.

To create a new database, right-click the Analysis Server (The Computer Name), and select New Database.

When the Database dialog box appears, type **Manufacturing** in the Database Name text box (see Figure 12.15). Click OK to create your database.

In the Analysis Manager, expand the Manufacturing Database node, and you will see folders to hold the cube, data sources, dimensions, mining models, and oles (permissions).

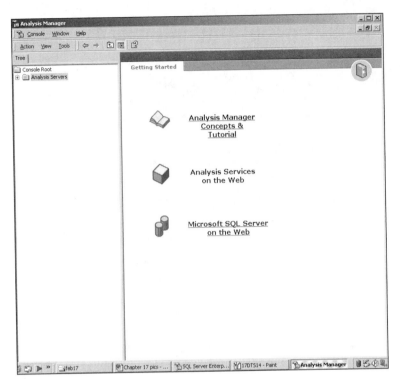

Figure 12.14 Getting to Analysis Services.

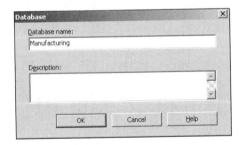

Figure 12.15 Creating an Analysis Services database.

Setting up a Data Source

Right-click the Data Sources node, and select new data source. The Data Link Properties dialog box will appear with four tabs (see Figure 12.16).

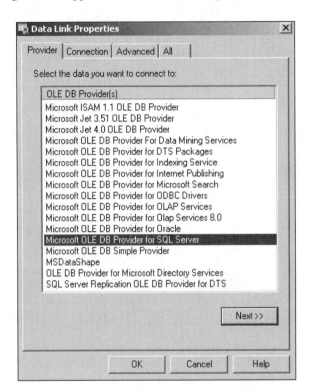

Figure 12.16 Selecting an OLE DB provider.

The first tab presents all of the OLE DB providers that are installed on the machine. Because you are connecting to SQL Server, choose the Microsoft OLE DB Provider for SQL Server, and then select Next. Now enter the name of the computer where SQL Server resides in the server name box. Enter the security information (see Figure 12.17).

Select the ManufacturingStar database from the drop-down list (see Figure 12.18). Test your connection. Click OK to save your data sources.

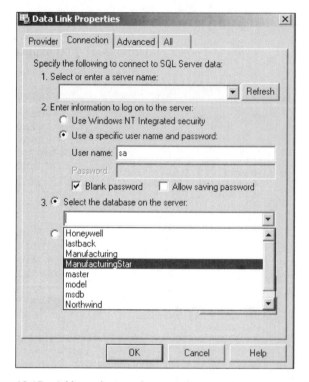

Figure 12.17   Adding a login and password to complete the connection.

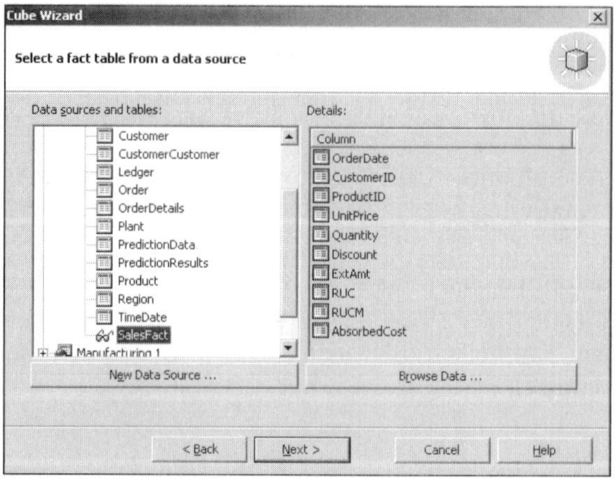

Figure 12.18   Finishing the connection.

Creating a Cube

Right-click the cube node, select New Cube, and then Wizard.

When prompted for a fact table, choose the view SalesFact (see Figure 12.19). Click Next. The next screen will ask you to identify the measure for your cube. Move UnitPrice, Quantity, ExtAmt, and AbsorbedCost to the right list box. Click Next.

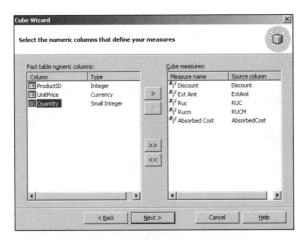

Figure 12.19 Choosing measures.

The next dialog box (see Figure 12.20) is used for defining the dimensions of the cube.

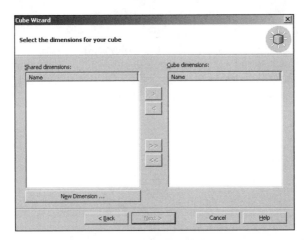

Figure 12.20 Cube Wizard.

Click New Dimension in the bottom-left corner. Customer is the first dimension you will create. All of the Customer data is contained in one table in the ManufacturingStar database. This is the definition of a star dimension. Select the Star Schema: a Single Dimension Table radio button and select Next. When presented with the available tables list box scroll down and choose the Customer table. Click Next (see Figure 12.21).

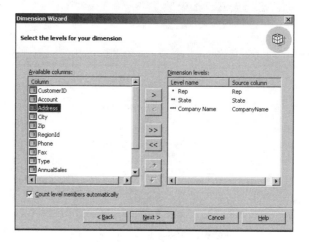

Figure 12.21 Dimension Wizard.

The Dimension Wizard will now ask you to define the levels for your dimension. Remember you want to list the most general levels first and levels with more detailed information as you work down the tree. Move Rep, State, and CompanyName to the right list box (see Figure 12.22). Select Next.

The next screen specifies the member Key column. In this case the member key column and the member name column are the same accept the defaults; select Next.

For this example, you will not be setting any advanced option. Click Next when the advanced options dialog box appears (see Figure 12.23).

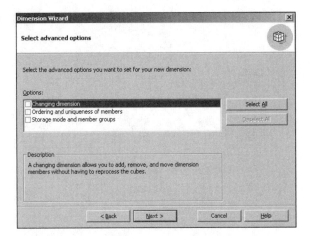

Figure 12.22 Advanced Options.

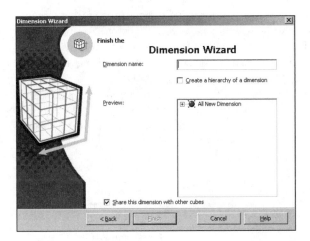

Figure 12.23 Finishing the dimension definition.

Name the dimension Customer, and make sure the Share This Dimension with Other Cubes check box is selected. Click Finish (see Figure 12.24).

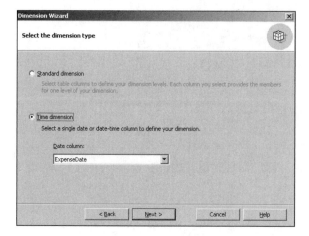

Figure 12.24 Naming a dimension.

You are now ready to make your second dimension, the time dimension. Click New Dimension, and choose star-schema as you did before. You will be using the TimeDate table for this dimension. Click Next. The next screen asks for Dimension type. Because this is a time dimension, select the second option, time dimension, and in the date column drop-down box select TransactionDate.

Select Next. In the Select time levels, drop the box down to see what options you have for time levels. Select Year, Quarter, Month, Day. The Dimension Wizard will build your dimension levels for you, using the datapart function applied to the transactionDate column from the TimeDate dimension table. Select Next to go to the advanced option screen, and then Next again. Name the dimension Time (see Figure 12.25).

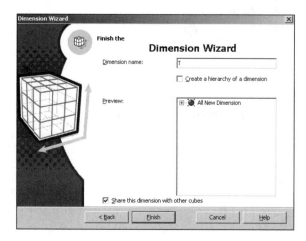

Figure 12.25 Finishing the time dimension.

The product dimension is the last dimension you will build for this cube. The data you need to build this dimension is contained in two related tables rather than one dimension table. You will be building a Snowflake dimension.

From the New Dimension dialog box, choose Snowflake dimension. When asked to choose tables, select both the businessline table and the product table. After selecting Next, you will be presented with the schema. Make sure that the tables are joined on productid = productid.

When choosing the levels, take businessline first, followed by businessunit and then product, respectively.

Name the dimension Product Line (see Figure 12.26).

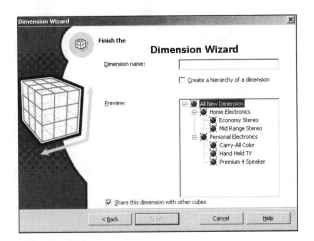

Figure 12.26   Finishing the Cube Wizard.

Now that you have all the dimensions identified, click Next, and name your cube Sales Analysis."

You will now be in the cube editor. Close the box and choose to save.

Right-click the cube, and choose Process (see Figure 12.27).

After the cube has processed, right-click the Sales Analysis cube and choose Browse Data to view the data. You have finished building your sales analysis cube.

You may want your cube to be refreshed with data on occasion. In fact, you may want to refresh your data every time you run your DTS package to update the data in the star schema. Fortunately, one of the DTS tasks you have to choose from is Analysis Service Processing Task. To utilize the task, edit the package that populates the ManufacturingStar, drag the Analysis Services Task onto the Designer screen, select your cube from the tree, select the refresh data option, and also select the Incrementally Update Dimension checkbox to ensure that your dimensions get refreshed as well (see Figure 12.28). Save the package.

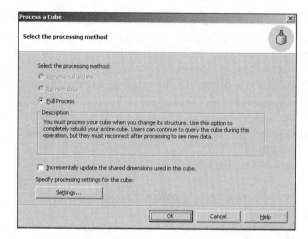

Figure 12.27   Processing the cube.

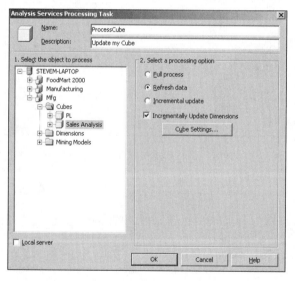

Figure 12.28   Adding the Analysis Services Task to a package.

For SQL Server 7.0 users, the OLAP Processing Task is available as a DTS add-in and can be downloaded from Microsoft's Web site, `http://www.microsoft.com/sql/downloads/OLAPaddin.htm`.

Summary

This chapter covered all of the steps for extracting data from multiple sources and consolidating the information into a SQL Server database. The SQL Server database was specially designed to hold information in a dimensional format. With the database populated, Microsoft Analysis Services 2000 was used as an Online Analytical Processing (OLAP) engine to store your data for easy querying.

13

DTS and Data Mining

DATA MINING AND THE DATA Mining Models are new features of Analysis Services with the Analysis Services 2000 release. Data mining technology analyzes data in relational databases and OLAP cubes to discover information of interest to users who cannot be intuitively or easily extracted from either a relational database or a data analysis cube.

Data mining is deducing knowledge by examining data. It can be thought of in this way:

- "Knowledge" = behavior patterns, clusters of data with common attributes, behavior decision trees, or association rules.

- Examining data = scanning samples of known facts about the situations we are interested in; these situations are known as cases.

For example, if we wanted to examine consumer buying patterns, the consumer is the case. We could use the consumers age, income, geographic location, and so on, as inputs to make predictions on the behavior of the case (Consumer).

After the knowledge is extracted, it is used to:

- Identify the cases you want to analyze
- Explain existing data
- Visualize data to aid humans

Data mining can answer many questions that can create value for an organization. For example:

- What demographic group is most likely to purchase a product or service?
- Which factors affect sales in a positive or negative fashion? This could be issues like weather, seasonality, or time of day.
- How can a consumer's previous buying patterns be used to predict future purchases?

Analyzing Data

Analysis Services 2000 includes two data mining algorithms: decision trees and cluster analysis for analyzing data. Data mining models are accessed through the Analysis Services manager under the mining model node. These are the steps and processes to analyzing data:

- Identify the result(s) you want to predict.
- Identify the input columns you want to use to make the prediction.
- Create the data mining model.
- Insert historical data into the mining model. This is called training the model.
- Use the results of the training to better understand historical results, or use the results for making prediction queries to forecast future results.

As illustrated in Figure 13.1, we start out with a raw set of data in the left column; we insert the selected data into a data mining algorithm that determines what factors weighed most heavily on the outcome. After the algorithm has stored the determining factors, known as content, you can then use this content to make *predictions* on data where the behavior is not yet known as shown in the third column.

Data Mining Model

Data mining uses historical information from existing databases. A data mining model is a table-like structure, which contains two types of data in columns. Data mining columns are used to define the inputs and outputs used by a data-mining model. The data-mining column also provides a standard structure against which familiar SQL syntax, such as INSERT for training data and SELECT for predictive analysis, can be used. Training data is data where the outcome is known and the inputs are known. For example, we know who bought stereo equipment last year, and if we have kept good data on our customers we know a lot of the attributes of those people as well. The mining model will "learn" from this data, and use it to make predictions about cases where the attributes are known and the outcome is not known.

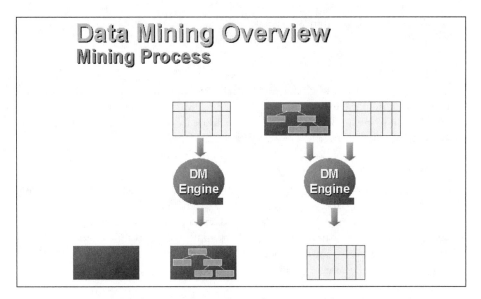

Figure 13.1 Data mining process overview—mining process.

The syntax for creating a mining model, as shown in Listing 13.1, is similar to the create table statement in SQL Server.

Listing 13.1 **Creating a Mining Model**

```
CREATE MINING MODEL [MyModel]
(
        [CustomerID]            LONG  KEY ,
        [CollegeDegree]    TEXT  DISCRETE ,
        [HouseholdIncome]  LONG  CONTINUOUS ,
        [IQ]               LONG  CONTINUOUS ,
        [StoreType]        TEXT  DISCRETE ,
        [ConsumerDecision] TEXT  DISCRETE          PREDICT_ONLY
)
USING [Microsoft_Decision_Trees]
```

The ConsumerDecision column is flagged as the predictable column with the PRE-DICT_ONLY flag. A predictable column can be used as an input to another prediction with the PREDICT flag. For example, if you are attempting to predict if a consumer will purchase a portable sound system, you can use this *predicted* purchase decision as an input into your mining model used to predict battery purchase.

After the data-mining model has been defined, data can be inserted into the model. Microsoft has shipped two data-mining algorithms with Analysis Services 2000. When applied to a data-mining model, these algorithms will create the content of the model.

The two algorithms that ship with Analysis Services 2000 are decision trees and clustering.

Decision Trees

A decision tree is a form of classification shown in a tree structure, in which a node in the tree structure represents each question used to further classify data. The various methods used to create decision trees have been used widely for decades, and there is a large body of work describing these statistical techniques.

Clustering

Like decision trees, clustering is a well-documented data mining technique. Clustering is the classification of data into groups based on specific criteria.

As you will discover in the "Data Mining Exercise" section later in this chapter, inserting data into a data-mining model is very similar to inserting data into a table using T-SQL. The model is then processed to produce the models content.

The syntax for training a mining model is as follows:

```
INSERT INTO [MyModel]
(
    CustomerID,CollegeDegree, HouseholdIncome, ConsumerDecision, IQ, StoreType
    )
OPENQUERY([Provider=SQLOLEDB],
'
    SELECT CustomerID, CollegeDegree, HouseholdIncome, ConsumerDecision
    FROM HistoricalData')
```

The above insert statement is using `CollegeDegree`, `HouseholdIncome`, `IQ`, and `StoreType` as inputs into the mining model, to make a prediction on `ConsumerDecision` about the "Case" CustomerID.

A data-mining model can be retrained as more data is collected.

Data Mining Model Content

A processed data-mining model contains content. The content is the insights/patterns/rules detected by the data mining algorithm as follows:

- Each node represents a "rule"
- A hierarchical graph for decision trees
- A flat graph for segmentation
- A single node for items that couldn't be separated
- The specific content of each node could vary with the algorithm

The content of a data-mining model can be used graphically, as in Figure 13.2, or it can be used in a prediction query. A trained mining model and a list of prospects with their related information, could be utilized to predict the results of future purchase decision. You could also calculate a probability as to the accuracy of the prediction.

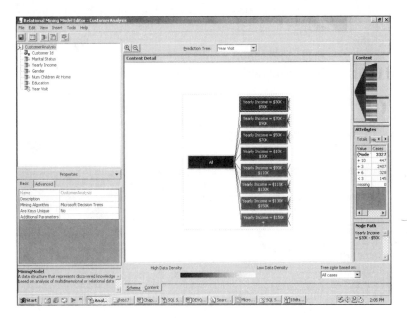

Figure 13.2   Mining model schema editor.

The SQL-like syntax for a prediction query against a trained mining model is as follows:

```
SELECT <columns to return or predict>
  FROM <dmm> PREDICTION JOIN
       <source data query> ON
       <join conditiond>
 WHERE ...
```

The above statement will allow you to select a dataset from data where the results are not known, that when joined in a prediction joined with a trained mining model will allow you to select not only the known data, but a *predicted* outcome based on the inputs attributes.

To automate this task for regular use, there is a DTS task available for use to run a data-mining prediction that will be incorporated into the Prediction Query Task exercise in the later section "Let the Analysis Begin."

Data Mining Exercise

From the data warehousing exercise in Chapter 12, "Building a Data Warehouse with DTS and Analysis Services," you imported a set of information about the Customers of the Customers when you included the CustomerCustomer table in your DTS package. You will use this CustomerCustomer as the basis for the exercises in the balance of this chapter.[1]

The intent is to create a data-mining model to predict how often a customer will visit the electronics store in a given year based on known information about a customer.

To access Microsoft data-mining models, open the Analysis Manager from the Start menu. Next, expand the Manufacturing database created in Chapter 12. You will see a node for mining models (see Figure 13.3).

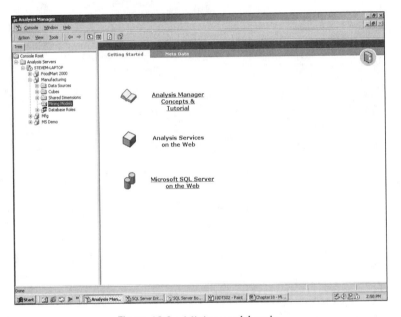

Figure 13.3   Mining model node.

The next step is to create a new mining model. Right-click the mining model node, and select new mining model. You will be presented with the Mining Model wizard as depicted in Figure 13.4.

---

1. All data files and scripts used in the book are available to be downloaded from http://www.magenic.com/publications or http://www.newriders.com. The self-extracting ZIP file will create a directory structure starting with DTS2000. You can extract the files to any drive or directory, but all file references in this book will be based on C:\DTS2000\.

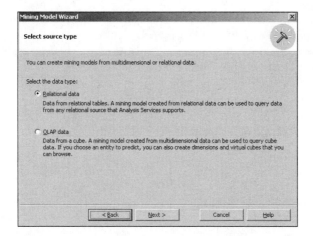

Figure 13.4   Mining Model Wizard.

The Customer data being utilized for this example is in the CustomerCustomer table residing in SQL server. Because it resides in SQL Server, it is considered relational data. So, select the Relational Data radio button on the wizard screen. Now select Next to go to the next screen.

All of the data to be mined is contained in the CustomerCustomer table. This will be the only case table to be selected from our ManufacturingStar data source. Select the CustomerCustomer table, and the columns will appear in the right list box. You should have a screen that resembles Figure 13.5.

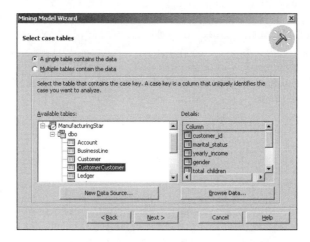

Figure 13.5   Select Case Tables.

In the select data mining technique dialog box, make sure Microsoft Decision Trees is selected in the drop-down list box. Select Next.

The next screen asks for the case key (see Figure 13.6). The case key is similar to a primary key in a database table. Because we have indicated this is a key and not a numeric input value for the mining model, the mining model will ignore the data from the customer_id key when the model is processed.

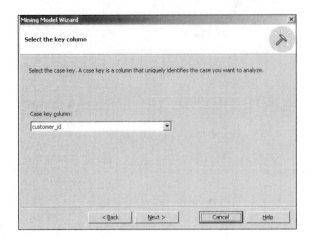

Figure 13.6 Case Key column.

If you have not already done so, select the next key to progress to the screen that allows you to select the input and predictable columns task. On this screen you will indicate the input columns, the data you want to use as a predictor, and the predictable columns. Move all columns EXCEPT customer_id and YearVisit to the list box labeled input columns. Move the predictable column, YearVisit, to the list box labeled Predictable Columns, as demonstrated in Figure 13.7

Click Next, and name the model CustomerPrediction. Choose the Save and Process Now radio button, and finish.

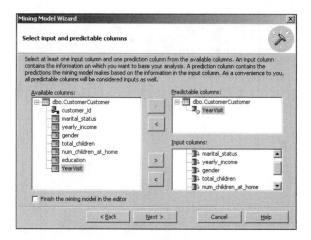

Figure 13.7 Input and predictable columns.

The mining model will then be created and trained with the data from the CustomerCustomer table. The mining model Editor dialog box will then be present (see Figure 13.8).

The useful data is contained in the content tab of the mining model editor. To switch to the content viewer, select the content tab at the bottom of the editor box.

Let the Analysis Begin

You should now have a screen similar to Figure 13.9.

With the All node selected, you can see in the attribute box at the right that the statistics break down as illustrated in Table 13.1.

Table 13.1 **Analyzing Content Browser Data**

Purchase Frequency	Number of Cases	Percent of Cases
(Tree Total)	10281	100.00%
+ 10	1198	11.66%
+ 3	5703	55.45%
+ 6	960	9.34%
< 3	2420	23.54%
missing	0	0.01%

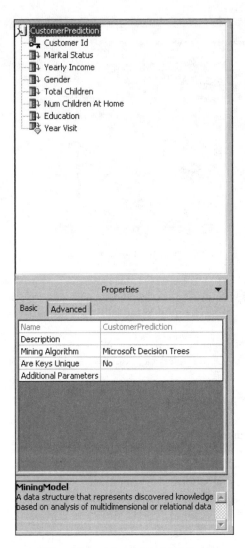

Figure 13.8   Mining Model Editor.

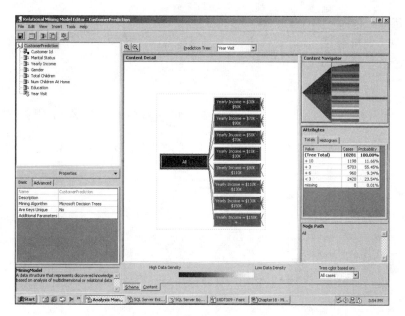

Figure 13.9 Model Content Browser.

This indicates that of all data used to create the mining model, there was

- 10281 rows of data

- 11.66 % shop in the electronics store at least 10 times per year

- 23.54 % shop less than three time per year

The next level of your tree holds different nodes with differing income amounts. The decision tree's algorithm deduced from the data that the single most important attribute related to shopping habits is the income level of the customer. Select the Yearly Income = 150k + node from the content detail screen. Your screen should look like Figure 13.10.

Again focusing on the attribute statistic box at the right, the statistics for folks in the 150k+ income range breaks out like this. Notice how the totals in Table 13.2 differ from Table 13.1.

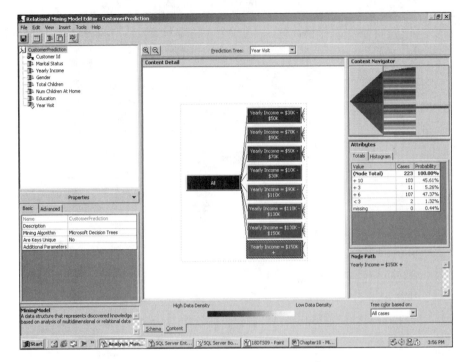

Figure 13.10 Browsing income nodes.

Table 13.2 **Browser Content for Incomes 150k +**

Purchase Frequency	Number of Cases	Percent of Cases
(Node Total)	223	100.00%
+ 10	103	45.61%
+ 3	11	5.26%
+ 6	107	47.37%
< 3	2	1.32%
missing	0	0.44%

In this group more than 45% shop more than 10 times per year versus the 11% from the whole group. And a whopping 98% shop more than 6 times per year. Clearly, income is a factor. But what is the next most important factor? Double-click the Yearly Income = 150k + node from the content detail screen. You will be taken down the tree one level, and you will notice that marital status is the next most important determining factor. Click on both the M and the S, and you will be able to view the statistics and determine that married higher income people tend to be more frequent shoppers than single people.

To see the real power of the tree, drill down into the 30–50k income range, and notice that here, marital status is not the next most important factor. Instead, it is the number of children at home (see Figure 13.11).

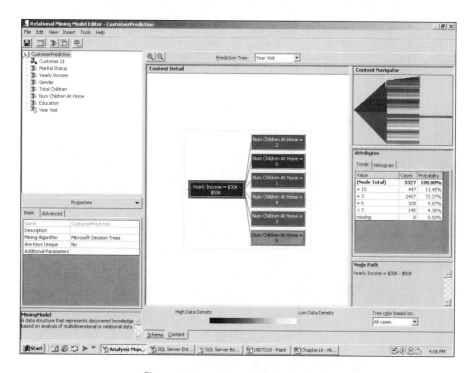

Figure 13.11   Browsing children node.

One of the ways to utilize a trained data mining model is to use the Data Mining Prediction Task available with a DTS package. In the sample MFG.mdb, there is a table ProspectList that can be used to make predictions using the CustomerPrediction.

In the SQL Server Enterprise Manager, make a new package. Drag the Data Mining Prediction Query Task onto the package Designer (see Figure 13.12). On the Mining Model tab, type the name of the server in the Server text box. In the database drop-down list, select the database name in Analysis Services that contains the Data Mining Model CustomerPrediction. Then highlight the CustomerPrediction Mining Model before advancing to the Query tab. Your screen should resemble Figure 13.13.

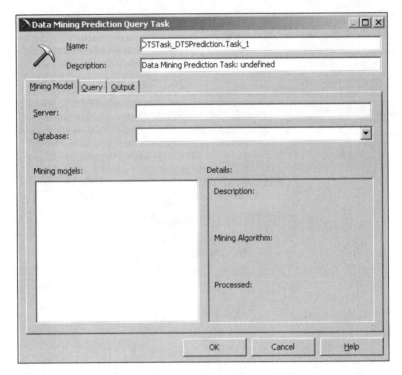

Figure 13.12 Prediction Query Task.

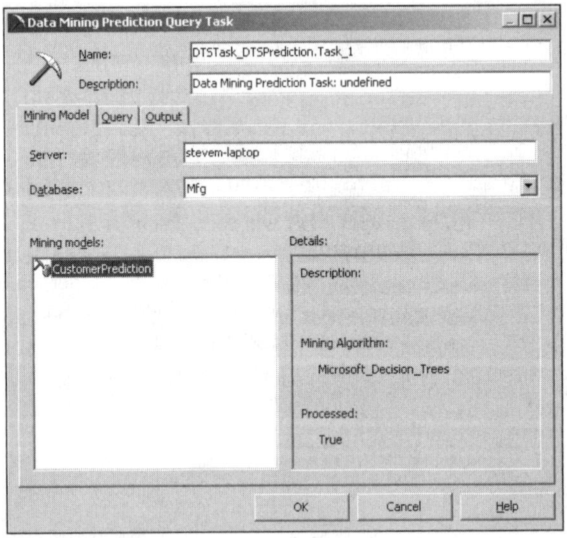

Figure 13.13 Selecting a Data mining model.

In the input data source text box, create a new Jet 4.0 OLE DB connection, and then browse to C:\DTS2000\Data\Manufacturing.mdb[2]. For the Prediction Query, select the New Query button to launch the query window. Select the ProspectList table as the case table in the query designer. Then map the mining model fields to the table fields. Make certain *not* to map the YearVisit column to anything in the Access table. It does not exist in the table, and it is the result that is being predicted. Therefore, make sure it is not selected as an input column. When completed, you should have a query that looks like Figure 13.14. Click Finish.

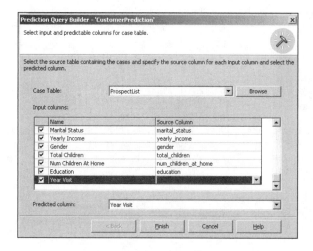

Figure 13.14 Mapping the case.

The Query designer has created a prediction query where you will join your prospect list with the mining model created earlier. You should have the same query in the Query window as shown in Listing 13.2.

Listing 13.2 **Data Prediction Query**

```
SELECT FLATTENED
  [T1].[Customer Id], [T1].[Marital Status], [T1].[Yearly Income], [T1].[Gender],
  [T1].[Total Children], [T1].[Num Children At Home], [T1].[Education],
  [CustomerPrediction].[Year Visit]
FROM
```

continues

2. If you want to follow along here, all data files and scripts used in the book are available to be downloaded from http://www.magenic.com/publications or http://www.newriders.com.

Listing 13.2   **Continued**

```
[CustomerPrediction]
PREDICTION JOIN
  OPENROWSET
  (
    'Microsoft.Jet.OLEDB.4.0',
    'Provider=Microsoft.Jet.OLEDB.4.0;Data
Source=C:\DTS2000\Data\Manufacturing.mdb;Persist Security Info=False',
    'SELECT `customer_id` AS `Customer Id`, `marital_status` AS `Marital
Status`, `yearly_income` AS `Yearly Income`, `gender` AS `Gender`,
`total_children` AS `Total Children`, `num_children_at_home` AS `Num Children At
Home`, `education` AS `Education` FROM `ProspectList` ORDER BY `customer_id`'
  )
  AS [T1]
  ON
    [CustomerPrediction].[Customer Id] = [T1].[Customer Id] AND
    [CustomerPrediction].[Marital Status] = [T1].[Marital Status] AND
    [CustomerPrediction].[Yearly Income] = [T1].[Yearly Income] AND
    [CustomerPrediction].[Gender] = [T1].[Gender] AND
    [CustomerPrediction].[Total Children] = [T1].[Total Children] AND
    [CustomerPrediction].[Num Children At Home] = [T1].[Num Children At Home] AND
    [CustomerPrediction].[Education] = [T1].[Education]
```

Like T-SQL, data mining has a set of functions available to use to return various statistics. In this case we want not only a prediction, but also a return value that reflects the probability the prediction is correct. We will add one more column to our SELECT statement.

```
,PredictProbability([CustomerPrediction].[Year Visit]) as Prob
```

The preceding comma is used as a column separator, and the `PredictProbabilty()` function accepts a predictable column as an argument.

The entire altered query should be like Listing 13.3.

Listing 13.3   **Modified Query in the Data Mining Prediction Query Task**

```
SELECT FLATTENED
  [T1].[Customer Id], [T1].[Marital Status], [T1].[Yearly Income], [T1].[Gender],
  [T1].[Total Children], [T1].[Num Children At Home], [T1].[Education],
  [CustomerPrediction].[Year Visit], PredictProbability([CustomerPrediction].[Year
  Visit])
FROM
  [CustomerPrediction]
  PREDICTION JOIN
    OPENROWSET
    (
      'Microsoft.Jet.OLEDB.4.0',
      'Provider=Microsoft.Jet.OLEDB.4.0;Data
Source=C:\DTS2000\Data\Manufacturing.mdb;Persist Security Info=False',
```

```
     'SELECT `customer_id` AS `Customer Id`, `marital_status` AS `Marital
Status`, `yearly_income` AS `Yearly Income`, `gender` AS `Gender`,
`total_children` AS `Total Children`, `num_children_at_home` AS `Num Children At
Home`, `education` AS `Education` FROM `ProspectList ` ORDER BY `customer_id`'
   )
AS [T1]
ON
  [CustomerPrediction].[Customer Id] = [T1].[Customer Id] AND
  [CustomerPrediction].[Marital Status] = [T1].[Marital Status] AND
  [CustomerPrediction].[Yearly Income] = [T1].[Yearly Income] AND
  [CustomerPrediction].[Gender] = [T1].[Gender] AND
  [CustomerPrediction].[Total Children] = [T1].[Total Children] AND
  [CustomerPrediction].[Num Children At Home] = [T1].[Num Children At Home] AND
  [CustomerPrediction].[Education] = [T1].[Education]
```

Now that you have successfully created a prediction query task, your prediction query task window should resemble Figure 13.15.

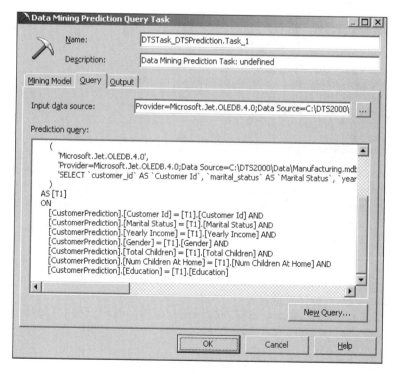

Figure 13.15   Prediction join query.

Now switch to the Output screen of the Data Mining Prediction Query Task dialog box. Indicate in the Output data source the ManufacturingStar database in SQL Server, and leave the Output table named PredictionResults. Click OK, save the Package as DataMining, and execute the package. Go to the ManufacturingStar database, and look at the results produced.

Singleton Prediction Queries

To perform a prediction on single data inputs instead of selecting a set of data from a table, you can pass in the values to be used in the prediction join as follows:

```
SELECT
  [T1].[Customer Id], [T1].[Marital Status], [T1].[Yearly Income], [T1].[Gender],
  [T1].[Total Children], [T1].[Num Children At Home], [T1].[Education],
  [CustomerPrediction].[Year Visit], PredictProbability([CustomerPrediction].[Year
  Visit])
FROM
  [CustomerPrediction]
  PREDICTION JOIN
    'SELECT 1 AS `Customer Id`, `m` AS `Marital Status`, `150 k+ ` AS `Yearly
  Income`, `m` AS `Gender`, 2 AS `Total Children`, 1 AS `Num Children At Home`,
  `High School` AS `Education` AS [T1] '
  ON
    [CustomerPrediction].[Customer Id] = [T1].[Customer Id] AND
    [CustomerPrediction].[Marital Status] = [T1].[Marital Status] AND
    [CustomerPrediction].[Yearly Income] = [T1].[Yearly Income] AND
    [CustomerPrediction].[Gender] = [T1].[Gender] AND
    [CustomerPrediction].[Total Children] = [T1].[Total Children] AND
    [CustomerPrediction].[Num Children At Home] = [T1].[Num Children At Home] AND
    [CustomerPrediction].[Education] = [T1].[Education]
```

The following script could be used as a SQL string to return an ADO resultset. When specifying the ADO connection string, you would utilize the MSOLAP Provider to communicate with the manufacturing database in Analysis Services as follows:

```
CONN_STR = "Provider=msolap;data source=localhost;Initial Catalog=Manufacturing;"
Rs.open (StrSQL,CONN_STR)
```

There are many functions that can be utilized for prediction queries. Table 13.3 from SQL Server Books On Line identifies the data mining functions available. Although the syntax for data mining appears SQL–like, it is actually syntax that conforms to OLE DB for Data Mining specification. The OLE DB for Data Mining specification can be found at www.microsoft.com\data\ole db\.

Table 13.3 **Available Functions within Mining Syntax**[3]

Function	Description
BottomCount	Returns a table containing a specified number of bottom-most rows in increasing order of rank based on a rank expression.
BottomPercent	Returns a table containing the smallest number of bottom-most rows, in increasing order of rank based on a rank expression, that meet a specified percent expression.
BottomSum	Returns a table containing the smallest number of bottom-most rows, in increasing order of rank based on a rank expression, that meet a specified sum expression.
Cluster	For clustering data mining models, returns the cluster identifier containing the highest probability of the input case.
ClusterDistance	Returns the distance between the input case and the center of the cluster that has the highest probability.
ClusterProbability	Returns the probability that the input case belongs to the cluster that has the highest probability.
Predict	Performs a prediction based on a specified column.
PredictAdjustedProbability	Retrieves the adjusted probability of the topmost histogram entry for a specified column.
PredictHistogram	Retrieves a table representing the histogram for a specified column.
PredictProbability	Retrieves the probability of the topmost histogram entry for a specified column.
PredictStdev	Retrieves the standard deviation value of the topmost histogram entry for a specified column.
PredictSupport	Retrieves the support value of the topmost histogram entry for a specified column.
PredictVariance	Retrieves the variance value of the topmost histogram entry for a specified column.
RangeMax	Retrieves the upper value of the predicted bucket discovered for a specified discretized column.
RangeMid	Retrieves the midpoint value of the predicted bucket discovered for a specified discretized column.
RangeMin	Retrieves the lower value of the predicted bucket discovered for a specified discretized column.

continues

Table 13.3 **Continued**

Function	Description
Sub-SELECT	Returns a table from a specified table expression.
TopCount	Returns a table containing a specified number of topmost rows in a decreasing order of rank based on a rank expression.
TopPercent	Returns a table containing the smallest number of topmost rows, in a decreasing order of rank based on a rank expression, that meet a specified percent expression.
TopSum	Returns a table containing the smallest number of topmost rows, in a decreasing order of rank based on a rank expression, that meet a specified sum expression.

3. *This table was copied from Microsoft SQL Server 2000 Version 8.00 Books On Line. This information is available on the SQL Server installation CD.*

Summary

Utilizing the tools demonstrated in this chapter, you can add functionality to your database and data warehouse applications. Rather than just reporting on data in your database, you will be able to provide explanations and insight as to why—instead of just what.

IV

Using the Tool—
Case Studies

14

Custom Error Logging with DTS

DTS SUPPORTS THREE KINDS OF LOGGING: data lineage logging, package execution logging, and error logging.

- **Data lineage logging**—Allows you to log all the data in the destination, the source, and any transformations applied. This is covered in much more detail in Chapter 18, "Data Lineage."

- **Package execution logging**—Is set in the package properties; it logs package and step information. For more information, please refer to Chapter 7, "Package."

- **Error logging**—Is a text-file log of the error and the current values at the time of the error. This has been expanded in SQL Server 2000 and is covered in more detail in Chapter 4, "DTS Tasks."

The focus of this chapter is about an alternative to the text-file log. The text-file log has good data, but it doesn't always give you what you want. You don't want to know just the values of the current record; you also want the key field names and their associated values, error field names and their associated values, and custom text on what the problem is. Hence, you need a custom error-logging design that will give you exactly what you desire.

Listings 14.1 and 14.2 are samples of the text-based error logs that are currently available in DTS for SQL Server 7.0 and 2000.

Listing 14.1 is a sample DTS transformation error log for SQL Server 7.0.

Listing 14.1 **Sample DTS Transformation Error Log for SQL Server 7.0**

```
DATA TRANSFORMATION SERVICES: Data Pump Exception Log


Package Name: (null)
Package Description: (null)
Package ID: {D93A6D97-F1DA-45AE-A331-55D64395D9F9}
Package Version: {D93A6D97-F1DA-45AE-A331-55D64395D9F9}
Step Name: DTSStep_DTSDataPumpTask_1
Execution Started: 10/29/2000 11:18:08 AM
Error during Transformation 'DTSTransformation__2' for Row number 1. Errors
encountered so far in this task: 1.

Error Source: Microsoft Data Transformation Services (DTS) Data Pump
Error Description:TransformCopy 'DTSTransformation__2' conversion error:
Conversion invalid for datatypes on column pair 1 (source column 'LastName'
(DBTYPE_WSTR), destination column 'LastName' (DBTYPE_I4)).
Error Help File:sqldts80.hlp
Error Help Context ID:30501
 1|D a v o l i o |N a n c y |S a l e s   R e p r e s e n t a t i v e |M s .
|12/8/1948|5/1/1992|5 0 7  -  2 0 t h   A v e .   E . A p t .   2 A |S e a t t l e |W
A |9 8 1 2 2 |U S A |( 2 0 6 )   5 5 5 - 9 8 5 7 |5 4 6 7 |||||

Execution Completed: 10/29/2000 11:18:08 AM
```

Listing 14.2 shows the contents of the log file, which contains four errors.

Listing 14.2 **Sample SQL Server 2000 DTS Source Data Log When a Record has an Error**

```
1|Davolio|Nancy|Sales Representative|Ms.|1948-12-08 00:00:00|1992-05-01
00:00:00|507 - 20th Ave. E.
Apt. 2A|Seattle|WA|98122|USA|(206) 555-9857|5467|||0|2|Fuller|Andrew|Vice President,
Sales|Dr.|1952-02-19 00:00:00|1992-08-14 00:00:00|908 W. Capital
Way|Tacoma|WA|98401|USA|(206) 555-9482|3457|||0|3|Leverling|Janet|Sales
Representative|Ms.|1963-08-30 00:00:00|1992-04-01 00:00:00|722 Moss Bay
Blvd.|Kirkland|WA|98033|USA|(206) 555-3412|3355|||0|4|Peacock|Margaret|Sales
Representative|Mrs.|1937-09-19 00:00:00|1993-05-03 00:00:00|4110 Old Redmond
Rd.|Redmond|WA|98052|USA|(206) 555-8122|5176|||0|
```

Solution Design

The solution requires you to create an error-log table and use the lookup query feature in the Transform Data Task to push data into that table. The table can reside in any valid data repository. I usually put the table in the SQL Server staging database where most of my processing happens. You can store any information you want at the time of the error. I like to store the task name, source and source data, destination data, detailed error message, and package information so that I always know the DTS package and execution date. The table layout I usually use is shown in Table 11.1.

Table 14.1 **Error-Logging Table**

Field Name	Data Type	Comment
ID	Int	AutoIncrement ID.
TaskName	VarChar(12)	Contains the name of the task that discovered the problem.
Source	VarChar(50)	This is the source database, table and field name where the data came from. I like database.table.field type notation.
SourceKey	VarChar(50)	Allows you to go back to the source table and look up the problem record. You can put in the field name and value by using the FieldName.Value notation.
SourceData	VarChar(25)	Contains the actual data that caused the problem.
Destination	VarChar(50)	This is the planned destination database, table, and field; it uses database.table.field notation.
DestinationKey	VarChar(50)	This is the key for the destination table, which is helpful when you record a default value at the destination and have to go back at a later date to fix it.
Error Message	VarChar(100)	Text that details the problem.
Critical	Bit	If True, this error stopped further processing.
Package	VarChar(50)	Tells you the package name and time it was run and uses Name.DateTime notation.

The lookup query of the Transform Data Task can execute any valid SQL statement. The last task in the package can query the Error Log Table for records and notify the administrator as appropriate.

Implementation

It's now time to put the design into practice by adding custom error handling for the package that you created in Chapter 2, "DTS—An Overview." If you did not build the package in Chapter 2, you can use the prebuilt package from C:\DTS2000\Packages\ CreateExcelReports.dts[1]. In this package, the Shipping Budget spreadsheet contains

---

1. All data files and scripts used in the book are available for download from http:// www.magenic.com/publications or http://www.newriders.com. The self-extracting ZIP file will create a directory structure starting with DTS2000. You can extract the files to any drive or directory, but all file references in this book will be based on C:\DTS2000\.

the list of products we want to report on. The current spreadsheet (Shipping Budget.xls) contains all valid products. The Shipping Budget Error.xls spreadsheet has several products misspelled; therefore, you cannot get any shipments for them. We will assume that if there are no shipments, there may be an error, and you will log in all products that have no shipments for a particular month.

Following is the process that we will go through:

1. Create the logging table.

2. Add a connection to it.

3. Change the data source from Shipping Budget.xls to Shipping Budget Error.xls.

4. Add the lookup query to insert the log entries.

5. Add the appropriate error-handling code.

Create Logging Table in SQL Server

The first step is to create the logging table in SQL Server. If you don't have a database already set up, create the database DTS2000. Then you can build the table described in Table 14.1 (refer to "Solution Design" earlier in this chapter) by using the New Table Wizard or by executing the script in Listing 14.3 in the Query Analyzer.

Listing 14.3 **SQL Statement That Creates the Custom Error-Logging Table**

```
CREATE TABLE [dbo].[ErrorLog] (
    [ID] [int] IDENTITY (1, 1) NOT NULL ,
    [TaskName] [varchar] (50) ,
    [Source] [varchar] (50) NULL ,
    [SourceKey] [varchar] (50) NULL ,
    [SourceData] [varchar] (25) NULL ,
    [Destination] [varchar] (50) NULL ,
    [DestinationKey] [varchar] (25) NULL ,
    [ErrorMsg] [varchar] (100) NULL ,
    [Critical] [bit] NULL ,
    [Package] [varchar] (50) NULL
) ON [PRIMARY]
```

Create Connection to Logging Table

The lookup query will perform best if you provide it a dedicated connection, so create a new SQL Server connection by using the Microsoft OLE DB Provider for SQL Server connection object. Add the name ErrorLog, set the correct server, and specify the DTS2000 database, as shown in Figure 14.1.

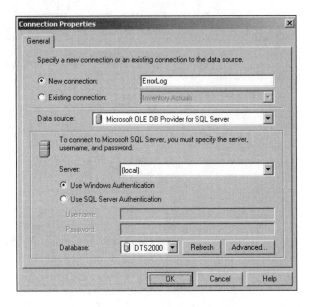

Figure 14.1   The SQL Server connection to support the lookup query for the error logging.

Change the Shipping Budget Excel Connection to Shipping Budget Error

Unfortunately, the original package did not have any errors, but you can get some by using another data source. Double-click on the Shipping Budget Excel Connection object in the DTS Designer main panel and change the filename from C:\DTS2000\ Data\Shipping Budget.xls to C:\DTS2000\Data\Shipping Budget Error.xls[2]. Then click OK. Figure 14.2 shows the new connection properties.

As soon as you click OK, you will see a warning dialog box titled Task References (see Figure 14.3). Because you have changed the data source, DTS wants to know whether any of the existing transformations need to be removed. Because Shipping Budget Error.xls is exactly like Shipping Budget.xls except for some misspelled product names, no changes are necessary. Make sure that the Clear Transformations check boxes have *not* been checked; then click OK to keep all your existing transformations as they were.

---

2. If you want to follow along here, all data files and scripts used in the book are available to be downloaded from http://www.magenic.com/publications or http://www.newriders.com.

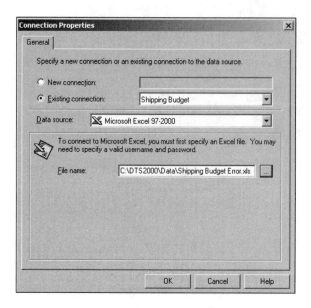

Figure 14.2 The new Shipping Budget connection, which contains errors.

Figure 14.3 The Task References warning you see when changing a data connection.

When you change the data source from Shipping Budget.xls to Shipping Budget Error.xls, SQL Server 7.0 will prompt you, "Do you want the transformations that have been designed using this connection to be reset?" Click No. Shipping Budget Error.xls has exactly the same format as Shipping Budget.xls, except that a few products are misspelled. All the transformations are still valid.

Create the Lookup Query to Insert the Log Transactions

Double-click on the Load Actuals Transform Data Task that connects the Shipping Budget and Shipping Report Excel Connections. Go to Lookups; then add a new lookup query called `InsertError`. Use the new `ErrorLog` connection, and click on the ellipsis button (...) to enter the SQL statement from Listing 14.4, which inserts the logging information (see Figure 14.4). Click OK to save the new query.

Listing 14.4   **The Lookup-Query SQL Statement That Inserts Data into a Table**

```
INSERT INTO ErrorLog
     (TaskName, Source, SourceKey, SourceData, Destination,
 DestinationKey, ErrorMsg, Critical, Package)
VALUES (?,?,?,?,?,?,?,?,?)
```

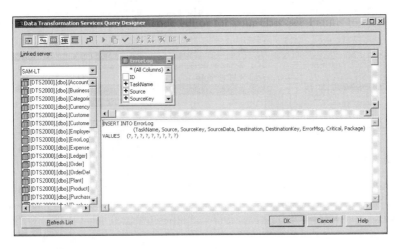

Figure 14.4   The DTS Query Designer dialog box with the logging insert statement.

Add Error-Handling Code to the Transform Data Script

The error-handling code in this case is straightforward. You need to get the return value of the `GetActualsCurrentMonth` lookup query and test to see whether it is zero. If it is, the number is suspect, and you will log it and continue processing. The original statement is:

```
DTSDestination(i+1) =
DTSLookups("GetActualsCurrentMonth").Execute(DTSSource("Product"),i,
DTSGlobalVariables("CurrentYear").Value)
```

This statement is a lookup query that passes in the source data product name, month, and year, and returns the actual shipment quantity from the lookup-query connection.

The new statement sets the lookup-query value to a variable named `CMActuals` and tests to see if it is zero. If the value is zero, the statement executes another lookup query to insert an error into the log. If the value is not zero, the statement sets the destination equal to `CMActuals` (see Listing 14.5).

Listing 14.5 **The Script that Executes a Lookup Query to Insert Custom Error Information into a Log Table**

```
CMActuals = DTSLookups("GetActualsCurrentMonth")
.Execute(DTSSource("Product"),DTSGlobalVariables("CurrentYear").Value,i)
If CMActuals = 0 then

        Set oPkg = DTSGlobalVariables.Parent
        Set oTask = oPkg.Tasks("DTSTask_DTSDataPumpTask_1")
        sTaskDescription = oTask.Properties("Description").Value
        Set oConnection = oPkg.Connections(oTask.Properties
                                    ("SourceConnectionID").Value)
        sDestination = oConnection.DataSource

DTSLookups("LoadErrors").Execute sTaskDescription,sSource,
        "Product." & DTSSource("Product"),
        "Month: " & i ,sDestination,NULL,"No Actuals for Product",0,
    oPkg.Name & Now()
Else
    DTSDestination(i+1) = CMActuals
End If
```

The parameters of the `LoadErrors` lookup query are:

- **TaskName**—Here, you put in the task description represented by the variable `sTaskDescription`. `sTaskDescription` can be picked up from DTS directly using the DTS object model. First, you need to get a reference to the package; the easiest way is to use the already-exposed `DTSGlobalVariables` object and request its parent—the package. Then use the package's `Tasks` collection to get access to the current task, `"DTSTask_DTSDataPumpTask_1"`.

  There are two ways to find the internal DTS name for a task: look at the task's Workflow Properties dialog box, or place a Dynamic Properties Task in your working area and refer to it for the task names and properties. After you have a reference to the task object, you can easily get its property values, such as Description. The VBScript in Listing 14.6 shows the steps needed to get the task description assigned to the variable `sTaskDescription`.

Listing 14.6 **VBScript That dynamically Gets the Active Task's Description from DTS**

```
Set oPkg = DTSGlobalVariables.Parent
Set oTask = oPkg.Tasks("DTSTask_DTSDataPumpTask_1")
sTaskDescription = oTask.Properties("Description").Value
```

- **Source**—Here, you specify the source table name, view, or file represented by the variable sSource. sSource can be easily picked up via the DTS object model, as shown in the following VBScript:

  ```
  sSource=oTask.Properties("SourceObjectName").Value)
  ```

- **SourceKey**—The key information for finding the problem is "Product." & DTSSource("Product").

- **SourceData**—This is the key data that caused the problem. Because you already have the product name, you can store the month number you are trying to get the shipments on: "Month: " & i.

- **Destination**—This is where you specify the destination table or file. Because this is a file you can actually query DTS to get the filename and location. The destination is represented by the variable sDestination, and you can pick it up by using the following code:

  ```
  Set oConnection =
  oPkg.Connections(oTask.Properties("SourceConnectionID").Value)
  sDestination = oConnection.DataSource
  ```

- **DestinationKey**—If a default value is loaded into the destination, this is where key information can be stored so that the default data can be fixed later. For this example, you can pass in NULL.

- **ErrorMsg**—Use any custom text that you want. For this situation, you can use "No Actuals for Product".

- **Critical**—This is not critical, just something that looks odd, so put in 0 (not critical).

- **Package**—This is the place to put the package name and the current date/time. The code is oPkg.Name & Now().

Finding DTS Objects and Properties for VBScript

When you are writing VBScript, you will find a great deal of power in dynamically pulling key information directly from the DTS object model. The easiest way to view the DTS objects and their properties, and to get the exact syntax, is to place a Dynamic Properties Task in the DTS Designer work area and use that task as your reference. For more information on the Dynamic Properties Task, please refer to Chapter 5, "More DTS Tasks." For more information on the DTS object model, please see Chapter 8, "Putting It All Together—An Extended DTS Example," and Chapter 9, "Building a Package Using Visual Basic."

Error Logging and the Multiphase Data Pump

Due to the added multiphase data pump in SQL Server 2000, you can save processing time by getting the dynamic information such as task name, data source, data destination, and package name in the PreSourceData transformation phase. This phase is executed only once; by contrast, the Row Transform function is executed for every row of data. For these functions to share information, you will need to declare your variables outside your functions or use global variables to store the values.

For more information on the multiphase data pump, see Chapter 4, "DTS Tasks."

When you have the extra code entered, click OK three times to return to the Package Designer.

Notifying the Administrator of Errors

There are several ways to notify an administrator of errors:

- DTS comes with a Send Mail Task that enables you to send a message with file attachments. If you wanted to send the errors, you would first need to save the information to a data file or an Excel spreadsheet and then attach that file to your message. See Chapter 5 for complete coverage of the Send Mail Task.

- You can use the Execute Process Task and run Net Send to notify the appropriate people of the package completion and review the error-log table. This is useful because it doesn't require a MAPI interface or account. The primary drawback to Net Send is that the recipient must be logged on and running Messenger Service at the time the package sends the message.

- You can write custom code in the ActiveX Script Task that can send email, a page, or any other kind of custom notification.

- You can use the extended stored procedure `xp_sendmail`. `xp_SendMail` is useful because you can attach the contents of the error-log table to the email message without having to save the contents to a data file. If you wanted to use the stored procedure, you would need to add an Execute SQL Task to the package, set the connection to `ErrorLog`, and set the SQL statement to something like Listing 14.7.

Listing 14.7 **SQL Statement that Emails the Contents of a Table to a Recipient**

```
EXEC master.dbo.xp_sendmail @recipients = 'jims@magenic.com',
  @query = 'SELECT * from DTS2000.dbo.ErrorLog',
  @subject = 'Create Excel Report Error Log',
  @message = 'The contents of the package error log',
  @attach_results = 'TRUE'
```

The `xp_sendmail` extended stored procedure has several parameters. In a situation such as this, however, all you would need to use are the recipients, subject line, and a short message, and you would make the `SELECT` statement `resultset` an attachment (see Figure 14.5). However, if you use the `xp_sendmail` stored procedure, you will need to set up SQL Server to be an email client. This procedure is well documented in Books on Line (BOL).

Execute Package

Now you can save and execute the package. The final package will look like Figure 14.6. When you run the package, you will see that the package executes without errors, but the error-log table will contain a number of entries in which actuals were zero.

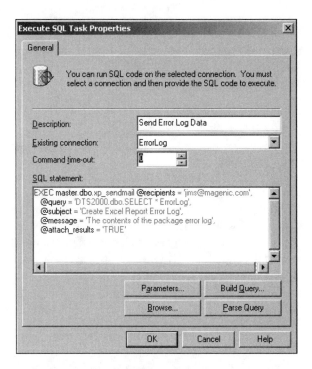

Figure 14.5 The Execute SQL Task Properties dialog box, using the `xp_sendmail` extended stored procedure to email the error log to an administrator.

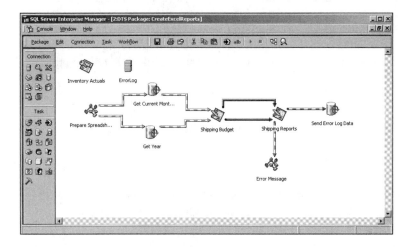

Figure 14.6 Final package.

Error-Logging Design Strengths and Weaknesses

As with all designs, this one has its strengths and weaknesses. The three major strengths are:

- You get the information you want.
- You can test for the conditions that are important to you.
- You can use this design with the Execute SQL Task, Execute Script Task, and the Data Driven Query Task.

The major drawbacks are:

- Not all tasks can use this design.
- You must use scripting in the Transform Data Task to catch and insert the errors into the log. The Transform Data Tasks that use Copy Column will use the DTS error logging and create a text file causing error logging to be in more than one location.
- Because this solution uses scripting, and because the script is compiled and run for each record, this error logging does have a significant impact on performance.

Custom Logging Using Execute SQL and Execute Scripting Tasks

This design is not limited to the Transform Data Task. You can include custom error logging in the Data Driven Query Task, Execute SQL Task, and the VBScript Task. Because the Data Driven Query Task uses the same VBScripting as the Transform Data Task, the solution is exactly the same as described in the example. For the Execute SQL Task and the Execute Script Task, you have slightly different scripting.

Execute SQL Task

Because the log is a table in SQL Server, it is easy to include an SQL INSERT statement in the log table for any problems you encounter. You may not have all the data for a full record, but the layout does provide appropriate fields for you to log problems.

Execute Script Task

Inserting data into a table from an ActiveX Script is a little more involved than the Execute SQL Task but still straightforward. What you need to do is create an ADO connection to SQL Server and execute an SQL INSERT statement through ADO. Listing 14.8 creates an ADO connection and executes the error-insertion SQL statement through the ADO command object.

Listing 14.8 **VBScript That Creates an ADO Connection to a SQL Server Database and Inserts Data**

```
Function Main()

dim myConn
dim myCommand

' instantiate the ADO objects
set myConn = CreateObject("ADODB.Connection")
set myCommand = CreateObject("ADODB.Command")

' setup the connection object to use the DTS2000 Database
myConn.Open = "Provider=SQLOLEDB.1;Data Source=(local); Initial
Catalog=DTS2000;user id = 'sa';password=''"

strSQL = "INSERT INTO ErrorLog (TaskName, ErrorMsg, Critical)"
strSQL = strSQL & "Values ('ActiveX Script Task', 'We have a Problem here', 0)"

Set myCommand.ActiveConnection = myConn
myCommand.CommandText = strSQL

myCommand.Execute

Main = DTSTaskExecResult_Success
End Function
```

Summary

Is this chapter the final word on custom error handling? No. With the new multiphase data pump in the SQL Server 2000 Transform Data Task, you have even more opportunities to validate your data and to respond to unexpected situations. You can also extend this concept to perform transaction logging. Logging all transactions does add overhead, but there are situations where logging all or specific transactions are more important than overall processing time. The point here is that the flexibility of DTS enables you to easily create custom solutions to a wide variety of business and technical problems.

15

Managing Distributed Databases with DTS and Message Queues

O NE OF THE NEW TASKS IN DTS FOR SQL Server 2000 is the Message Queue Task. This task is designed to allow DTS to participate in all design situations in which message queues are useful.

Message queuing is all about moving data between loosely coupled, highly distributed applications and systems. Message queuing has an infrastructure in many ways similar to email systems, but instead of sending mail to people, you send messages to queues. Instead of people looking in their inboxes for mail, applications monitor a queue. When a message arrives, the application can open the message and extract any embedded data, perform actions on the data, and return the message with new data back to the sender. Queue messages can be encrypted and auto-returned if they are not picked up in a predefined amount of time. Best of all, the systems do not have to have reliable communication lines for queues to work.

Message queues are useful in many situations:

- When communication lines are unreliable and the sender is not dependent on a reply from the recipient. The sender sends the message and then moves on to do additional work. If the communication lines are down, the messages will stack up and wait until the communication lines come up again. When the lines are open, the messages move on to their intended recipient queues. An example is a Web site that takes orders and sends the transactions to the accounting system or an order-processing system. We will build this example in this chapter.

- When the time to reply does not need to be immediate, but you do need a processed reply back with contained data, such as in an order-processing system that needs to do a credit-rating check before proceeding. The system can send the request for the customer's credit rating and then continue working on other tasks. When the reply message comes back with the customer's actual credit rating, the system will continue processing the order.

- When the recipient may not be able to keep up during high peak times. Messages will stack up in the queue and wait until the recipient can get around to processing them.

- In load-balancing situations. You can have several computers monitor the same queue, and as a computer is available for work, it will take the next available message and start processing it.

- When you want to pass information to several systems. The information can be identical or different. The sender just sends a message with the appropriate data to each recipient. For example, if a repair-order message has been received, the main processing system can send a work-order notification to the accounting system, send a work schedule to the scheduling system, and send a replacement-part request to the inventory control system.

- In cross-platform situations. With the products already on the market, you can send messages across Windows, UNIX, AS/400, Tandem, Digital, VMS, CICS/MVS, and more.

These are just some of the situations in which message queues have been useful in today's environment.

Example Design

To work this example, you must have access to a Microsoft message queue. If you are working on Windows 2000 or Windows NT 4.0 with the option pack installed, you can create a private queue that can work with this example.

Discussing how to install message queuing or create a message-queue domain is beyond the scope of this book. However, at the Microsoft Message Queue Home Page (www.microsoft.com/msmq/), you will find great information, including demos, white papers, case studies, and links to technical information. We will discuss how to create a private queue that can be used during a package's execution phase, a package that sends data via a queue, and a package that listens to a queue to pick up the messages and processes the contained data.

In the example used here, the Web server is selling products. But the server is in a different geographic location from the manufacturing database. You are concerned that the network communication lines between the two systems may be down sometimes; you also are concerned about workload. You do not want to slow down the e-commerce service if the manufacturing database starts to slow down and choke on the high volumes. Also, you want to have the orders coming in as they are placed, one transaction at a time.

Figure 15.1 shows the process this example will follow. The e-commerce site (DTS Package Queue Sender) will take the order, pack it into an XML document, and send it to the manufacturing database via a message-queue message. The manufacturing database has a DTS package (Queue Receiver) that is monitoring the queue and loads the order data into the correct tables as they arrive. For this exercise, you will need the new SQL Server 2000 feature OpenXML to insert the data into multiple tables.

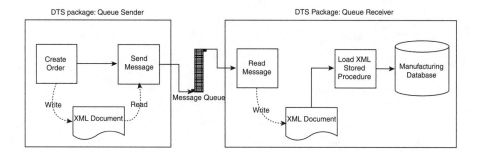

Figure 15.1   The two DTS packages moving the order from creation to the message queue to the manufacturing database.

Implementation

Because you don't have a real Web site that creates orders, the first of two packages will simulate the e-commerce site by creating and sending multiple product orders. To better represent a transaction system, this first package will contain a loop and issue 10 orders at a time, each for a different customer.

Step 1: Create Queue

To create a queue in Windows 2000, you need to go to the Computer Management window. If message queuing is installed, you will see a Message Queuing node inside the Services and Applications node. Select Private Queue. Then choose New from the Action menu and Private Queue from the submenu. The Queue Name dialog box opens. Type the queue name in the text box. For this example, type **DTSOrders**. Do not check the Transactional check box. Then click OK to create the queue (see Figure 15.2).

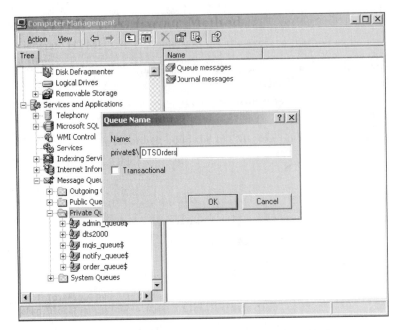

Figure 15.2   Creating a new queue in Windows 2000.

Creating a Queue in Windows NT 4.0

NT 4.0 did not include message queuing in the basic installation, but you can add it through the option pack, which is available free from Microsoft (`www.microsoft.com/ntserver/nts/downloads/recommended/nt4optpk`). After message queuing is installed, you can access it through the Start menu; choose Programs > Windows NT 4.0 Option Pack > Microsoft Message Queue > Explorer. When the MSMQ Explorer tool opens, you can click on your server's node to select it. Right-click on the server node object to display the shortcut menu, choose New, and then select Queue (see Figure 15.3). In the Create New Queue dialog box, type the queue name. For this example, type **DTSOrders**.

Step 2: Create the Recipient Database

Now we need to insert an order into a SQL Server-based manufacturing database. Using the SQL Server Enterprise Manager, create a new database called

Manufacturing. Then use the Data Import Wizard to import all the tables and data from the Access database C:\DTS2000\Data\Manufacturing.mdb[1]. You will be bringing in 17 tables from Access.

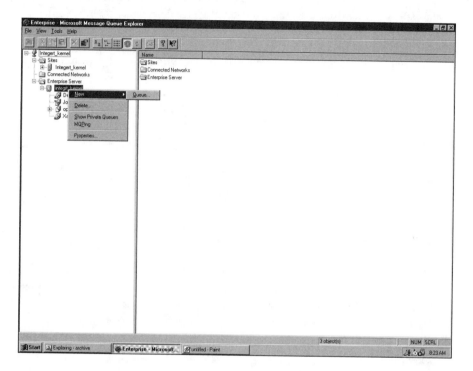

Figure 15.3   Creating a new queue in Windows NT 4.0.

Step 3: Create the Sending Data Package

Create a new, empty DTS package, and save it as Queue Sender. Next, you need to create a global variable that will count the number of orders sent. Right-click the package and choose Package Properties from the shortcut menu to open the Package Properties dialog box. Click the Global Variables tab. Create one global variable called Counter, and set the type as integer with a value of 0.

---

1. All data files and scripts used in the book are available to be downloaded from http:// www.magenic.com/publications or http://www.newriders.com. The self-extracting ZIP file will create a directory structure starting with DTS2000. You can extract the files to any drive or directory, but all file references in this book will be based on C:\DTS2000\.

Step 4: Create an ActiveX Script Task

Create an ActiveX Script task called Order Generator to create an order, and save it as an XML document. This task will create a random order with data for customer, freight expense, order data, and required date; then it will generate multiple-order detail records containing product, quantity, and unit price. The task will package the order in an XML string and save it to disk. The really cool feature about using XML is that with one XML document, you can create a new order that will update multiple tables.

The key components of the script will generate random numbers and create the XML string. Generating random numbers is easy with VBScript. First, you initialize the randomization engine by using the Randomize command. Then you can create any integer value between two numbers by using the Rnd function in the following algorithm:

```
Int((HighValue * Rnd) + LowValue )
```

For instance if you want to generate a random integer between 18 and 136, the formula is:

```
Int((136 * Rnd) + 18)
```

XML

Extensible Markup Language (XML) is a hypertext programming language used to describe the contents of a set of data. XML can even contain information about how the data should be displayed. Like the other markup languages, XML uses tags to explain the data. XML is flexible enough to represent an unlimited variation of data relationships.

Listing 15.1 shows customers and their corresponding orders. The first Customer is Company1, the CustomerID is XYZZ, and the Contact is Joe. Company1 placed an order on August 8 and one on October 3. The second customer is Company2, with only one order on June 13. You can see that each topic or node has a begin and end tag. For example, "<Customer" is the topic and the field name is CustomerID. CustomerID is followed by the CustomerID value XYZAA. The customer-related data ends with the </Customer> tag. The whole string begins with the <root> tag and ends with the </root> tag. As you can see, XML easily (and in a somewhat readable format) represents the data that would be split into several tables in a normalized RDBMS.

Listing 15.1 **Sample XML Document That Contains Several Orders**

```
<ROOT>
      <Customers CustomerID="XYZAA" ContactName="Joe" CompanyName="Company1">
       <Orders CustomerID="XYZAA" OrderDate="2000-08-25T00:00:00"/>
       <Orders CustomerID="XYZAA" OrderDate="2000-10-03T00:00:00"/>
      </Customers>
      <Customers CustomerID="XYZBB" ContactName="Steve" CompanyName="Company2">
       <Orders CustomerID=" XYZBB " OrderDate="2000-06-13T00:00:00"/>
      </Customers>
</ROOT>
```

The XML string that you will need to create looks like this:

```
<OrderRoot><OrderData CustomerID="5" Freight="37.47" OrderDate="03/24/1998"
RequiredDate="5/29/1998"><OrderDetailData OrderID="??OrderID??" ProductID="11"
Quantity="361"/><OrderDetailData OrderID="??OrderID??" ProductID="14"
Quantity="76"/><OrderDetailData OrderID="??OrderID??" ProductID="10"
Quantity="71"/></OrderData></OrderRoot>
```

The string starts with `<OrderRoot>` and ends with `</OrderRoot>`. The order header data starts with the tag `<OrderData>`, which maps into the Order table at the recipient system. The Order table needs CustomerID, Freight Expense, OrderDate, and Required Date. Two fields in the recipient system, EmployeeID and Shipdate, cannot be filled in, because the product was sold via the Web and the product hasn't been shipped yet

The next part of the XML string contains the `OrderDetailData` for three items. This information maps to the OrderDetail table in the recipient system. That table has a foreign-key reference to the Order table, using the OrderID, and needs ProductID, Quantity, and UnitPrice. This order is closed with the `</OrderData>` tag.

Careful inspection will show that XML can easily represent many items in one order and even many orders all within one string. To be closer to a real-life situation, we will allow up to 20 items per order. You will notice that there is no OrderID in the `OrderDetailData` string; you have it filled with the keyword `OrderID`, wrapped by question marks before and after. This keyword holds the place for the OrderID. When the order is placed, you will have the actual ID value, and you can replace the string with the ID and then update the order detail items.

To build the XML document, you will use the Microsoft XML Document Object Model (DOM). The object model lets you create node objects to which you can assign a name and values, and nest these objects in parent–child relationships, as order details are nested inside an order. The DOM will handle the XML syntax and make sure that all the beginning and ending tags are in place. To build the document, follow these steps:

1. Create an empty document, as follows:

   ```
   Set oDoc = CreateObject("MSXML.DOMDocument")
   ```

2. Create the root node called Order Root, and add it to the document by using the `Append Child` method, as follows:

   ```
   Set nodBase = oDoc.createNode(1, "OrderRoot", "")
   oDoc.appendChild nodBase
   ```

3. Create the order header node called `OrderData`, as follows:

   ```
   Set nodOrder = oDoc.createNode(1, "OrderData", "")
   ```

   You will not add this node to the document until after you add all the data to the order.

4. Add data fields and values for the order (such as Customer, Purchase Date, and Required Date), as follows:

```
Set nodDataValue = oDoc.createAttribute("CustomerID")
nodDataValue.Text = Int((21 * Rnd) + 1 )
nodOrder.Attributes.setNamedItem nodDataValue
```

For example, you will add Customer by creating the Customer node, adding the CustomerID to the Text property of the node, and then adding the CustomerID node to the OrderData node.

5. After you populate the Order header, you need to populate the order details (such as Product, Purchase Price, and Quantity):

```
Set nodOrderDetail = oDoc.createNode(1, "OrderDetailData", "")
```

To hold the data, first to create an Order Detail node, just as you would need to create an Order Detail table in a normalized database.

6. Create the order detail data (such as ProductID), as follows:

```
'Create a random Product(between 1-16)
    Set nodDataValue = oDoc.createAttribute("ProductID")
    nodDataValue.Text = Int((16 * Rnd) + 1 )
    nodOrderDetail.Attributes.setNamedItem nodDataValue
```

You create this data the way you did the order header data: create the node, assign it a value, and then add the node to the `OrderDetailData` node.

7. Save the file to disk.

DTS provides three ways to pack data into a message: string, global variable, and data file. The data file allows you to transport the largest amount of data (up to 4MB) and therefore is the best choice. To generate the XML data file, all you need to do is execute the `Save` method on the DOM and specify the file location and name, as follows:

```
oDoc.save "C:\DTS2000\Data\OrderOut.XML"
```

Listing 15.2 shows the full code to generate a purchase order randomly and persist it to file.

Listing 15.2 **VBScript to Create an XML-Based Order by Using the Microsoft XML Document Object**

```
Function Main
  Dim iRandomValue
  Dim iTotalItemCount
  Dim i
  Dim sTransDate
  Dim oDoc
  Dim nodBase
```

```
Dim nodOrder
Dim nodDataValue
Dim nodOrderDetail

'Create an initiate of the random-number generator.
Randomize

  'Create an instance of the Microsoft XML Document Object
Set oDoc = CreateObject("MSXML.DOMDocument")

Set nodBase = oDoc.createNode(1, "OrderRoot", "")
oDoc.appendChild nodBase

Set nodOrder = oDoc.createNode(1, "OrderData", "")

'Create a random Customer(between 1-21)
Set nodDataValue = oDoc.createAttribute("CustomerID")
nodDataValue.Text = Int((21 * Rnd) + 1 )
nodOrder.Attributes.setNamedItem nodDataValue

'Create a random Freight Expense(between $10.00 and $100.00)
Set nodDataValue = oDoc.createAttribute("Freight")
nodDataValue.Text = Int((10000 * Rnd) + 1000 ) / 100
nodOrder.Attributes.setNamedItem nodDataValue

'For the OrderDate we will send all the transactions during May 1998. Format is
03/DD/1998
  Set nodDataValue = oDoc.createAttribute("OrderDate")
  sTransDate = "03/" & Int((31 * Rnd) + 1 ) & "/1998"
  nodDataValue.Text = sTransDate
  nodOrder.Attributes.setNamedItem nodDataValue

'Required Date will be between 5 and 100 days from Order Date
  Set nodDataValue = oDoc.createAttribute("RequiredDate")
  nodDataValue.Text = DateAdd( "d" ,Int((100 * Rnd) + 5 ) , sTransDate )
  nodOrder.Attributes.setNamedItem nodDataValue

'Append the Order Items for the Order. There can be from 1 to 20 items ordered
per order
  iTotalItemCount = Int((20 * Rnd) + 1)
  For i = 1 to iTotalItemCount

    Set nodOrderDetail = oDoc.createNode(1, "OrderDetailData", "")

    'We don't know the OrderID but we can put in a placeholder until we do
    Set nodDataValue = oDoc.createAttribute("OrderID")
    nodDataValue.Text = "??OrderID??"
    nodOrderDetail.Attributes.setNamedItem nodDataValue
```

continues

Listing 15.2   **Continued**

```
    'Create a random Product(between 1-16)
    Set nodDataValue = oDoc.createAttribute("ProductID")
    nodDataValue.Text = Int((16 * Rnd) + 1 )
    nodOrderDetail.Attributes.setNamedItem nodDataValue

    'Create a random Quantity Order (between 5-100 Units)
    Set nodDataValue = oDoc.createAttribute("Quantity")
    nodDataValue.Text = Int((100 * Rnd) + 5 )
    nodOrderDetail.Attributes.setNamedItem nodDataValue
    nodOrder.appendChild nodOrderDetail

    'Create a random Unit Price (between 25-500 Dollars)
    Set nodDataValue = oDoc.createAttribute("UnitPrice")
    nodDataValue.Text =Int((500 * Rnd) + 25 )
    nodOrderDetail.Attributes.setNamedItem nodDataValue
    nodOrder.appendChild nodOrderDetail
  Next

  nodBase.appendChild nodOrder
  oDoc.save "C:\DTS2000\Data\OrderOut.XML"

  Main = DTSTaskExecResult_Success

End Function
```

Step 5: Send the Message with the XML String to the Message Queue

In the DTS Designer, add the Message Queue task to the package. Set the description to "Send Order," the message property to Send Message, and the queue to *Computer Name\Queue Type\Queue Name*—in this case, sam-lt\private$\DTSOrders. Remember to add the dollar sign ($) after the queue type. Figure 15.4 shows the Message Queue Task Properties screen.

To create the message to send, click the Add button to open the Message Queue Message Properties dialog box. Type **Data File Message** in the Message Type text box; then, in the File Name text box, type the path and filename that you entered in the VBScript earlier: **C:\DTS2000\Data\OrderOut.XML** (see Figure 15.5).

Figure 15.4   The Message Queue Task Properties dialog box with one message added.

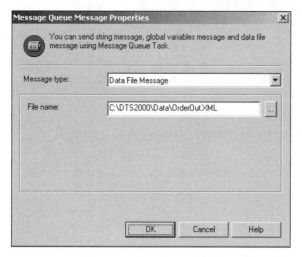

Figure 15.5   Adding a data file message to the Message Queue Task Message.

Step 6: Make the Package Loop to Create Many Records

Connect the Order Generator Task with the Send Message Task by using an On
Completion workflow connection. If you run the package now, the tasks will create a
single order and send it to the queue. To better simulate a real system, you need to
generate multiple orders. Therefore, you need to make the package loop many times.

To keep things contained, you will have the package loop 10 times (creating 10
orders) every time you run the package. To do so, you need to add an ActiveX Script
Task and have it reset the execution status of the Order Generator Task waiting to
execute DTSStepExecStat_Waiting. This setting restarts the task and has it generate
another purchase order. You do this for 10 iterations, using the global variable Counter
and increasing the count every time work comes to this ActiveX Script Task.

Drag an ActiveX Script Task from the taskbar, and place it to the right of the
Message Queue Task. Double-click the new task, and set the description to Loop
Package. Add the script in Listing 15.3 to make the package loop 10 times.

Listing 15.3   **VBScript to Loop a Package 10 Times**

```
Function Main()

    Dim oPkg
    DTSGlobalVariables("Counter").Value = _
    DTSGlobalVariables("Counter").Value + 1

    If DTSGlobalVariables("Counter").Value < 10 THEN
      Set oPkg = DTSGlobalVariables.Parent

      'Set the Order Generator Step to Waiting
  oPkg.Steps("DTSStep_DTSActiveScriptTask_1").ExecutionStatus = _
        DTSStepExecStat_Waiting

    Else
      DTSGlobalVariables("Counter").Value = 0
    END IF

         Main = DTSTaskExecResult_Success

End Function
```

The steps involved with setting another task's status is to first get an instance of the
current package object using the following code.

```
"Set oPkg = DTSGlobalVariables.Parent".
```

Then set the step's execution status to waiting, as follows:

```
oPkg.Steps("DTSStep_DTSActiveScriptTask_1").ExecutionStatus = _
DTSStepExecStat_Waiting
```

To know how to reference the step name for a task, right-click the task, choose Workflow from the shortcut menu, and then choose Workflow Properties to bring up the Workflow Properties dialog box. The Options tab has a read-only name property that contains the step name you need to reference—in this case, `DTSStep_DTSActiveScriptTask_1`. Finally, be sure to reset the global variable `Counter` back to zero. After the package has run 10 times, set `Counter = 0`.

After the code is entered and parsed for syntax correctness, click OK to get back to the package; then add an On Completion workflow from Send Message to Loop Package. Save the package and run it a few times to stack up messages in the queue. The completed package should look like Figure 15.6.

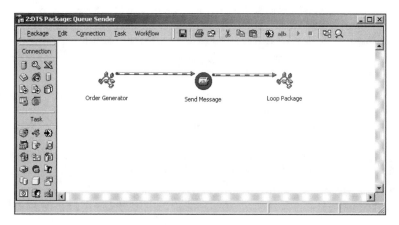

Figure 15.6   Queue Sender package.

Create Package to Receive and Process the Messages

The second package you need to create is the Queue Receiver package, which will listen to the message queue and process the orders as they come in. The basic work-flow of this package will be to have a Message Queue Task listen to the queue. When an appropriate message arrives, the package saves the data file to disk and loads the XML document into the appropriate tables by using one of SQL Server 2000's new XML features.

Step 1: Create the Stored Procedure

The stored procedure will process the XML string. Before you start working on the package, create the stored procedure that will process the XML document. The stored procedure named `LoadXMLData` takes one parameter: the XML document. The stored procedure then uses the `sp_xml_preparedocument` stored procedure in SQL Server to parse the text by using the MSXML parser (msxml2.dll) in a form that can be referenced. The `sp_xml_preparedocument` system stored procedure will return a handle for use throughout the current connection.

SQL Server and XML

SQL Server 2000 supports both XML composition and decomposition. The composition is done through the `SELECT` statement clause `for XML`. This easy-to-use clause tells SQL Server to convert the return data to an XML string that is complete with all the tags.

The decomposition is done through OpenXML. OpenXML provides a mechanism to parse and store an XML document in a SQL Sever internal cache and then query the document much like you query a table or view. You can do regular selects to get data from the cached documents or, better yet, insert or update data in your database based on the data contained in the cached documents. But be careful: *OpenXML will use one-eighth of the memory available to SQL Server.* Always release the documents when you are done working with them.

After the document has the internal reference, you execute an `INSERT` SQL statement specifying the XML document reference and the portion of the XML document that is applicable. In this case, the section tagged `OrdersData` is what you want to insert. You can do this easily, because the field names match in the XML document and the table. This is not a requirement; you can create a field mapping to do the translation. This topic is covered well in BOL.

After the order has been created, you need to pick up the newly created Order ID and place it inside the XML document for the order detail item. From there, you can use the `replace` function to replace the `??OrderID??` key with the correct ID. You then have to pass the XML document back through the parser and create the internal representation with the correct IDs for order detail items.

Now you can load all the order item details into the OrderDetail table. This is done just like the `INSERT` into Orders statement, but with the OrderDetail table referencing the `<OrderDetailData>` tag. If you had multiple order items in the XML document, SQL Server will load them all with this single command.

The final step in this stored procedure is to free up the resources and remove the documents from memory by using the `sp_xml_remove document` system stored Procedure. The handle to the document is provided as an input parameter to the `sp_xml_remove_document` stored procedure. Listing 15.4 shows the full storedprocedure text.

Listing 15.4 **Stored Procedure that Accepts an XML Document and Decomposes it into Multiple SQL Server Tables**

```
CREATE PROCEDURE LoadXMLData @xmldoc varchar(1000) AS

Declare @h int
```

```
— Create an internal representation of the XML Document
EXEC sp_xml_preparedocument @h OUTPUT, @xmldoc

—Insert the data from the XML Document directly into the Orders Table
Insert into Orders
select * from OpenXML(@h, '//OrderData',1) with Orders

—Set the OrderID for the newly created order in each OrderItem
Set @xmldoc= Replace (@xmldoc,'??OrderID??',@@Identity)

—Reload the XML Document into the Internal Representation
EXEC sp_xml_preparedocument @h OUTPUT, @xmldoc

—Insert the Orders Details directly into the Order Detail Table
Insert into OrderDetails
select * from OpenXML(@h, '//OrderDetailData',1) with OrderDetails

—Free up resources by removing the internal representation of the document
EXEC sp_xml_removedocument @h
GO
```

Step 2: Create a New Package

Create a new package to monitor a message queue for messages, and name it Queue
Receiver. Next, create a Message Queue Task, and name it Queue Listener. Set the
`Messages` property to `Receive Messages`. Specify the same queue as you did in the
Queue Sender: sam-lt\private$\DTSOrders. Set the message type to Data File
Message, and fill in the path and filename to specify a location for the file. For this
example, type **C:\DTS2000\Data\OrderIn.XML**.

You can also specify a filter—such as pick up messages only from a particular package. Filters are handy when you have several packages or applications monitoring one
queue for messages. You won't have worry about that here. However, you are doing
some filtering. Because you set the message type to Data Files, this task will ignore all
other messages except ones that are from a DTS package and that contain a data file.

Be sure to check the Remove from Message queue so that you don't process the
same order over and over. Also, put in a time to live of 5 seconds to make sure that the
package doesn't sit forever when the queue is empty of messages (see Figure 15.7).

Step 3: Add Connections

Before you can add the Text File Source connection, you need to add a dummy text
file to point to. All you need to do is use Notepad to save a file with the word
XMLData (anything will do). Then press Enter to put in a carriage return and line
feed, and save the file in the directory where your Message Queue Task is saving the
incoming data files: C:\DTS2000\Data\OrderIn.XML. Now you can add a Text File
Source connection. Set the name as Order XML Doc, and set it to read the file you
just created (see Figure 15.8).

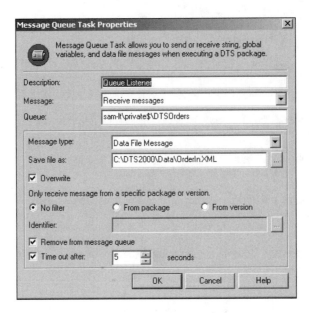

Figure 15.7 Message Queue Task Properties dialog box set up to listen to a queue.

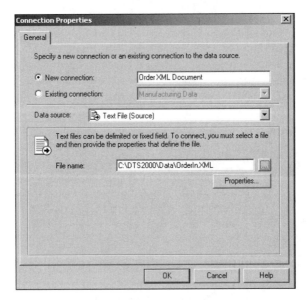

Figure 15.8 The Text File Source Data connection set to load the XML document saved by the Message Queue Task.

Inside the Connection Properties dialog box, click on the Properties button, set the file format to Delimited, and set the Text Qualifier to <none>. Click on Next, and set the delimiter to Tab. You want to make sure that you read the whole document as one long string. Now click on Finish and OK to return to the Designer.

Next, add a SQL Server Data connection, set the database to the Manufacturing database that you have created, and call the connection Manufacturing Data.

Step 4: Add a Transform Data Connection

Add a Transform Data connection from the Text File Source to the SQL Server Manufacturing Destination. Inside the Transform Data Task Properties dialog box, click on the Source tab, set the Description to Load Orders. Next, click on the Destination tab, set the Destination Table to Orders.

Before you create the script to process the orders, you need to create a lookup query that will run the LoadXMLData stored procedure and pass in the XML document. Inside the Transform Data Task Properties dialog box, click on the Lookups tab; then click on Add. Set the name to InsertOrder, make the connection Manufacturing Data, and click on the ellipsis button (...) to enter your SQL statement. Because all you are doing is executing the stored procedure that you created, just type **Execute LoadXMLData** in the SQL pane of the Data Transformation Services Query Designer dialog box.

When you try to close the Query Designer, you receive the error message: "The Query Designer does not support the EXECUTE SQL construct." Click OK. This error comes from the fact that the Designer cannot graphically display the Execute SQL. If you hide the Diagram pane, you will not receive this error message. This returns you to the Transform Data Task Properties dialog box.

Now you are ready to write the ActiveX Script that will grab the source text file containing the XML document and pass it to the stored procedure LoadXMLData. At the Transform Data Task Properties dialog box, click on the Transformation tab, and click on col1 in Source Columns to select it. Click on the New Transformation button and select ActiveX Script from the Create New Transformations dialog box. Type **Pass on XML Documents** in the Name field located in the Transformations dialog box. Now click on the Destination Columns tab, and make sure no Destination columns appear. These columns are not necessary, because you will use the lookup query and stored procedure to insert the data.

Click OK to return to the Transformation Options dialog box. Click on the Properties button. The script that you need is very short. All you need to do is execute the lookup query InsertOrder and pass in source column, Col001. First make sure that the Language tab is selected in the ActiveX Script Transformations Properties dialog box. Next, type the following code from Listing 15.5 in the right window pane. Close the script by letting the data pump know that everything is OK (see Listing 15.5). Click OK three times to get back to the Designer.

Listing 15.5 **VBScript Using the Lookup Query to Pass in an XML Document to a SQL Server Stored Procedure**

```
Function Main()
    DTSLookups("InsertOrder").Execute(DTSSource("Col001"))
    Main = DTSTransformStat_OK
End Function
```

Step 5: Create a Looping Mechanism

Create a looping mechanism to process all messages in the queue. In the first package, you created a workflow script to loop the package, and you can do the same thing in this step. Because you do not need to keep track of the count, you can use the Dynamic Properties Task to create the looping.

Add a Dynamic Properties Task to the package. Inside the Dynamic Properties Task Properties dialog box, type **Loop** in the Description field. Click on the Add button and double-click on Steps to expand it. Double-click on the DTSStep_DTSMessageQueueTask_1 step to expand it. Click on Execution Status Line in the right pane; then click on the Set button. In the Add/Edit Assignment dialog box, change the Source to Constant, set the Constant value to 1 (Waiting), and click OK twice (see Figure 15.9).

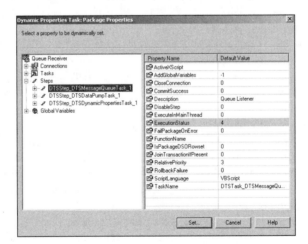

Figure 15.9 Setting the execution status for the Message Queue Task by using the Dynamic Properties Task.

Step 6: Add Workflow.

Add an On Success workflow from Queue Listener to Order XML Doc. Then add an On Success workflow from Manufacturing Data to Loop (see Figure 15.10).

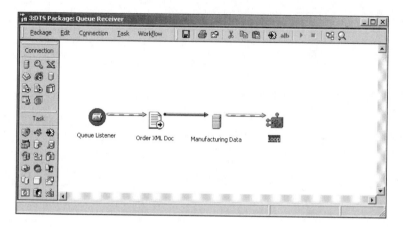

Figure 15.10 The Queue Receiver package.

Now all you have to do is run the Queue Sender package and the Queue Receiver package.

If you want, you can have the receiver package run with no Message Queue Task timeout, or you can have it scheduled to run every so many minutes or hours to process all the accumulated messages.

Summary

Although the DTS Message Queue task does not expose all the features and properties available, you can work around that situation easily by using the ActiveX Script task to interact with message queues or by building a custom task that exposes the particular properties that interest you. The major design issue you need to be aware of is that the creator and the consumer must have a common understanding of the tags in the XML document. If the creator uses CID for CustomerID, the consumer must know what that term means.

Combining message queuing and DTS into a solution can have a great impact on your system's flexibility and reliability. You can use one package to send many messages to different queues, and you can have many packages monitor a queue from many senders. You can even use message queues within transactions; the sending system waits for a reply message either with a transaction-completion notice or with processed return data.

16

Creating Your Own Custom Task

IT PROBABLY WOULDN'T SURPRISE YOU IF you were told that DTS is written with Microsoft's Component Object Model (COM) technology. Because of COM, many of the features inside DTS can be extended using any programming environment that supports COM. In fact, some of the "built-in" features of DTS are mere extensions of a base COM object, which certainly is true for tasks. All the DTS tasks that were introduced in Chapter 4, "DTS Tasks," and Chapter 5, "More DTS Tasks," are COM objects that implement interfaces defined in the base DTS task object. As such, they really are just another regular custom task, which means that you can create your very own DTS task and add it to DTS Designer or use it as a component in a DTS application that you are developing. This chapter will show you how to build a custom task.

DTS Applications

A *DTS application* is an application that creates instances of DTS objects outside the DTS Designer environment. The application can then execute tasks by calling the Execute method of the package under its control and destroy them when it's done.

You have plenty of options when deciding which development tool to use, because many tools support COM. Among the Microsoft offerings, Visual Basic and Visual C++ are popular choices. For high performance and more control of all programming aspects, Visual C++ is the choice. For example, if you want to create a custom task that needs to gain access to OLE DB—as in enumerating the available servers, databases, and tables—you will need to develop with Visual C++.

Note that Visual Basic support for multithreading is limited to apartment threading, a topic that is well beyond the scope of this book. Suffice it to say that you need to evaluate carefully whether VB's apartment threading is sufficient for your needs. If not, consider developing your custom task with Visual C++.

For less complex tasks, Visual Basic usually is sufficient. The example presented in this chapter is developed using Visual Basic. The custom-task example will take ADO recordset data previously saved (by an `Execute` SQL task) in a global variable. The custom task will generate an HTML table containing the recordset data and write the HTML text to a text file. Then you can include the file in a Web page and display it easily.

The custom task has a custom Properties dialog box that allows the user to select the global variable to be accessed by the custom task. This window also allows the user to specify the filename and the location where the HTML text will be saved.

Setting up a Custom Task-Development Project

It is very easy to use Microsoft's Visual Basic (VB) development environment to create a custom task. Open VB, and double-click the ActiveX DLL icon to create a new Microsoft ActiveX DLL project (see Figure 16.1).

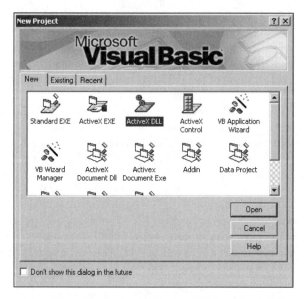

Figure 16.1 Creating a new ActiveX DLL project in VB.

This will create an in-process COM server, which you can add to the DTS Designer environment in SQL Server's Enterprise Manager.

DTS Designer Requires an In-Process COM Server

When creating the VB project, you must choose ActiveX DLL to make it an in-process COM server. This is required if you want to add the custom task to the DTS Designer environment.

Next, you need to add a reference to the DTS object library so that VB (and your custom task) will know how to access the DTS objects. From the Project menu, click on References to bring up the References dialog box (see Figure 16.2).

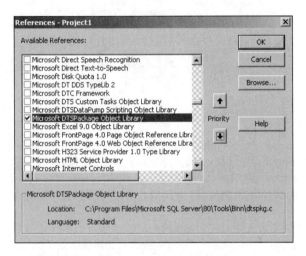

Figure 16.2   Setting a reference to the DTS Package Object Library.

Make sure that the Microsoft DTSPackage Object Library check box is checked. If you cannot find this option in the Available References window, click the Browse button and find the file named dtspkg.dll. This file is installed during the SQL Server installation and normally is in the folder C:\Program Files\Microsoft SQL Server\80\Tools\Binn. Click the OK button. Now you should be able to reference DTS objects within your project.

From the Project menu, click on [*Project1* Properties], where *Project1* is the default name VB gives your newly created project. This will bring up the Project Properties dialog box (see Figure 16.3).

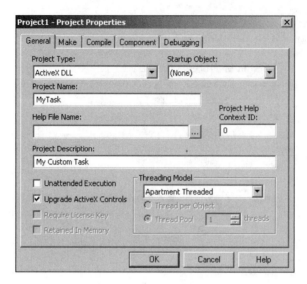

Figure 16.3 The Project Properties dialog box.

If you want to change the default names that VB assigns to your project and class, now is the time. Change the project name to a more meaningful one, such as `MyTask`. Change the class name to `clsMyTask`. Although these names are important to the current project, they do not necessarily affect the naming of the task when you add it to the DTS Designer.

Other housekeeping chores that you need to take care of include the following:

- **Startup Object**—In the Project Properties dialog box, click on the General tab, and make sure that Startup Object is set to None.

- **Threading Model**—In the Project Properties dialog box, click on the General tab, and make sure that Threading Model is set to Apartment Threaded.

- **Version Compatibility**—In the Project Properties dialog box, click on the Component tab, and make sure that Version Compatibility is set to Project Compatibility.

- **Instancing**—Click on the class object (`clsMyTask`), and make sure that its `Instancing` property is set to `MultiUse`.

These options will ensure that your COM server is built and instantiated properly. If you save the project now, you should have in your project folder the files named MyTask.vbp and clsMyTask.cls. (We saved our example in C:\DTS2000\Custom Task\).

One of the objects exposed by the DTSPackage Object Library is the DTS task object. This object in turn exposes two COM interfaces: CustomTask and CustomTaskUI.

You use the CustomTask interface to implement the processing to be done by your custom task. You use the CustomTaskUI interface to implement an optional graphical user interface, often called the *property page*, for setting and saving the property values of your custom task.

The Custom Task Interface

If you followed the steps for setting up the Visual Basic development environment earlier in this chapter, you can now implement the COM interface exposed by the base DTS task object. As explained above, you don't use the task object directly. DTS defines a COM interface called CustomTask, which implements the properties and methods of the base task object. All other custom task implementations derive from this secondary COM interface.

Make sure that clsMyTask is selected in VB's Project window. Then choose Code from the View menu to open the code editor for your class (see Figure 16.4).

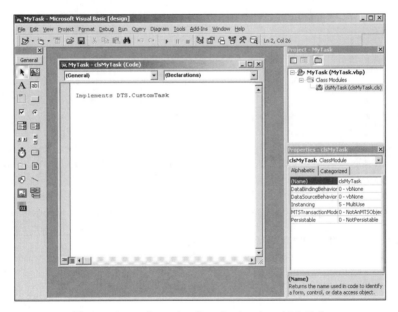

Figure 16.4   The code editor for the class clsMyTask.

(General) should be shown as the selected item on the Object list box on the left side of the dialog box, and (Declarations) should be the selected item in the Procedure list box on the right side. At the top of the code-editing area, type the code

Implements DTS.CustomTask. As soon as you do, CustomTask will be added to the Object list box. Select the CustomTask item, and then open the Procedure list box. This will display all the elements of the CustomTask COM interface, which you *must* implement (see Figure 16.5).

Figure 16.5 Elements of the CustomTask interface.

When you select each one of the interface elements from the Procedure list box, Visual Basic generates placeholder code called *event procedures*. These procedures are termed placeholders because they are valid `Sub` or `Function` procedures even though they don't do anything. Even if you don't add any code to these empty functions, they are considered to be implemented. They can be called, but because there is no code inside to execute, they will not do anything. Of course, you need to add code to at least some of these placeholders or your custom task will not be doing much either.

Implementing the COM Interface

Although COM requires that all the interface's elements be implemented, some of these implementations can be mere placeholders that do nothing. The Visual Basic compiler may strip out the event procedure if it is empty, so be sure that you have at least a comment line inside each placeholder.

The CustomTask COM interface exposes the following interface elements:

- A `Description` property
- A `Name` property
- A `Properties` collection
- An `Execute` method

As you can see, there are two property interface elements, a collection interface element (which is just a special property interface), and a method interface element.

Note that the property interface elements represent the property values of the base DTS custom task, *not your custom task.* You can have your own public variables and properties for your custom task. If you don't plan to add a custom user interface to your custom task, DTS provides default services for managing the public variables and properties of your custom task and saving them in a Properties collection. In SQL Server's Enterprise Manager, the DTS Designer will display a default property page so that these can be updated (see Figure 16.6).

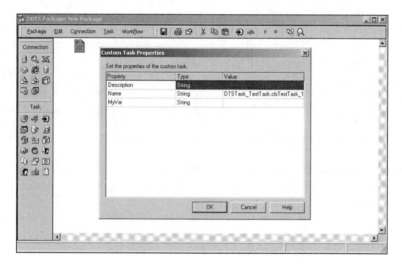

Figure 16.6   The default Custom Task Properties window.

In Figure 16.6, despite the fact that we've named the public variables `Description` and `Name`, these variables have nothing to do with the similarly named properties of the base DTS custom task; they simply are variables in *your* custom task. To make the association between your `Description` and `Name` variables and the base DTS custom task's properties, you need to implement those properties and have them point to your variables.

As you've seen, if your variables happen to be public, you don't have to do anything else. The DTS default properties provider will recognize the variables and take care of saving them in the Properties collection. The traditional way to implement property values, however, is to use private variables and declare the property as public. When you make your variables private, DTS will not be able to see them, so you need to declare in your custom task public properties that provide access to those private variables. You will take this approach in building a custom task, and as a result, you will need to take the extra step of declaring your own public property values.

Below the `Implements DTS.CustomTask` line, type the following:

```
Private m_strDescription As String
Private m_strName As String
```

These variables will store the `Description` and `Name` properties of the custom task. Now you are ready to implement the base DTS custom task's properties.

The *Description* Property

To implement the `Description` property, select Description [PropertyGet] and Description [PropertyLet] from the Procedure list box. This will generate empty place-holders for the `Description` property. As noted earlier, this satisfies the minimum COM requirement for implementing this interface element.

You can register the custom task and use it in DTS even with empty placeholders for the `Description` property. When you add the custom task to a package in DTS Designer, DTS gives the task a label consisting of the name used to register the task in DTS plus the string ": undefined". If you implement an empty placeholder for the `Description` property, the task will not be able to retain this label.

> **Implementing an Empty Placeholder for Description**
>
> When you use a custom task in DTS Designer, no label will be attached to the icon if you implement empty placeholders for the `Description` property.

Therefore, you need to properly implement the `Description` property by adding the following boldfaced statements:

```
Private Property Let CustomTask_Description(ByVal RHS As String)
    m_strDescription = RHS
End Property

Private Property Get CustomTask_Description() As String
    CustomTask_Description = m_strDescription
End Property
```

Because these property methods (and the variable where the property value is stored) are private, you need to implement in your custom task a public property that points to the same private variable. This will effectively tie the two `Description` properties together. Following is the code you use:

```
Public Property Let Description(ByVal RHS As String)
    m_strDescription = RHS
End Property

Public Property Get Description() As String
    Description = m_strDescription
End Property
```

The Description property is added to your custom task's Properties collection, allowing it to be persisted properly in the Custom Task Properties window in DTS Designer. To allow users to set and modify this property with a custom property page, you must implement a CustomTaskUI interface for your custom task (see section, "Using the Custom Task UI Interface," later in this chapter).

The *Name* Property

Within a DTS package, task objects are identified by their Name property. When you add any task to a DTS package, DTS Designer assigns it a unique name. A custom task must save this assigned name, because DTS will use this name to reference the task thereafter. This means that, unlike the Description property, you cannot use a custom task in DTS Designer if you have only empty placeholders for its Name property. Therefore, you must implement fully the Name property of the CustomTask interface.

To do so, select the Name [PropertyGet] and Name [PropertyLet] items from the Procedure list box. This will generate empty placeholders for the Name property. Then add the following boldfaced statements:

```
Private Property Let CustomTask_Name(ByVal RHS As String)
    m_strName = RHS
End Property

Private Property Get CustomTask_Name() As String
    CustomTask_Name = m_strName
End Property
```

This will allow the Name property to be persisted properly. Because DTS will always use this preassigned name to refer to the task, you should not allow the name to be changed. Therefore, *do not implement a separate public Name property for your custom task,* as you did with the Description property.

Never Expose the *Name* Property of Your Custom Task

If the custom task will be used in DTS Designer, do not implement a class-specific Name property for your custom task. Instead, implement only the Name property of the CustomTask COM interface.

If you will be using the custom task in a DTS application, you can allow the task's name to be modified. However, the application must ensure that task names are unique whenever a task is added to the Tasks collection.

The *Properties* Collection

When you implement class-specific properties of your custom task (that is, not the CustomTask's property interface elements), the `Property` object is stored in the Properties collection. This means that a Properties collection must be implemented somewhere. By now, you should be saying, "Oh, great, just how I was looking to waste my time." Fortunately, you do not have to deal with property bags and property persistence yourself. As mentioned earlier in this chapter, DTS provides a default properties provider that takes care of it. The bottom line is that you can choose to handle the implementation of the Properties collection yourself or have DTS do it for you.

To implement the Properties collection, select the Properties [PropertyGet] item in the Procedure list box. This will generate an empty placeholder for the `Property Get` event of the Properties collection. To have DTS take care of managing the task's properties, return `Nothing` in this placeholder, as in the following code:

```
Private Property Get CustomTask_Properties() As DTS.Properties
    Set CustomTask_Properties = Nothing
End Property
```

This will enable the proper persistence of any property that you define for your custom task through the default properties provider.

The *Execute* Method

The `Execute` method is where you put all the code that you want the custom task to execute. DTS calls this method at the proper time during package execution. When DTS calls the `Execute` method, it passes four parameters that you can use within the method: `pPackage, pPackageEvents, pPackageLog,` and `pTaskResult`.

The *pPackage* Parameter

The `pPackage` parameter is a reference to the `Package2` object in the DTS object model. (Note that the `Package2` object exists only in DTS 2000.) Use this parameter to access other objects in the package where your custom task is used. You can access such objects as the Tasks collection, the Steps collection, and global variables, including the extended properties and methods of a DTS package object.

You must ensure that the parameter is not set to `Nothing` before you use it within the `Execute` method.

The *pPackageEvents* Parameter

The `pPackageEvents` parameter is a reference to a `PackageEvents` object in the DTS object model. Use this parameter to raise events in the package. You can raise the following events:

- **OnStart**—Indicates the start of a task or step.
- **OnQueryCancel**—Terminates the task.

- **OnProgress**—Provides information about the progress of the task's execution.

- **OnFinish**—Indicates completion of a task's execution.

- **OnError**—Indicates that an error occurred and provides information about the error.

You must ensure that the parameter is not set to Nothing before using it within the method. To use the pPackageEvent parameter, declare a local variable as a DTS PackageEvents object, as follows:

```
Dim oPkgEvent As DTS.PackageEvents
Set oPkgEvent = [Parameter name specified for pPackageEvents]
```

You can then use this local variable to raise events from within your custom task. Typically, the first event that you raise is the OnStart event. This event lets the host application know that the step in which your task executes has started, as follows:

```
oPkgEvent.OnStart "MyTask" 'Declare that MyTask has started
```

You can notify the host application of the progress in your task's processing by raising the OnProgress event, as follows:

```
oPkgEvent.OnProgress "MyTask", "Records Processed", 27, 1, rst.RecordCount
```

You can verify that DTS actually handles this event. When you execute the package, DTS displays the status as specified by your invocation of OnProgress in the Executing Package status window (see Figure 16.7).

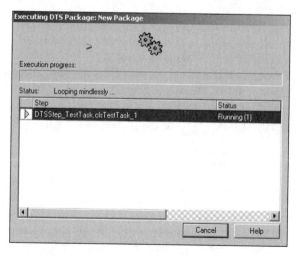

Figure 16.7   The Executing Package status window.

If you want to allow the process to be canceled, you can provide the user with that option by raising the OnQueryCancel event like this:

```
Dim bCancel As Boolean

oPkgEvent.OnQueryCancel "MyTask", bCancel
If bCancel Then
   pTaskResult = DTSTaskExecResult_Failure
   Exit Sub    'Exits the Execute Method
End If
```

Again, you can verify that DTS handles this event. In the Executing Package status window (refer to Figure 16.7) if you click the Cancel button, DTS will actually return `true` to your invocation of `OnQueryCancel`, which then allows you to terminate the task gracefully by setting `pTaskResult` and exiting the `Execute` method.

For error handling, you can use the `OnError` event (see Listing 16.1) to notify the host application that an error has occurred. The `OnError` event has many parameters. Listing 16.1 shows an example of how to code an `OnError` event.

Listing 16.1 **How to Raise an Error from a Custom Task**

```
Dim bCancel As Boolean

 oPkgEvent.OnError "MyTask", 102, "ADODB", "Unable to open recordset",,, bCancel
 If bCancel Then
   pTaskResult = DTSTaskExecResult_Failure
   Exit Sub    'Exits the Execute Method
 End If
```

As with `OnQueryCancel`, you need to check the last parameter to see whether you need to terminate the processing within the custom task. The other parameters allow you to provide more information about the error.

The last event that you typically raise is the `OnFinish` event. This event lets you notify the host application that the step in which your custom task executes has completed its processing. Here is an example of how this event is coded:

```
oPkgEvent.OnFinish "MyTask" 'Declare that MyTask has finished
```

The *pPackageLog* Parameter

A DTS package logs critical events to the msdb database in SQL Server if its `LogToSQLServer` property is set. You can have your custom task adhere to this convention by implementing logging yourself.

Using the `pPackage` parameter discussed earlier in this chapter, check whether the `LogToSQLServer` property is set. If so, you can choose to implement logging within your custom task.

The `pPackageLog` parameter is a reference to the `PackageLog` object in the DTS object model. You use this parameter to write log records to a log table in SQL Server's msdb database.

You must ensure that the parameter is not set to Nothing before you use it within the method. The first thing you need to do is add a log record to the log table. This log record represents the main log for the current execution of your custom task. Here is an example of how to add a log record:

```
If Not pPackageLog Is Nothing Then
    pPackageLog.WriteTaskRecord 300, "MyCustom Task Error"
End If
```

After the log record has been added, you can append log strings to this log record. Log strings are accumulated for the step in which the task is being executed. You can append multiple log strings to the log record. Here is an example of how to write a log string:

```
If Not pPackageLog Is Nothing Then
    pPackageLog.WriteStringToLog "Getting global variables"
End If
```

You can see what gets written to the log by viewing the package's logs in Enterprise Manager. Right-click on the DTS package that contains your custom task, and click on Package Logs to display the DTS Packages Logs window (see Figure 16.8).

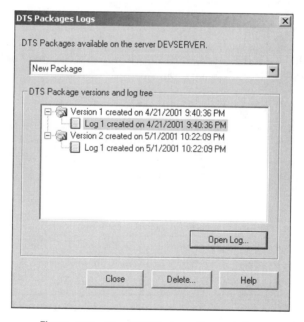

Figure 16.8   The DTS Packages Logs window.

Click on the Open Log button to display the Log Detail window (see Figure 16.9). Click the More Info button to expand the Log Detail window and show the task details.

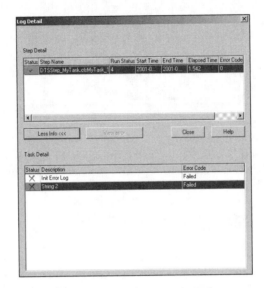

Figure 16.9 The Log Detail window.

If logging to SQL Server is turned off, you can specify a filename in the Error Handling section of the Logging tab of the DTS Package Properties window (see Figure 16.10). In fact, if you specify a filename here, logs are written to this error file whether or not SQL Server logging is on.

The *pTaskResult* Parameter

When the Execute method is invoked by DTS, the task must inform DTS of the results of its execution. To facilitate this communication, DTS passes a pTaskResult parameter, which you must set before returning from the Execute method. This parameter is a reference to the DTSTaskExecResult object in the DTS object model. Depending on the result of the custom task's execution, set the pTaskResult parameter to one of these values:

- **DTSTaskExecResult_Failure**—Task execution failed.
- **DTSTaskExecResult_RetryStep**—Retry the step that fires the custom task. This parameter effectively repeats the execution of the task.
- **DTSTaskExecResult_Success**—Task executed successfully.

If you do not return a result, DTS assumes that an error occurred, and package execution fails as well.

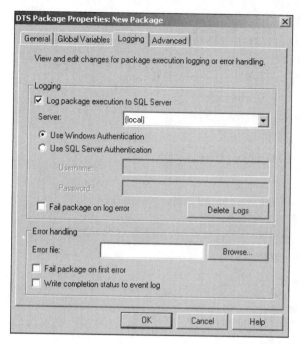

Figure 16.10 The Logging tab of the DTS Package Properties window.

> ### Task Result Handling in SQL 7.0
> In SQL 7.0, if you do not return a result from your custom task, DTS reports that package execution was successful.

For example, to tell DTS the that the task executed successfully, use the following code:

```
Private Sub CustomTask_Execute(ByVal pPackage As Object, _
                        ByVal pPackageEvents As Object, _
                        ByVal pPackageLog as Object, _
                        pTaskResult As DTS.DTSTaskExecResult)

    ...
    (other code here)
    ...
    pTaskResult = DTSTaskExecResult_Success
End Sub
```

Generate HTML Task: *Execute* Method

For the Generate HTML Task example, you use the `Execute` method to perform the following steps:

- Get the global variable specified by the user
- Open the text file for writing
- Output the HTML table's start tag
- For each row in the recordset, build the HTML row and then output the row
- Output the HTML table's end tag
- Close the text file

Listing 16.2 shows the code to get the global variable.

Listing 16.2 **Custom Task Accessing a DTS Global Variable**

```
Set oPkg = pPackage

'Get the global variable
For i = 1 To oPkg.GlobalVariables.Count
  If oPkg.GlobalVariables(i).Name = GlobalVarName Then
    Set rst = CreateObject("ADODB.Recordset")
    Set rst = oPkg.GlobalVariables(i).Value
    Exit For
  End If
Next i
```

Basically, you are iterating through the global-variables collection of the containing package to find the one that the user specified. You need to create the local variable as an `ADODB.Recordset` before copying the global variable into it.

You can then open the text file for output, like this:

```
Dim html As String

'Open the HTML file for output
If Mid(Pathname, 2, 1) = ":" Then
  html = Pathname & "\" & Filename
Else
  html = Pathname & "/" & Filename
End If
Open html For Output As #1
```

This code just allows for the possibility of the path being specified in UNC format (*//servername/path/filename*).

Here is the code for generating the start of the HTML table:

```
'Generate start of HTML table
Print #1, "<TABLE Border='1'>"
```

In Listing 16.3, you see the main code that does most of the work. From accessing the rowset data, converting it to HTML script, and then writing it out to the text file, the code is surprisingly short.

Listing 16.3   **Creating an HTML Table from an ADODBRecordset**

```
'Generate HTML table rows
rst.MoveFirst
Do Until rst.EOF
  'Build the row
  td = ""
  For j = 0 To rst.Fields.Count - 1
    tmp = ""
    If IsObject(rst.Fields(j).Value) Then
      tmp = " "
    ElseIf IsEmpty(rst.Fields(j).Value) Then
      tmp = " "
    ElseIf IsNull(rst.Fields(j).Value) Then
      tmp = " "
    ElseIf IsMissing(rst.Fields(j).Value) Then
      tmp = " "
    ElseIf IsArray(rst.Fields(j).Value) Then
      tmp = " "
    ElseIf IsNumeric(rst.Fields(j).Value) Then
      tmp = CStr(rst.Fields(j).Value)
    ElseIf IsDate(rst.Fields(j).Value) Then
      tmp = CStr(rst.Fields(j).Value)
    Else
      tmp = rst.Fields(j).Value
    End If
    td = td & "<TD>" & tmp & "</TD>"
  Next j

  'Write the row
  Print #1, vbTab & "<TR>" & td & "</TR>"

  rst.MoveNext
Loop
```

Essentially, in this code, you are going through each field in each row of the recordset. You are taking the value of each field (with the proper conversions to string) to build the row to be displayed. You then "print" the current row before moving on to the next row.

The important part of this code is determining what kind of data is coming in so that the code can handle its conversion to string properly. You will have to anticipate all the possible scenarios if you want the custom task to be robust.

Finally, you need to generate the HTML table's end tag and close the file:

```
'Generate end of HTML table
Print #1, "</TABLE>"

'Close the HTML file
Close #1
```

This section completes the *minimum* implementation of the CustomTask COM interface. If your custom task requires them, you can easily add more property elements, because they will automatically be added to the Properties collection and managed by the DTS properties provider.

For the example, you will need three more properties:

- A GlobalVarName property

- A PathName property

- A FileName property

The code to handle these properties is shown in Listing 16.4.

Listing 16.4 **Creating Custom Properties for the Custom Task**

```
Private m_strGlobalVarName As String
Private m_strPathname As String
Private m_strFilename As String

Public Property Let GlobalVarName(ByVal RHS As String)
    m_strGlobalVarName = RHS
End Property

Public Property Get GlobalVarName () As String
    GlobalVarName = m_strGlobalVarName
End Property

Public Property Let Pathname(ByVal RHS As String)
    m_strPathname = RHS
End Property

Public Property Get Pathname () As String
    Pathname = m_strPathname
End Property

Public Property Let Filename(ByVal RHS As String)
    m_strFilename = RHS
End Property

Public Property Get Filename () As String
    Filename = m_strFilename
End Property
```

Now you can move on to implementing a user interface for your custom task.

Creating the Property Page

A *property page* is typically used to display all the properties of an object. The default properties provider in DTS Designer will display a default property page if you do not implement a custom task user interface for your custom task. If you plan to provide a user interface for your custom task, now is the time to create the form that will be the property page for that user interface.

In VB, choose Add Form from the Project menu to bring up the Add Form dialog box (see Figure 16.11).

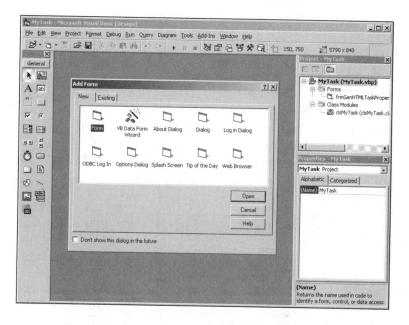

Figure 16.11   The Add Form dialog box.

Make sure that the icon named Form is selected; then click on the Open button. This will add a regular form named Form1 to your project. Change the name of the form to frmGenHTMLTaskProperties (or whatever form name you prefer). Also, change the form's caption to Generate HTML Task Properties.

With the form selected in the Project window, choose Object from the View menu to display the blank form. Add the form elements in Table 16.1 to the form.

Table 16.1 **Form Elements for the Property Page**

Object	Name	Text/Caption	Style
Frame	fraDescription	Description	
Frame	fraSource	Source	
Frame	fraDestination	Destination	
Textbox	txtDescription	Generate HTML Task: undefined	
Textbox	txtFilename		
Label	lblGlobalVar	Global Variable:	
Label	lblFilename	Filename:	
Combobox	cboGlobalVars		2-Drop-down List
DriveListBox	drvDestination		
DirListBox	dirDestination		
FileListBox	filDestination		
CommandButton	cmdCancel	Cancel	
CommandButton	cmdClose	Close	

After you add the form elements, the form should look something like Figure 16.12.

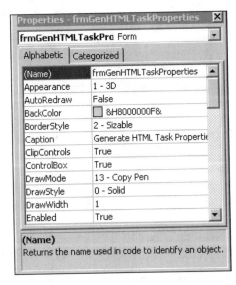

Figure 16.12 The frmGenHTMLTaskProperties form.

The form needs a `TaskObject` property that will contain the instance of the task object provided to the form during run time. When this property is set, it needs to do several things:

- Display the task description in the form
- Load the names of global variables into the combo box
- Select the current global variable in the combo box (if already set)
- Set the drive, path, and filename in `DriveListBox`, `DirListBox`, and `FileListBox`
- Display the current filename in the form

Listing 16.5 shows the code that does all these things.

Listing 16.5   **Initializing a Properties Form for the Custom Task**

```
Private oTask As DTS.Task
Private oCustomTask As clsMyTask

Public Property Set TaskObject (ByVal pTask As DTS.Task)
    Dim oTasks As DTS.Tasks
    Dim oPkg As DTS.Package
    Dim i As Integer
    Dim SaveIndex As Integer

    On Error Resume Next

    If Not pTask Is Nothing Then
        If TypeOf pTask Is DTS.Task Then
          Set oTask = pTask
          Set oCustomTask = pTask.CustomTask

          'Display the custom task's description
          txtDescription.Text = oCustomTask.Description

          'Get a reference to the containing package
          Set oTasks = oTask.Parent
          Set oPkg = oTasks.Parent

          'Load the names of the global variables into the combobox
          For i = 1 To oPkg.GlobalVariables.Count
            'Add only variables of type recordset
            If TypeName(oPkg.GlobalVariables(i).Value) = "Recordset" Then
              cboGlobalVars.AddItem oPkg.GlobalVariables(i).Name
            End If
          Next I

          'Select the current global variable in the combobox
          If oCustomTask.GlobalVarName <> "" Then
```

continues

Listing 16.5 **Continued**

```
                For i = 0 To cboGlobalVars.ListCount - 1
                    If cboGlobalVars.List(i) = oCustomTask.GlobalVarName Then
                        cboGlobalVars.ListIndex = I
                        Exit For
                    End If
                Next i
            End If


            'Display the current path and file names
            drvDestination.Drive = Left(oCustomTask.Pathname, 1)
            dirDestination.Path = oCustomTask.Pathname
            filDestination.Filename = oCustomTask.Filename
            txtFilename.Text = oCustomTask.Filename
        Else
            Err.Raise 1027 + vbObjectError, Me.Name, "Parameter pTask is not a Task
"
        End If
    Else
        Err.Raise 1027 + vbObjectError, Me.Name, "Parameter pTask is Nothing"
    End If
End Property

When the Cancel button is clicked, the form will have to be unloaded:
Private Sub cmdCancel_Click()
    Unload Me
End Sub
```

Finally, when the Close button is clicked, the properties have to be updated, and the form has to be unloaded (see Listing 16.6).[1]

Listing 16.6 **Setting the Custom Task's Custom Properties**

```
Private Sub cmdClose_Click()
    If txtDescription.Text = "" Then
        MsgBox "Please enter a description.",, "Description"
        Exit Sub
    Else
        oCustomTask.Description = txtDescription.Text
    End If
```

1. You can get the code for the event handlers of the DriveListBox, DirListBox, and FileListBox, together with the full source code for the custom-task VB project, by downloading CustomTask.Zip from www.newriders.com or www.magenic.com/publications.

```
    If cboGlobalVars.Text = "" Then
        MsgBox "Please select a global variable.",,"Global Variable"
        Exit Sub
    Else
        oCustomTask.GlobalVarName = cboGlobalVars.Text
    End If

    oCustomTask.Pathname = dirDestination.Path

    If txtFilename.Text = "" Then
        MsgBox "Please enter a filename.",, "Filename"
        Exit Sub
    Else
        oCustomTask.Filename = txtFilename.Text
    End If

    Unload Me
End Sub
```

The Custom Task UI Interface

As noted earlier in this chapter, if you want your users to be able to set some of the properties of your custom task, you have to implement the CustomTaskUI interface. This is the COM interface that displays and saves a property page for your custom task.

The CustomTaskUI COM interface exposes the following interface elements:

- An `Initialize` method
- A `New` method
- An `Edit` method
- A `Delete` method
- A `Help` method
- A `GetUIInfo` method
- A `CreateCustomToolTip` method

When you add your custom task to DTS, the DTS Designer calls these methods appropriately as needed whenever the property page for the custom task is displayed. In a DTS application, you must call these methods yourself.

To see these interface elements in your VB project, start with the keyword Implements as you did with the CustomTask COM interface. In the VB code editor, after the line `Implements DTS.CustomTask`, type the line **Implements DTS.Custom TaskUI**. This line adds the CustomTaskUI item to the Object list box. Select the CustomTaskUI item; then open the Procedure list box. You should now see the interface elements of the CustomTaskUI COM interface that you need to implement (see Figure 16.13).

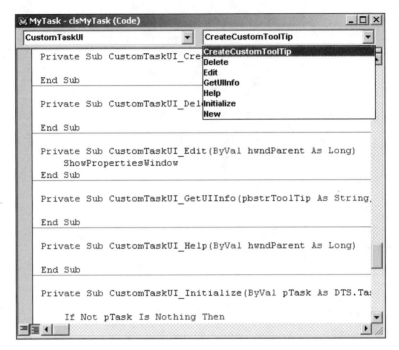

Figure 16.13   Elements of the CustomTask UI interface.

As you have done previously, select each of these interface elements to let VB generate the empty placeholder code. Now you are ready to implement each element.

The *Initialize* Method

The `Initialize` method is called whenever the custom task is opened. DTS will call the method automatically when the custom task is dropped on the DTS Designer sheet, when the custom task's property window is opened, and even when the custom task is deleted. You should note that `Initialize` is always the first method called. When you add the custom task to a DTS application, make sure that you call this method ahead of all the others to be consistent.

> ### *Initialize* Method Is Always Called
> In DTS Designer, the `Initialize` method is always called first—before the New, Edit, and Delete methods. In a DTS application, you should call `Initialize` before calling the other methods.

When the `Initialize` method is called, a task object is passed in as a parameter. You must save this object in a module-level object variable so that you can access the task object's properties and methods from anywhere within your custom task object. The

`Initialize` method is also used to set default values for certain properties of your custom task. Typically, you will want to set the `Description` property to a default description. Listing 16.7 shows the code.

Listing 16.7   **Code to Allow DTS to Initiate the Display of the Custom Task Property Page**

```
Private m_objTask As DTS.Task

Private Sub CustomTaskUI_Initialize(ByVal pTask As DTS.Task)

    If Not pTask Is Nothing Then
        If TypeOf pTask Is DTS.Task Then
            Set m_objTask = pTask

            If Description = "" Then
                Description = "Generate HTML Table: undefined"
            End If

            ... other code here

        Else
            Err.Raise 1027 + vbObjectError, "CustomTaskUI Initialize", "Parameter
pTask is not a Task "
        End If
    Else
        Err.Raise 1027 + vbObjectError, "CustomTaskUI Initialize", "Parameter
pTask is Nothing"
    End If
End Sub
```

The *New* Method

The `New` method is called whenever an instance of your custom task is created. In DTS Designer, this happens automatically when a user drops the icon representing your custom task on the DTS Designer sheet.

In a DTS application, you typically create a Tasks collection first and then call its `New` method to create the custom task. After the custom task object is created, you should call this `New` method.

Because the custom task object is newly created at this point, it should display all the default property values and let the user customize those that have been configured as user-modifiable. This is usually done with the property page. Because the code to display a property page is shared with the `Edit` method (discussed later in this chapter), you should create a private `Sub` procedure to contain it, as shown in Listing 16.8.

Listing 16.8   **Code to Display the Custom Task Property Page**

```
Private frmProperties As frmGenHTMLTaskProperties

Private Sub ShowPropertiesWindow()

    If Not pTask Is Nothing Then
        If TypeOf pTask Is DTS.Task Then
            Set frmProperties = New frmGenHTMLTaskProperties
            Set frmProperties.TaskObject = m_objTask

            frmProperties.Show vbModal
            DoEvents

            Set frmProperties = Nothing
        Else
            Err.Raise 1027 + vbObjectError, "ShowPropertiesWindow", "Parameter pTask
is not a Task "
        End If
    Else
        Err.Raise 1027 + vbObjectError, "ShowPropertiesWindow", "Parameter pTask
is Nothing"
    End If
End Sub
```

The code to display the property page from the New method should look like this:

```
Private Sub CustomTaskUI_New(ByVal hwndParent As Long)
    ShowPropertiesWindow
End Sub
```

The *Edit* Method

The Edit method is called when the property page needs to be displayed so that property values can be updated. In DTS Designer, DTS calls this method when the user right-clicks on the custom task and chooses Properties from the shortcut menu or when the user double-clicks the task icon. The Edit method displays the property page, using the same procedure invoked by the New method, as follows:

```
Private Sub CustomTaskUI_Edit(ByVal hwndParent As Long)
    ShowPropertiesWindow
End Sub
```

The *Delete* Method

The Delete method is called when the custom task is removed from the DTS Designer's design sheet. If the custom task is used only in DTS Designer, you normally do not have to do anything in this method; it can be a placeholder. In a DTS application, this method gives you the opportunity to perform cleanup code. Here is the `Delete` method as a placeholder:

```
Private Sub CustomTaskUI_Delete(ByVal hwndParent As Long)

End Sub
```

The *Help* Method

The `Help` method is called whenever a user right-clicks on the custom task and selects Help from the shortcut menu. This method gives you the opportunity to display a help screen. You can use message boxes, launch a custom help application, or use .hlp files. Here is the code for implementing the `Help` method:

```
Private Sub CustomTaskUI_Help(ByVal hwndParent As Long)
    ... code to display help
End Sub
```

The *GetUIInfo* Method

The `GetUIInfo` method is not called from DTS Designer. You can use this method in a DTS application to obtain a custom task's description and version information, as well as its ToolTips text.

```
Private Sub CustomTaskUI_GetUIInfo(pbstrToolTip As String, _
                                   pbstrDescription As String, _
                                   plVersion As Long, _
                                   pFlags As DTS.DTSCustomTaskUIFlags)
    ... code to retrieve the custom task's Description and ToolTipText
End Sub
```

The `GetUIInfo` method is also used to return a `DTSCustomTaskUIFlag` status, which can be one of the following:

- **DTSCustomTaskUIFlags_Default**—Indicates a default user interface.
- **DTSCustomTaskUIFlags_DoesCustomToolTip**—Indicates that the task supports custom ToolTips.

The *CreateCustomToolTip* Method

If you used `GetUIInfo` to query the custom task (if it supports custom ToolTips), you can use the `CreateCustomToolTip` method to create the ToolTip. Here is the placeholder for the method:

```
Private Sub CustomTaskUI_CreateCustomToolTip(ByVal hwndParent As Long,
                                    ByVal x As Long,_
                                    ByVal y As Long,_
                                    plTipWindow As Long)
    ... code to create the custom task's tooltip
End Sub
```

Adding a Custom Icon to the Custom Task

When you register the custom task with DTS Designer, DTS displays an icon associated with your custom task to represent it in the Task toolbar and on the design sheet. If you don't add a custom icon to your custom task, DTS uses a default icon. You can add a custom icon to your custom task to differentiate it from other custom tasks that may be installed on the server.

You add custom icons by creating a *resource file*—a container file for bitmaps, icons, cursors, text strings, and other user-interface elements that can be modified without having to recompile the application.

You can create a resource file by using a standard text editor. You will have to learn the syntax, but it's not complicated. You can find out about the syntax for creating resource files in Resource.txt, located in the \Tools directory in which VB is installed.

After you create the resource file, you compile it by using a resource compiler. The resource compiler for VB, called Rc.exe, can be found in the directory \Tools\Resource\Rc32 in which VB is installed.

To add the resource file to your custom task VB project, choose Add File from the Project menu to bring up the Add File dialog box (see Figure 16.14).

The compiled resource file has the .res extension. To locate your resource file, you have to specify Resource Files as the file type. Locate your file; then click the Open button to add the resource file to the project.

When you register your custom task with DTS Designer, all icons contained in your resource file will be presented as choices. You can select one to be associated with your custom task in DTS Designer.

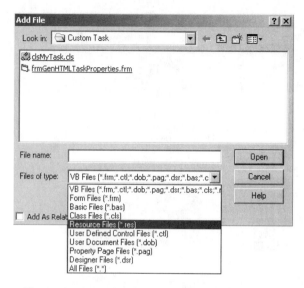

Figure 16.14 Adding a resource file to the VB project.

Registering the Custom Task

After you complete the required elements for the custom task VB project, you need to compile it. This generates the .dll file for the custom task. This file is used to register the custom task with DTS in SQL Server's Enterprise Manager.

Before you generate the .dll file, first make sure that you have saved the latest version of your VB project by choosing Save Project from the File menu. Then, click on the File menu again and select choose Make MyTask.dll (The name of the file may be different if you chose a different name.) This will compile your VB project and generate the MyTask.dll file (see Figure 16.15).

Now you can register the custom task in DTS Designer. You do so inside a DTS package. Launch SQL Server's Enterprise Manager, and open the Data Transformation Services folder. Right-click Local Packages; then select New Package from the shortcut menu to open the DTS Designer for a new package.

Click on the Task menu and then select Register Custom Task, which is one of the two options at the bottom of the menu (see Figure 16.16). The Register Custom Task dialog box opens (see Figure 16.17).

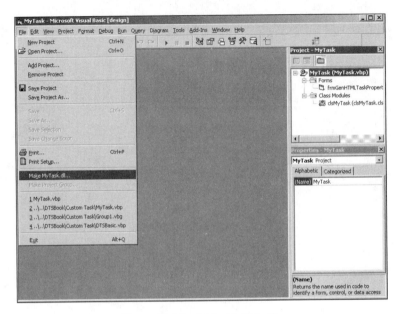

Figure 16.15 Make MyTask.dll.

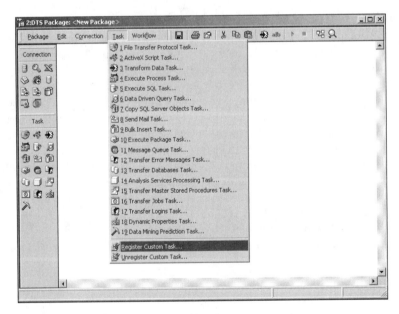

Figure 16.16 Registering a custom task.

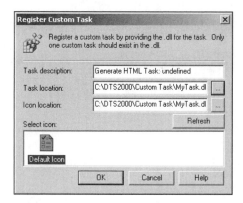

Figure 16.17   The Register Custom Task dialog box.

The description you enter in this dialog box becomes the default description for the custom task, regardless of any default setting done in the VB code. (The default setting in the VB code will apply in a DTS application.) This is because the description is saved in the custom task's Properties collection. When the custom task is used in a DTS package, the `Description` property already has a value, and the default-setting code does not execute. Therefore, make sure that the description you set in this dialog box is the one that you really want your custom task to have. Don't worry, though; if you change your mind later, you can unregister the custom task and register it again.

Registering Overrides Default Task Description

When you register and add the custom task in DTS Designer, the description that you give the task overrides what has been coded as the default in VB.

The next thing you need to do is locate the .dll file that contains the custom task. You can enter the location directly or browse to it by clicking the ellipsis (…) button inside the Register Custom Task dialog box. Choose an icon, if you have multiple icons to choose from; then click the OK button. When the icon appears on the Task toolbar on the left side of the window, the custom task has been registered successfully (see Figure 16.18).

That's it! You should now have a working custom task registered with DTS Designer, complete with its own Properties window.

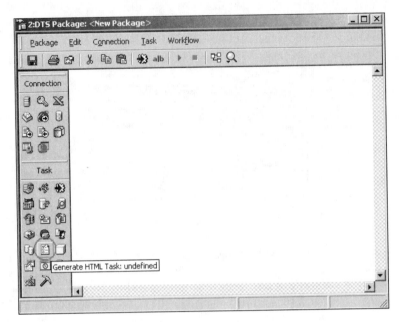

Figure 16.18   The custom-task icon on the Task toolbar.

Component Registration and DTS Caching

When you register your custom task, it becomes one of many components that DTS must keep track of. DTS organizes the information about these components by using the following collections:

- OLEDBProviderInfos

- ScriptingLanguageInfos

- TaskInfos

- TransformationInfos

Within the TaskInfos collection, a TaskInfo object stores the class information for a task (including your custom task). As efficient as it is in accessing the system registry, DTS allows you to boost performance even more by caching these entries. Even though the cache itself also is in the registry, the membership information has been predetermined and is readily available, making for a more efficient retrieval.

You can turn on this caching by right-clicking on the Data Transformation Services folder in the Enterprise Manager console and selecting Properties from the shortcut menu to bring up the Package Properties dialog box. Then check the Turn On Cache option. DTS will now scan the cache instead of the full registry whenever it needs component information.

When you develop your custom components, be aware that you may find yourself in situations where caching may get in the way. You may need to refresh the cache to have it show up or be removed, depending on what you are doing.

Also, you should know that you also can access the component information programmatically by using the Application object, which owns the collections mentioned earlier in this section. See Chapter 9, "Building a Package Using Visual Basic," and Chapter 10, "Interacting with a Package Using Visual Basic," for information about how to use VB to navigate through the DTS object model.

Using the Custom Task

To use the example custom task in a DTS package, add a connection to the package. Create a global variable that can store a rowset—a global variable with the data type <Other>. Next, add an ExecuteSQL task that queries a table and returns a result set. Configure its Parameters setting to store its result set in the global variable you created earlier. Save the package, and give it an appropriate name.

Saving a Package with an <Other> Global Variable
You might see the error "Type Mismatch" when you try to save the package. If so, try executing the package once and then try saving it again.

Drag and drop the custom task's icon to the design sheet to add it to the package. The Connection Properties dialog box appears where you can configure the custom task by selecting the global variable from the drop-down menu and specifying an output file.

Figure 16.19 shows the Generate HTML Task Properties dialog box with a global variable selected and a filename specified for output. You should make sure that the custom task will execute after the ExecuteSQL task by adding a workflow between the two tasks as shown in the figure.

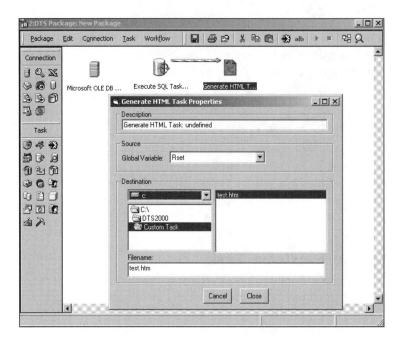

Figure 16.19   The Generate HTML Task Properties dialog box in DTS Designer.

Summary

In this chapter, you saw how to set up a Visual Basic project in which to develop a custom task. You learned about the COM interfaces that need to be implemented. You gained a clear understanding of how the custom task is launched and how it communicates with its host application, be it the DTS run-time system or a DTS application. In addition, you learned how a custom task interacts with DTS Designer to display and update its property values. Finally, you saw how a custom task is registered and added to DTS Designer.

17

Executing a DTS Package from a Stored Procedure

NOW THAT YOU HAVE A DTS PACKAGE designed to provide the functionality you desire, you will have to determine where and when to execute the package. In previous chapters, you executed your packages by using the following methods:

- Manual execution from the SQL Enterprise Manager
- Scheduling execution with the SQL Agent
- Executing the package from another package
- Initiating the package from custom application code

All the examples described in this chapter use the DTS package you created in Chapter 2, "DTS—An Overview," called `CreateExcelReports`.[1]

Executing DTS Packages from T-SQL

In many instances, you may want to execute your package within a SQL Server stored procedure. This chapter outlines several strategies to accomplish this task.

---

1. This package can be downloaded from www.magenic.com\publication\ or www.newriders.com.

You cannot always anticipate when to run DTS packages for the users. For example, you may want to create Excel reports on demand. If the logic for executing the DTS package is incorporated into a stored procedure, your problem is solved. You give users, through their application, execute permission on the stored procedure, ensuring that the reports will be generated on *their* schedule.

You could use the xp_cmdshell extended stored procedure to facilitate an on-demand package execution. xp_cmdshell is one of the two methods we will explore in this chapter.

In many cases, you do not want DTS packages to run until other preliminary processes finish executing. In such cases, you may choose to use Object Linking and Embedding (OLE) automation to execute the desired package. OLE automation is the other alternative outlined in this chapter.

Executing DTS Packages with *xp_cmdshell*

The xp_cmdshell extended stored procedure is available in the master database. This section provides examples of the command string you need to pass to the xp_cmdshell extended stored procedure to execute existing DTS packages. The command-line structure to execute dtsrun is:

```
dtsrun
[/?] |
[
  [
    /[~]S server_name[\instance_name]
    { {/[~]U user_name [/[~]P password]} | /E }
  ]
  {
    {/[~]N package_name }
    | {/[~]G package_guid_string}
    | {/[~]V package_version_guid_string}
  }
  [/[~]M package_password]
  [/[~]F filename]
  [/[~]R repository_database_name]
  [/A global_variable_name:typeid=value]
  [/L log_file_name]
  [/W NT_event_log_completion_status]
  [/Z] [/!X] [/!D] [/!Y] [/!C]
]
```

Table 17.1, which comes directly from SQL Server Books Online (BOL), lists each command-line switch and explains the parameters you will pass with the command-line command.

Table 17.1 **Command-Line Switches**[2]

Command-Line Switch	Definition
/?	Displays the command prompt options.
~	Specifies that the parameter to follow is hexadecimal text representing the encrypted value of the parameter; can be used with the /S, /U, /P, /N, /G, /V, /M, /F, and /R options. Using encrypted values increases the security of the command used to execute the DTS package because the server name, password, and similar items are not visible. Use /!Y to determine the encrypted command.
/S server_name[\instance_name]	Specifies the instance of SQL Server to connect to. Specify server_name to connect to the default instance of SQL Server on that server. Specify server_name\instance_name to connect to a named instance of SQL Server 2000 on that server.
/U user_name	Specifies a login ID used to connect to an instance of SQL Server.
/P password	Specifies a user-specified password used with a login ID.
/E	Specifies a trusted connection (password not required).
/N package_name	Specifies the name of a DTS package assigned when the package was created.
/G package_guid_string	Specifies the package ID assigned to the DTS package when it was created. The package ID is a GUID.
/V package_version_guid_string	Specifies the version ID assigned to the DTS package when it was first saved or executed. A new version ID is assigned to the DTS package each time it is modified. The version ID is a GUID.
/M package_password	Specifies an optional password assigned to the DTS package when it was created.
/F filename	Specifies the name of a structured storage file containing DTS packages. If server_name is also specified, the DTS package retrieved from SQL Server is executed and that package is added to the structured storage engine.

continues

Table 17.1 **Continued**

Command-Line Switch	Definition
/R repository_database_name	Specifies the name of the repository database containing DTS packages. If no name is specified, the default database name is used.
/A global_variable_name:typeid=value	Specifies a package global variable(s), where typeid equals the type identifier for the data type of the global variable. The entire argument string can be quoted. This argument can be repeated to specify multiple global variables.
/L log_file_name:	Specifies the name of the package log file.
/W Windows_Event_Log	Specifies whether to write the completion status of the package execution to the Windows Application Log. Specify True or False.
/Z	Indicates that the command line for dtsrun is encrypted with SQL Server 2000 encryption.
/!X	Blocks execution of the selected DTS package. Use this command parameter when you want to create an encrypted command line without executing the DTS package.
/!D	Deletes the DTS package from an instance of SQL Server. The package is not executed. You cannot delete a specific DTS package from a structured storage file.

2. Most of this table was copied from Microsoft SQL Server 2000 Version 8.00 Books Online. This information is available on the SQL Server installation CD.

Working with Global Variables

If you need to specify more than one global-variable value, you may use the /A switch more than once.

Also, to set global variables with the dtsrun command, you must have Owner permission for the package or the package must have been saved without DTS password protection enabled. If you do not have Owner permission, you can specify global variables, but the values used will be those set in the package, not those specified with the /A command switch.

The syntax for executing packages varies somewhat, depending on how you have chosen to save your DTS packages. Although the basic syntax is similar, following are the syntax differences for executing packages saved as COM-structured storage files, SQL Server packages, and repository packages.

To execute a DTS package saved as a COM-structured storage file, use this syntax:

```
dtsrun /Ffilename /Npackage_name /Mpackage_password
```

To execute a DTS package saved in the SQL Server msdb database, use this syntax:

```
dtsrun /Sserver_name /Uuser_nName /Ppassword /Npackage_name /Mpackage_password
```

To execute a DTS package saved in Meta Data Services, use this syntax:

```
dtsrun /Sserver_name /Uusernrame /Ppassword /Npackage_name /Mpackage_password
/Rrepository_name
```

To execute a DTS package saved in the SQL Server msdb database, pass a value to the global variable "CustomerID" with an integer data type, and pass the value of 45 for the "CustomerID" global variable, use this syntax:

```
dtsrun /Sserver_name /Uuser_nName /Ppassword /Npackage_name /Mpackage_password /A
"CustomerID":"18"="45"
```

The 18 after the semicolon in the /A switch represents the ID of the global-variable data type of integer. It is important not only to pass in the global variable, but to ensure proper execution of the package, you also must indicate the proper type ID of the global variable.

Table 17.2, which is from SQL Server BOL, shows the global-variable data types and their corresponding type IDs.

Table 17.2 **Data Types and The Corresponding Type IDs**[3]

Data Type	Type ID
Integer (small)	2
Integer	3
Real (4-byte)	4
Real (8-byte)	5
Currency	6
Date	7
String	8
Boolean	11
Decimal	14
Integer (1-byte)	16
Unsigned int (1-byte)	17

continues

Table 17.2 **Continued**

Data Type	Type ID
Unsigned int (2-byte)	18
Unsigned int (4-byte)	19
Integer (8-byte)	20
Int	22
Unsigned int	23
HRESULT	25
Pointer	26
LPSTR	30
LPWSTR	31

3. *This table was copied from Microsoft SQL Server 2000 Version 8.00 Books Online. This information is available on the SQL Server installation CD.*

For an example, if you wanted to execute the DTS package called CreateExcelReports, you would use the code in Listing 17.1. Figure 17.1 shows how this code looks on-screen.

Listing 17.1 **Executing a DTS Package from T-SQL with the *dtsrun* Utility**

```
Create Procedure sp_EXECPackage
as
/*
/S represents the ServerName
/U User ID
/P User Password
/N Name of Package
/M Package Password
*/

exec master.dbo.xp_cmdshell

'dtsrun /Sstevem-laptop /Usa /P /NCreateExcelReports /M'
```

You may have noticed that the stored procedure you created references the master database with a standard three-part naming convention. The master database is where the xp_cmdshell extended stored procedure is located.

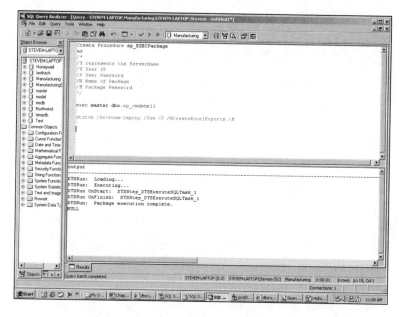

Figure 17.1   Creating a stored procedure using `dtsrun`.

Running the *dtsrun* Utility from the Command Prompt

To run the command directly from the command prompt, choose Run from the Start menu and paste in the command `dtsrun /Sstevem-laptop /Usa /P /NCreateExcelReports /M` (see Figure 17.2). Your reports should then be refreshed.

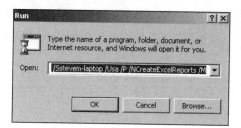

Figure 17.2   Using dtsrun from the command prompt.

Using *dtsrunui*

The `dtsui` is a graphical interface you can use to set up your `dtsrun` command line, including parameters for executing your DTS packages.

The dtsrunui interface is launched from the command prompt or by clicking on the Start button at the bottom left corner of your desktop and selecting Run from the Start menu. For an example, see Figure 17.3.

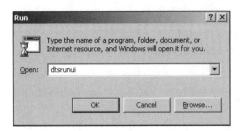

Figure 17.3 Launching the dtsrunui utility.

After you load the DTS Run dialog box, in the Package Name text box, type the version of the package you want to execute (see Figure 17.4).

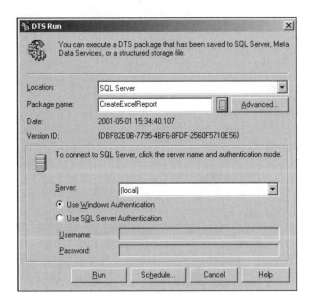

Figure 17.4 Specifying the package to execute.

After you specify the version of the package you want to execute, click the Advanced button next to the Package Name text box. The Advanced DTS Run dialog box opens. This dialog box allows you to do the following:

- Specify global variables and the values you want to pass in
- Specify a log file to record events

- Generate command-line code
- Encrypt the command-line code
- Specify that the command line be generated in SQL Server version 7.0 format

Type **CustomerID** as the global variable, and give it a data type of `integer` and a value of 36. Then click the Generate button to see the command string built. You also may want to check the Encrypt the Command check box and regenerate your command string to see an encrypted line (see Figure 17.5).

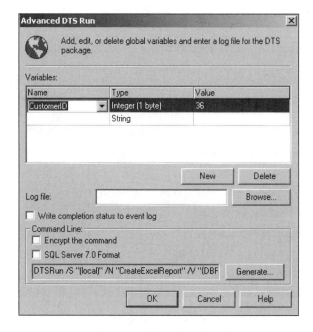

Figure 17.5 Advanced DTS Run dialog box.

Executing DTS Packages with OLE Automation

You can execute packages from T-SQL by using OLE automation. You may use this technique for any object library available on the server. OLE automation is documented in BOL. The following sections describe the available commands.

sp_OACreate

`sp_OACreate` is used to create an instance of an object. It returns an integer, which represents an object token. The argument passed to the procedure is either the `progid` (such as `MyObject.MyClass`) or the `clsid` (such as {nnnnnnnn-nnnn-nnnn-nnnn-nnnnnnnnnnnn}). You will be creating an instance of the DTS package object library. Your syntax should look like this:

```
declare @hr int
-- Holds Result of Execution 0 indicates success, -- Other Results indicate an
error
declare @DTSpkg int
-- Holds an integer representing the Object Token
EXEC @hr = sp_OACreate 'DTS.Package', @DTSpkg OUT
```

sp_OAMethod

Now that you have successfully created an instance of `DTS.Package`, you will use the `LoadFromSQLServer` method to load your `CreateExcelReports` package. To do so, you will pass in the instance of DTS you created earlier (by referencing the `objecttoken`), and pass in the appropriate arguments. `LoadFromSQLServer` accepts the following arguments:

- `Sub LoadFromSQLServer(ServerName As String)`
- `[ServerUserName As String]`
- `[ServerPassword As String]`
- `[Flags As DTSSQLServerStorageFlags = DTSSQLStgFlag_Default]`
- `[PackagePassword As String]`
- `[PackageGuid As String]`
- `[PackageVersionGuid As String]`
- `[PackageName As String]`
- `[pVarPersistStgOfHost]`

Your T-SQL code should look like this:

```
EXEC @hr = sp_OAMethod @DTSpkg,
   'LoadFromSQLServer("stevem-laptop", "sa", "", , , , , , "CreateExcelReports")'
```

> **Using the `clsid` or Package Name with the `LoadFromSQLServer` method**
> You also specify which package to load by its `clsid` to ensure that you run the same version each time. If you want to run the latest version of the package, you will be better served by calling the package by name.

Now that your object `@DTSpkg` has used the `LoadFromSQLServer` method of the `DTS.Package` library to specify which package you want to reference, it is time to execute the package.

Again, you should use `sp_OAMethod` to run the `Execute` method of the package object to run your DTS package as follows:

```
EXEC @hr = sp_OAMethod @DTSpkg, 'Execute'
```

sp_OADestroy

After you execute your package, it would be wise to destroy the package object. This procedure is simple—just use this code:

```
EXEC @hr = sp_OADestroy @DTSpkg
```

sp_displayoaerrorinfo

sp_displayoaerrorinfo is not an intrinsically available stored procedure, but it is fully documented in BOL. If an OLE automation call fails, it will be returned as an error (a non-zero result) to your @hr variable. sp_displayoaerrorinfo allows you to decode the error into more meaningful information. The command works in two steps; it takes in the @hr error code and then calls sp_hexidecimal to decode the binary error code. Listing 17.2 shows the complete code, which is also available in BOL.

Listing 17.2 **Handling OLE Automation Errors in T-SQL**

```
CREATE PROCEDURE sp_hexadecimal
  @binvalue varbinary(255),
  @hexvalue varchar(255) OUTPUT
AS
DECLARE @charvalue varchar(255)
DECLARE @i int
DECLARE @length int
DECLARE @hexstring char(16)
SELECT @charvalue = '0x'
SELECT @i = 1
SELECT @length = DATALENGTH(@binvalue)
SELECT @hexstring = '0123456789abcdef'
WHILE (@i <= @length)
BEGIN
DECLARE @tempint int
DECLARE @firstint int
DECLARE @secondint int
SELECT @tempint = CONVERT(int, SUBSTRING(@binvalue,@i,1))
SELECT @firstint = FLOOR(@tempint/16)
SELECT @secondint = @tempint - (@firstint*16)
SELECT @charvalue = @charvalue +
SUBSTRING(@hexstring, @firstint+1, 1) +
SUBSTRING(@hexstring, @secondint+1, 1)
SELECT @i = @i + 1
END
SELECT @hexvalue = @charvalue

CREATE PROCEDURE sp_displayoaerrorinfo
  @object int,
  @hresult int
```

continues

Listing 17.2   **Continued**

```
AS
DECLARE @output varchar(255)
DECLARE @hrhex char(10)
DECLARE @hr int
DECLARE @source varchar(255)
DECLARE @description varchar(255)
PRINT 'OLE Automation Error Information'
EXEC sp_hexadecimal @hresult, @hrhex OUT
SELECT @output = ' HRESULT: ' + @hrhex
PRINT @output
EXEC @hr = sp_OAGetErrorInfo @object, @source OUT, @description OUT
IF @hr = 0
BEGIN
SELECT @output = ' Source: ' + @source
PRINT @output
SELECT @output = ' Description: ' + @description
PRINT @output
END
ELSE
BEGIN
  PRINT ' sp_OAGetErrorInfo failed.'
  RETURN
END
```

Putting It Together

Now that you have all the pieces, putting everything together is a simple matter.
First, run the SQL scripts `sp_hexadecimal.sql` and `sp_displayoaerrorinfo.sql` from
C:\DTS2000\scripts.[4] Then use the OLE automation stored procedures to do the rest
of the work. Your code should look similar to Listing 17.3.

Listing 17.3   **Using OLE Automation to Execute a DTS Package from T-SQL**

```
Create Procedure sp_OLEAutomationPackage as

declare @hr int
declare @DTSpkg int
-- Create DTS package Object
EXEC @hr = sp_OACreate 'DTS.Package', @DTSpkg OUT
IF @hr <> 0
BEGIN
  PRINT 'Create Package Failed'
  EXEC sp_displayoaerrorinfo @DTSpkg, @hr
```

4. To follow along, run the SQL scripts `sp_hexadecimal.sql` and `sp_displayoaerrorinfo.`
`sql` from C:\DTS2000\scripts.

```
    RETURN
END
--Execute Load Method of Package Object
--Load Method Has The Following Parameters
/*
Sub LoadFromSQLServer(ServerName As String, [ServerUserName As String],
[ServerPassword As String], [Flags As DTSSQLServerStorageFlags =
DTSSQLStgFlag_Default],
[PackagePassword As String], [PackageGuid As String], [PackageVersionGuid As
String],
[PackageName As String], [pVarPersistStgOfHost])

*/

EXEC @hr = sp_OAMethod @DTSpkg,
 'LoadFromSQLServer("stevem-laptop", "sa", "", , , , , "CreateExcelReports")'

IF @hr <> 0
BEGIN
  PRINT 'Failed to Load Package'
  EXEC sp_displayoaerrorinfo @DTSpkg, @hr
  RETURN
END
--Execute the Package Execute Method
EXEC @hr = sp_OAMethod @DTSpkg, 'Execute'
IF @hr <> 0
BEGIN
  PRINT ' Failed Execution'
  EXEC sp_displayoaerrorinfo @DTSpkg , @hr
  RETURN
END
--CleanUp
EXEC @hr = sp_OADestroy @DTSpkg
```

OLE Automation Versus *xp_cmdshell*

In choosing between the two strategies covered in this chapter, you need to consider
two factors:

- **xp_cmdshell**—By default, only members of the sysadmin role may execute the
  xp_cmdshell extended stored procedure, but you can grant execute permissions
  to any users you want. Additionally, you may choose to have no output values
  returned to the stored procedure. xp_cmdshell runs synchronously, meaning that
  control is not returned to SQL Server until the command has finished running.

- **OLE automation**—Only members of sysadmin may execute OLE automation
  stored procedures. In addition, when an in-process DLL is executed from OLE
  automation, the created object shares memory and resources with SQL Server
  and may produce unpredictable results.

Summary

This chapter covered two ways to execute DTS packages from T-SQL. The first is a simple method that executes the dtsrun utility from within a stored procedure. The second method uses the OLE automation commands available through T-SQL. Although it is somewhat more cumbersome than the other method, OLE automation gives you exposure to all the properties and methods associated with the DTS object model.

18

Data Lineage

STARTING WITH MICROSOFT SQL SERVER 7.0, Microsoft included the Microsoft Repository for storing and managing meta data, models, components and objects for reusability, interoperability, team development, data resource management, and dependency tracking. The Microsoft Repository is known as Meta Data Services in SQL Server 2000. By using Meta Data Services, you can track the source, transformation, and destination of the data used in the package over time. You will find this capability very useful with data warehousing (refer to chapters 11, 12, and 13). Data lineage that is stored via Meta Data Services can be used to validate or research the data used in the warehouse. When you save a package to Meta Data Services, you have an entirely new level of data tracking available for your package.

Introduction to Microsoft's Meta Data Services

Microsoft first included Microsoft Repository 2 in SQL Server 7.0 and Visual Studio 6. SQL Server 2000 uses Repository 3, which is completely backward compatible with version 2. Both versions use the Open Information Model (OIM). Meta data repositories use information models to define the meta data. Microsoft developed the OIM but has handed it off to the Meta Data Coalition (MDC).

The OIM contains meta data specifications that allow the meta data to be used and shared between tools and systems. The idea behind OIM is that the meta data can be used by systems other than SQL Server. The OIM uses the Universal Modeling Language (UML) to describe the meta data that is stored in the repository.

The OIM includes many subject areas, including relational database schemas, data transformation details, data analysis descriptions, and COM objects. It also includes business and knowledge management subject areas. For more information on the Open Information Model, refer to the Meta Data Services SDK at `http://msdn.microsoft.com/repository/downloads/sdk/default.asp`.

The data repository engine is installed by default in the msdb database in both versions of SQL Server. The tables that are part of the repository have the following prefixes: Rtbl, Dbm, Dtm, Dts, Gen, Mds, Ocl, Olp, Tfm, Uml, and Umx. The stored procedures have the prefix r_i. Although SQL Server can host multiple repositories, DTS works with only one repository, and the repository must be hosted in msdb.

Meta Data Services and DTS

As noted in the preceding section, DTS uses only the repository stored in msdb. Thus, when you save the package and any versions of the package to Meta Data Services, meta data is generated in msdb.

Package Property Settings

Chapter 7, "Package," covers package properties. The following sections cover the properties specific to Meta Data Services and data lineage. Figure 18.1 shows the Advanced tab of the DTS Package Properties dialog box, where you can set the meta data properties for the package.

When you check the Show Lineage Variables as Source Columns check box, you can have lineage variables added to the package without writing them to Meta Data Services. Then you can use the global variables that were created for use in custom tasks to track lineage and auditing information.

If you want to track the lineage by using Meta Data Services, you must check the Write Lineage to Repository check box. When this option is selected, the data lineage will be saved to the repository each time the package is saved or run.

Scanning Options

The OLE DB Scanner included in SQL Server can scan the data schema from an OLE DB source and record it to the repository as meta data. To set up the scanning from DTS, use the Options button in the Advanced tab of the DTS Package Properties dialog box or, when saving the package to Meta Data Services, click the Scanning button in the Save dialog box. To set scanning from DTS, you must choose the Resolve Package References to Scanned Catalog Meta Data option in the Scanning Options dialog box (see Figure 18.2). This option links the package to the meta data stored in Meta Data Services. The next two sections of the dialog box determine the rules for scanning catalogs for use with DTS.

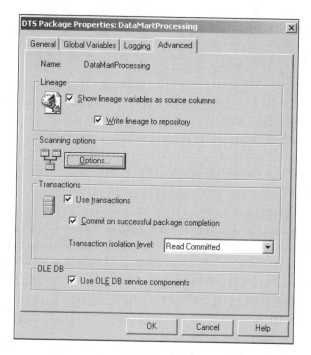

Figure 18.1   DTS Package Properties dialog box, Advanced tab.

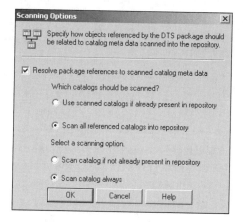

Figure 18.2   Scanning Options dialog box (Package Properties
and Save to Meta Data Services).

First, you need to determine which catalogs should be scanned. If the meta data has
already been imported or scanned and has not changed, you can use the Use Scanned

Catalogs If Already Present in Repository option, which uses these previously scanned catalogs. This option can be useful if you are pressed for time, but it is imperative that the meta data has not changed. If the meta data has changed, the references to this meta data might not be meaningful. The safer choice is to scan all referenced catalogs into the repository. Therefore, any changes made in the meta data will be reflected in the repository and will have meaningful references. This option costs more in terms of time and resources, however.

Next, you need to specify a scanning option. You can choose Scan Catalog If Not Already Present in Repository. This option is the default option for a DTS package. The other option is Scan Catalog Always. The catalogs will be scanned according to these rules each time the package is saved.

Importance of Scanning the Catalogs

If you choose not to use the scanning options for the catalogs with DTS, you will not be able to track the lineage accurately. When you do not scan the source and destination catalogs explicitly, DTS will create DTS local catalogs that will be used for referencing the data. These catalogs are temporary, in that they are re-created each time the package is saved (meta data is scanned). This will make finding the actual data locations nearly impossible and will remove any descriptive comments added to the catalogs.

Saving DTS Packages as Meta Data

When you save the package, select the Meta Data Repository for any valid SQL Server 2000 instance (not available with SQL Server 7.0 instances). At this point, you can set up the scanning options for the catalogs (refer to the preceding section, "Scanning Options"). To open the DTS package from the SQL Server Enterprise Manager console tree, expand by clicking on the Data Transformation Services object. Click to expand the Meta Data Services Packages folder. Double-click on the package.

In SQL Server 7.0, you can save the DTS package to the repository. Meta Data Services, which uses Microsoft Repository 3, is available only with SQL Server 2000, whereas the Microsoft Repository 2 is used in SQL Server 7.0. If you used SQL Server 7.0 initially, remember that the repository engine that shipped with SQL Server 2000 is completely backward compatible with previous versions of the repository. If you upgrade from SQL Server 7.0 to 2000, however, the new repository engine is not installed by default, and you will get an error if you try to save a package to Meta Data Services.

Viewing DTS Packages as Meta Data

The easiest way to view the DTS package meta data is to choose the Meta Data option in Data Transformation Services (see Figure 18.3). This option shows you the hierarchical view of the package and allows you to drill down in an organized manner to the meta data that you want to see. You also can track the lineage and version information. (The lineage data is not viewable in the Meta Data browsers—only in Data Transformation Services.) You can also use the Meta Data browser to view the meta data, as described in the following section.

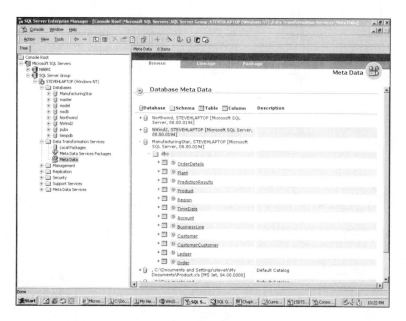

Figure 18.3 Browsing meta data in DTS.

Using the Meta Data Browser

You can use the Meta Data browser to browse the meta data for scanned catalogs. You can access the Meta Data browser from two locations. First, you can use the Meta Data browser that is part of Enterprise Manager. This browser allows you to view (in read-only mode) the meta data that you create that is stored in msdb. You can view the meta data created for the relational databases, analytical databases, and Data Transformation Services. You can find this browser in the Contents folder of Meta Data Services (see Figure 18.4).

You can also run the browser as a standalone snap-in in the Microsoft Management Console (see Figure 18.5). This version of the browser has a wider range of functionality and works with other SQL Server repository databases. You can use this browser to view repositories stored in SQL Server v6.5, 7.0, and 2000. To use the browser, however, you must use Repository 3, which comes with SQL Server 2000.

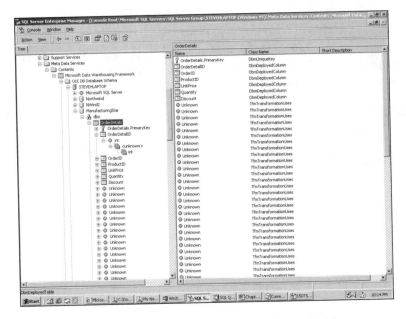

Figure 18.4   Meta Data browser in SQL Server Enterprise Manager.

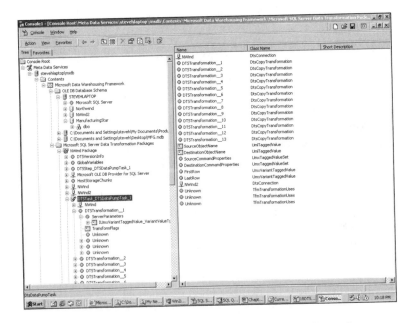

Figure 18.5   Meta Data browser as a standalone MMC snap-in.

How to Use Data Lineage

Data lineage can help you create an audit trail for your packages. You need to develop a plan before you implement data lineage, to determine whether you need row lineage, column lineage, or both. The performance of the package can be affected when you implement data lineage.

Row-Level Data Lineage

Row-level data lineage is concerned with the actual data content and is tracked each time the package is executed. By using row-level lineage options, you can track the source, the transformation, and the destination of the data. The lineage values stored by the meta data services for each package include: a global unique identifier (GUID), the user and server name necessary for package execution, and the recorded time of last package execution. To effectively use these lineage values you need to add them to the transformation process. The lineage value is set by the package and can be passed along to the destination system. Then you can query the destination table by using the lineage information and determine the original source of the data through the lineage value(s) in Meta Data Services.

Column-Level Data Lineage

Column-level data lineage tracks changes in the schema of the source or destination systems; it provides information about the package version and the database tables and columns used as source or destinations. The information resulting from column-level data lineage tracking allows you to verify or validate columns in the source or destination system.

Data Lineage Applied to a Package

This section illustrates data lineage by saving the package DataMartProcessing to Meta Data Services and viewing the meta data and data lineage that are generated.

Overview of the Package

The purpose of this package is to move data from the Manufacturing database to the ManufacturingStar database for use in Analysis Server. The following sections take you through the process of setting up this package in Meta Data Services and tracing the lineage through the process.

Steps to Set Up Meta Data

To use Meta Data Services, you need to save the package to Meta Data Services. In the Save As dialog box, select Meta Data Services as the location to save the package. Before saving the package, set the scanning options; click the Scanning button in the Save dialog box to display the Scanning Options dialog box (refer to Figure 18.2).

In the Scanning Options dialog box, click Resolve Package References To Scanned Catalog Metadata. Under Which Catalogs Should Be Scanned?, click Scan All Referenced Catalogs Into Repository. Under Select a Scanning Option, click Scan Catalog Always. Now you can proceed to save the package. (You don't need to change the name of the package, because it will be saved in a different format and location.)

Next, you need to set the appropriate package properties. Open the DTS Package Properties dialog box and go to the Advanced tab (refer to Figure 18.1). In the Lineage section, check both check boxes. The first option lets you use the lineage data as source columns; the second option writes the lineage to the repository. You do not need to set the scanning options in this dialog box, because they were set when you saved the package. At this point, you are done with the property settings necessary for using data lineage.

When you have the properties set correctly, you need to add columns to the destination tables in the ManufacturingStar database to receive the lineage values from the transformation. You can name the columns anything you want to use. For the purposes of this exercise, name them Lineage_Full, with a data type of uniqueidentifier, and Lineage_Short, with the data type of int. These columns need to be added to any table in which you want to track the lineage. In this example, you are adding them to the Order and Product tables (see Figure 18.6).

Finally, you will need to edit the Data Transformation tasks to accept the data-lineage values. For the two tasks affecting the tables you are referencing, add Copy Column transformations between the source columns (DTSLineage_Full and DTSLineage_Short) and your recently created destination columns (Lineage_Full and Lineage_Short). When the transformation tasks are executed, they will record the package lineage information to the destination tables.

Viewing the Data Lineage

When all the steps are completed, you need to save the package and then execute it. After the execution, you will be able to view the lineage data. In this section, you'll trace the lineage of Order ID 10248. First, you need to query the ManufacturingStar database for the lineage values for the data. Use this query to trace the data lineage of Order 10248:

```
SELECT Lineage_Full, Lineage_Short FROM [Order] WHERE OrderID = 10248
```

When you have the lineage values in hand, you will be able to use them in Meta Data Services to track their source.

Next, copy the value from Lineage_Short. This value will be used for the remainder of the trace because it is simpler to work with than a GUID is.

When you have the lineage value, open Enterprise Manager, and go to the Meta Data node below the Data Transformation Services folder. When you select this node, the Browse tab should show the meta data for the databases you scanned (see Figure 18.7).

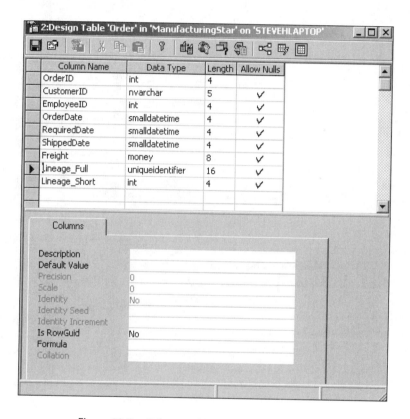

Figure 18.6   Columns added for data-lineage values.

The Meta Data node has two other tabs. The second tab is Lineage (see Figure 18.8). In this tab, you can filter Meta Data Services by lineage.

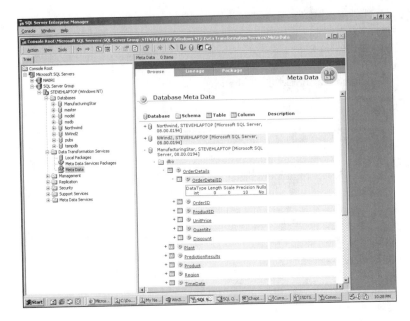

Figure 18.7   Browsing database Meta Data.

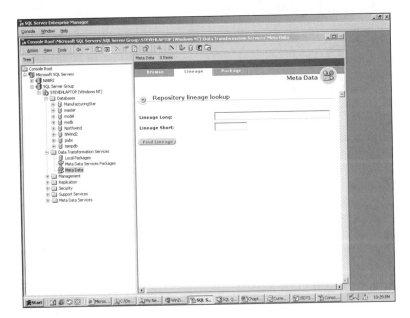

Figure 18.8   Lineage filter.

Before applying the filter, look at the Package tab. In this tab, you can see the packages that have been saved to Meta Data Services and their version and lineage data (see Figure 18.9).

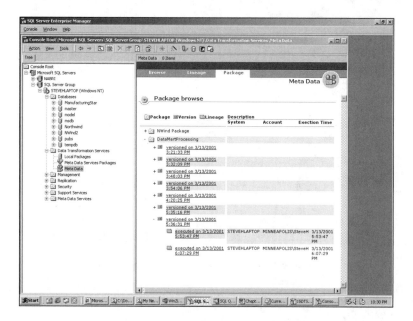

Figure 18.9   Browsing package Meta Data.

Now return to the Lineage tab and filter for the lineage value you copied. You see a screen similar to the one shown in Figure 18.10. This screen displays information about the package, including when it was run, which version was executed, and who executed it. When you know the version of the package that was executed, you can open it and determine what rules and systems were used to transform Order ID 10248. The level of detail you will be able to pursue for this piece of data depends on your source data systems.

Although this example is rather simple for purposes of explanation, the value of data lineage becomes more significant when the way data is transformed changes over time. If the rules businesses use to determine a profit change, for example, you will have values stored in your OLAP cubes that are compared as though they are the same but are really different in the nature of their calculations. You can use the data lineage to trace which calculations were used to produce the values you are reviewing.

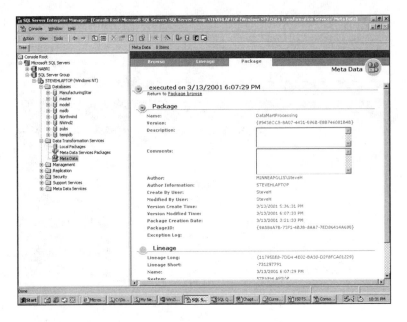

Figure 18.10 Browsing lineage data in DTS.

Take Extra Caution

Use caution when implementing Meta Data Services. Your performance will take a hit when you save and execute the package with logging activated.

Summary

Now you can see the value in using Meta Data Services with data-lineage values for what is essentially row-level logging. The tools you use to track the transformation of data in DTS will help you find any errors or inconsistencies that might occur. Used in conjunction with logging, error handling, and exception handling, data lineage can be a real force in validating the data you are generating from the packages you create.

Index

F

N

O

U-V

VOICES THAT MATTER

VISIT OUR WEBSITE

WWW.NEWRIDERS.COM

On our website, you'll find information about our other books, authors, tables of contents, and book errata. You will also find information about book registration and how to purchase our books, both domestically and internationally.

EMAIL US

Contact us at: **nrfeedback@newriders.com**

- If you have comments or questions about this book
- To report errors that you have found in this book
- If you have a book proposal to submit or are interested in writing for New Riders
- If you are an expert in a computer topic or technology and are interested in being a technical editor who reviews manuscripts for technical accuracy

Contact us at: **nreducation@newriders.com**

- If you are an instructor from an educational institution who wants to preview New Riders books for classroom use. Email should include your name, title, school, department, address, phone number, office days/hours, text in use, and enrollment, along with your request for desk/examination copies and/or additional information.

Contact us at: **nrmedia@newriders.com**

- If you are a member of the media who is interested in reviewing copies of New Riders books. Send your name, mailing address, and email address, along with the name of the publication or website you work for.

BULK PURCHASES/CORPORATE SALES

If you are interested in buying 10 or more copies of a title or want to set up an account for your company to purchase directly from the publisher at a substantial discount, contact us at 800-382-3419 or email your contact information to corpsales@pearsontechgroup.com. A sales representative will contact you with more information.

WRITE TO US

New Riders Publishing
201 W. 103rd St.
Indianapolis, IN 46290-1097

CALL/FAX US

Toll-free (800) 571-5840
If outside U.S. (317) 581-3500
Ask for New Riders
FAX: (317) 581-4663

New
Riders

WWW.NEWRIDERS.COM

RELATED NEW RIDERS TITLES

Inside XML

Steven Holzner

Inside XML is a foundation book that covers both the Microsoft and non-Microsoft approach to XML programming. It covers in detail the hot aspects of XML, such as DTD's versus XML Schemas, CSS, XSL, XSLT, XLinks, XPointers, XHTML, RDF, CDF, parsing XML in Perl and Java, and much more.

ISBN: 0735710201
1152 pages
US $49.99

C++ XML

Fabio Arciniegas

The demand for robust solutions is at an all-time high. Developers and programmers are asking the question, "How do I get the power performance found with C++ integrated into my web applications?" Fabio Arciniegas knows how. He has created the best way to bring C++ to the web. In this book, he shares the secrets developers and programmers worldwide are searching for.

ISBN: 073571052X
300 pages with CD-ROM
US $39.99

ISBN: 0735711127
384 pages
US $44.99

XML and SQL Server 2000

John Griffin

XML and SQL Server 2000 enables SQL developers to understand and work with XML, the preferred technology for integrating eBusiness systems. SQL Server 2000 has added several new features that SQL Server 7.0 never had that make working with and generating XML easier for the developer. XML and SQL Server 2000 provides a comprehensive discussion of SQL Server 2000's XML capabilities.

ISBN: 0735710899
768 pages with CD-ROM
US $49.99

XML, XSLT, Java and JSP: A Case Study in Developing a Web Application

Westy Rockwell

A practical, hands-on experience in building web applications based on XML and Java technologies, this book is unique because it teaches the technologies by using them to build a web chat project throughout the book. The project is explained in great detail, after the reader is shown how to get and install the necessary tools to be able to customize this project and build other web applications

ISBN: 0735711364
640 pages
US $49.99

Inside XSLT

Steven Holzner

Inside XSLT is designed to be a companion guide to the highly succesful *Inside XML*. This example oriented book covers XML t HTML, XML to Music, XML with Java, stylesheet creation and usage, nodes and attributes, sorting data, creating XPath expressions, using XPath and XSLT functions, namespaces, names, templates, name variables, desig ing stylesheets and using XSLT processor API's, the 56 XSL formatting objects, the XSLT DTD, and much more.

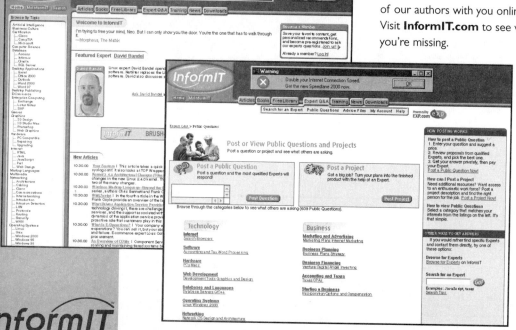

Colophon

The image on the cover of this book is that of the Inca ruins Machu Picchu. The ruins, captured here by photographer Emanuele Taroni, are considered by many to be the Eighth Wonder of the World. Located on a ridge a mile and a half high in the Andes Mountains in southeastern Peru, Machu Picchu is a complex of about 200 structures connected by alleys and side streets. This carefully planned "lost city" included homes, stores, temples, terraced farming plateaus, and a water supply system.

A popular tourist site, Machu Picchu has become the subject of much controversy as the Peruvian government has provided land for a public railway system that would support new tourism. Current plans also include a hotel and a cable car to the site. Scientists fear the ensuing increase in tourist activity will destroy the ruins. This development would be in violation of existing Peruvian laws and international heritage agreements.

This book was written and edited in Microsoft Word, and laid out in QuarkXPress. The font used for the body text is Bembo and MCPdigital. It was printed on 50# Husky Offset Smooth paper at R.R. Donnelley & Sons in Crawfordsville, Indiana. Prepress consisted of PostScript computer-to-plate technology (filmless process). The cover was printed at Moore Langen Printing in Terre Haute, Indiana, on Carolina, coated on one side.